My Little Monster

9

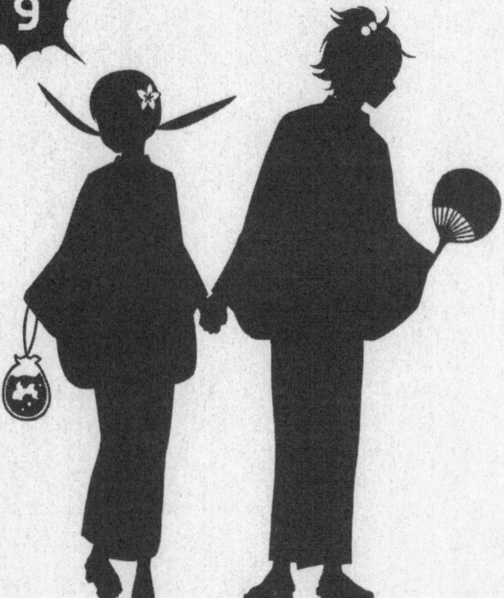

Robico

CONTENTS

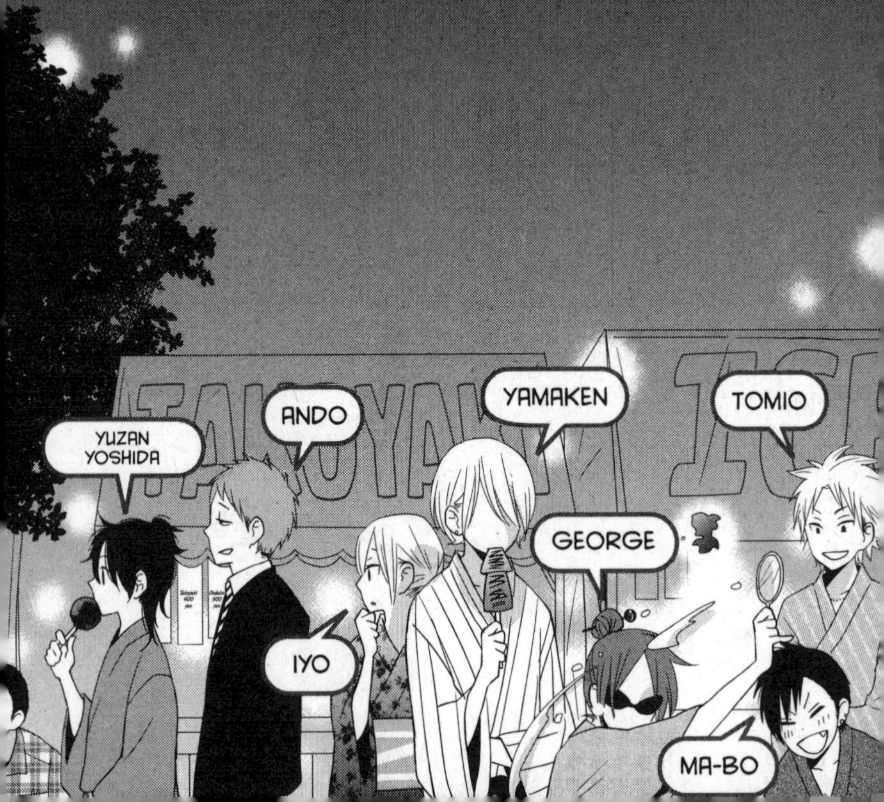

TOMIO
YAMAKEN
ANDO
YUZAN YOSHIDA
GEORGE
IYO
MA-BO

[redacted]

When Shizuku Mizutani does a fa[redacted]or for problem child Haru Yoshida, who sat next to her in school, he develops a huge crush on her. Attracted to his innocence, she eventually falls for him, too, but when she asks him out, he inexplicably turns her down. After that, the couple repeatedly fail to find themselves on the same page as they eventually move on to their second year of high school. Shizuku still has no response to her third confession of love to Haru, but Yamaken's younger sister Iyo has just enrolled at their school, and gets the ball rolling for Yamaken, who gets put in a position where he has to confess his secret crush to Shizuku. Shizuku turns Yamaken down, Haru admits that he loves Shizuku, and Haru and Shizuku finally become a couple. However, they go on a camping trip for summer vacation and...?!

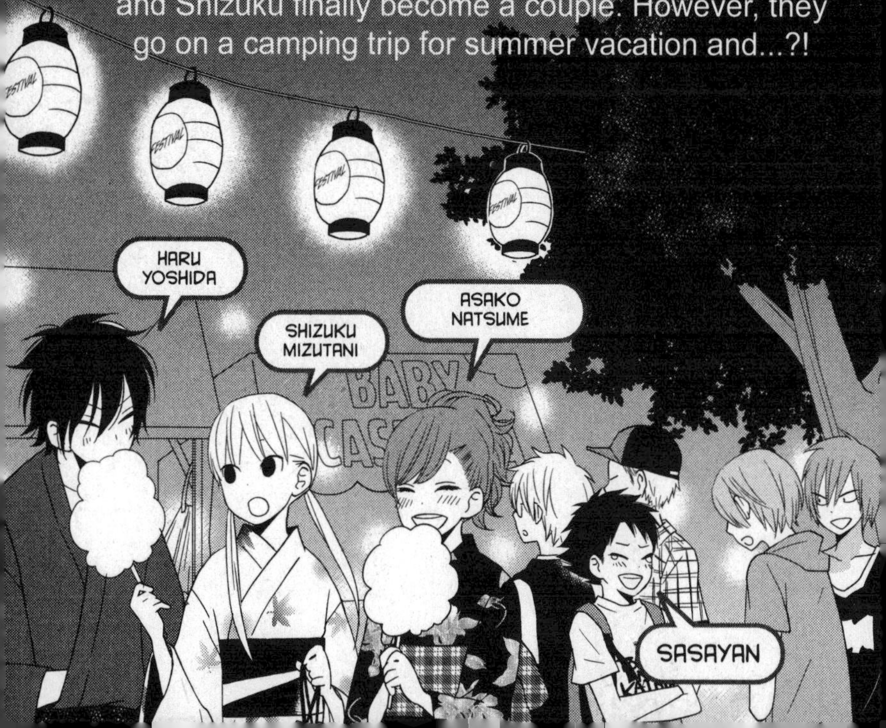
ASAKO NATSUME
SHIZUKU MIZUTANI
HARU YOSHIDA
SASAYAN

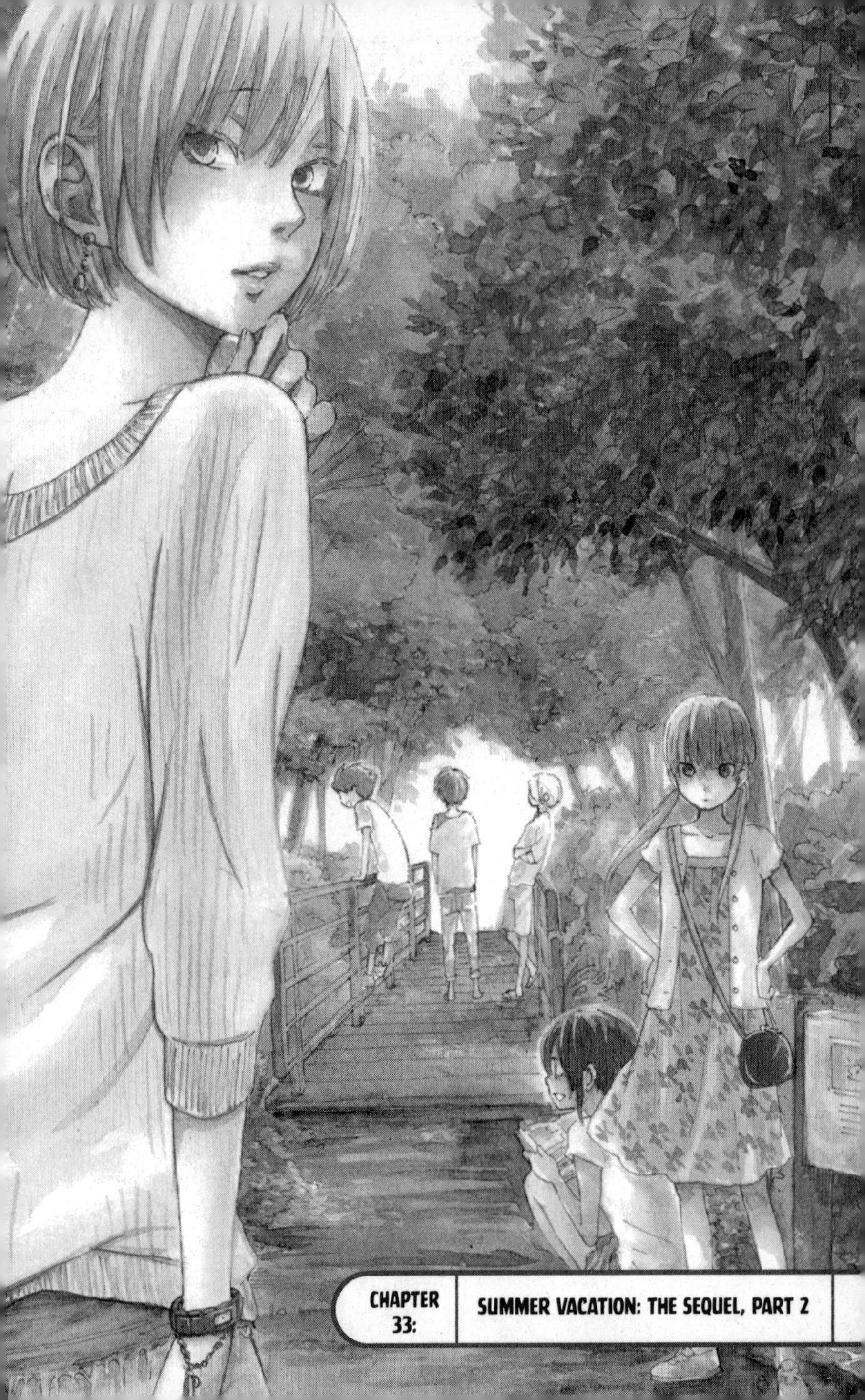

CHAPTER 33: SUMMER VACATION: THE SEQUEL, PART 2

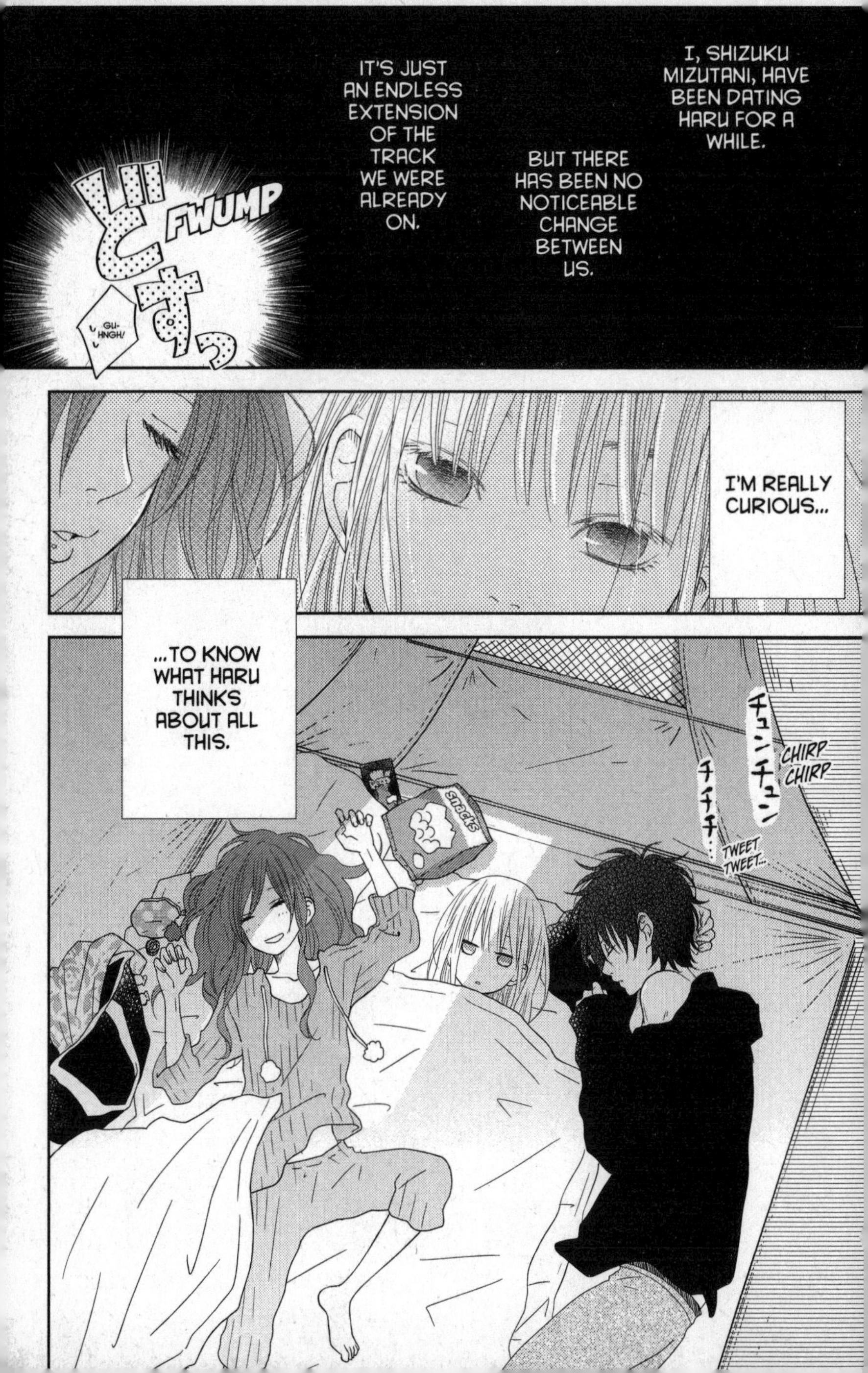

I, SHIZUKU MIZUTANI, HAVE BEEN DATING HARU FOR A WHILE.
BUT THERE HAS BEEN NO NOTICEABLE CHANGE BETWEEN US.
IT'S JUST AN ENDLESS EXTENSION OF THE TRACK WE WERE ALREADY ON.
どすっ
FWUMP
GU-HNGH!
I'M REALLY CURIOUS...
...TO KNOW WHAT HARU THINKS ABOUT ALL THIS.
チュンチュン
CHIRP CHIRP
チチチ...
TWEET TWEET...
snacks

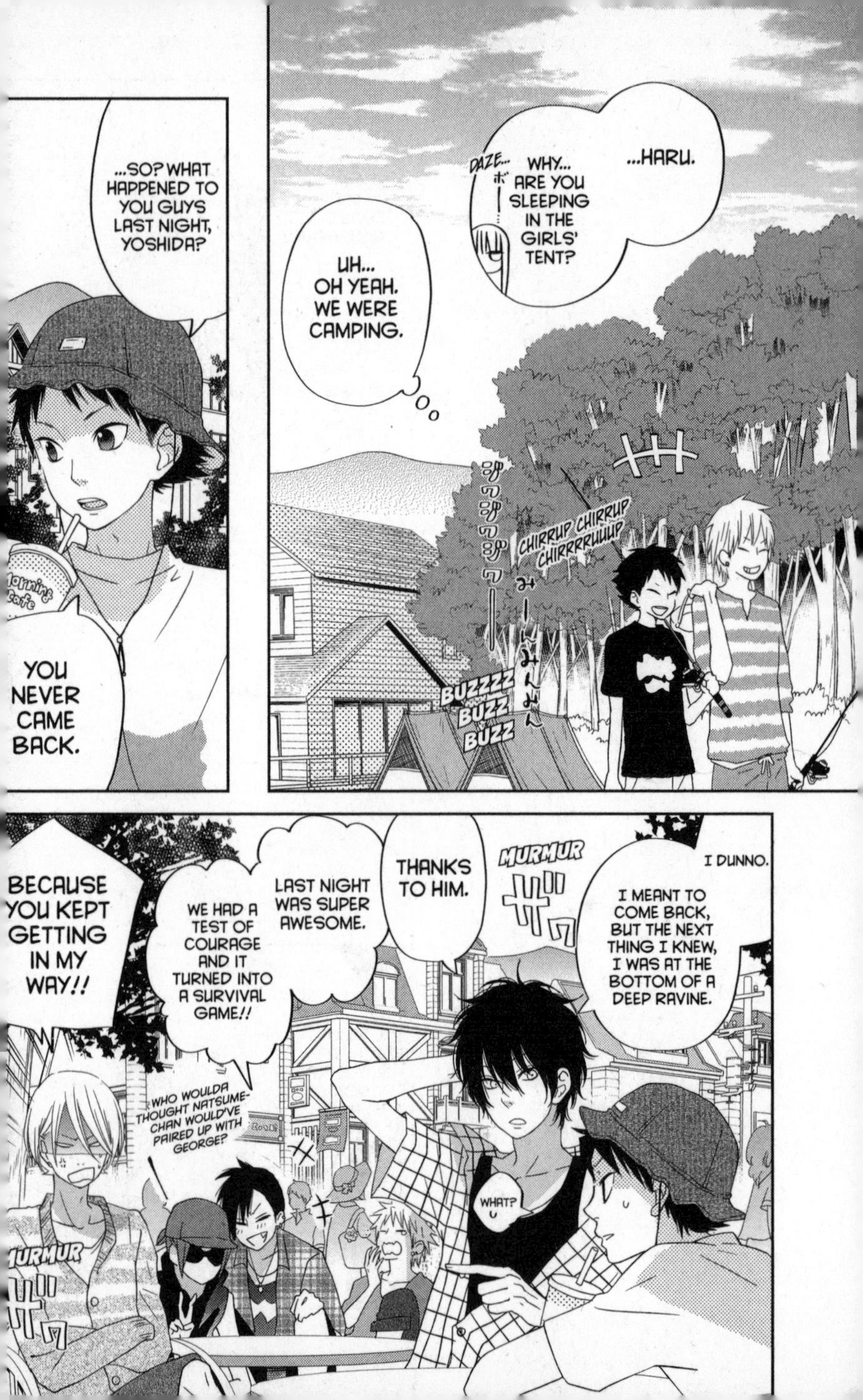
...HARU.
DAZE...
WHY... ARE YOU SLEEPING IN THE GIRLS' TENT?
UH... OH YEAH. WE WERE CAMPING.
CHIRRUP CHIRRUP CHIRRRRUUUP
BUZZZZ BUZZ BUZZ
...SO? WHAT HAPPENED TO YOU GUYS LAST NIGHT, YOSHIDA?
YOU NEVER CAME BACK.
I DUNNO.
I MEANT TO COME BACK, BUT THE NEXT THING I KNEW, I WAS AT THE BOTTOM OF A DEEP RAVINE.
MURMUR
THANKS TO HIM.
LAST NIGHT WAS SUPER AWESOME.
WE HAD A TEST OF COURAGE AND IT TURNED INTO A SURVIVAL GAME!!
BECAUSE YOU KEPT GETTING IN MY WAY!!
WHAT?
WHO WOULDA THOUGHT NATSUME-CHAN WOULD'VE PAIRED UP WITH GEORGE?
MURMUR

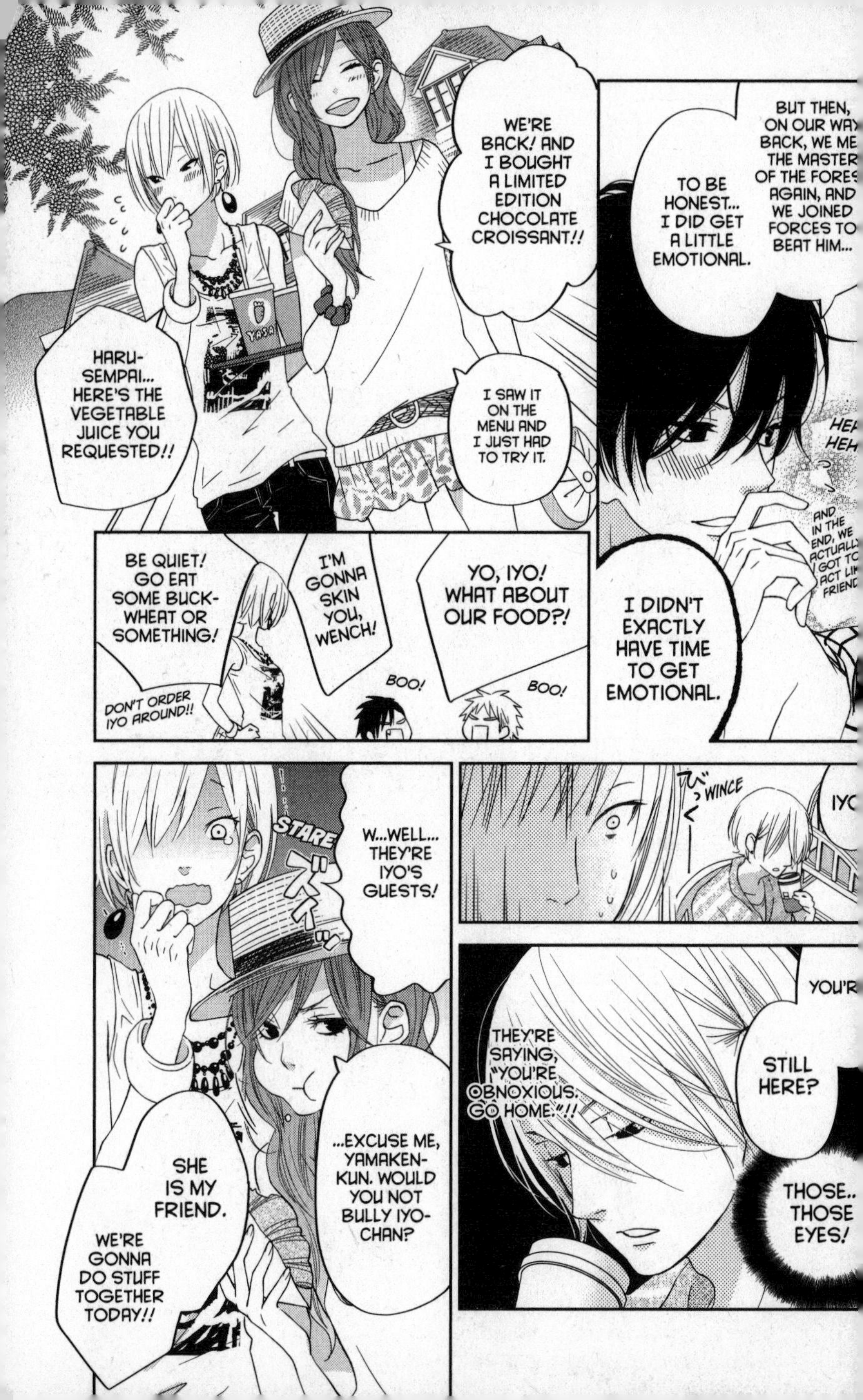

BUT THEN, ON OUR WA BACK, WE ME THE MASTER OF THE FORES AGAIN, AND WE JOINED FORCES TO BEAT HIM...
TO BE HONEST... I DID GET A LITTLE EMOTIONAL.
HEH HEH
AND IN THE END, WE ACTUALL GOT TO ACT LIK FRIEND
I DIDN'T EXACTLY HAVE TIME TO GET EMOTIONAL.
WE'RE BACK! AND I BOUGHT A LIMITED EDITION CHOCOLATE CROISSANT!!
I SAW IT ON THE MENU AND I JUST HAD TO TRY IT.
YASAI
HARU-SEMPAI... HERE'S THE VEGETABLE JUICE YOU REQUESTED!!
YO, IYO! WHAT ABOUT OUR FOOD?!
BOO!
I'M GONNA SKIN YOU, WENCH!
BOO!
BE QUIET! GO EAT SOME BUCK-WHEAT OR SOMETHING!
DON'T ORDER IYO AROUND!!
IYO
WINCE
YOU'R STILL HERE?
THEY'RE SAYING, "YOU'RE OBNOXIOUS. GO HOME."!!
THOSE.. THOSE EYES!
W...WELL... THEY'RE IYO'S GUESTS!
STARE
...EXCUSE ME, YAMAKEN-KUN. WOULD YOU NOT BULLY IYO-CHAN?
SHE IS MY FRIEND.
WE'RE GONNA DO STUFF TOGETHER TODAY!!

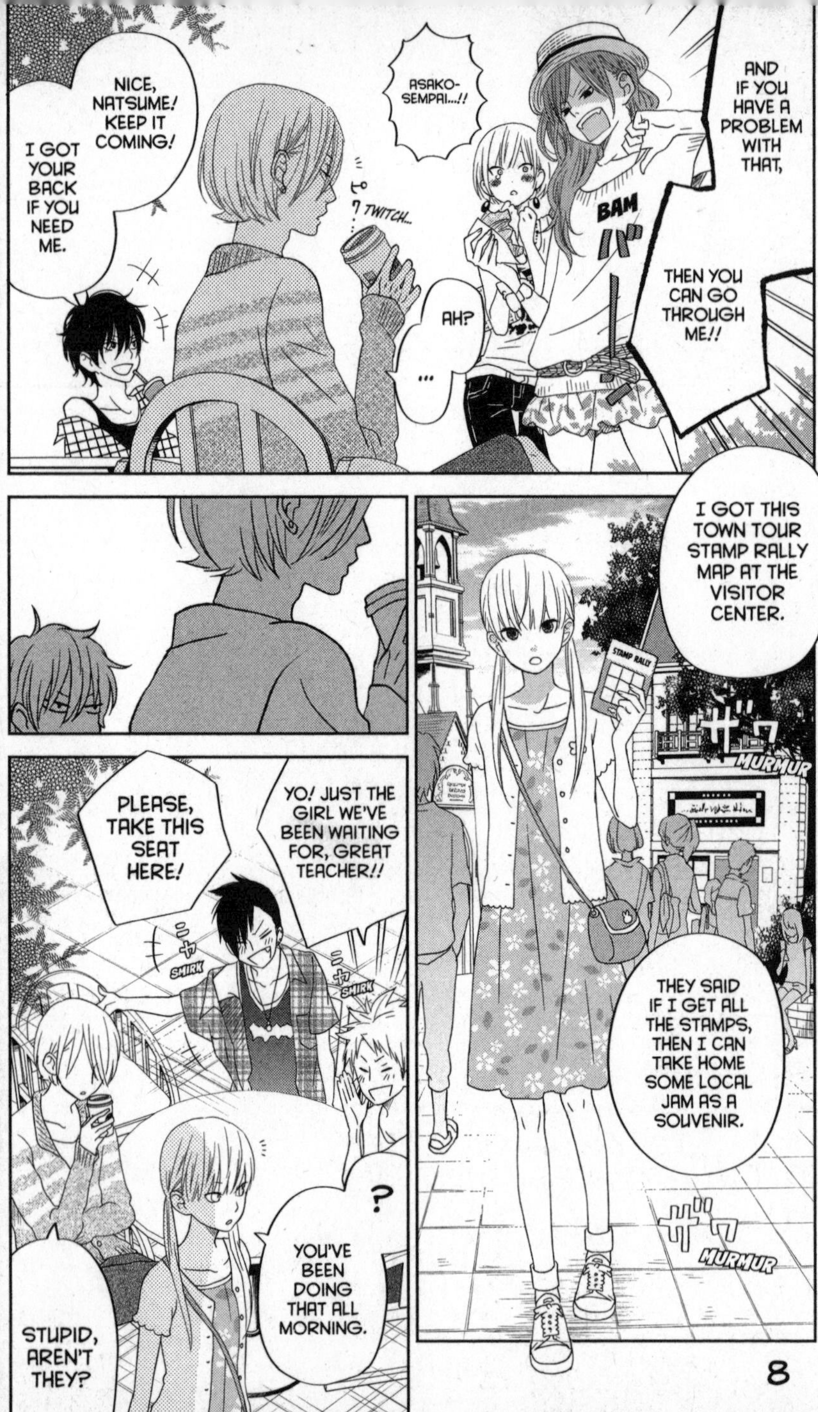
AND IF YOU HAVE A PROBLEM WITH THAT,
THEN YOU CAN GO THROUGH ME!!
BAM
ASAKO-SEMPAI...!!
AH?
...
TWITCH...
NICE, NATSUME! KEEP IT COMING!
I GOT YOUR BACK IF YOU NEED ME.
I GOT THIS TOWN TOUR STAMP RALLY MAP AT THE VISITOR CENTER.
STAMP RALLY
MURMUR
THEY SAID IF I GET ALL THE STAMPS, THEN I CAN TAKE HOME SOME LOCAL JAM AS A SOUVENIR.
MURMUR
YO! JUST THE GIRL WE'VE BEEN WAITING FOR, GREAT TEACHER!!
PLEASE, TAKE THIS SEAT HERE!
SMIRK
SMIRK
?
YOU'VE BEEN DOING THAT ALL MORNING.
STUPID, AREN'T THEY?

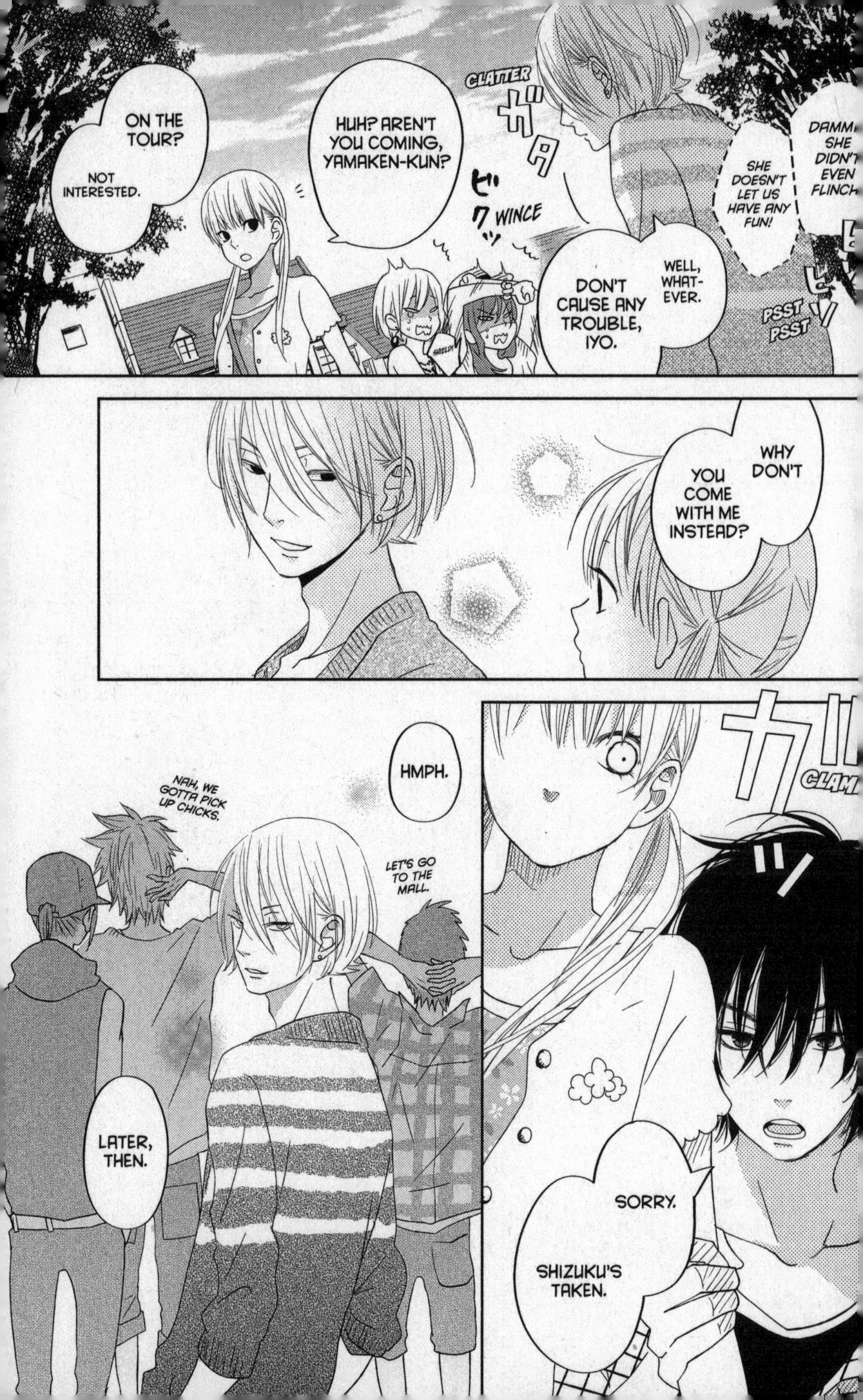
DAMMI SHE DIDN'T EVEN FLINCH
SHE DOESN'T LET US HAVE ANY FUN!
PSSST PSSST
WELL, WHAT-EVER.
DON'T CAUSE ANY TROUBLE, IYO.
CLATTER
WINCE
HUH? AREN'T YOU COMING, YAMAKEN-KUN?
SHIELD!
ON THE TOUR?
NOT INTERESTED.
WHY DON'T YOU COME WITH ME INSTEAD?
CLAM
SORRY.
SHIZUKU'S TAKEN.
HMPH.
LET'S GO TO THE MALL.
NAH, WE GOTTA PICK UP CHICKS.
LATER, THEN.

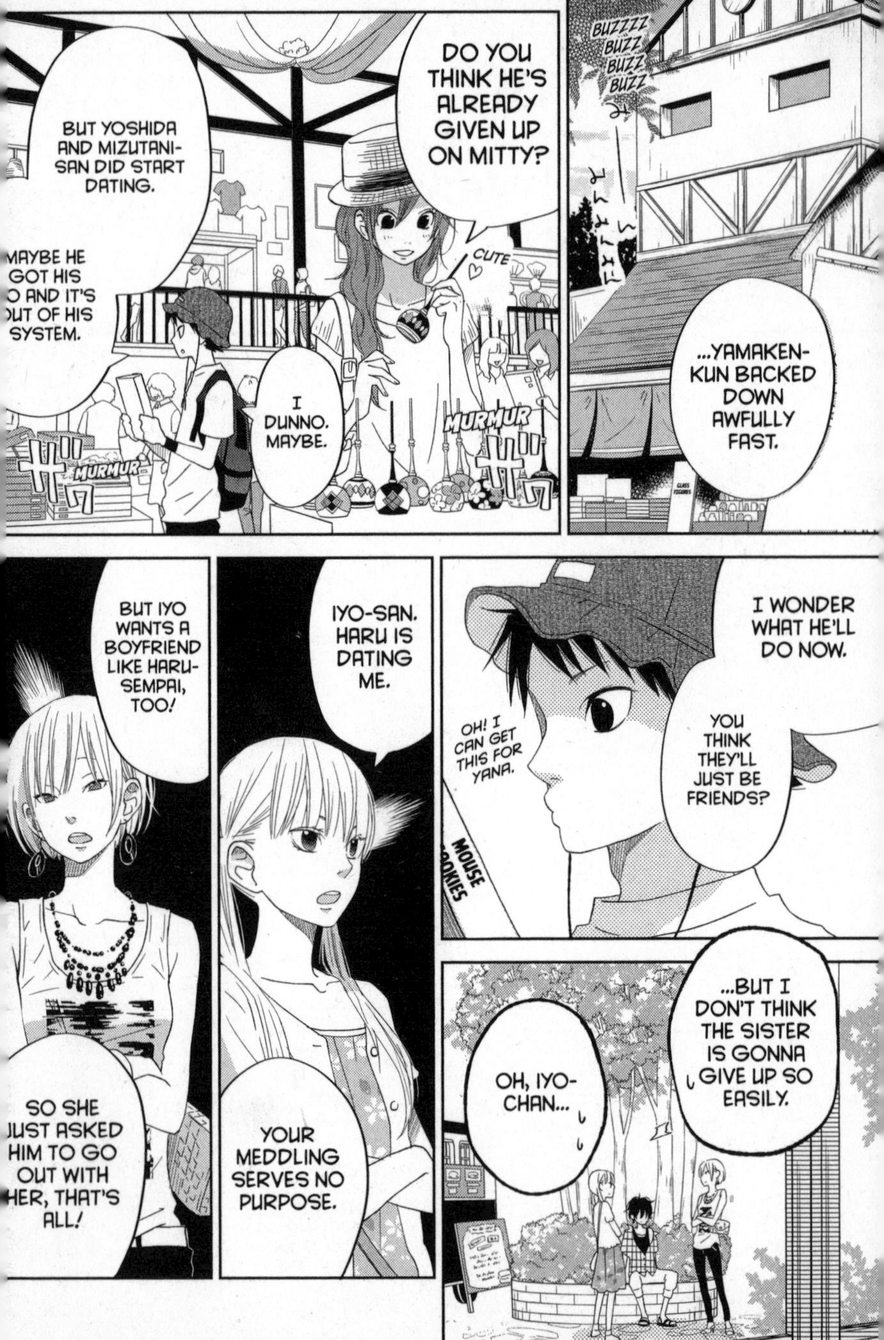
BUZZZZ BUZZ BUZZ BUZZ
...YAMAKEN-KUN BACKED DOWN AWFULLY FAST.
DO YOU THINK HE'S ALREADY GIVEN UP ON MITTY?
CUTE
BUT YOSHIDA AND MIZUTANI-SAN DID START DATING.
MURMUR
ザワ
I DUNNO. MAYBE.
MAYBE HE GOT HIS O AND IT'S UT OF HIS SYSTEM.
MURMUR
ザワ
I WONDER WHAT HE'LL DO NOW.
YOU THINK THEY'LL JUST BE FRIENDS?
OH! I CAN GET THIS FOR YANA.
MOUSE COOKIES
...BUT I DON'T THINK THE SISTER IS GONNA GIVE UP SO EASILY.
OH, IYO-CHAN...
IYO-SAN. HARU IS DATING ME.
YOUR MEDDLING SERVES NO PURPOSE.
BUT IYO WANTS A BOYFRIEND LIKE HARU-SEMPAI, TOO!
SO SHE JUST ASKED HIM TO GO OUT WITH HER, THAT'S ALL!

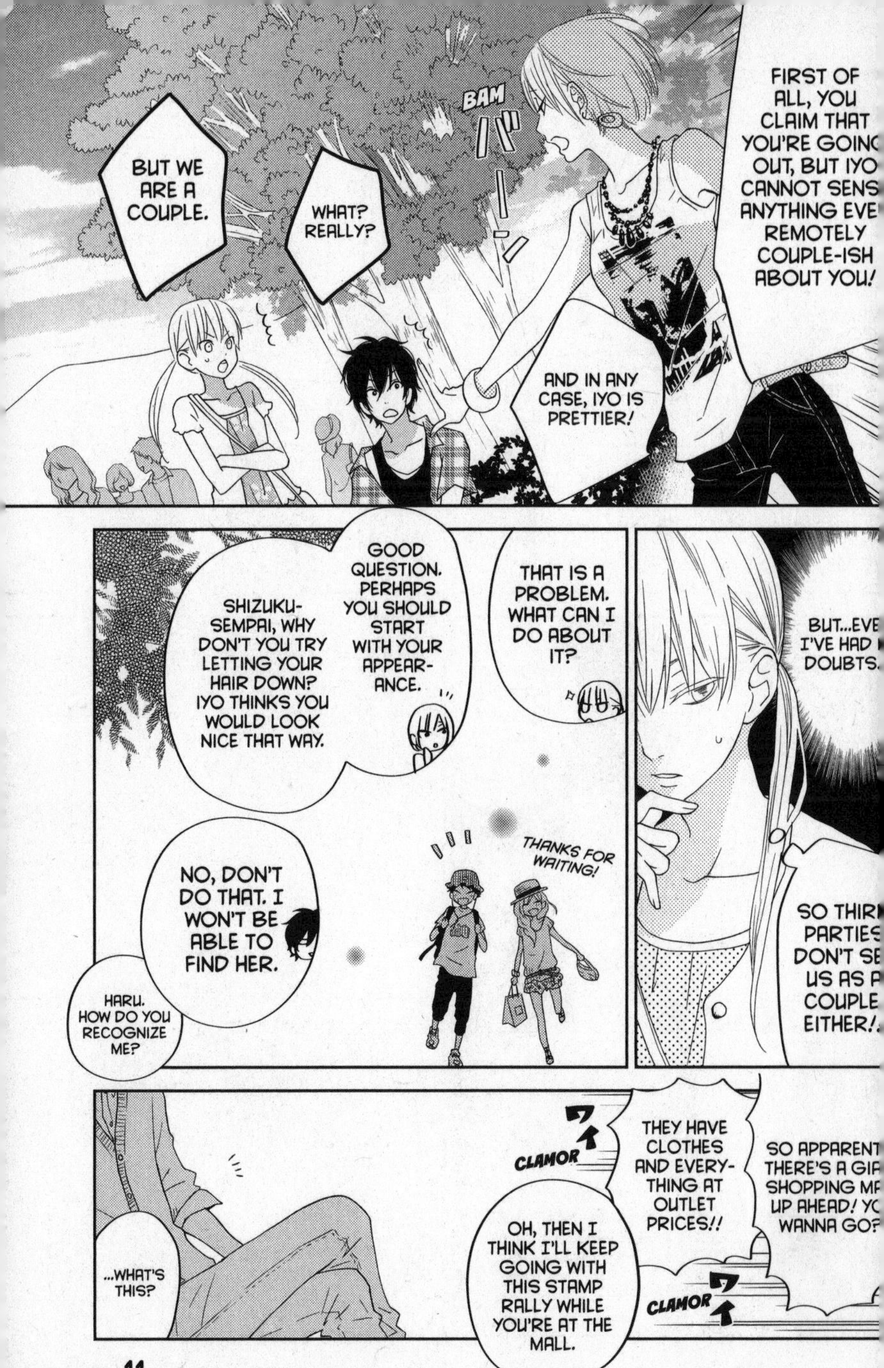
FIRST OF ALL, YOU CLAIM THAT YOU'RE GOING OUT, BUT IYO CANNOT SENS ANYTHING EVE REMOTELY COUPLE-ISH ABOUT YOU!
BAM
AND IN ANY CASE, IYO IS PRETTIER!
WHAT? REALLY?
BUT WE ARE A COUPLE.
BUT...EVE I'VE HAD DOUBTS.
SO THIR PARTIES DON'T SE US AS A COUPLE EITHER!.
THAT IS A PROBLEM. WHAT CAN I DO ABOUT IT?
GOOD QUESTION. PERHAPS YOU SHOULD START WITH YOUR APPEAR-ANCE.
SHIZUKU-SEMPAI, WHY DON'T YOU TRY LETTING YOUR HAIR DOWN? IYO THINKS YOU WOULD LOOK NICE THAT WAY.
THANKS FOR WAITING!
NO, DON'T DO THAT. I WON'T BE ABLE TO FIND HER.
HARU. HOW DO YOU RECOGNIZE ME?
SO APPARENT THERE'S A GI SHOPPING M UP AHEAD! YO WANNA GO?
THEY HAVE CLOTHES AND EVERY-THING AT OUTLET PRICES!!
CLAMOR
OH, THEN I THINK I'LL KEEP GOING WITH THIS STAMP RALLY WHILE YOU'RE AT THE MALL.
CLAMOR
...WHAT'S THIS?

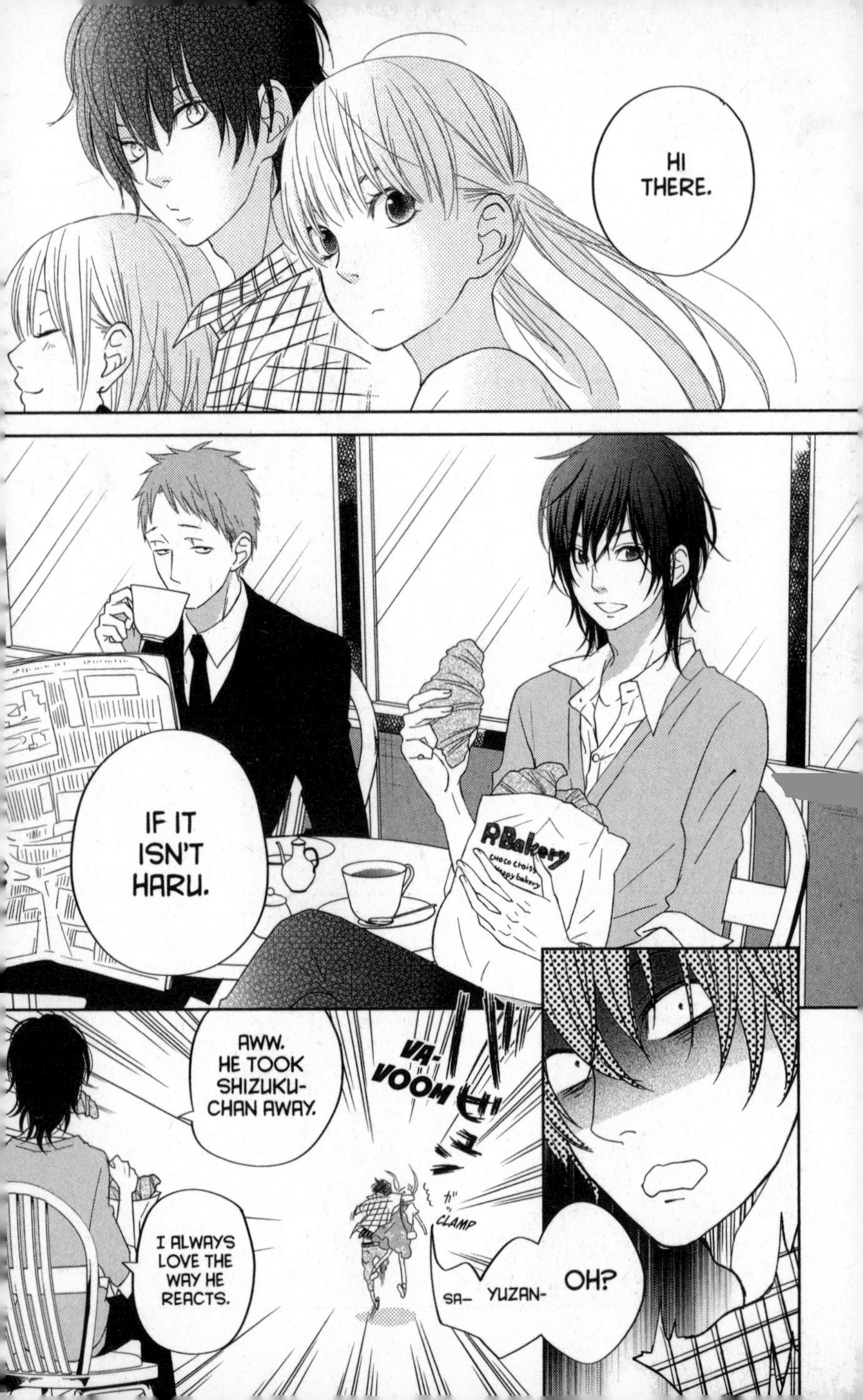

HI THERE.
IF IT ISN'T HARU.
RBakery
OH?
SA— YUZAN-
VA-VOOM
CLAMP
AWW. HE TOOK SHIZUKU-CHAN AWAY.
I ALWAYS LOVE THE WAY HE REACTS.

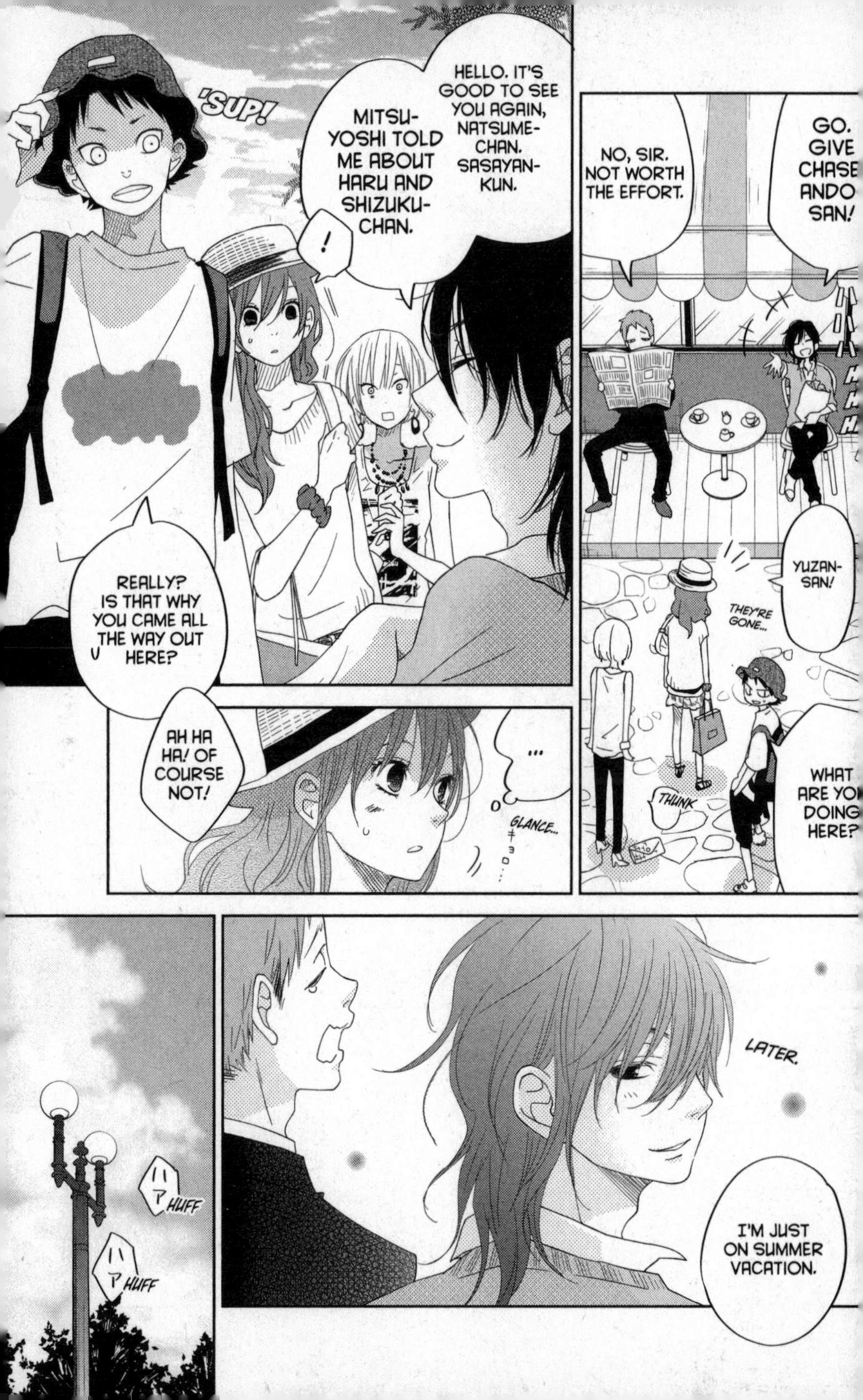
GO. GIVE CHASE ANDO SAN!
NO, SIR. NOT WORTH THE EFFORT.
YUZAN-SAN!
THEY'RE GONE...
WHAT ARE YO DOING HERE?
THUNK
'SUP!
HELLO. IT'S GOOD TO SEE YOU AGAIN, NATSUME-CHAN. SASAYAN-KUN.
MITSUYOSHI TOLD ME ABOUT HARU AND SHIZUKU-CHAN.
!
REALLY? IS THAT WHY YOU CAME ALL THE WAY OUT HERE?
...
GLANCE...
AH HA HA! OF COURSE NOT!
LATER.
I'M JUST ON SUMMER VACATION.
HUFF
HUFF

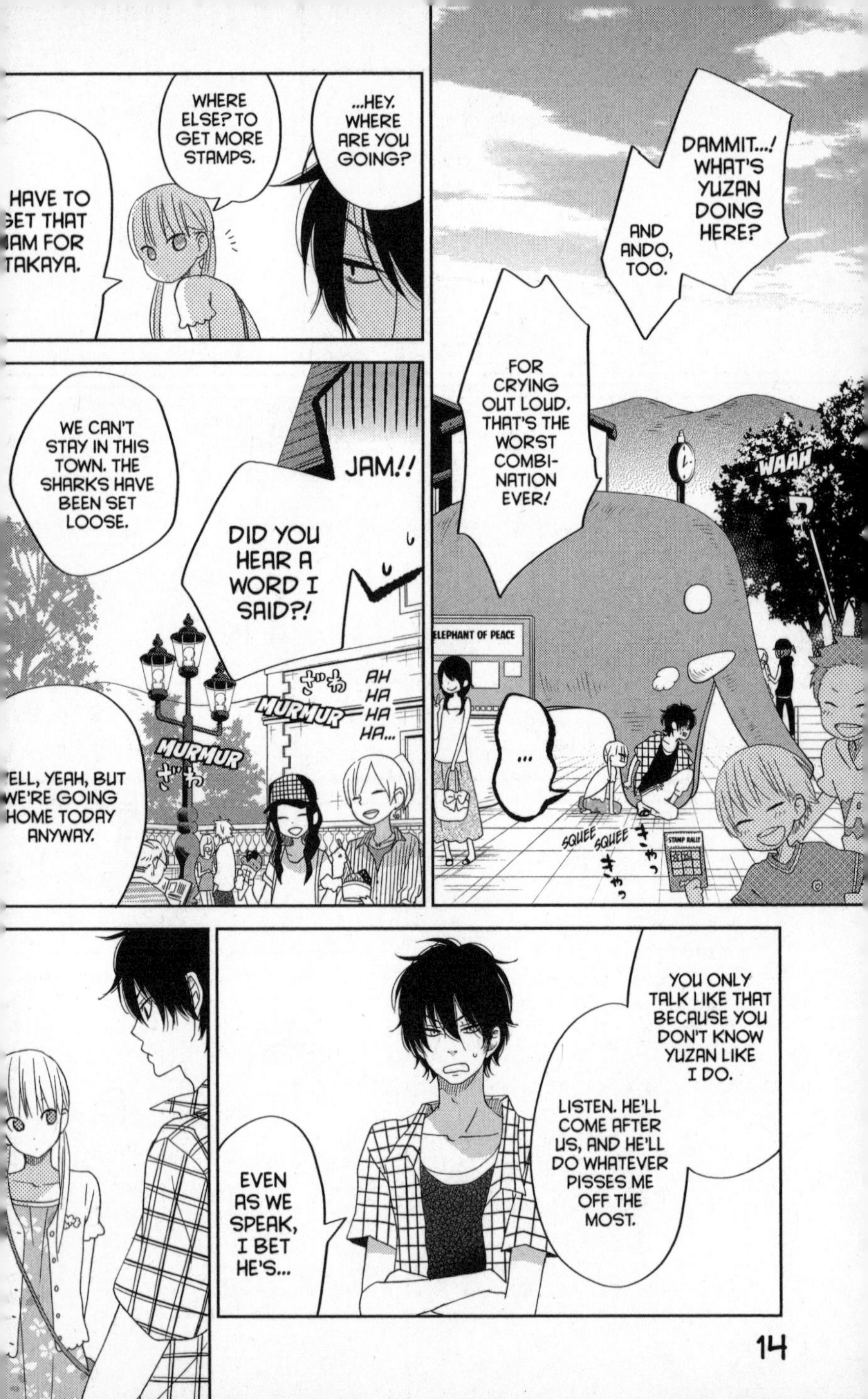
DAMMIT...! WHAT'S YUZAN DOING HERE?
AND ANDO, TOO.
FOR CRYING OUT LOUD. THAT'S THE WORST COMBI-NATION EVER!
WAAH
ELEPHANT OF PEACE
...
SQUEE SQUEE
STAMP RALLY
...HEY. WHERE ARE YOU GOING?
WHERE ELSE? TO GET MORE STAMPS.
HAVE TO GET THAT JAM FOR TAKAYA.
JAM!!
DID YOU HEAR A WORD I SAID?!
WE CAN'T STAY IN THIS TOWN. THE SHARKS HAVE BEEN SET LOOSE.
MURMUR
AH HA HA HA...
MURMUR
WELL, YEAH, BUT WE'RE GOING HOME TODAY ANYWAY.
YOU ONLY TALK LIKE THAT BECAUSE YOU DON'T KNOW YUZAN LIKE I DO.
LISTEN. HE'LL COME AFTER US, AND HE'LL DO WHATEVER PISSES ME OFF THE MOST.
EVEN AS WE SPEAK, I BET HE'S...

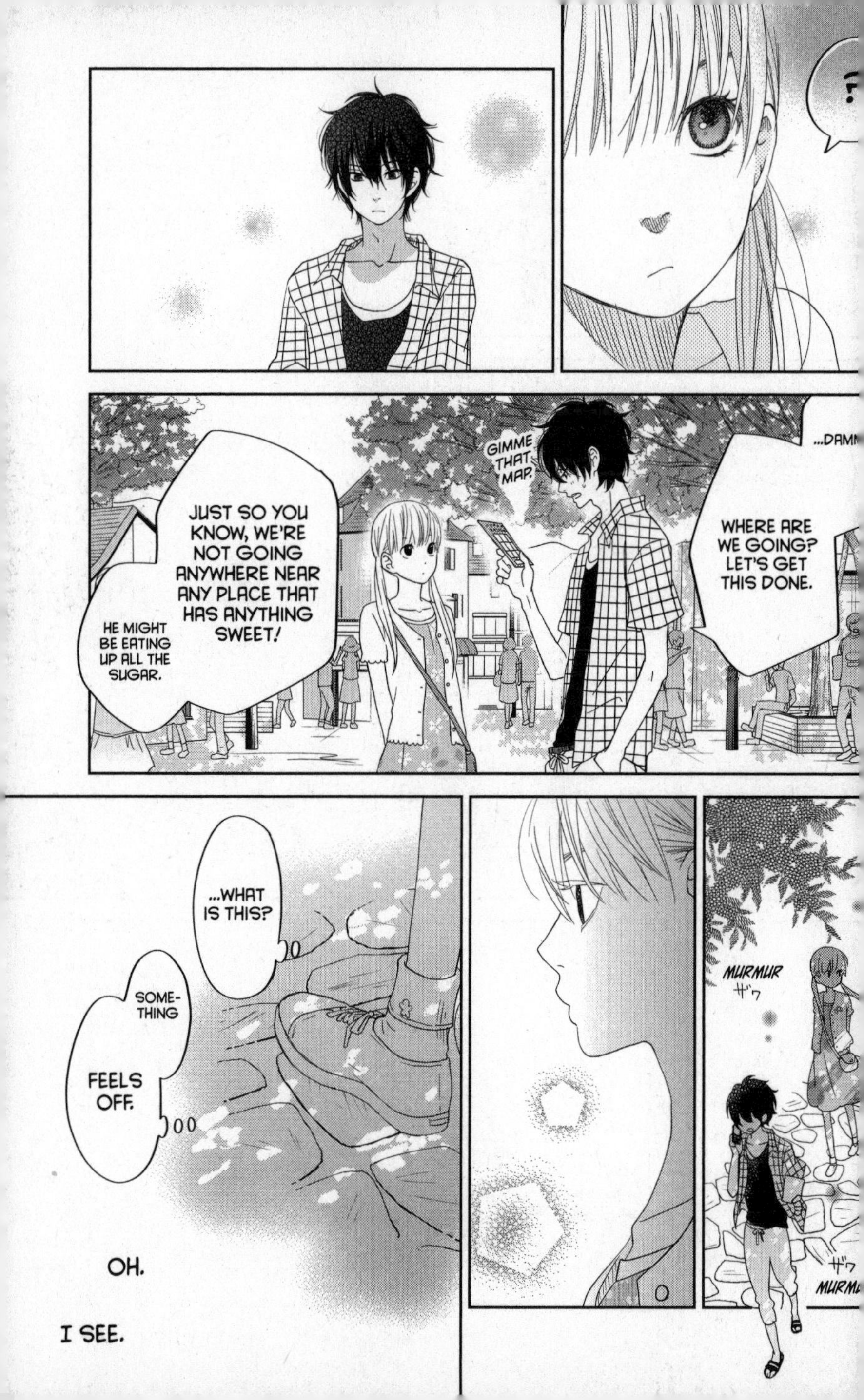
!?
...DAMN
WHERE ARE WE GOING? LET'S GET THIS DONE.
GIMME THAT MAP.
JUST SO YOU KNOW, WE'RE NOT GOING ANYWHERE NEAR ANY PLACE THAT HAS ANYTHING SWEET!
HE MIGHT BE EATING UP ALL THE SUGAR.
MURMUR
ザワ
ザワ
MURMU
...WHAT IS THIS?
SOME-THING FEELS OFF.
OH.
I SEE.

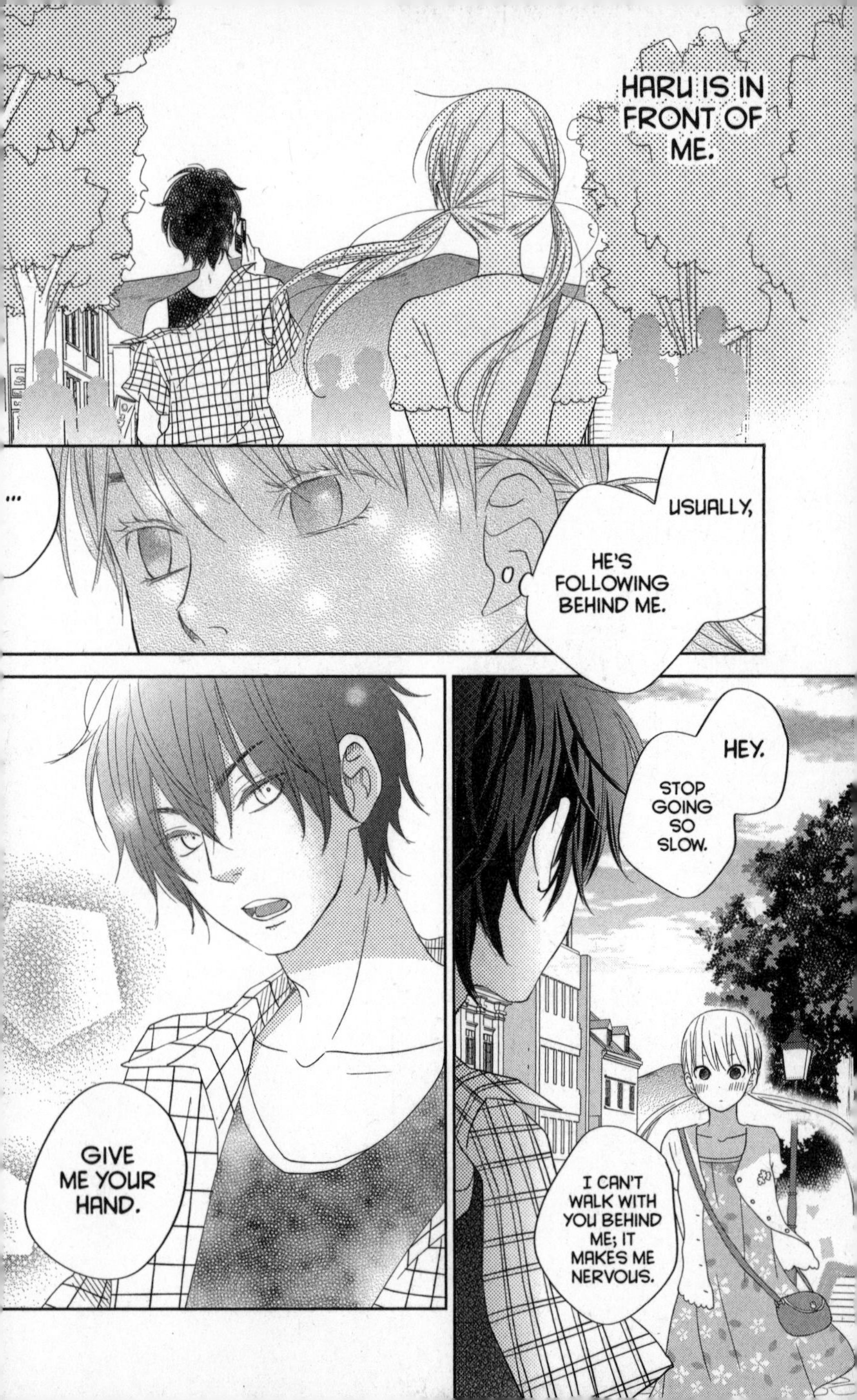
HARU IS IN FRONT OF ME.
USUALLY,
HE'S FOLLOWING BEHIND ME.
...
HEY.
STOP GOING SO SLOW.
I CAN'T WALK WITH YOU BEHIND ME; IT MAKES ME NERVOUS.
GIVE ME YOUR HAND.

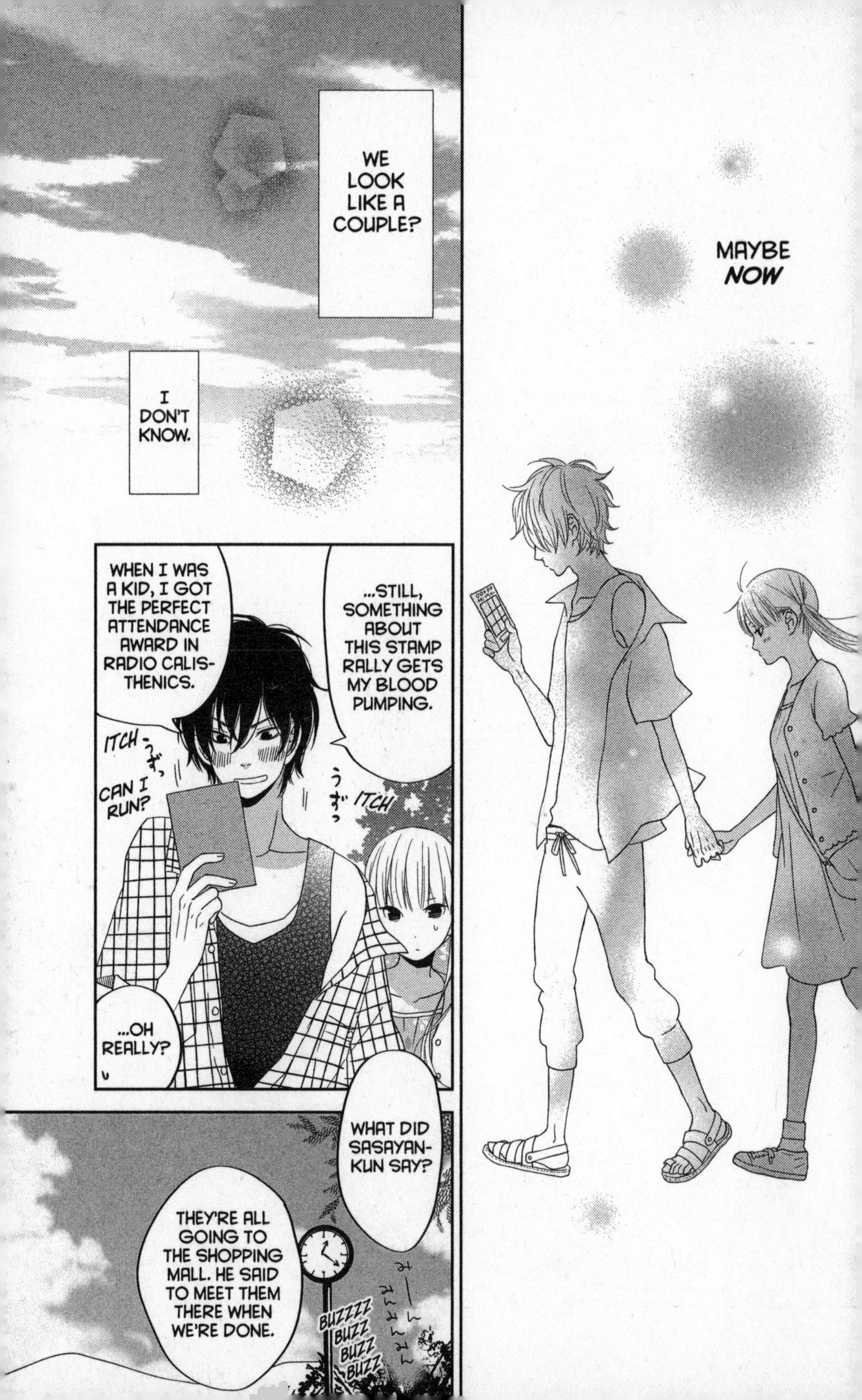
MAYBE NOW
WE LOOK LIKE A COUPLE?
I DON'T KNOW.
...STILL, SOMETHING ABOUT THIS STAMP RALLY GETS MY BLOOD PUMPING.
WHEN I WAS A KID, I GOT THE PERFECT ATTENDANCE AWARD IN RADIO CALIS-THENICS.
うずっ ITCH
ITCH うずっ
CAN I RUN?
...OH REALLY?
WHAT DID SASAYAN-KUN SAY?
THEY'RE ALL GOING TO THE SHOPPING MALL. HE SAID TO MEET THEM THERE WHEN WE'RE DONE.
みーんみんみんみん
BUZZZZ BUZZ BUZZ BUZZ

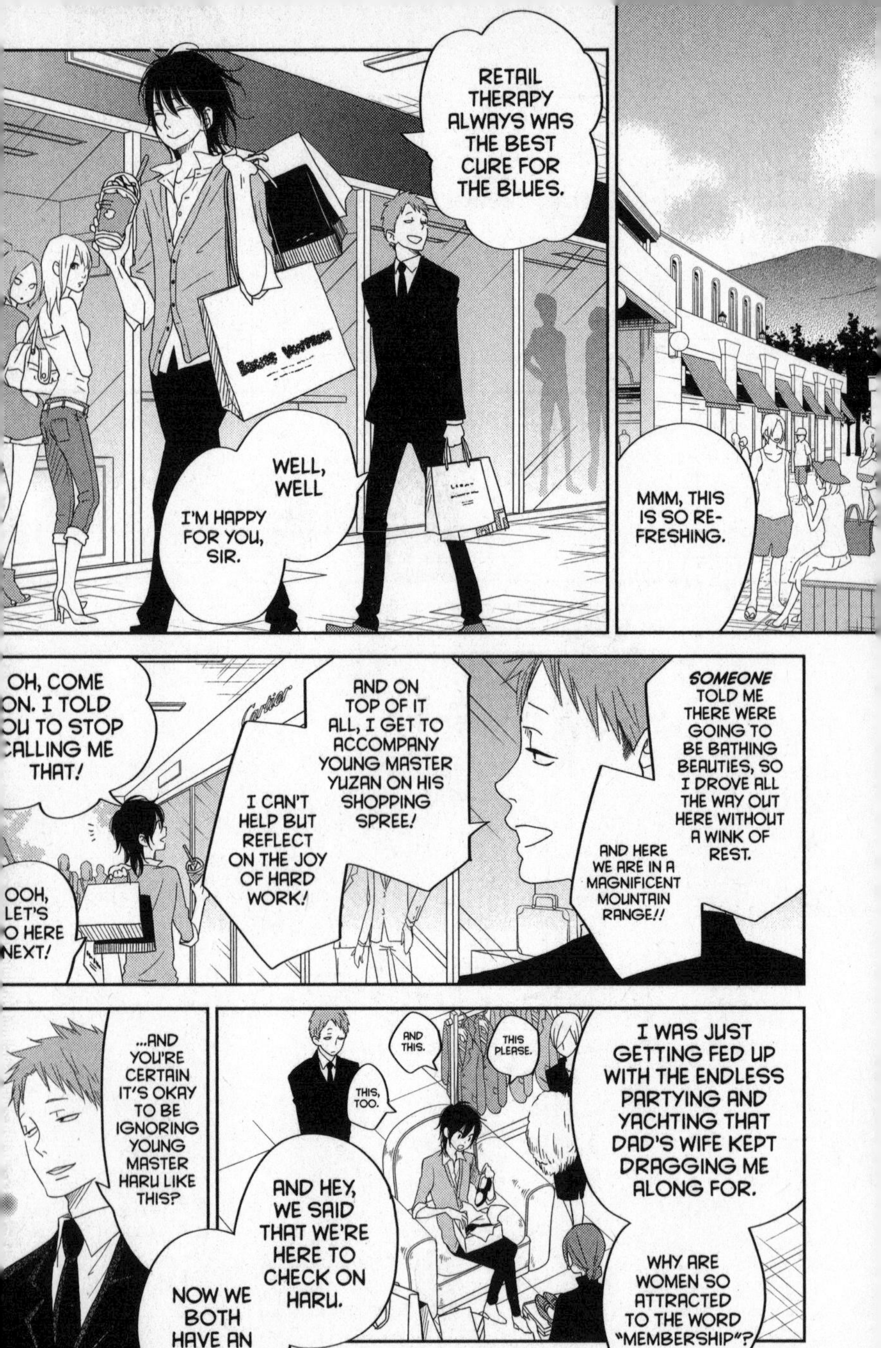
MMM, THIS IS SO RE-FRESHING.
RETAIL THERAPY ALWAYS WAS THE BEST CURE FOR THE BLUES.
WELL, WELL
I'M HAPPY FOR YOU, SIR.
SOMEONE TOLD ME THERE WERE GOING TO BE BATHING BEAUTIES, SO I DROVE ALL THE WAY OUT HERE WITHOUT A WINK OF REST.
AND HERE WE ARE IN A MAGNIFICENT MOUNTAIN RANGE!!
AND ON TOP OF IT ALL, I GET TO ACCOMPANY YOUNG MASTER YUZAN ON HIS SHOPPING SPREE!
I CAN'T HELP BUT REFLECT ON THE JOY OF HARD WORK!
OH, COME ON. I TOLD OU TO STOP CALLING ME THAT!
OOH, LET'S O HERE NEXT!
I WAS JUST GETTING FED UP WITH THE ENDLESS PARTYING AND YACHTING THAT DAD'S WIFE KEPT DRAGGING ME ALONG FOR.
WHY ARE WOMEN SO ATTRACTED TO THE WORD "MEMBERSHIP"?
THIS PLEASE.
AND THIS.
THIS, TOO.
AND HEY, WE SAID THAT WE'RE HERE TO CHECK ON HARU.
NOW WE BOTH HAVE AN EXCUSE.
...AND YOU'RE CERTAIN IT'S OKAY TO BE IGNORING YOUNG MASTER HARU LIKE THIS?

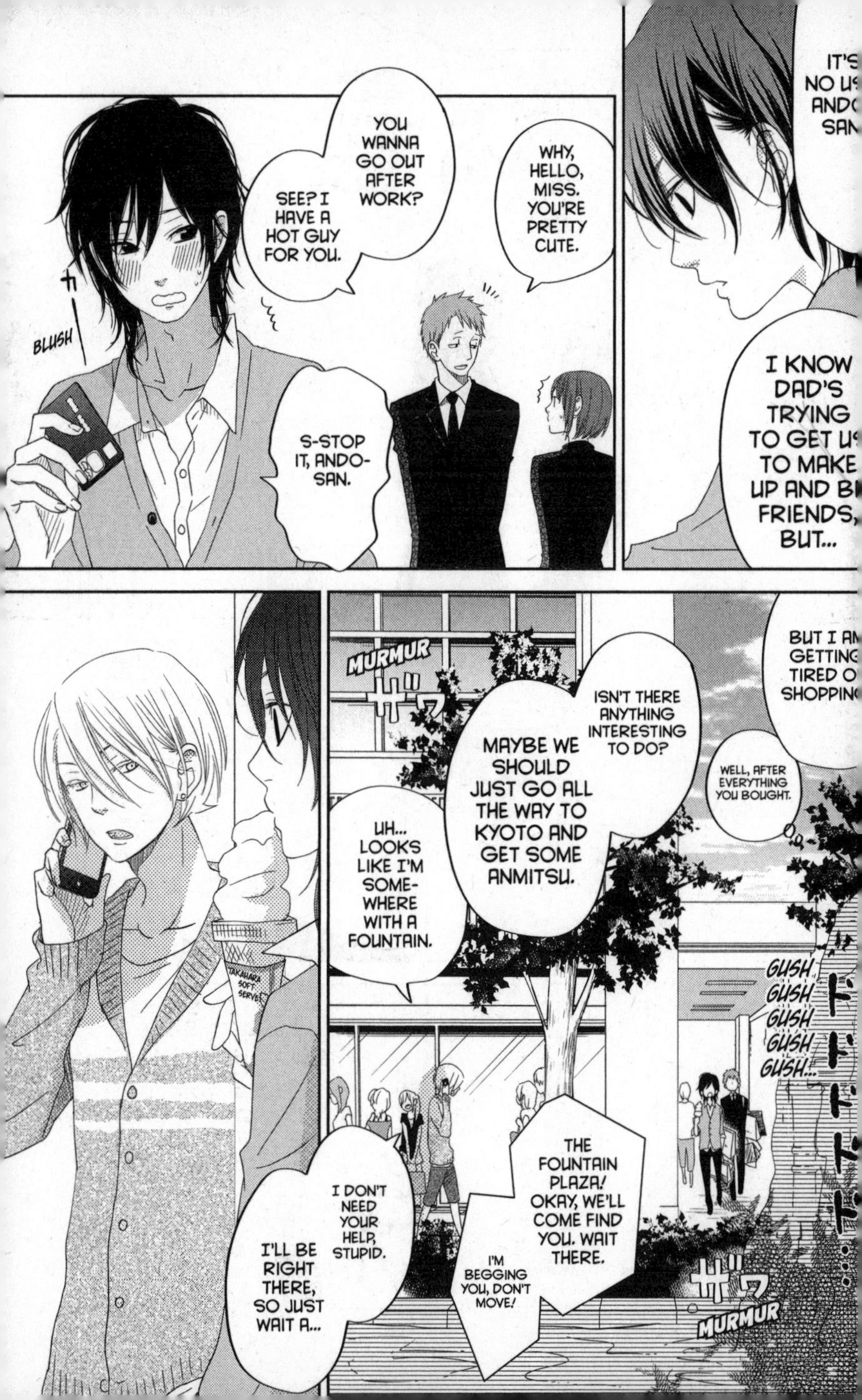
IT'S NO U ANDO SAN
I KNOW DAD'S TRYING TO GET U TO MAKE UP AND B FRIENDS, BUT...
WHY, HELLO, MISS. YOU'RE PRETTY CUTE.
YOU WANNA GO OUT AFTER WORK?
SEE? I HAVE A HOT GUY FOR YOU.
BLUSH
S-STOP IT, ANDO-SAN.
BUT I A GETTIN TIRED O SHOPPIN
WELL, AFTER EVERYTHING YOU BOUGHT.
ISN'T THERE ANYTHING INTERESTING TO DO?
MAYBE WE SHOULD JUST GO ALL THE WAY TO KYOTO AND GET SOME ANMITSU.
MURMUR
UH... LOOKS LIKE I'M SOME-WHERE WITH A FOUNTAIN.
GUSH GUSH GUSH GUSH GUSH...
THE FOUNTAIN PLAZA! OKAY, WE'LL COME FIND YOU. WAIT THERE.
I'M BEGGING YOU, DON'T MOVE!
MURMUR
I DON'T NEED YOUR HELP, STUPID.
I'LL BE RIGHT THERE, SO JUST WAIT A...
TAKAHARA SOFT SERVE

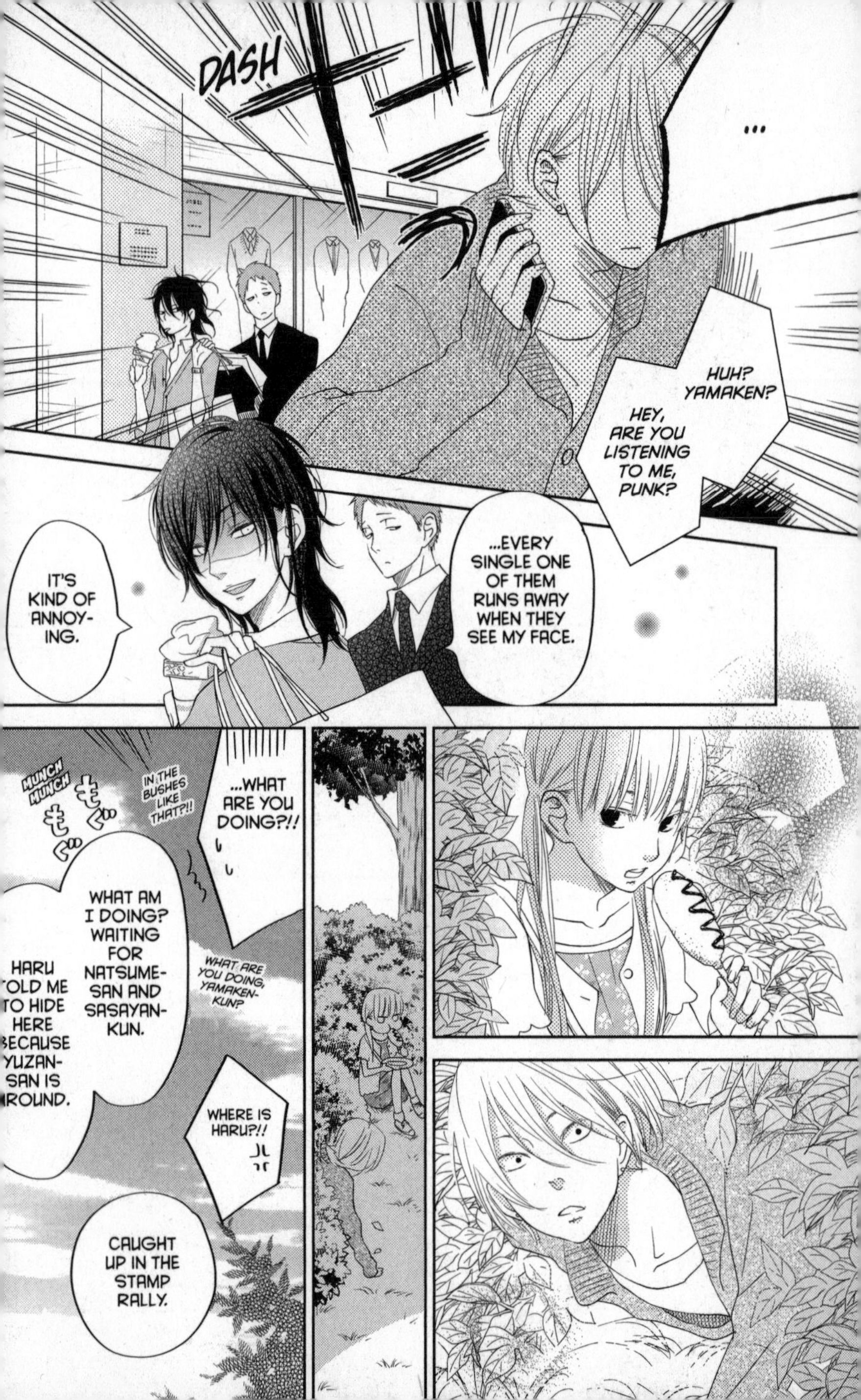
DASH
...
HUH? YAMAKEN?
HEY, ARE YOU LISTENING TO ME, PUNK?
...EVERY SINGLE ONE OF THEM RUNS AWAY WHEN THEY SEE MY FACE.
IT'S KIND OF ANNOYING.
WHAT ARE YOU DOING, YAMAKEN-KUN?
...WHAT ARE YOU DOING?!!
IN THE BUSHES LIKE THAT?!!
MUNCH MUNCH
WHAT AM I DOING? WAITING FOR NATSUME-SAN AND SASAYAN-KUN.
HARU TOLD ME TO HIDE HERE BECAUSE YUZAN-SAN IS AROUND.
WHERE IS HARU?!!
CAUGHT UP IN THE STAMP RALLY.

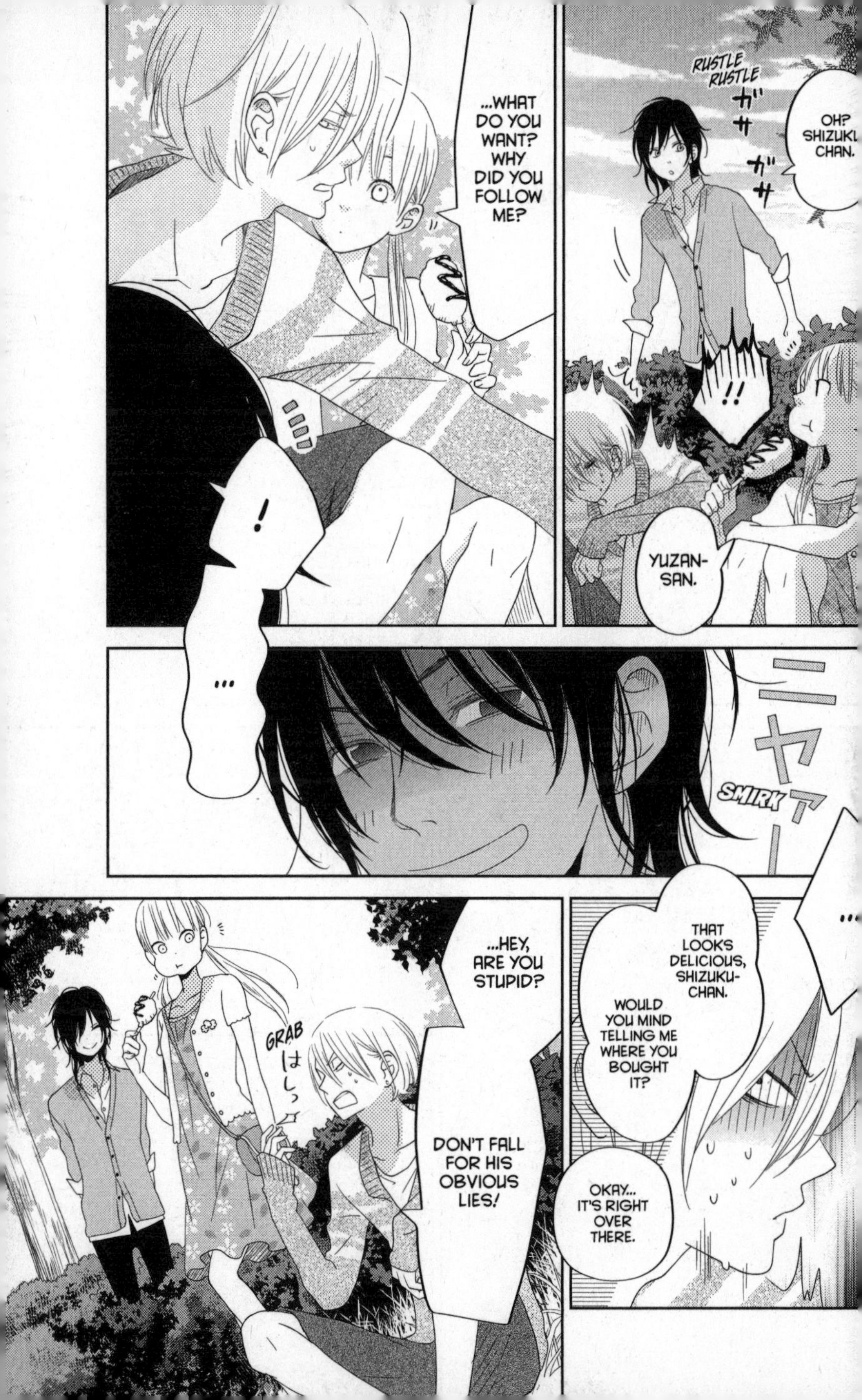
RUSTLE RUSTLE
ガサ ガサ
OH? SHIZUKU-CHAN.
!!
YUZAN-SAN.
...WHAT DO YOU WANT? WHY DID YOU FOLLOW ME?
!
SMIRK
ニヤー
...
...
THAT LOOKS DELICIOUS, SHIZUKU-CHAN.
WOULD YOU MIND TELLING ME WHERE YOU BOUGHT IT?
OKAY... IT'S RIGHT OVER THERE.
...HEY, ARE YOU STUPID?
GRAB
はしっ
DON'T FALL FOR HIS OBVIOUS LIES!

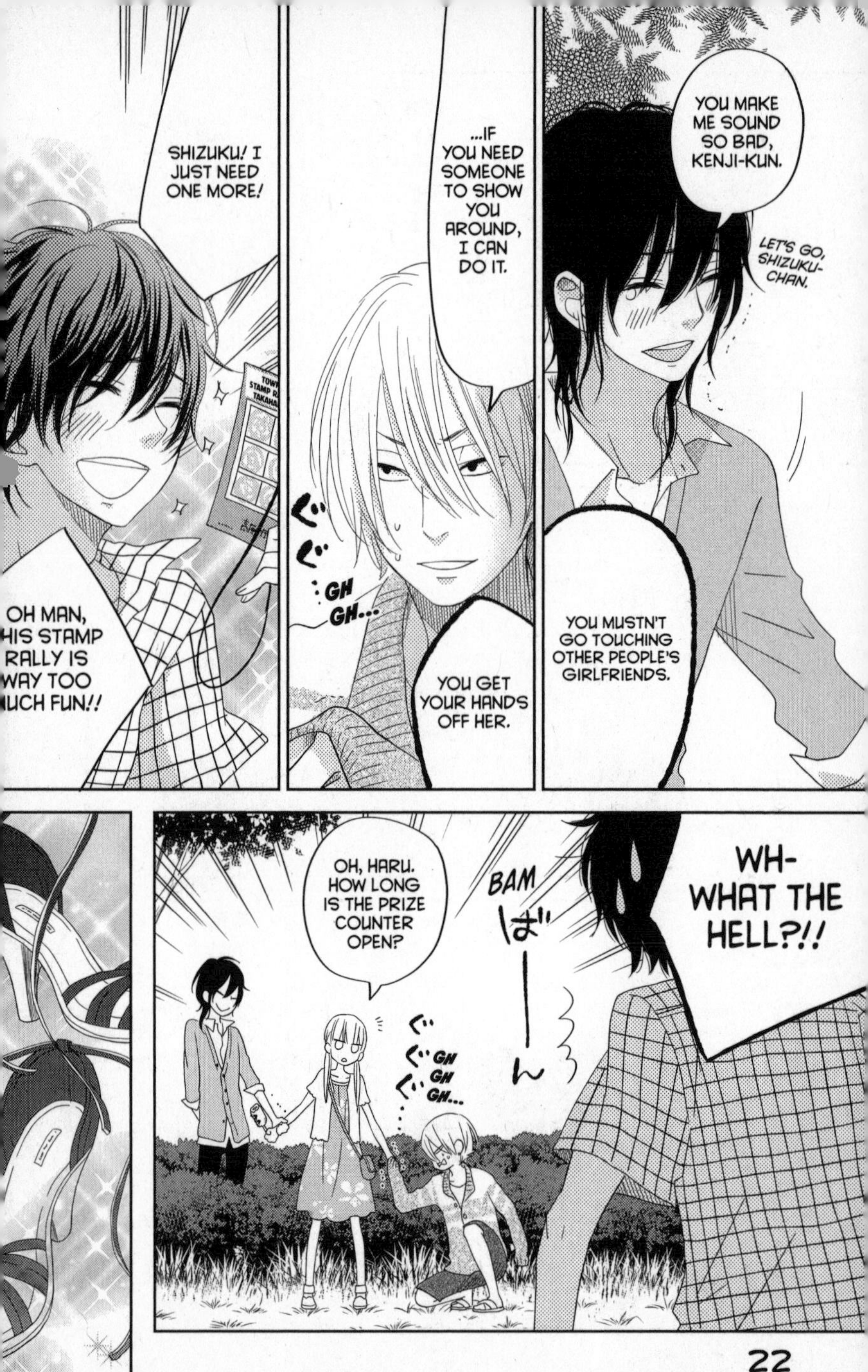
YOU MAKE ME SOUND SO BAD, KENJI-KUN.
LET'S GO, SHIZUKU-CHAN.
YOU MUSTN'T GO TOUCHING OTHER PEOPLE'S GIRLFRIENDS.
...IF YOU NEED SOMEONE TO SHOW YOU AROUND, I CAN DO IT.
ぐぐ
GH GH...
YOU GET YOUR HANDS OFF HER.
SHIZUKU! I JUST NEED ONE MORE!
OH MAN, HIS STAMP RALLY IS WAY TOO UCH FUN!!
WH-WHAT THE HELL?!!
BAM
ばーん
OH, HARU. HOW LONG IS THE PRIZE COUNTER OPEN?
ぐぐぐ
GH GH GH...

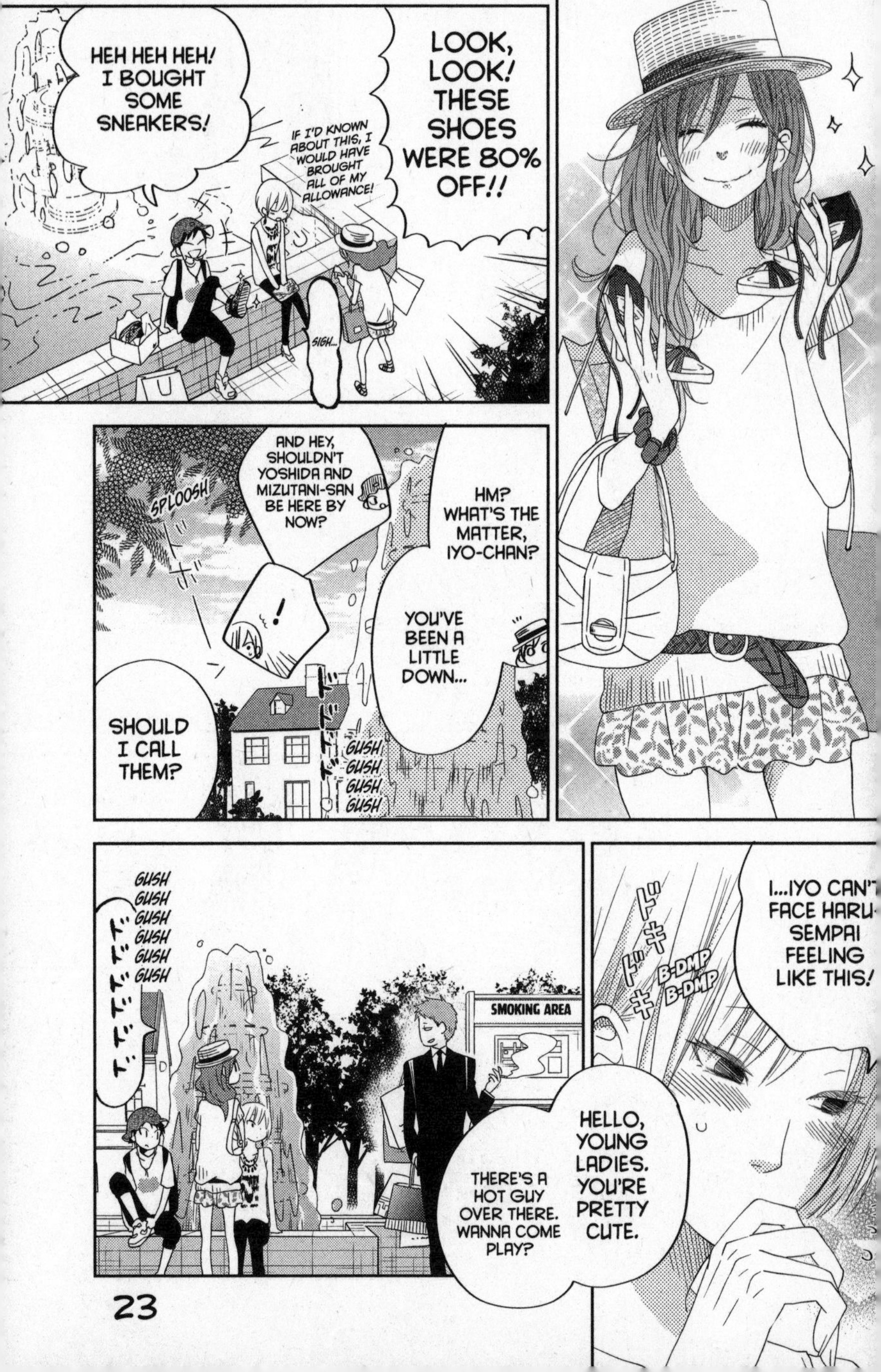
LOOK, LOOK! THESE SHOES WERE 80% OFF!!
IF I'D KNOWN ABOUT THIS, I WOULD HAVE BROUGHT ALL OF MY ALLOWANCE!
HEH HEH HEH! I BOUGHT SOME SNEAKERS!
SIGH...
HM? WHAT'S THE MATTER, IYO-CHAN?
YOU'VE BEEN A LITTLE DOWN...
AND HEY, SHOULDN'T YOSHIDA AND MIZUTANI-SAN BE HERE BY NOW?
!
SPLOOSH
GUSH GUSH GUSH GUSH
SHOULD I CALL THEM?
I...IYO CAN'T FACE HARU-SEMPAI FEELING LIKE THIS!
B-DMP B-DMP
HELLO, YOUNG LADIES. YOU'RE PRETTY CUTE.
THERE'S A HOT GUY OVER THERE. WANNA COME PLAY?
SMOKING AREA
GUSH GUSH GUSH GUSH GUSH GUSH

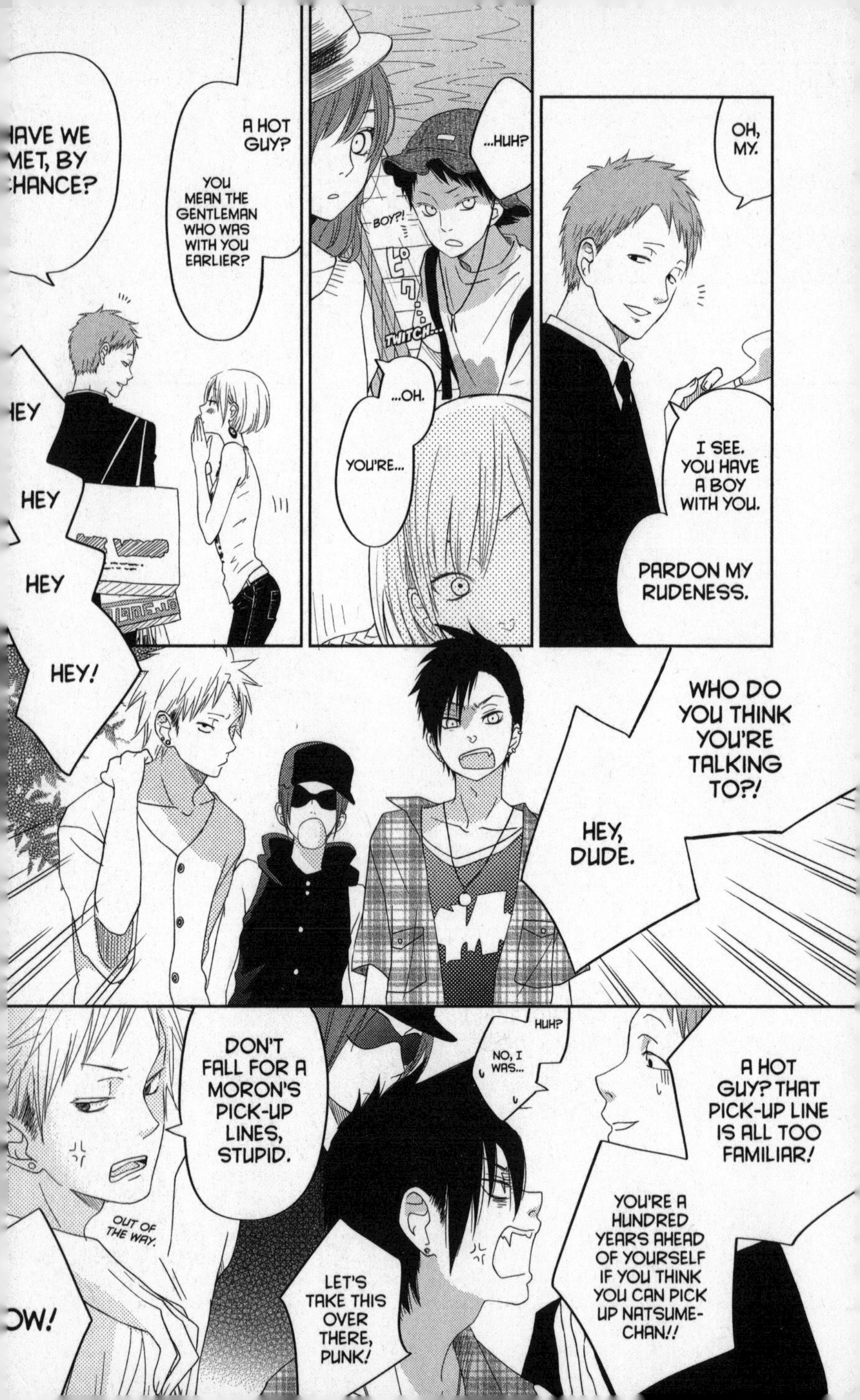
OH, MY.
I SEE. YOU HAVE A BOY WITH YOU.
PARDON MY RUDENESS.
...HUH?
BOY?!
TWITCH...
...OH.
YOU'RE...
A HOT GUY?
YOU MEAN THE GENTLEMAN WHO WAS WITH YOU EARLIER?
HAVE WE MET, BY CHANCE?
HEY
HEY
HEY
HEY!
WHO DO YOU THINK YOU'RE TALKING TO?!
HEY, DUDE.
A HOT GUY? THAT PICK-UP LINE IS ALL TOO FAMILIAR!
YOU'RE A HUNDRED YEARS AHEAD OF YOURSELF IF YOU THINK YOU CAN PICK UP NATSUME-CHAN!!
HUH?
NO, I WAS...
LET'S TAKE THIS OVER THERE, PUNK!
DON'T FALL FOR A MORON'S PICK-UP LINES, STUPID.
OUT OF THE WAY.
OW!

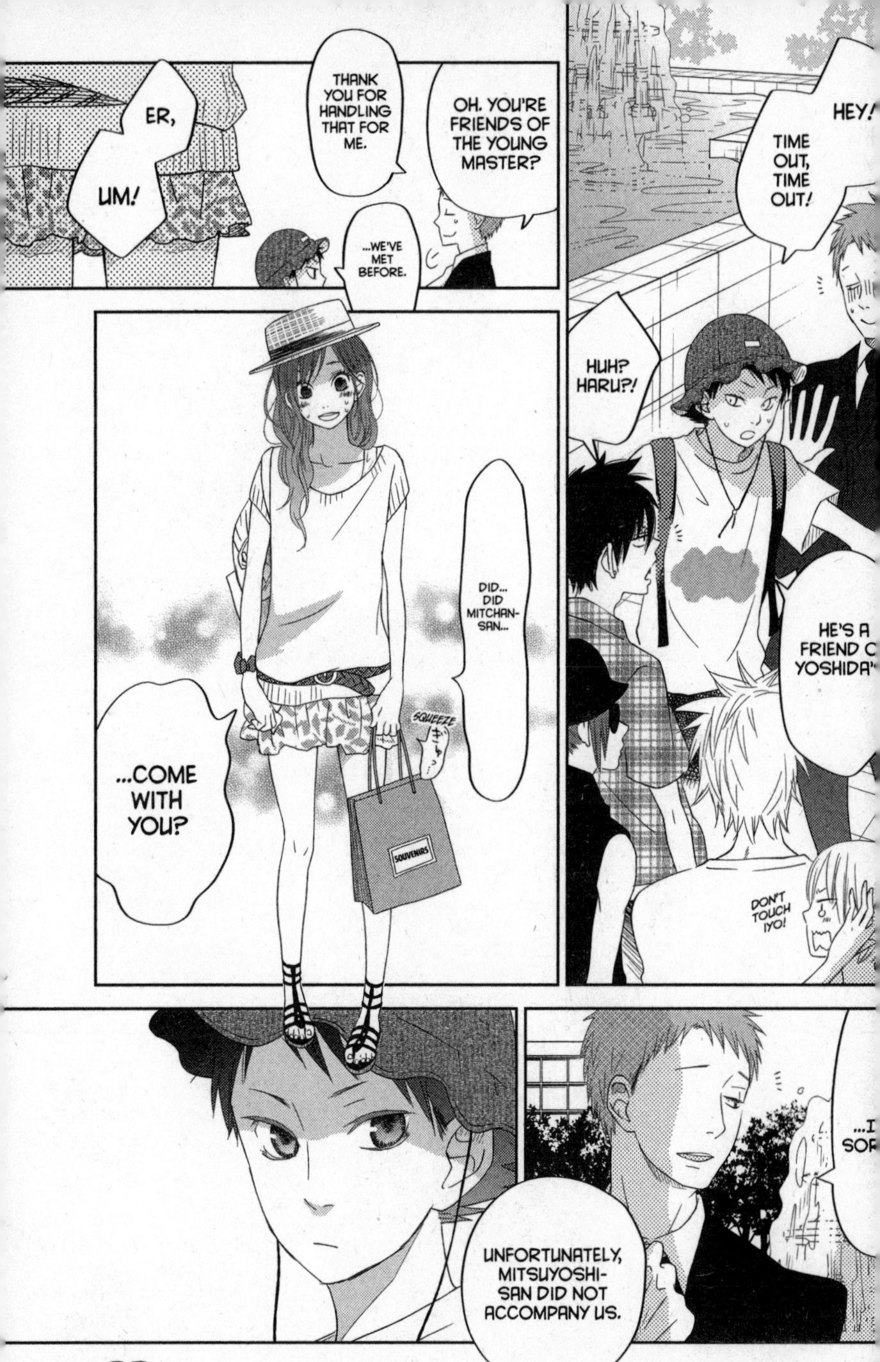
HEY!
TIME OUT, TIME OUT!
HUH? HARU?!
HE'S A FRIEND O YOSHIDA'
DON'T TOUCH IYO!
OH. YOU'RE FRIENDS OF THE YOUNG MASTER?
THANK YOU FOR HANDLING THAT FOR ME.
...WE'VE MET BEFORE.
ER,
UM!
DID... DID MITCHAN-SAN...
SQUEEZE
SOUVENIRS
...COME WITH YOU?
...I SOR
UNFORTUNATELY, MITSUYOSHI-SAN DID NOT ACCOMPANY US.

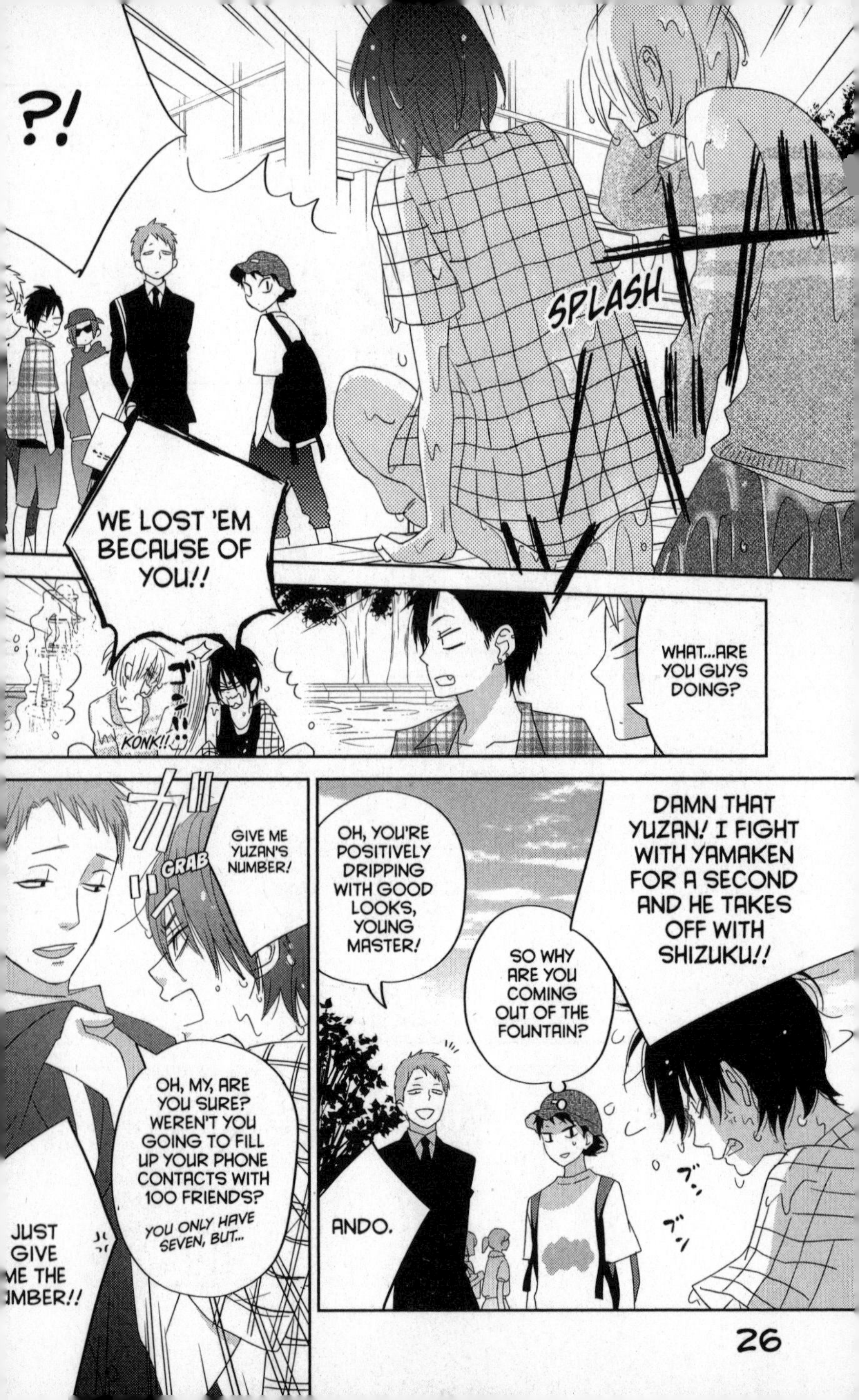
SPLASH
?!
WE LOST 'EM BECAUSE OF YOU!!
WHAT...ARE YOU GUYS DOING?
KONK!!
DAMN THAT YUZAN! I FIGHT WITH YAMAKEN FOR A SECOND AND HE TAKES OFF WITH SHIZUKU!!
SO WHY ARE YOU COMING OUT OF THE FOUNTAIN?
OH, YOU'RE POSITIVELY DRIPPING WITH GOOD LOOKS, YOUNG MASTER!
ANDO.
GIVE ME YUZAN'S NUMBER!
GRAB
OH, MY, ARE YOU SURE? WEREN'T YOU GOING TO FILL UP YOUR PHONE CONTACTS WITH 100 FRIENDS?
YOU ONLY HAVE SEVEN, BUT...
JUST GIVE ME THE UMBER!!

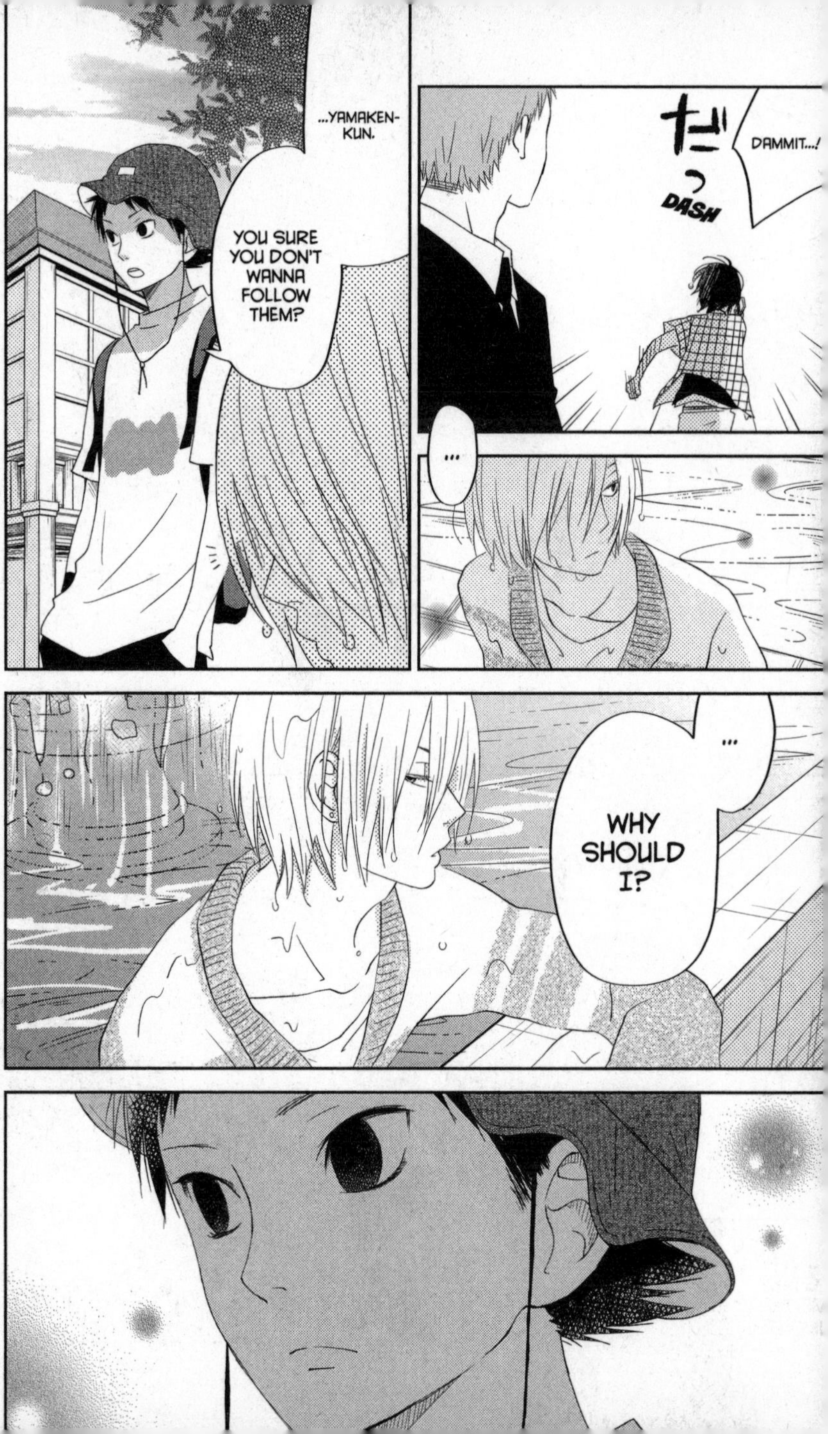
だっ
DASH
DAMMIT...!
...
...YAMAKEN-KUN.
YOU SURE YOU DON'T WANNA FOLLOW THEM?
...
WHY SHOULD I?

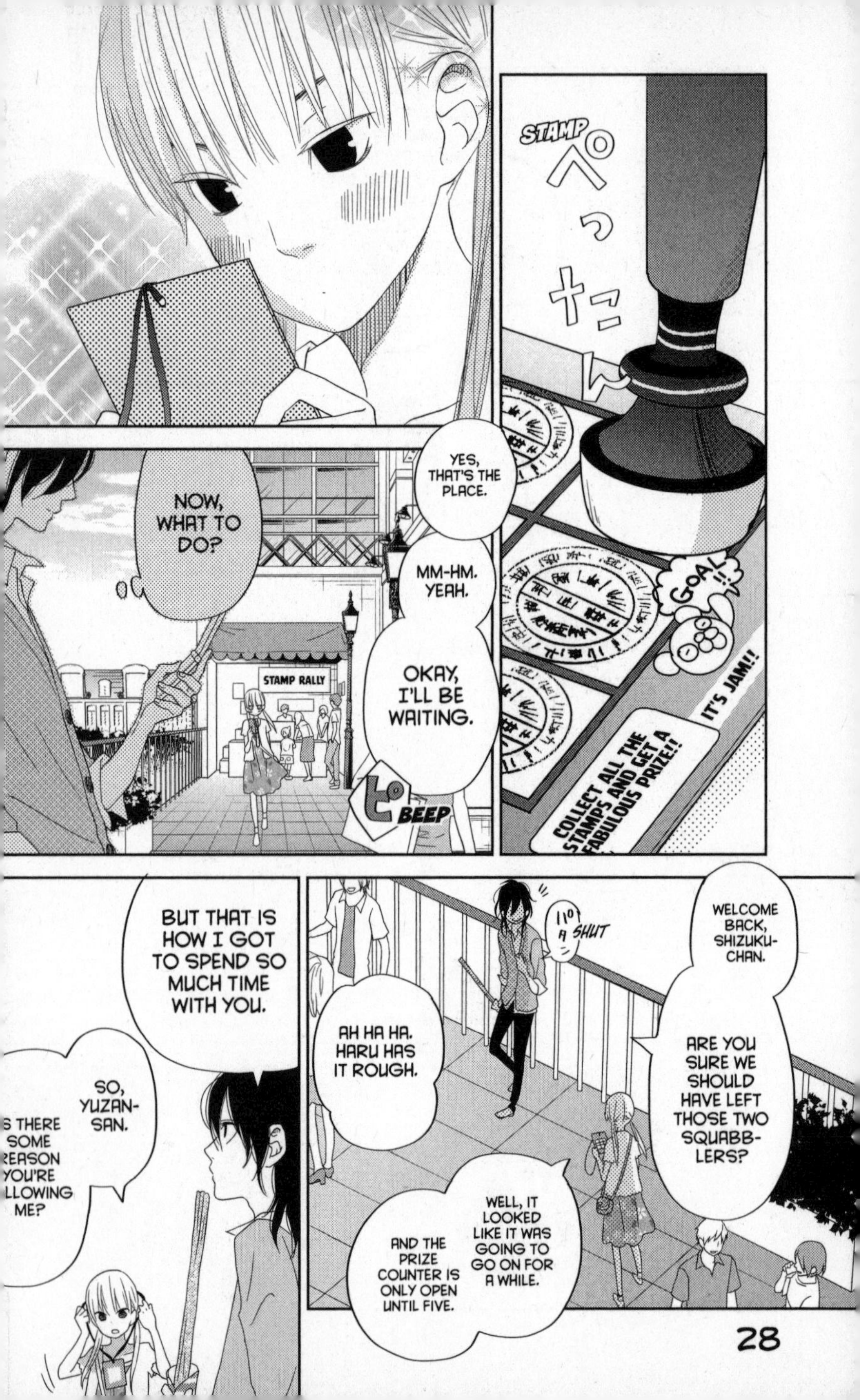
STAMP
ぺったん
GOAL!!
IT'S JAM!!
COLLECT ALL THE STAMPS AND GET A FABULOUS PRIZE!!
YES, THAT'S THE PLACE.
NOW, WHAT TO DO?
MM-HM. YEAH.
STAMP RALLY
OKAY, I'LL BE WAITING.
ピ BEEP
WELCOME BACK, SHIZUKU-CHAN.
SHUT
ARE YOU SURE WE SHOULD HAVE LEFT THOSE TWO SQUABB-LERS?
AH HA HA. HARU HAS IT ROUGH.
WELL, IT LOOKED LIKE IT WAS GOING TO GO ON FOR A WHILE.
AND THE PRIZE COUNTER IS ONLY OPEN UNTIL FIVE.
BUT THAT IS HOW I GOT TO SPEND SO MUCH TIME WITH YOU.
SO, YUZAN-SAN.
S THERE SOME REASON YOU'RE LLOWING ME?

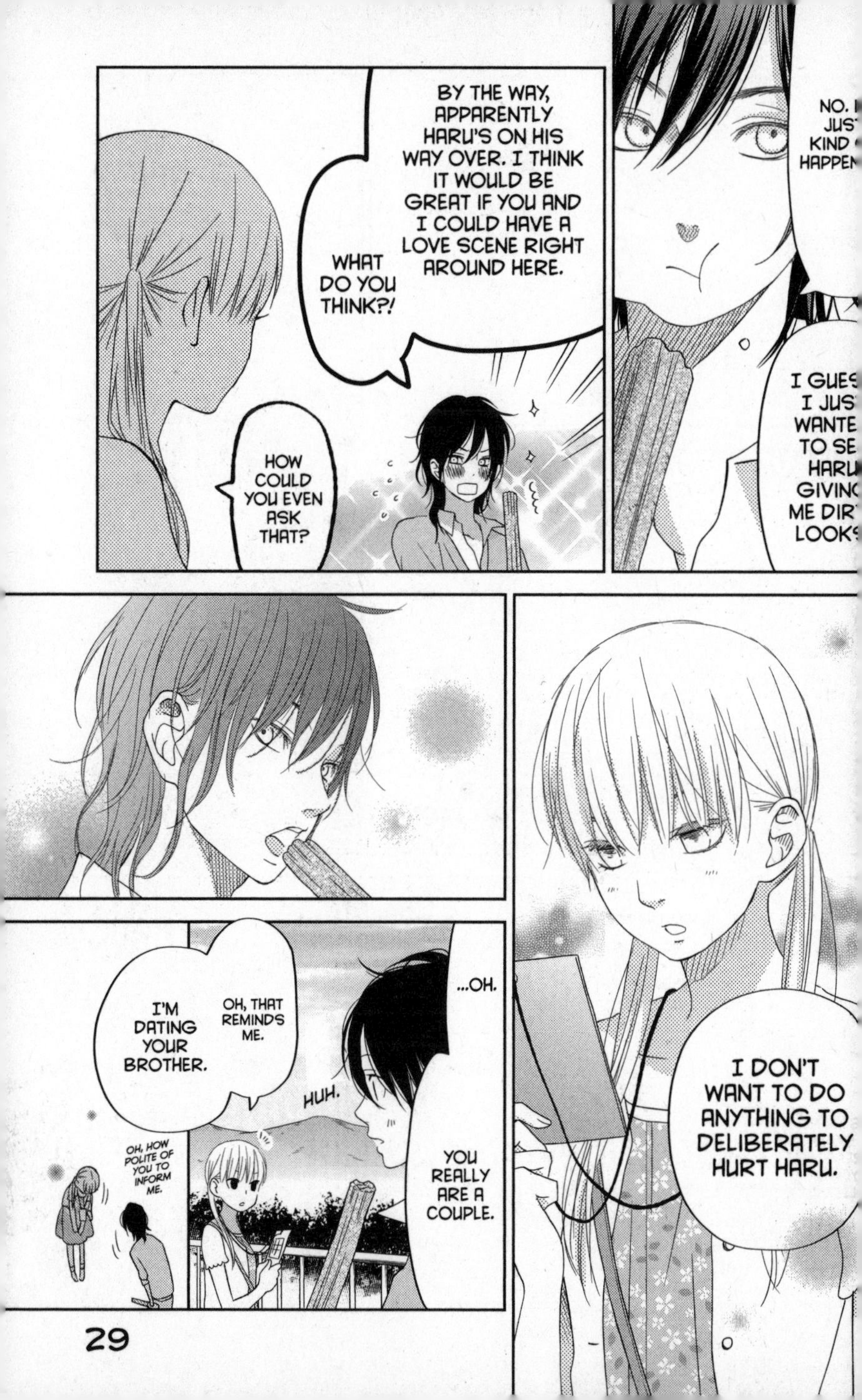
NO. I JUST KIND HAPPEN
I GUES I JUS WANTE TO SE HARU GIVING ME DIRT LOOKS
BY THE WAY, APPARENTLY HARU'S ON HIS WAY OVER. I THINK IT WOULD BE GREAT IF YOU AND I COULD HAVE A LOVE SCENE RIGHT AROUND HERE.
WHAT DO YOU THINK?!
HOW COULD YOU EVEN ASK THAT?
I DON'T WANT TO DO ANYTHING TO DELIBERATELY HURT HARU.
...OH.
YOU REALLY ARE A COUPLE.
OH, THAT REMINDS ME.
I'M DATING YOUR BROTHER.
HUH.
OH, HOW POLITE OF YOU TO INFORM ME.

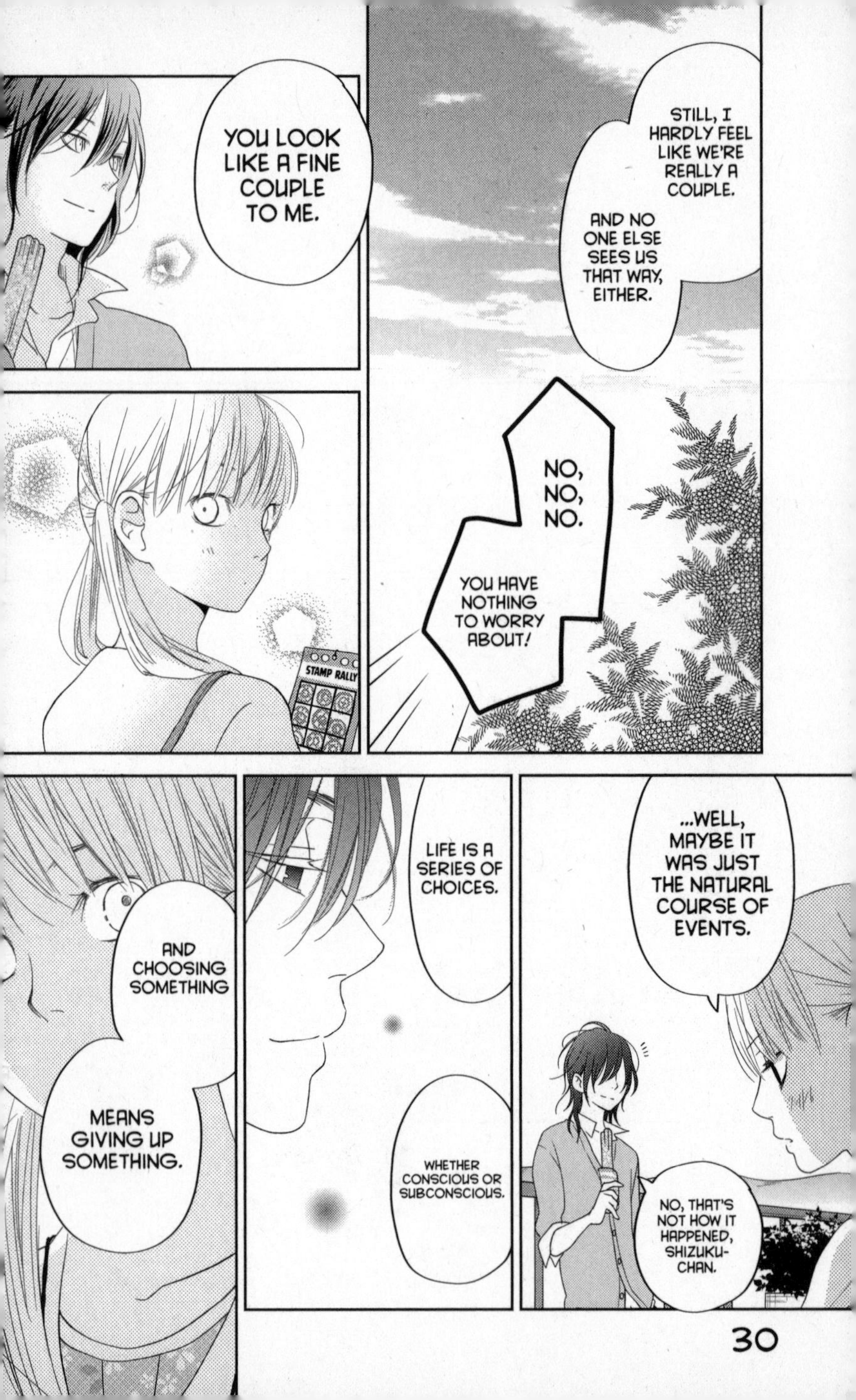
STILL, I HARDLY FEEL LIKE WE'RE REALLY A COUPLE.
AND NO ONE ELSE SEES US THAT WAY, EITHER.
NO, NO, NO.
YOU HAVE NOTHING TO WORRY ABOUT!
YOU LOOK LIKE A FINE COUPLE TO ME.
STAMP RALLY
...WELL, MAYBE IT WAS JUST THE NATURAL COURSE OF EVENTS.
NO, THAT'S NOT HOW IT HAPPENED, SHIZUKU-CHAN.
LIFE IS A SERIES OF CHOICES.
WHETHER CONSCIOUS OR SUBCONSCIOUS.
AND CHOOSING SOMETHING
MEANS GIVING UP SOMETHING.

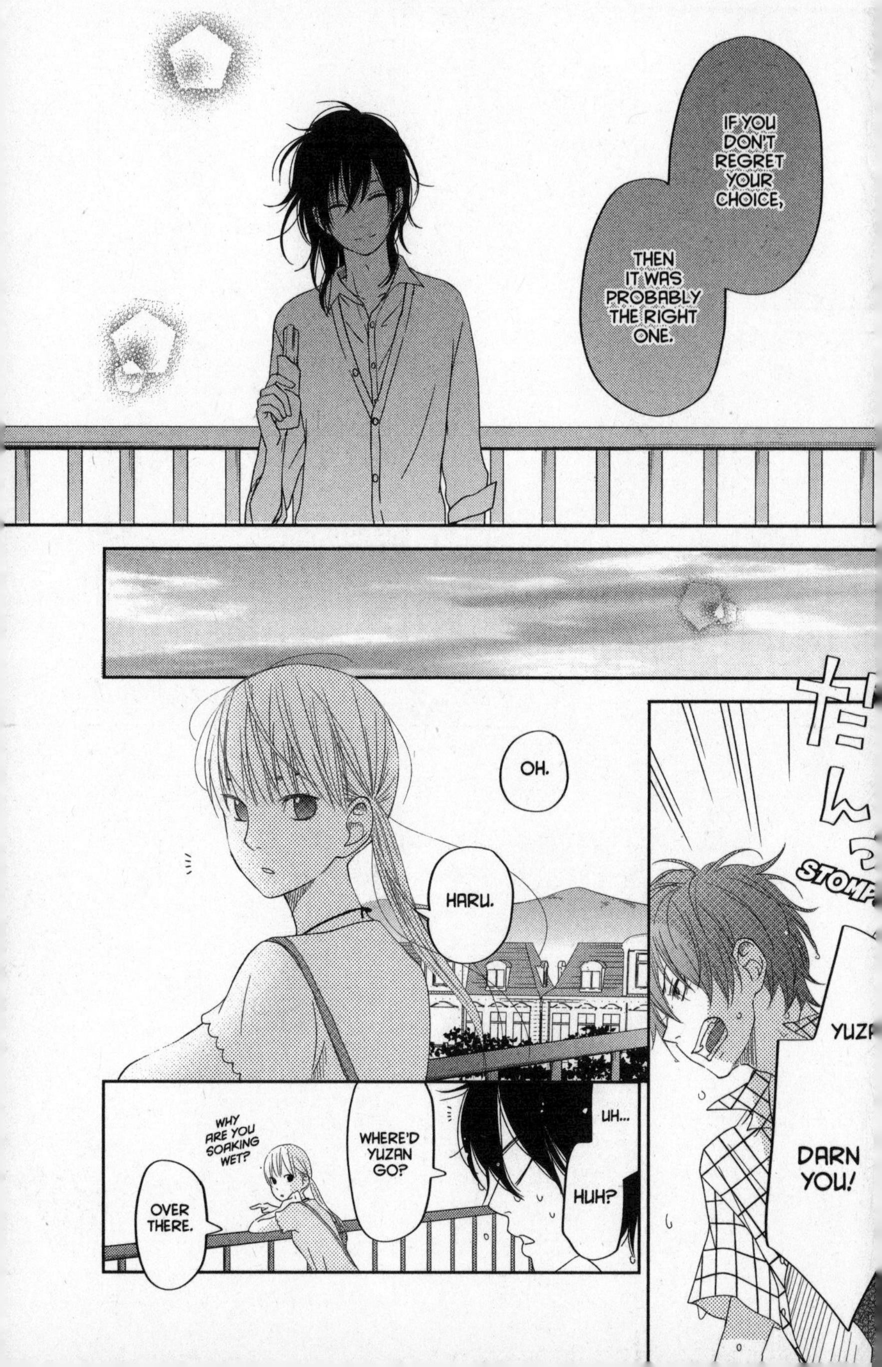
IF YOU DON'T REGRET YOUR CHOICE,
THEN IT WAS PROBABLY THE RIGHT ONE.
だんっ
STOMP
YUZA
DARN YOU!
OH.
HARU.
UH...
HUH?
WHERE'D YUZAN GO?
WHY ARE YOU SOAKING WET?
OVER THERE.

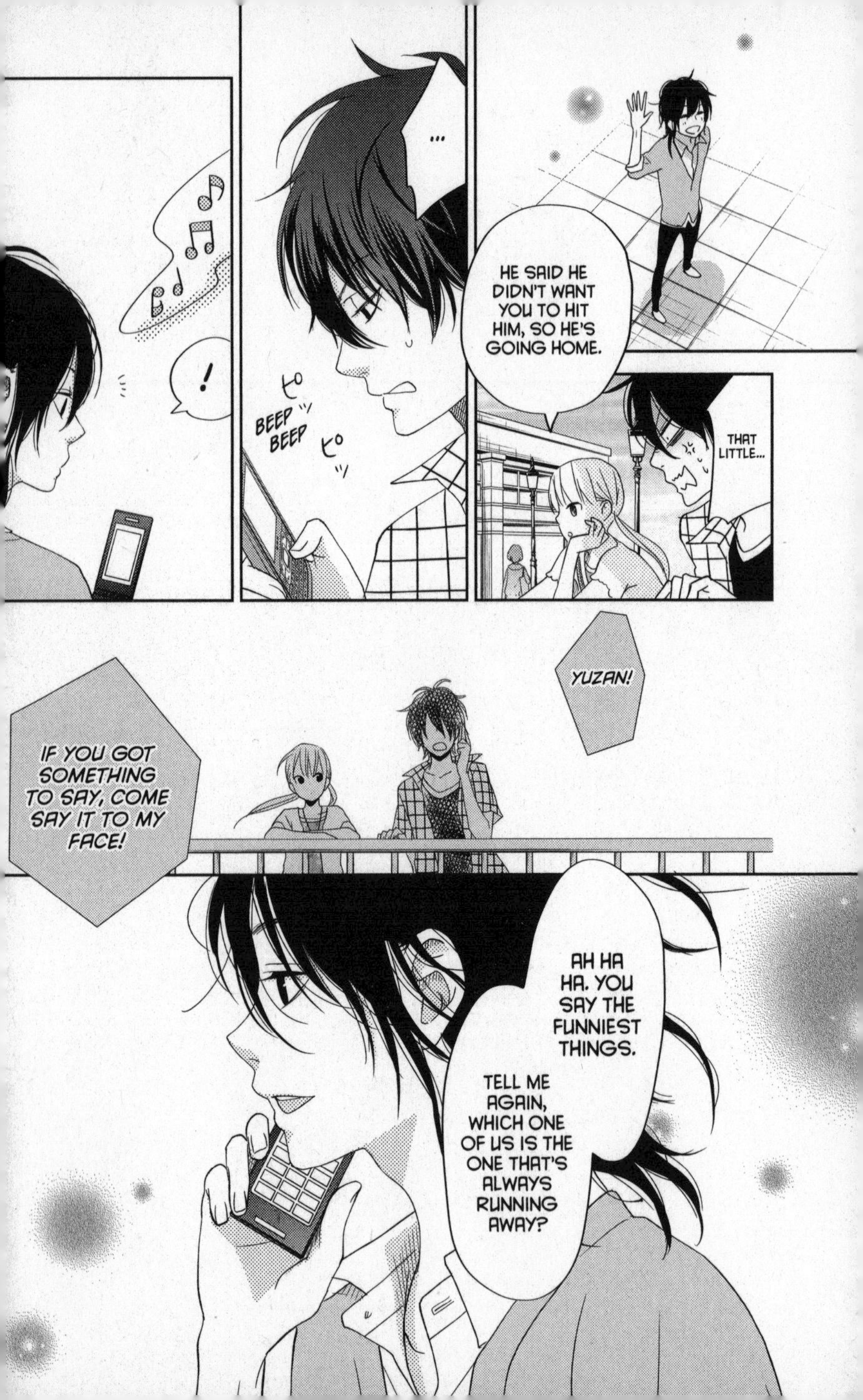
HE SAID HE DIDN'T WANT YOU TO HIT HIM, SO HE'S GOING HOME.
THAT LITTLE...
...
ピッ
BEEP BEEP
ピッ
!
YUZAN!
IF YOU GOT SOMETHING TO SAY, COME SAY IT TO MY FACE!
AH HA HA. YOU SAY THE FUNNIEST THINGS.
TELL ME AGAIN, WHICH ONE OF US IS THE ONE THAT'S ALWAYS RUNNING AWAY?

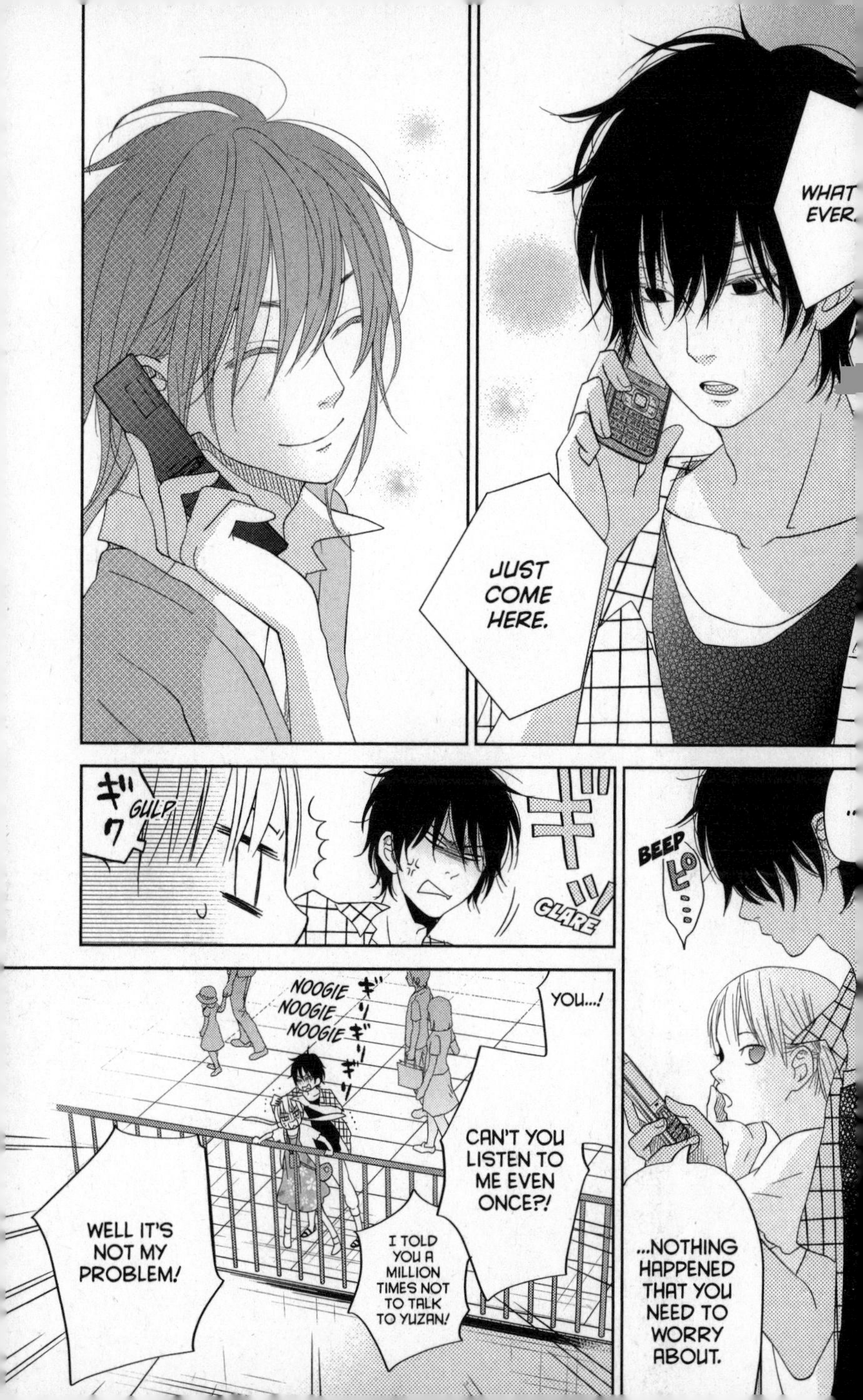
WHAT EVER.
JUST COME HERE.
...
BEEP
ピ...
...NOTHING HAPPENED THAT YOU NEED TO WORRY ABOUT.
ギッ
GLARE
ギク
GULP
YOU...!
CAN'T YOU LISTEN TO ME EVEN ONCE?!
NOOGIE NOOGIE NOOGIE
ギリギリギリ
I TOLD YOU A MILLION TIMES NOT TO TALK TO YUZAN!
WELL IT'S NOT MY PROBLEM!

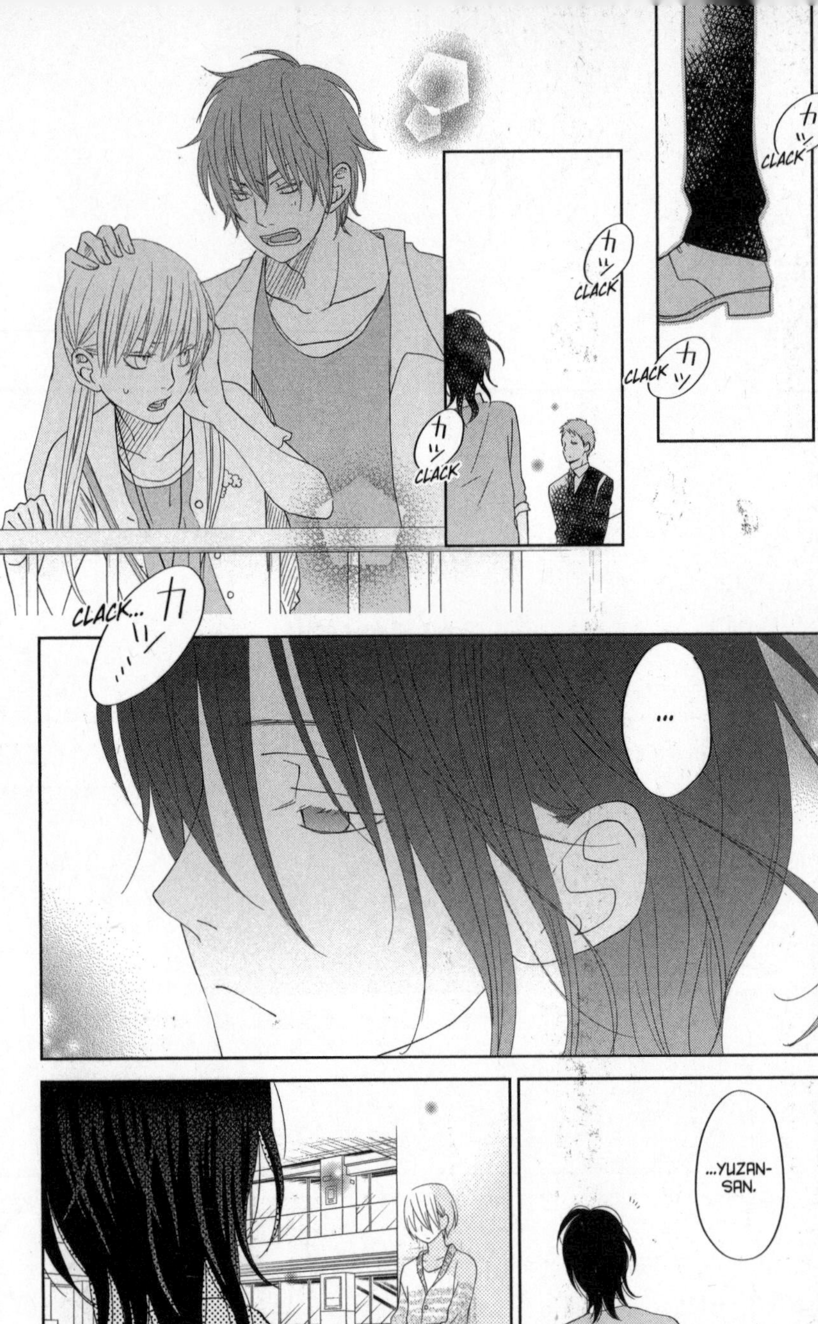

カッ
CLACK
カッ
CLACK
カッ
CLACK
カッ
CLACK
CLACK...
カッ...
...
...YUZAN-SAN.

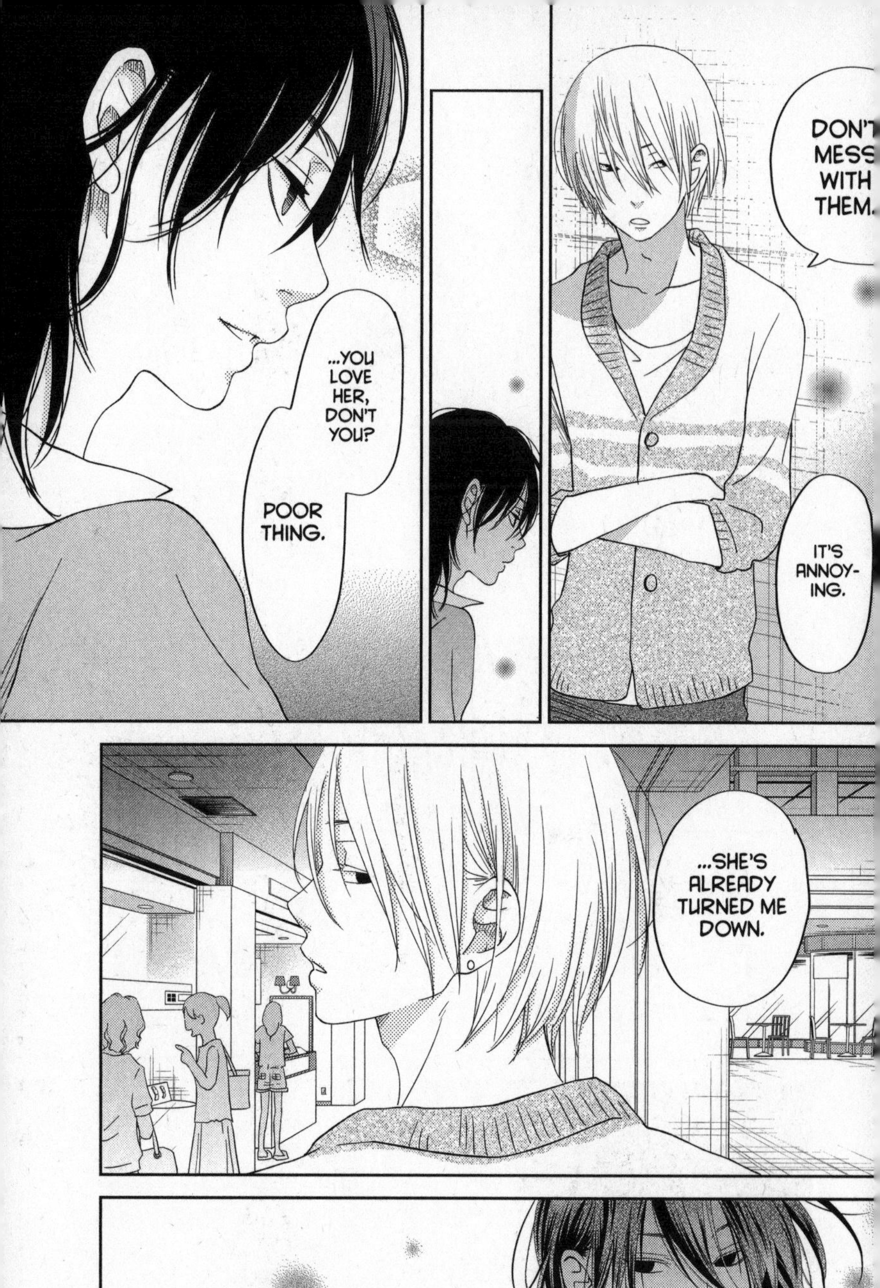
DON'T MESS WITH THEM.
IT'S ANNOYING.
...YOU LOVE HER, DON'T YOU?
POOR THING.
...SHE'S ALREADY TURNED ME DOWN.

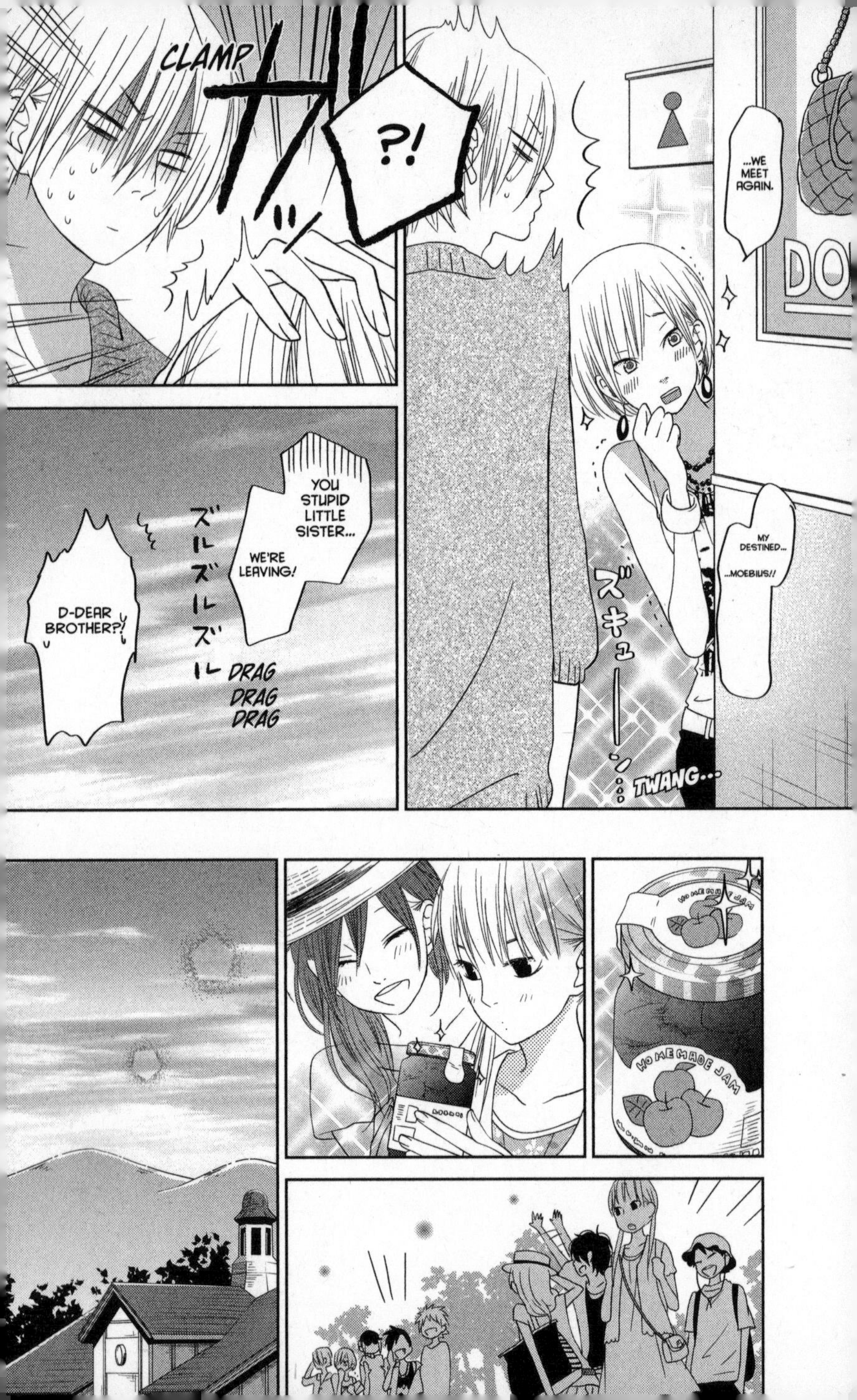
...WE MEET AGAIN.
MY DESTINED...
...MOEBIUS!!
ズキューーン…
TWANG...
CLAMP
?!
YOU STUPID LITTLE SISTER...
WE'RE LEAVING!
D-DEAR BROTHER?!
ズルズルズル
DRAG DRAG DRAG

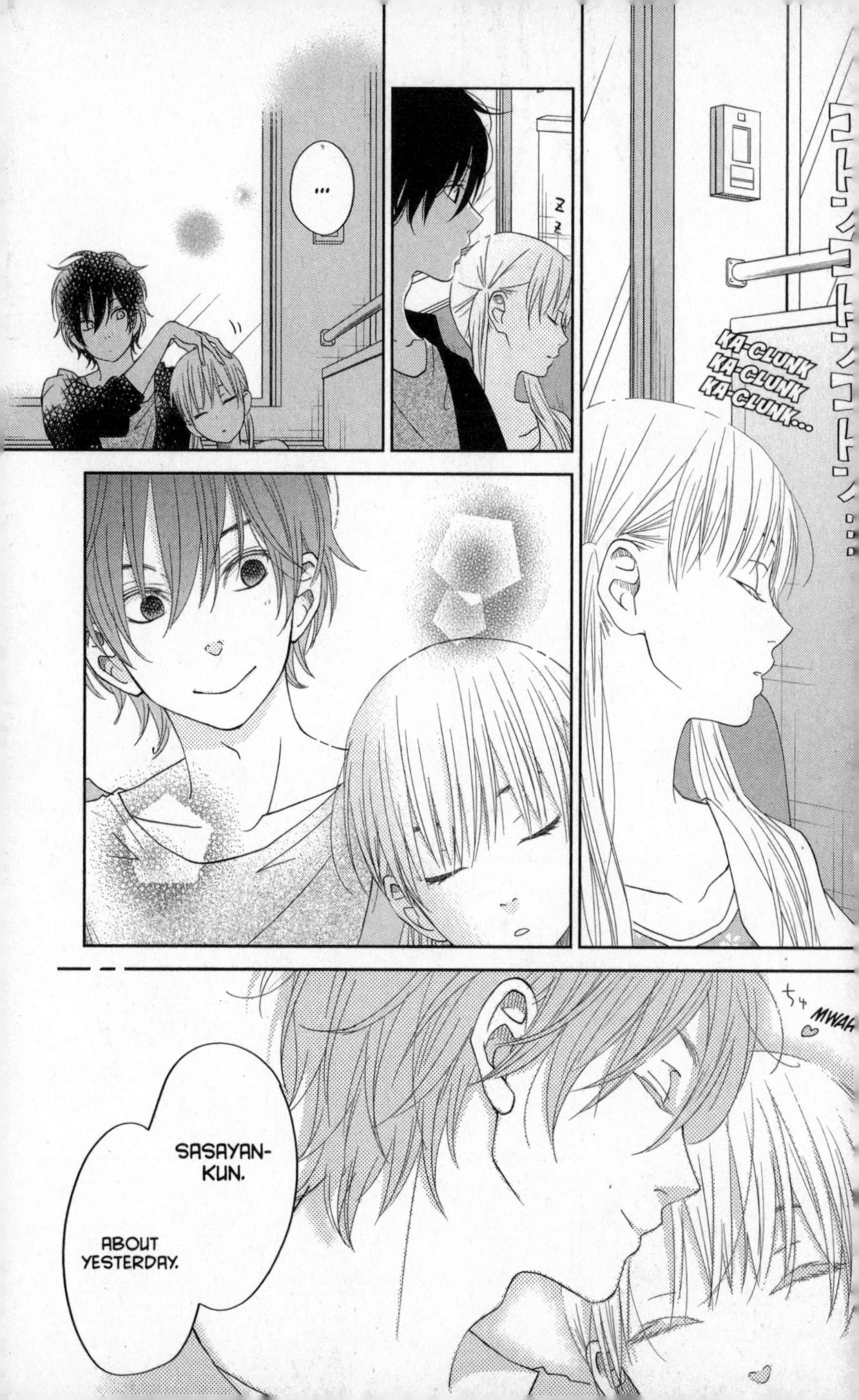
コトンコトンコトン…
KA-CLUNK
KA-CLUNK
KA-CLUNK...
Z
Z
...
ちゅ
MWAH
SASAYAN-KUN.
ABOUT YESTERDAY.

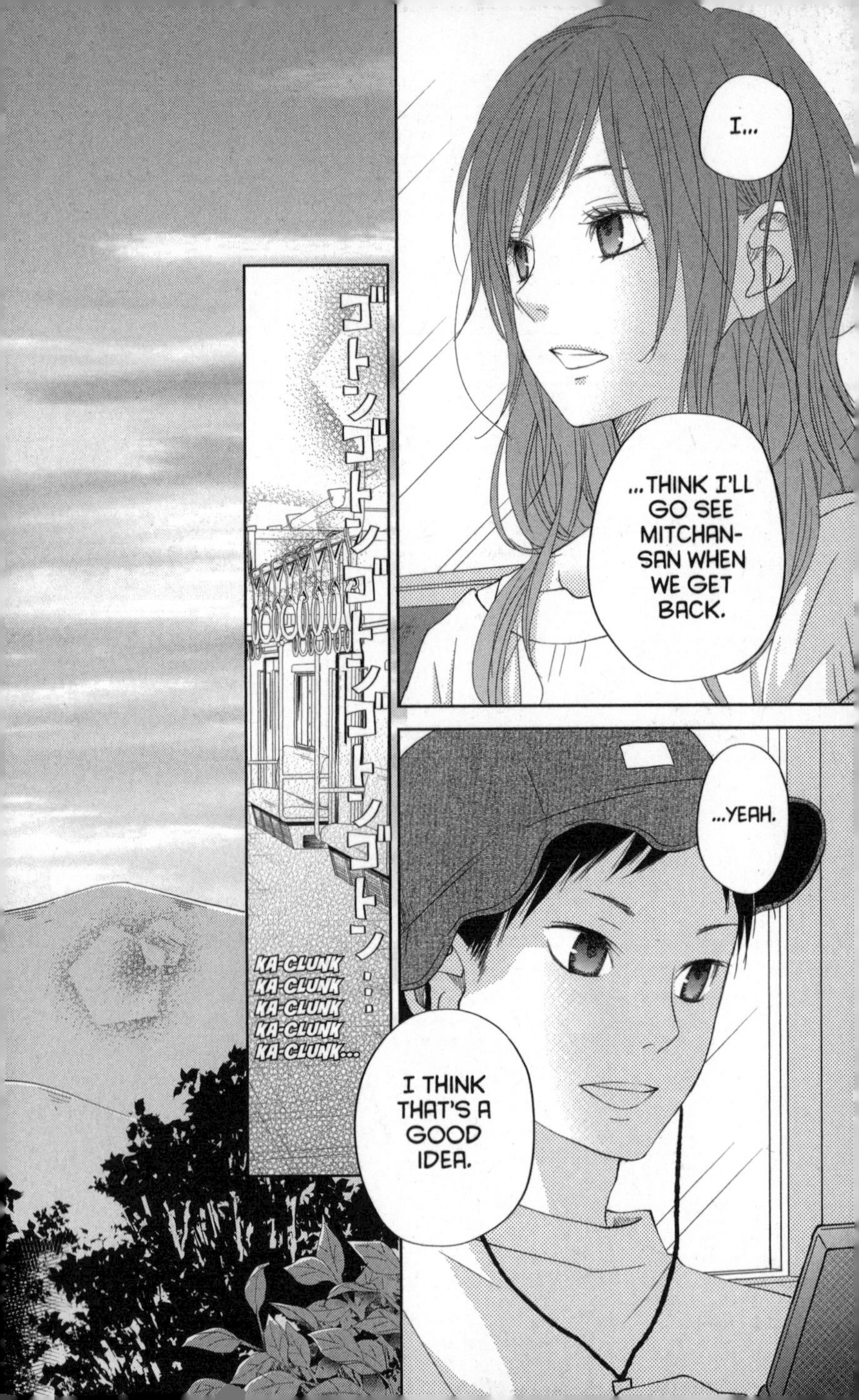

I...
...THINK I'LL GO SEE MITCHAN-SAN WHEN WE GET BACK.
...YEAH.
I THINK THAT'S A GOOD IDEA.
ゴトンゴトンゴトンゴトンゴトン・・・
KA-CLUNK KA-CLUNK KA-CLUNK KA-CLUNK KA-CLUNK...

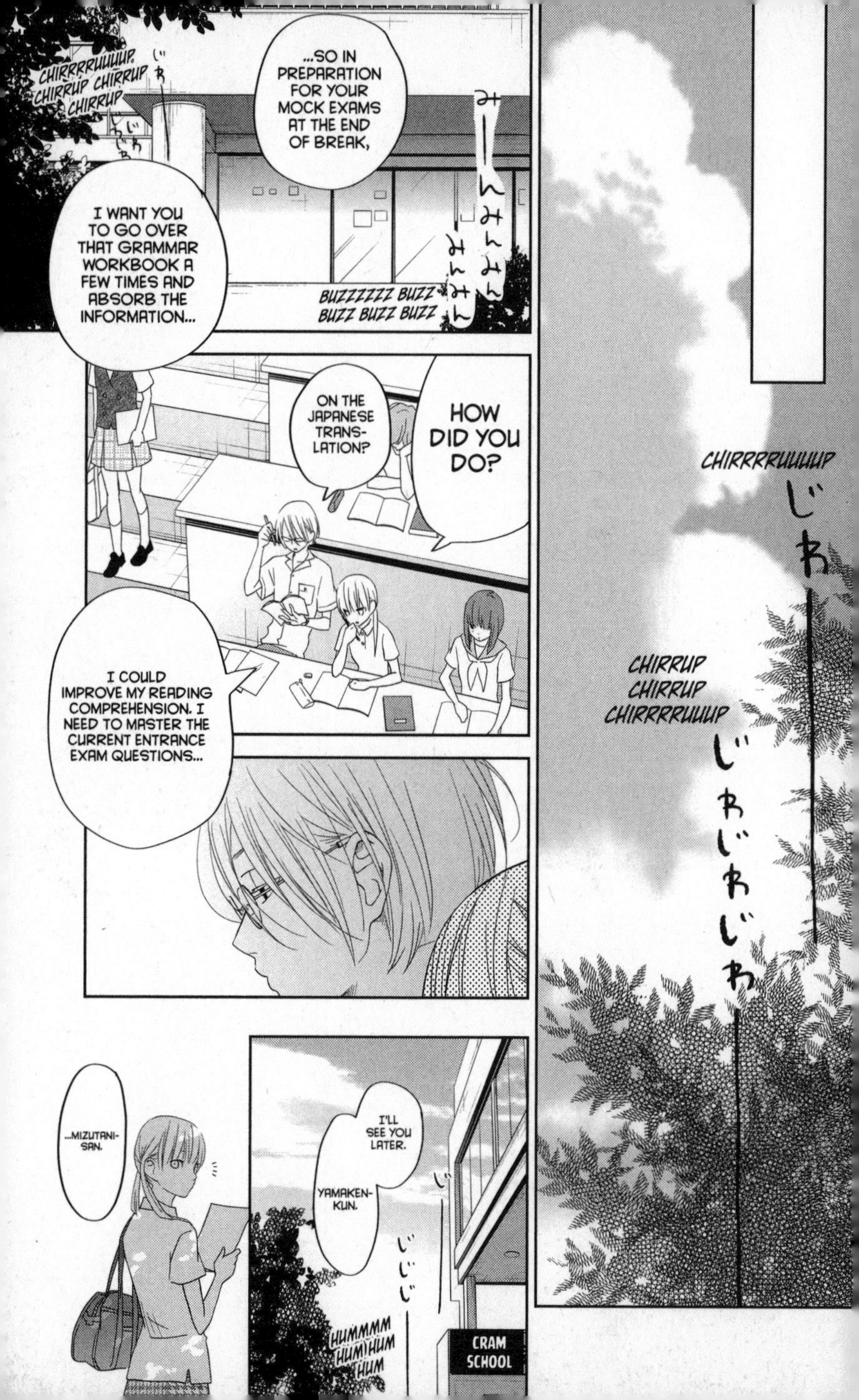
CHIRRRRUUUUP
じわ
CHIRRUP CHIRRUP CHIRRRRUUUP
じわじわじわ
...SO IN PREPARATION FOR YOUR MOCK EXAMS AT THE END OF BREAK,
みーんみんみん みんみん
CHIRRRRUUUUP CHIRRUP CHIRRUP CHIRRUP
I WANT YOU TO GO OVER THAT GRAMMAR WORKBOOK A FEW TIMES AND ABSORB THE INFORMATION...
BUZZZZZZ BUZZ BUZZ BUZZ BUZZ
HOW DID YOU DO?
ON THE JAPANESE TRANS-LATION?
I COULD IMPROVE MY READING COMPREHENSION. I NEED TO MASTER THE CURRENT ENTRANCE EXAM QUESTIONS...
I'LL SEE YOU LATER.
YAMAKEN-KUN.
じ
じじじ
HUMMMM HUM HUM HUM
CRAM SCHOOL
...MIZUTANI-SAN.

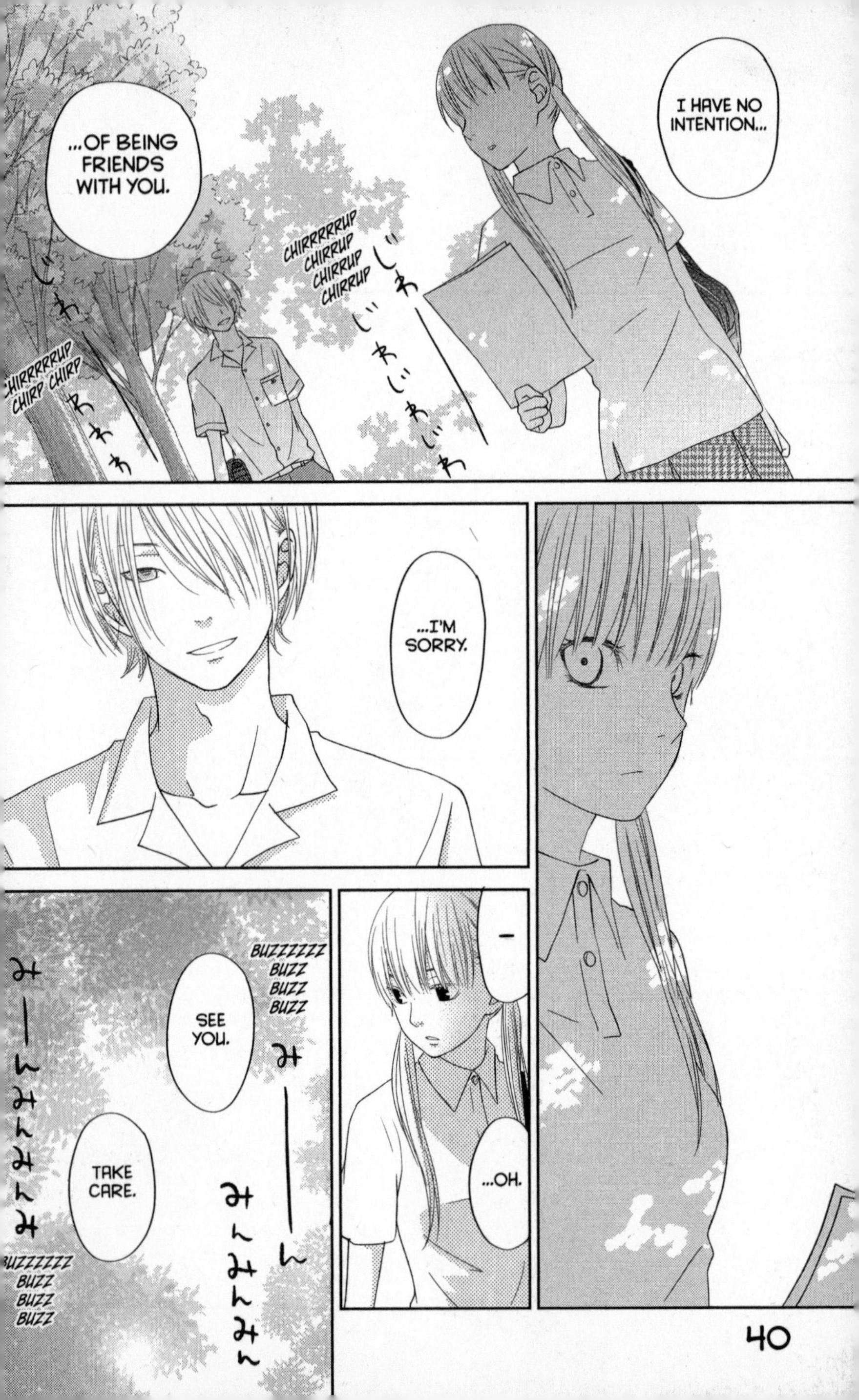
I HAVE NO INTENTION...
...OF BEING FRIENDS WITH YOU.
CHIRRRRRUP CHIRRUP CHIRRUP CHIRRUP
CHIRRRRRUP CHIRP CHIRP
...I'M SORRY.
–
...OH.
BUZZZZZZ BUZZ BUZZ BUZZ
SEE YOU.
TAKE CARE.
BUZZZZZZ BUZZ BUZZ BUZZ

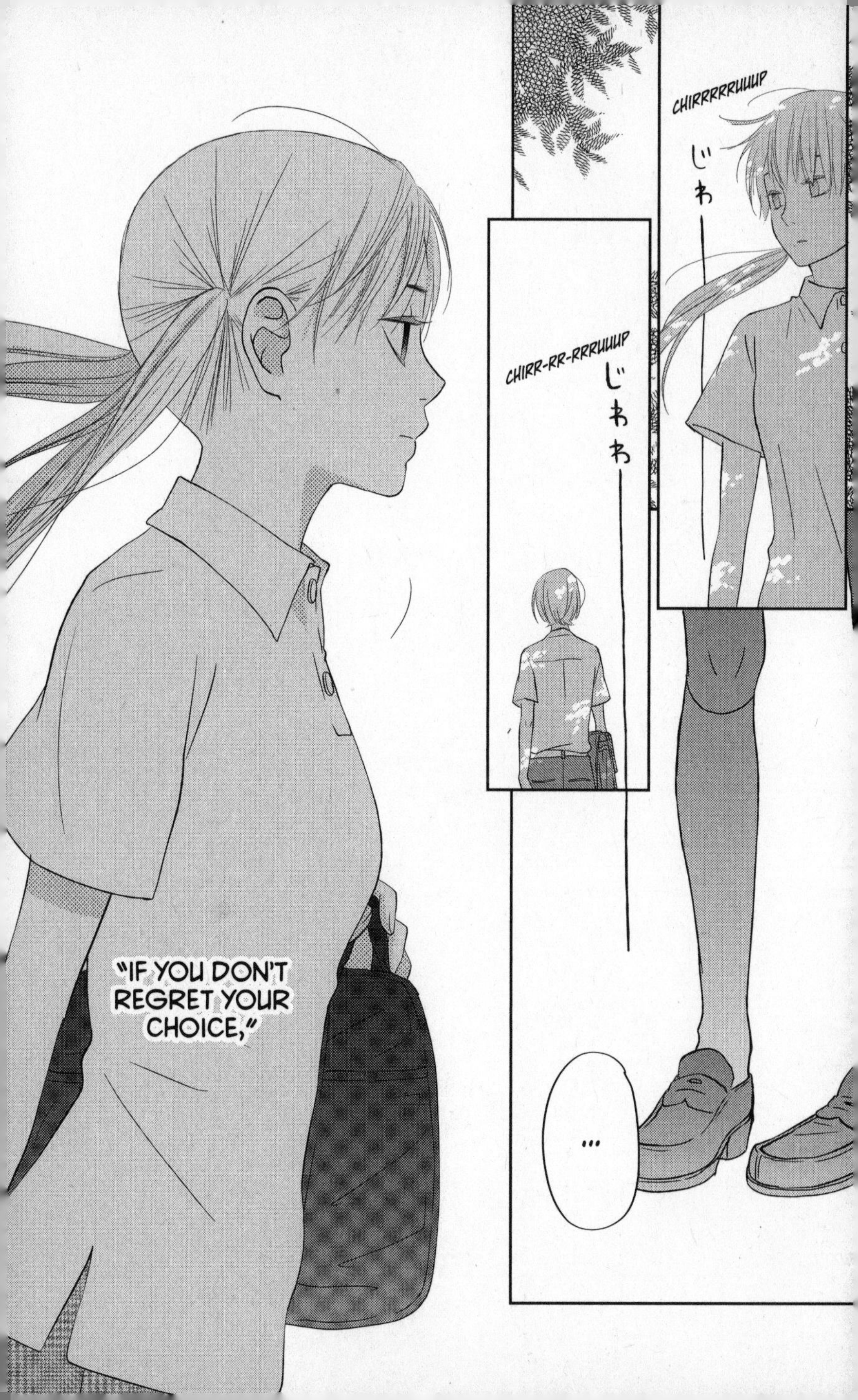

CHIRRRRRUUUP
じわー
CHIRR-RR-RRRUUUP
じわわー
...
"IF YOU DON'T REGRET YOUR CHOICE,"

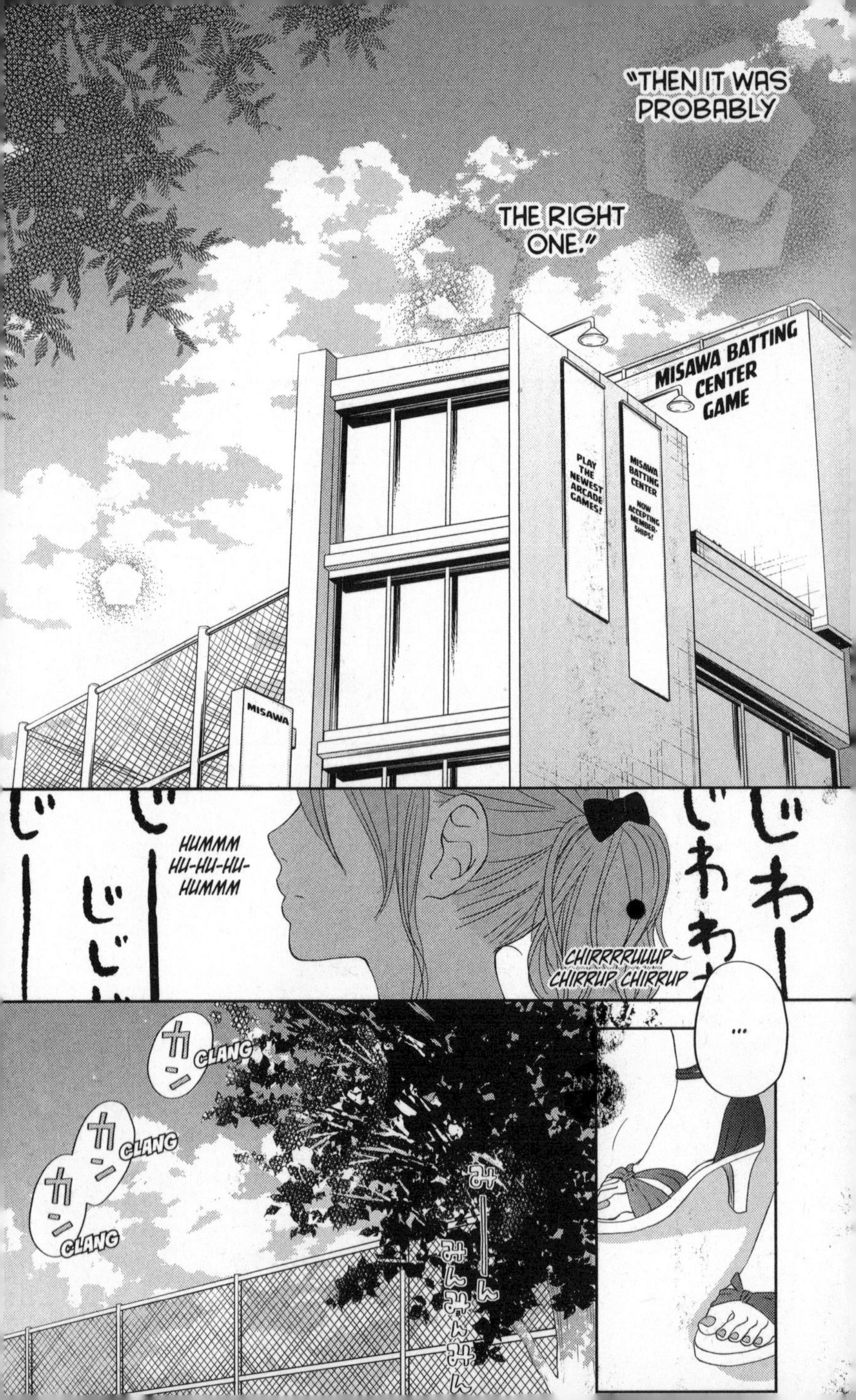

"THEN IT WAS PROBABLY
THE RIGHT ONE."
MISAWA BATTING CENTER GAME
MISAWA BATTING CENTER NOW ACCEPTING MEMBERSHIPS!
PLAY THE NEWEST ARCADE GAMES!
MISAWA
じわーじわわ
CHIRRRRUUUP CHIRRUP CHIRRUP
HUMMM HU-HU-HU-HUMMM
じーじじじ
...
みーんみんみんみん
カン CLANG
カン CLANG
カン CLANG

IN THE CAR

YUZAN & ANDO-SAN HAPPILY ON THEIR WAY TO THEIR VACATION DESTINATION.
ARE WE THERE YET?
NOT FOR ABOUT TWO HOURS.
AWW, THAT LONG?
BORED
I'M BORED. LET'S PLAY WORD CHAIN.
CAKE-MIX.
JUST KIDDING. ALL DONE.
HA HA HA
HA HA HA
(ACTING NICE)
...WE DO NOT GET ALONG.
I'M GOING TO SLEEP. WAKE ME UP WHEN WE GET THERE.
GO RIGHT AHEAD.
WHEN THEY'RE TOGETHER TOO LONG, TENSIONS RISE.

SHELTERED GIRL

CAMPING ADJOURNED.
SEE YOU LATER!
IN THE END, IYO DIDN'T GET ANY CLOSER TO HARU-SEMPAI... BUT IT WAS FUN.
HEE HEE!
HUH? IYO, YOU'RE COMING WITH US?
I THOUGHT YOU'D GO HOME WITH THEM.
WELL, THEY SAID IT WOULD TAKE THEM THREE HOURS TO GET HOME BY TRAIN.
THAT DOESN'T MAKE ANY SENSE.
(LOL).
SHE HAS YET TO EXPERIENCE THE TRUE CHARM OF TRAVELING WITH FRIENDS.

AMUSING THEMSELVES WITH NATSUME-SAN'S FORGOTTEN UNO CARDS.

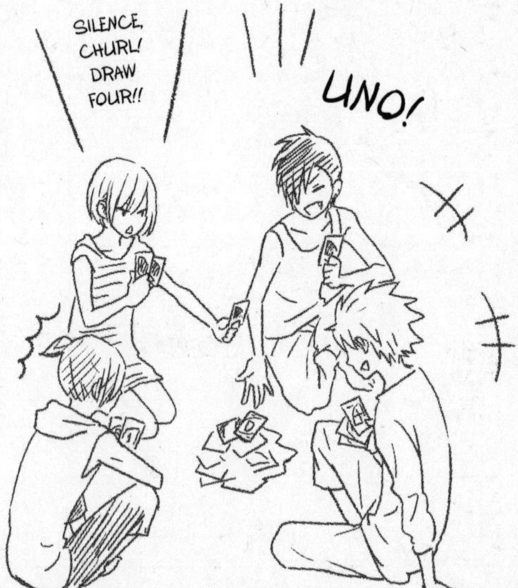
UNO!
SILENCE, CHURL! DRAW FOUR!!

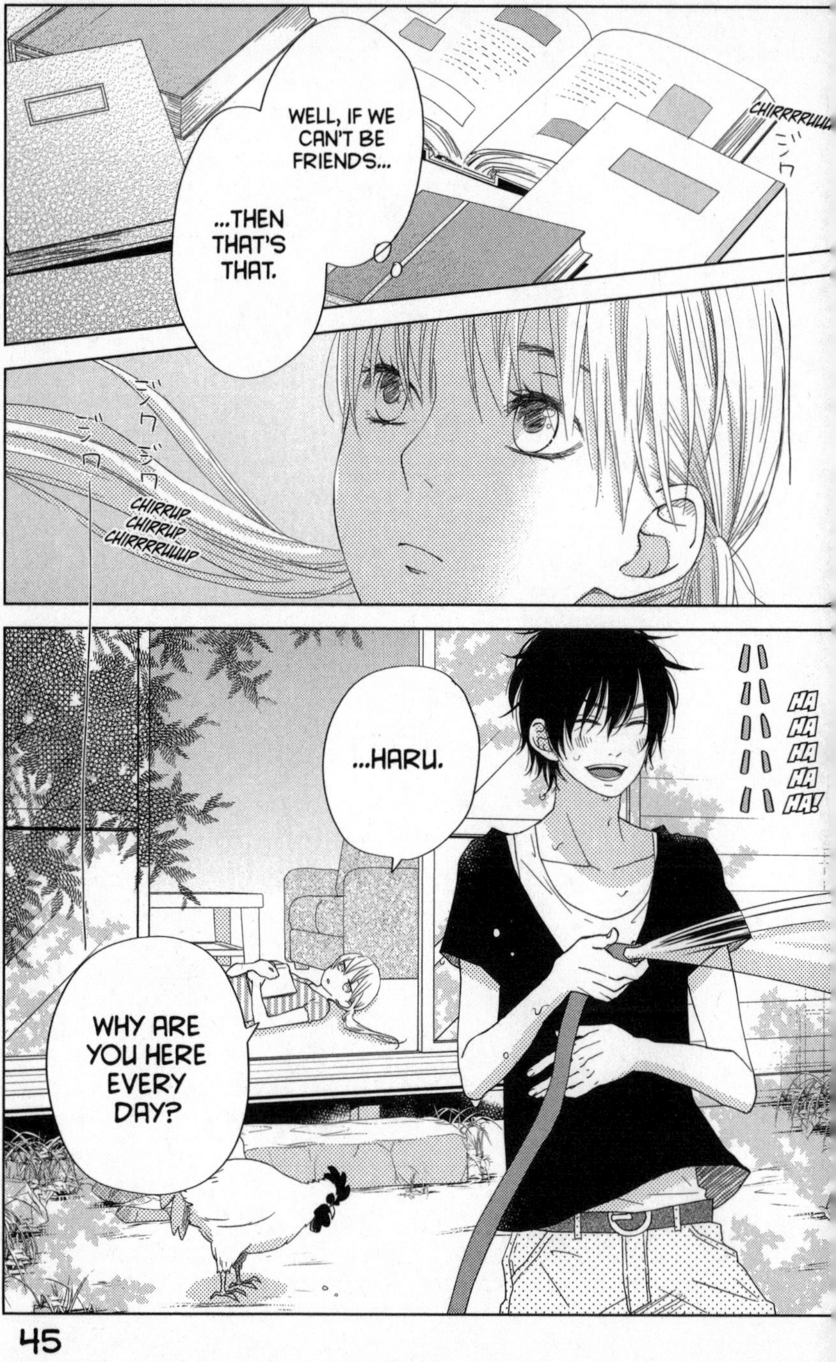
WELL, IF WE CAN'T BE FRIENDS...
...THEN THAT'S THAT.
CHIRRRRUUU
ジワ
ジワジワ
ジワ
CHIRRUP CHIRRUP CHIRRRRUUUP
HA HA HA HA HA!
...HARU.
WHY ARE YOU HERE EVERY DAY?

CHAPTER 34: SUMMER VACATION: THE SEQUEL, PART 3: THE LAST OF SUMMER

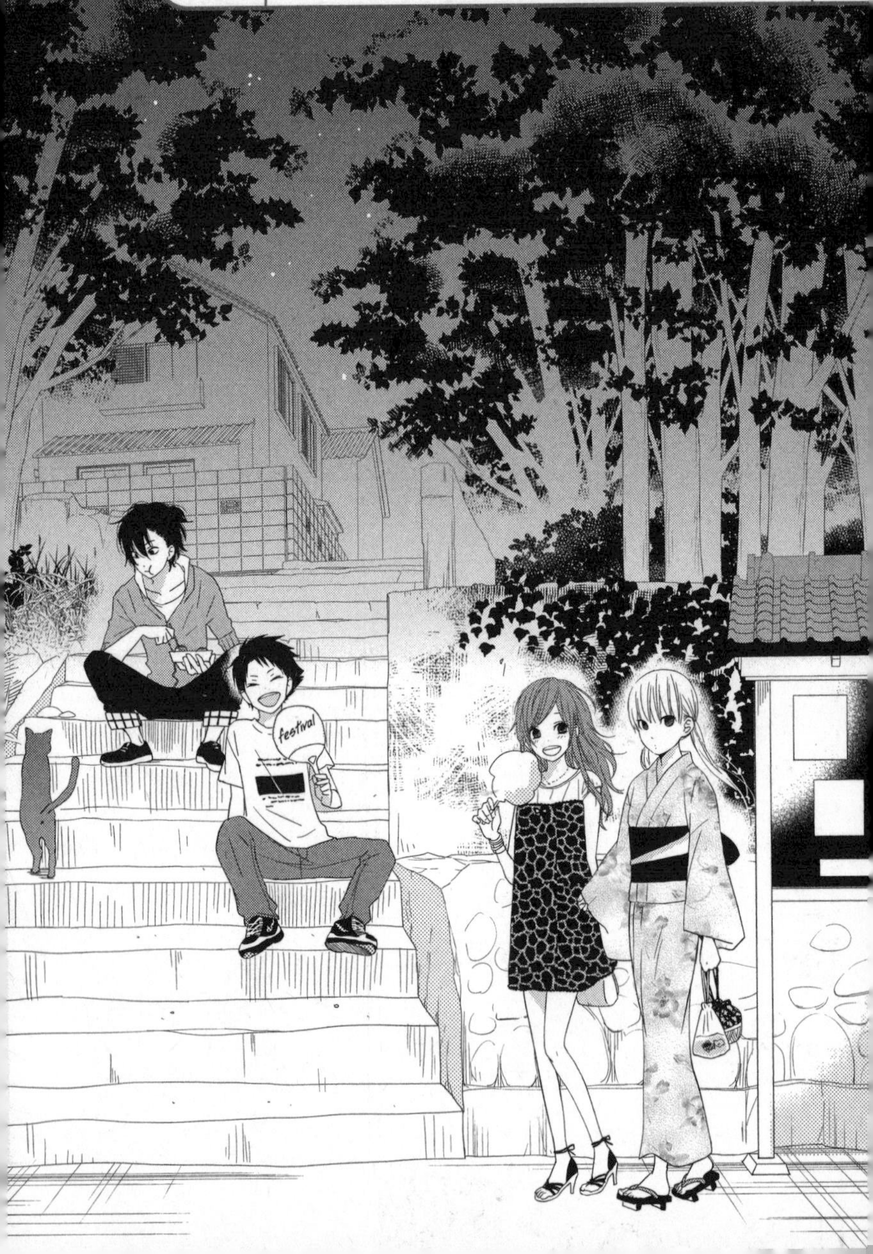
festival

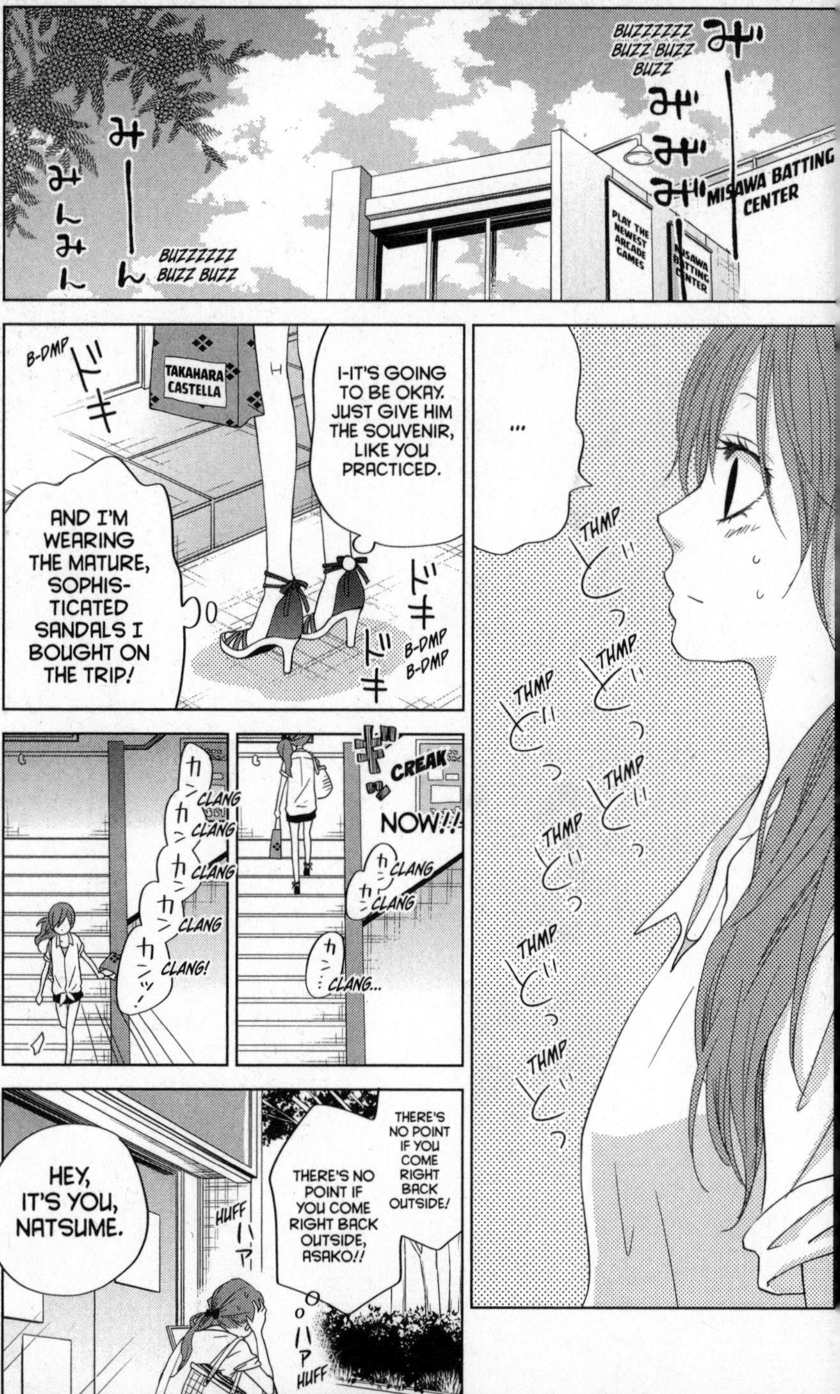
BUZZZZZZ BUZZ BUZZ BUZZ
みーみ゛み゛み゛ー
MISAWA BATTING CENTER
PLAY THE NEWEST ARCADE GAMES
MISAWA BATTING CENTER
みーーん みんみん
BUZZZZZZ BUZZ BUZZ
...
THMP
THMP
THMP
THMP
THMP
THMP
THMP
I-IT'S GOING TO BE OKAY. JUST GIVE HIM THE SOUVENIR, LIKE YOU PRACTICED.
TAKAHARA CASTELLA
ドキ B-DMP
AND I'M WEARING THE MATURE, SOPHISTICATED SANDALS I BOUGHT ON THE TRIP!
ドキ ドキ B-DMP B-DMP
ギィ CREAK
NOW!!
カンカン CLANG CLANG
カン... CLANG...
カン CLANG
カン CLANG
カン CLANG
カン CLANG
カンッ! CLANG!
THERE'S NO POINT IF YOU COME RIGHT BACK OUTSIDE!
THERE'S NO POINT IF YOU COME RIGHT BACK OUTSIDE, ASAKO!!
ハァ HUFF
ハア HUFF
HEY, IT'S YOU, NATSUME.

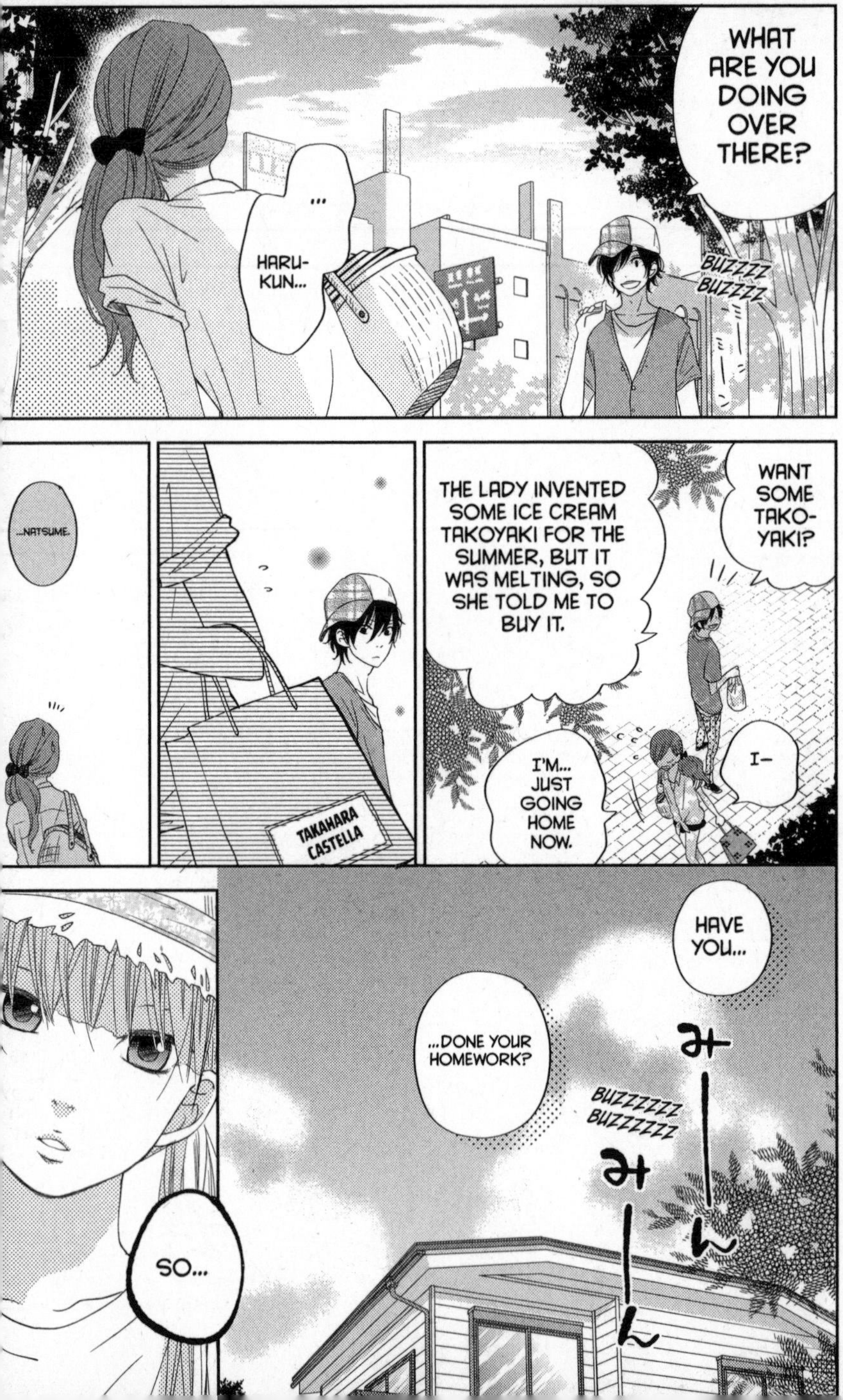
WHAT ARE YOU DOING OVER THERE?
BUZZZZ BUZZZZ
...
HARU-KUN...
WANT SOME TAKO-YAKI?
THE LADY INVENTED SOME ICE CREAM TAKOYAKI FOR THE SUMMER, BUT IT WAS MELTING, SO SHE TOLD ME TO BUY IT.
I—
I'M... JUST GOING HOME NOW.
TAKAHARA CASTELLA
...NATSUME.
HAVE YOU...
...DONE YOUR HOMEWORK?
BUZZZZZZZ BUZZZZZZZ
みーん
みーん
SO...

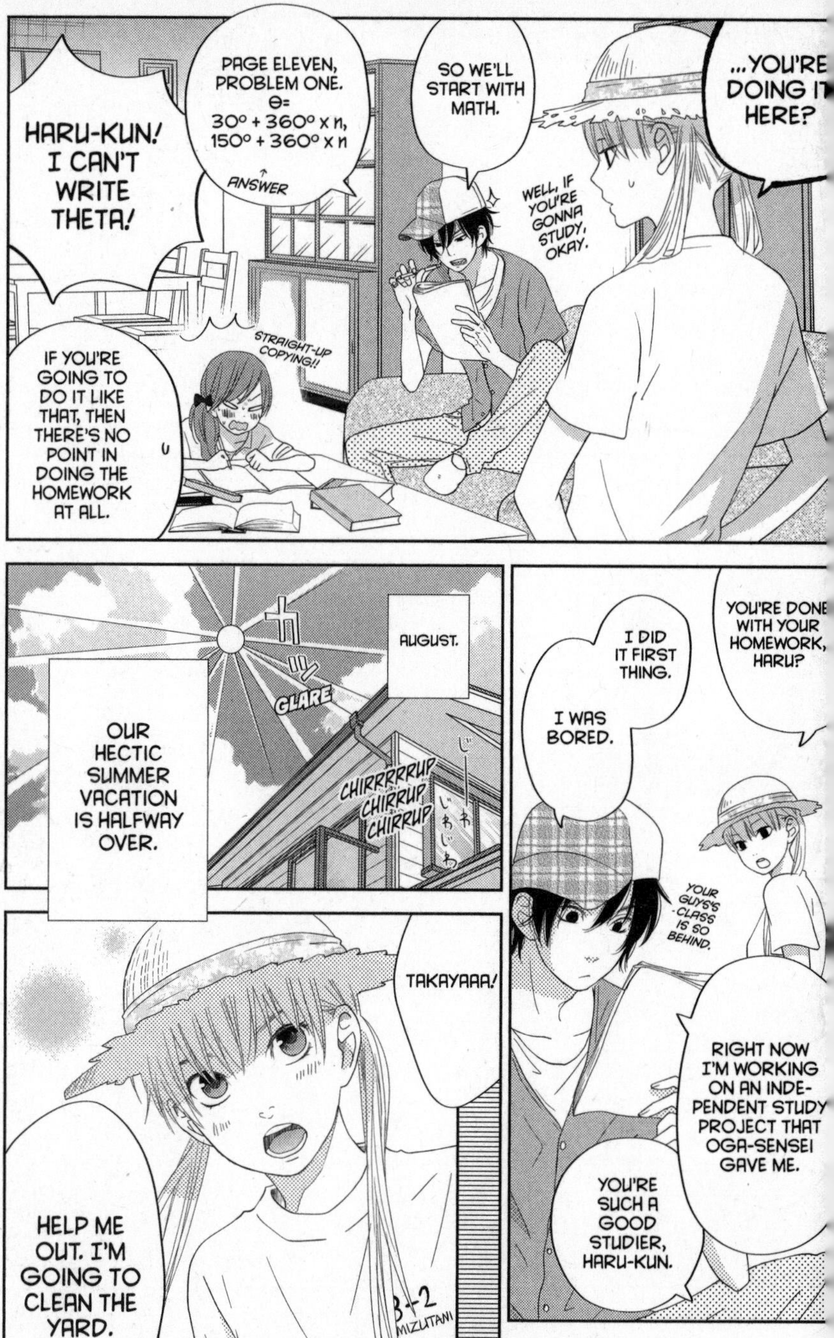
...YOU'RE DOING IT HERE?
WELL, IF YOU'RE GONNA STUDY, OKAY.
SO WE'LL START WITH MATH.
PAGE ELEVEN, PROBLEM ONE. θ= 30° + 360° x n, 150° + 360° x n
ANSWER
HARU-KUN! I CAN'T WRITE THETA!
STRAIGHT-UP COPYING!!
IF YOU'RE GOING TO DO IT LIKE THAT, THEN THERE'S NO POINT IN DOING THE HOMEWORK AT ALL.
YOU'RE DONE WITH YOUR HOMEWORK, HARU?
I DID IT FIRST THING.
I WAS BORED.
YOUR GUYS'S CLASS IS SO BEHIND.
RIGHT NOW I'M WORKING ON AN INDE-PENDENT STUDY PROJECT THAT OGA-SENSEI GAVE ME.
YOU'RE SUCH A GOOD STUDIER, HARU-KUN.
AUGUST.
GLARE
OUR HECTIC SUMMER VACATION IS HALFWAY OVER.
CHIRRRRRUP CHIRRUP CHIRRUP
TAKAYAAA!
HELP ME OUT. I'M GOING TO CLEAN THE YARD.
3-2
MIZUTANI

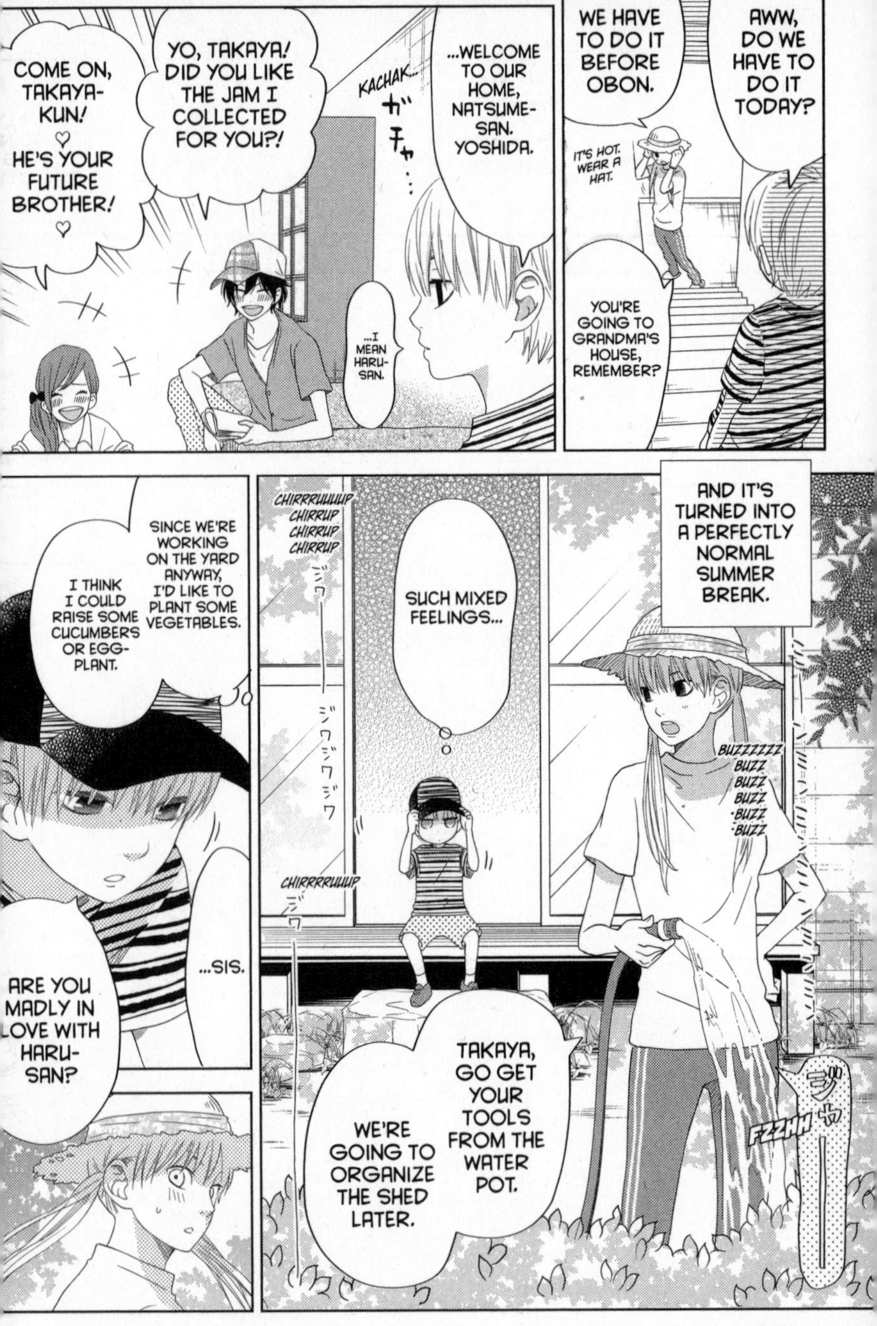
AWW, DO WE HAVE TO DO IT TODAY?
WE HAVE TO DO IT BEFORE OBON.
IT'S HOT. WEAR A HAT.
YOU'RE GOING TO GRANDMA'S HOUSE, REMEMBER?
...WELCOME TO OUR HOME, NATSUME-SAN. YOSHIDA.
KACHAK...
...I MEAN HARU-SAN.
YO, TAKAYA! DID YOU LIKE THE JAM I COLLECTED FOR YOU?!
COME ON, TAKAYA-KUN! ♡ HE'S YOUR FUTURE BROTHER! ♡
AND IT'S TURNED INTO A PERFECTLY NORMAL SUMMER BREAK.
BUZZZZZZ BUZZ BUZZ BUZZ BUZZ BUZZ
SUCH MIXED FEELINGS...
CHIRRRUUUUP CHIRRUP CHIRRUP CHIRRUP
CHIRRRRUUUP
TAKAYA, GO GET YOUR TOOLS FROM THE WATER POT.
WE'RE GOING TO ORGANIZE THE SHED LATER.
FZZHH
SINCE WE'RE WORKING ON THE YARD ANYWAY, I'D LIKE TO PLANT SOME VEGETABLES.
I THINK I COULD RAISE SOME CUCUMBERS OR EGG-PLANT.
...SIS.
ARE YOU MADLY IN LOVE WITH HARU-SAN?

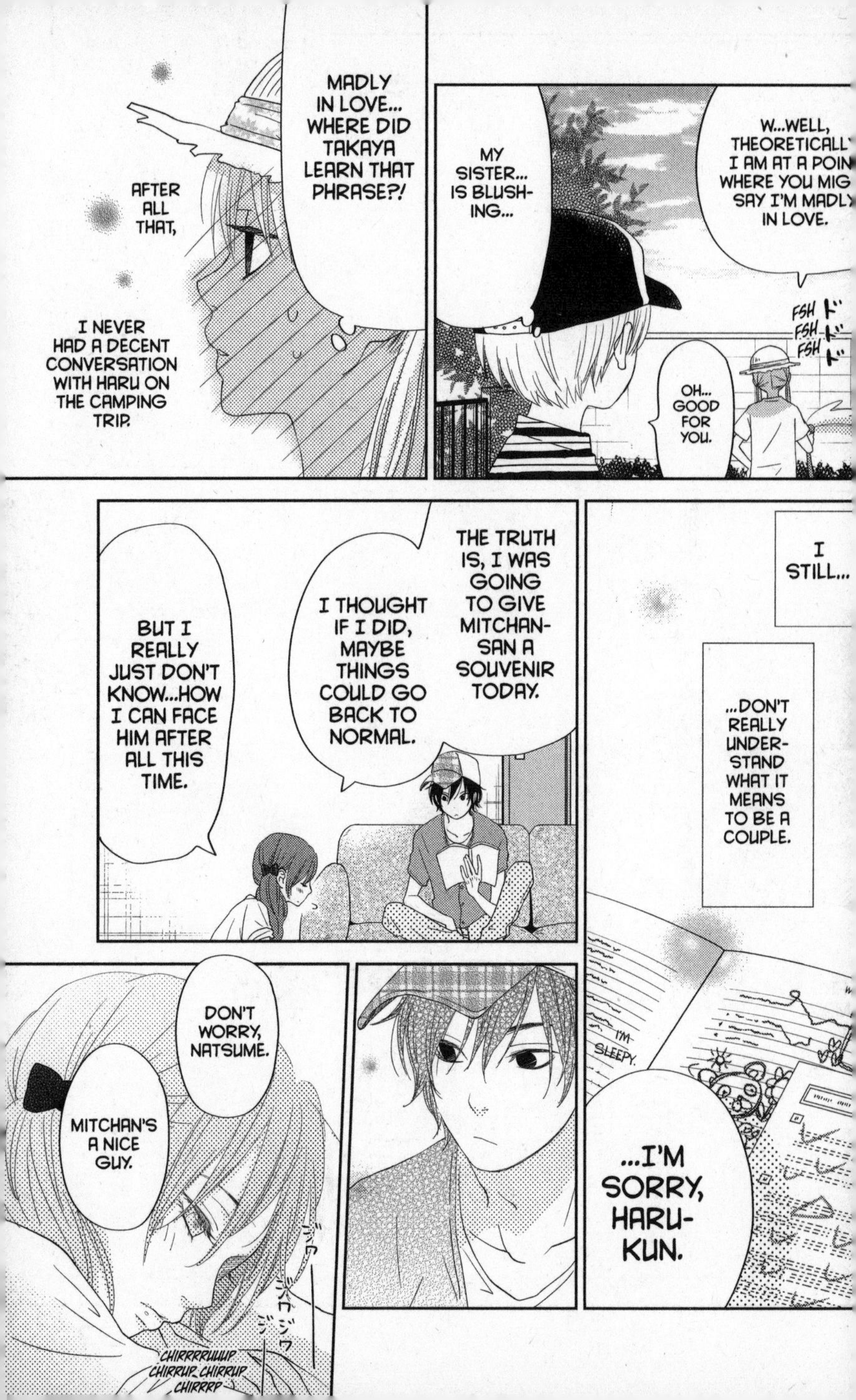
W...WELL, THEORETICALL I AM AT A POIN WHERE YOU MIG SAY I'M MADL IN LOVE.
FSH ド FSH ド FSH ド
OH... GOOD FOR YOU.
MY SISTER... IS BLUSH-ING...
MADLY IN LOVE... WHERE DID TAKAYA LEARN THAT PHRASE?!
AFTER ALL THAT,
I NEVER HAD A DECENT CONVERSATION WITH HARU ON THE CAMPING TRIP.
I STILL...
...DON'T REALLY UNDER-STAND WHAT IT MEANS TO BE A COUPLE.
I'M SLEEPY.
...I'M SORRY, HARU-KUN.
THE TRUTH IS, I WAS GOING TO GIVE MITCHAN-SAN A SOUVENIR TODAY.
I THOUGHT IF I DID, MAYBE THINGS COULD GO BACK TO NORMAL.
BUT I REALLY JUST DON'T KNOW...HOW I CAN FACE HIM AFTER ALL THIS TIME.
DON'T WORRY, NATSUME.
MITCHAN'S A NICE GUY.
CHIRRRRUUUP CHIRRUP CHIRRUP CHIRRRP

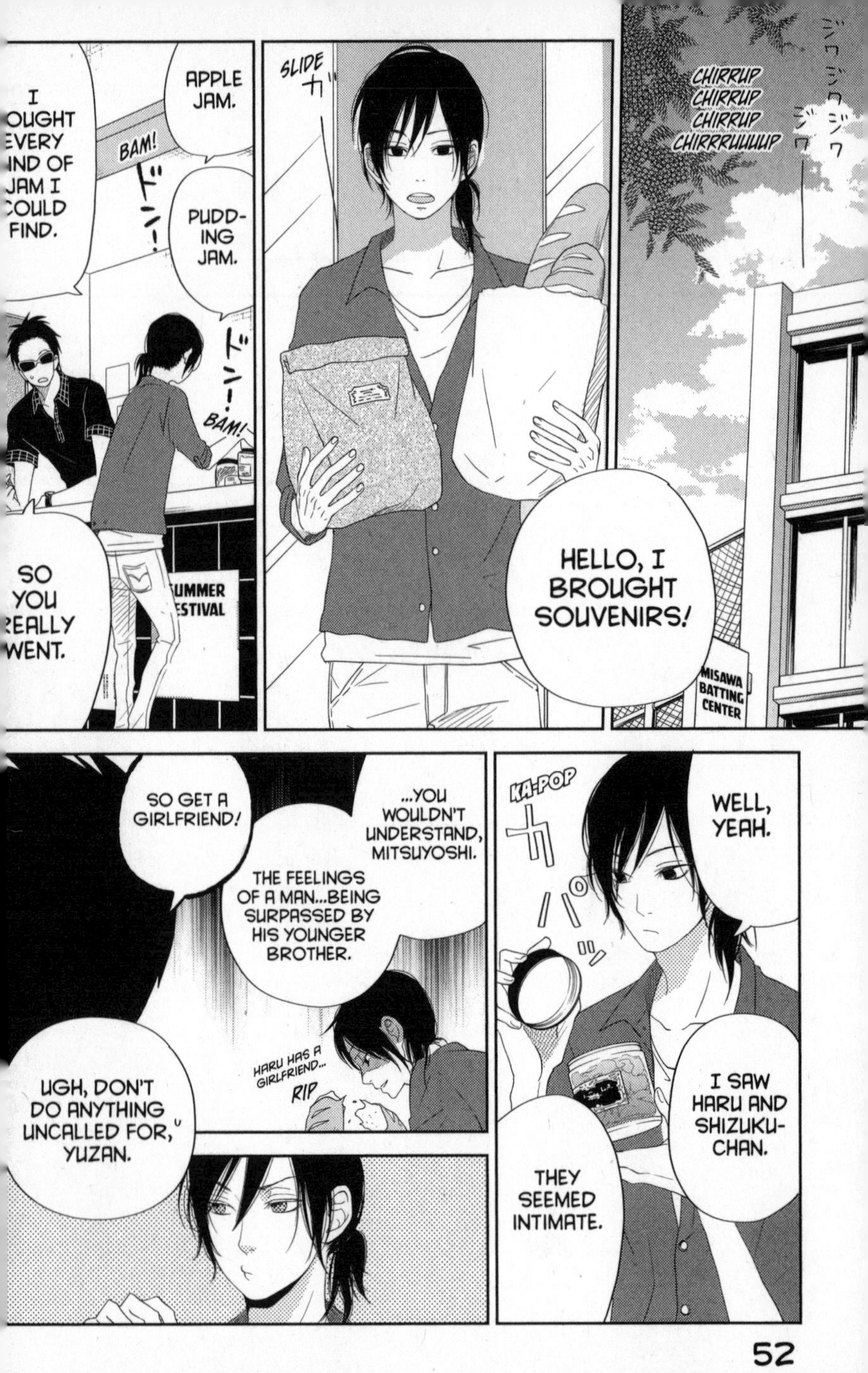
CHIRRUP CHIRRUP CHIRRUP CHIRRRUUUUP
MISAWA BATTING CENTER
SLIDE
ガ
HELLO, I BROUGHT SOUVENIRS!
APPLE JAM.
BAM!
ドン!
PUDDING JAM.
ドン!
BAM!
I OUGHT EVERY IND OF JAM I COULD FIND.
SUMMER ESTIVAL
SO YOU EALLY WENT.
KA-POP
カパッ
WELL, YEAH.
I SAW HARU AND SHIZUKU-CHAN.
THEY SEEMED INTIMATE.
...YOU WOULDN'T UNDERSTAND, MITSUYOSHI.
THE FEELINGS OF A MAN...BEING SURPASSED BY HIS YOUNGER BROTHER.
SO GET A GIRLFRIEND!
HARU HAS A GIRLFRIEND...
RIP
UGH, DON'T DO ANYTHING UNCALLED FOR, YUZAN.

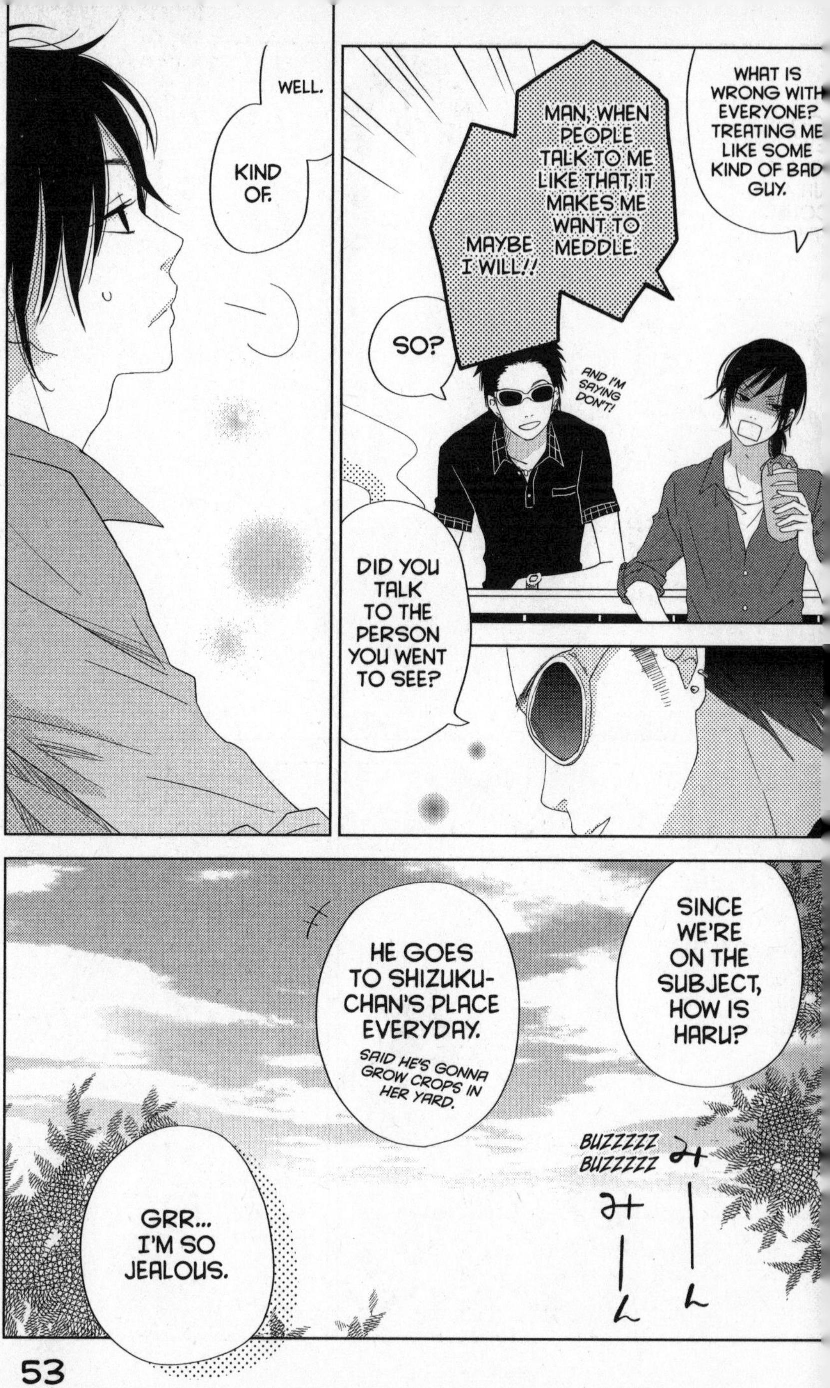
WHAT IS WRONG WITH EVERYONE? TREATING ME LIKE SOME KIND OF BAD GUY.
MAN, WHEN PEOPLE TALK TO ME LIKE THAT, IT MAKES ME WANT TO MEDDLE.
MAYBE I WILL!!
AND I'M SAYING DON'T!
SO?
DID YOU TALK TO THE PERSON YOU WENT TO SEE?
WELL.
KIND OF.
SINCE WE'RE ON THE SUBJECT, HOW IS HARU?
BUZZZZZ BUZZZZZ
みーん
みーん
HE GOES TO SHIZUKU-CHAN'S PLACE EVERYDAY.
SAID HE'S GONNA GROW CROPS IN HER YARD.
GRR... I'M SO JEALOUS.

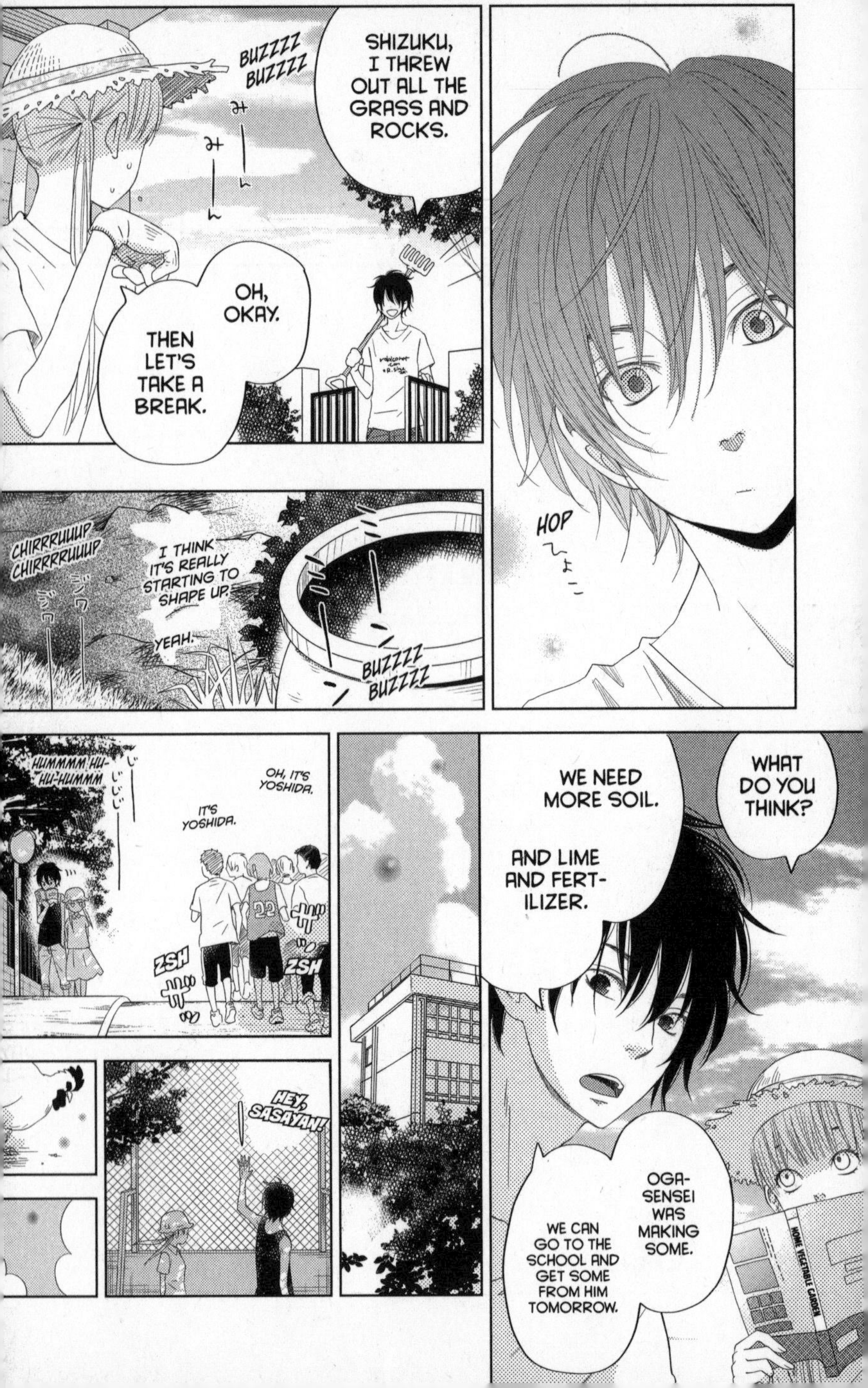
HOP
SHIZUKU, I THREW OUT ALL THE GRASS AND ROCKS.
BUZZZZ BUZZZZ
OH, OKAY.
THEN LET'S TAKE A BREAK.
CHIRRRUUUP CHIRRRRUUUP
I THINK IT'S REALLY STARTING TO SHAPE UP.
YEAH.
BUZZZZ BUZZZZ
WHAT DO YOU THINK?
WE NEED MORE SOIL.
AND LIME AND FERT-ILIZER.
OGA-SENSEI WAS MAKING SOME.
WE CAN GO TO THE SCHOOL AND GET SOME FROM HIM TOMORROW.
HOME VEGETABLE GARDEN
HUMMMM HU-HU-HUMMM
OH, IT'S YOSHIDA.
IT'S YOSHIDA.
ZSH
ZSH
HEY, SASAYAN!

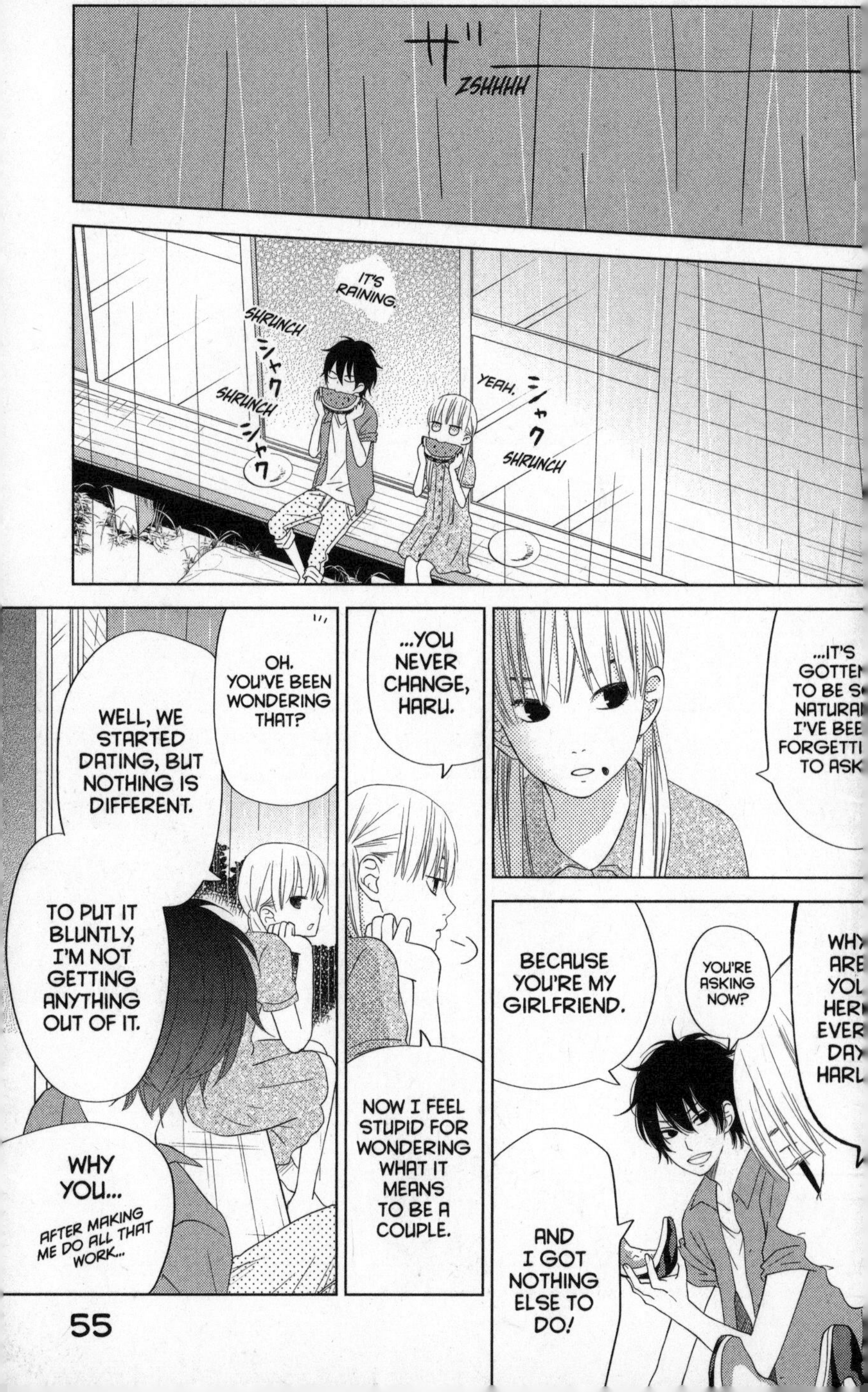
ザ
ZSHHHH
シャク
SHRUNCH
YEAH.
IT'S RAINING.
SHRUNCH
シャク
SHRUNCH
シャク
...IT'S GOTTEN TO BE S NATURA I'VE BEE FORGETTI TO ASK
WHY ARE YOU HER EVER DAY HARU
YOU'RE ASKING NOW?
BECAUSE YOU'RE MY GIRLFRIEND.
AND I GOT NOTHING ELSE TO DO!
...YOU NEVER CHANGE, HARU.
NOW I FEEL STUPID FOR WONDERING WHAT IT MEANS TO BE A COUPLE.
OH. YOU'VE BEEN WONDERING THAT?
WELL, WE STARTED DATING, BUT NOTHING IS DIFFERENT.
TO PUT IT BLUNTLY, I'M NOT GETTING ANYTHING OUT OF IT.
WHY YOU...
AFTER MAKING ME DO ALL THAT WORK...

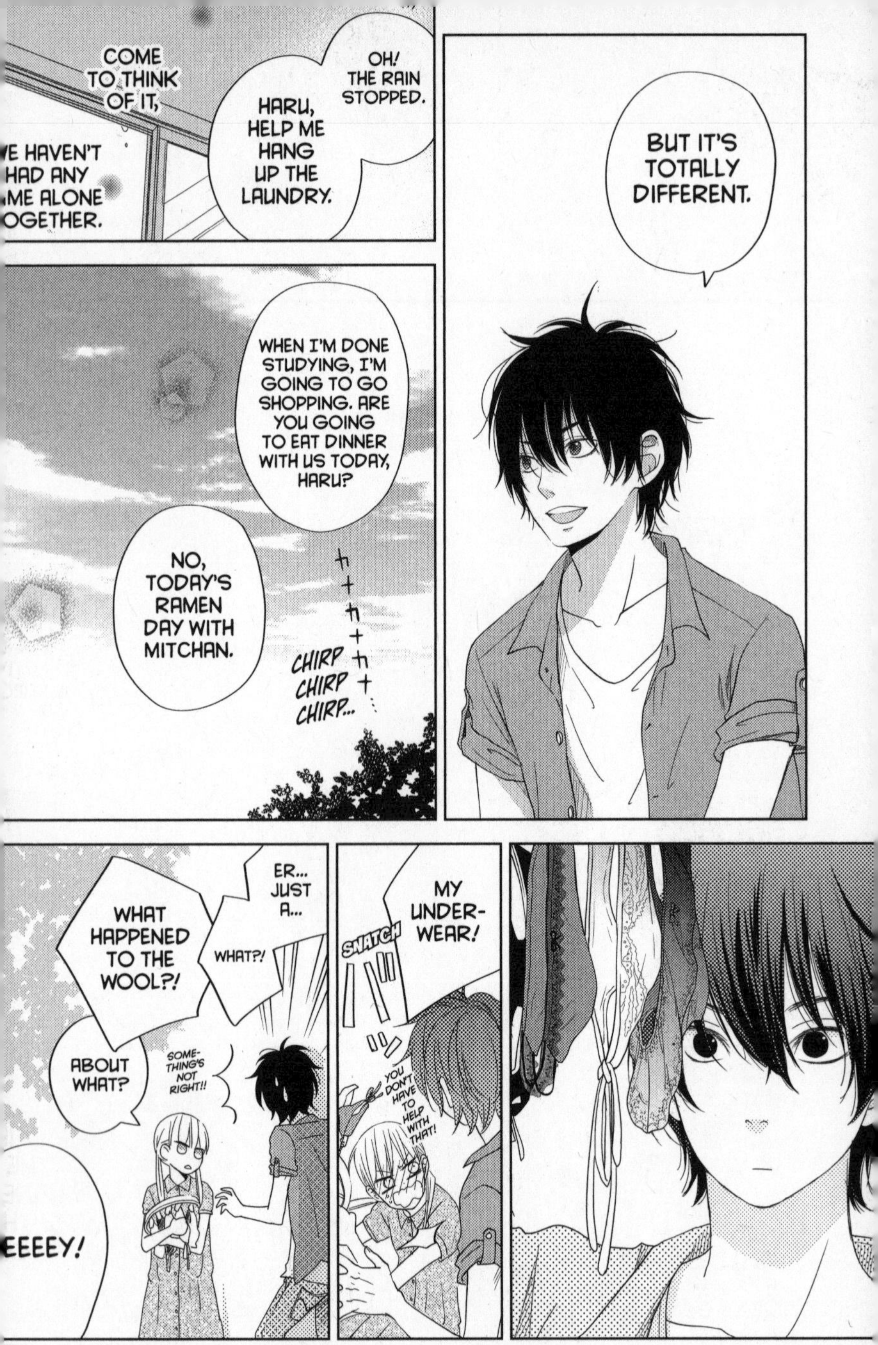
BUT IT'S TOTALLY DIFFERENT.
OH! THE RAIN STOPPED.
HARU, HELP ME HANG UP THE LAUNDRY.
COME TO THINK OF IT,
E HAVEN'T HAD ANY ME ALONE OGETHER.
WHEN I'M DONE STUDYING, I'M GOING TO GO SHOPPING. ARE YOU GOING TO EAT DINNER WITH US TODAY, HARU?
NO, TODAY'S RAMEN DAY WITH MITCHAN.
CHIRP CHIRP CHIRP...
MY UNDER-WEAR!
SNATCH
YOU DON'T HAVE TO HELP WITH THAT!
ER... JUST A...
WHAT?!
WHAT HAPPENED TO THE WOOL?!
SOME-THING'S NOT RIGHT!!
ABOUT WHAT?
EEEEY!

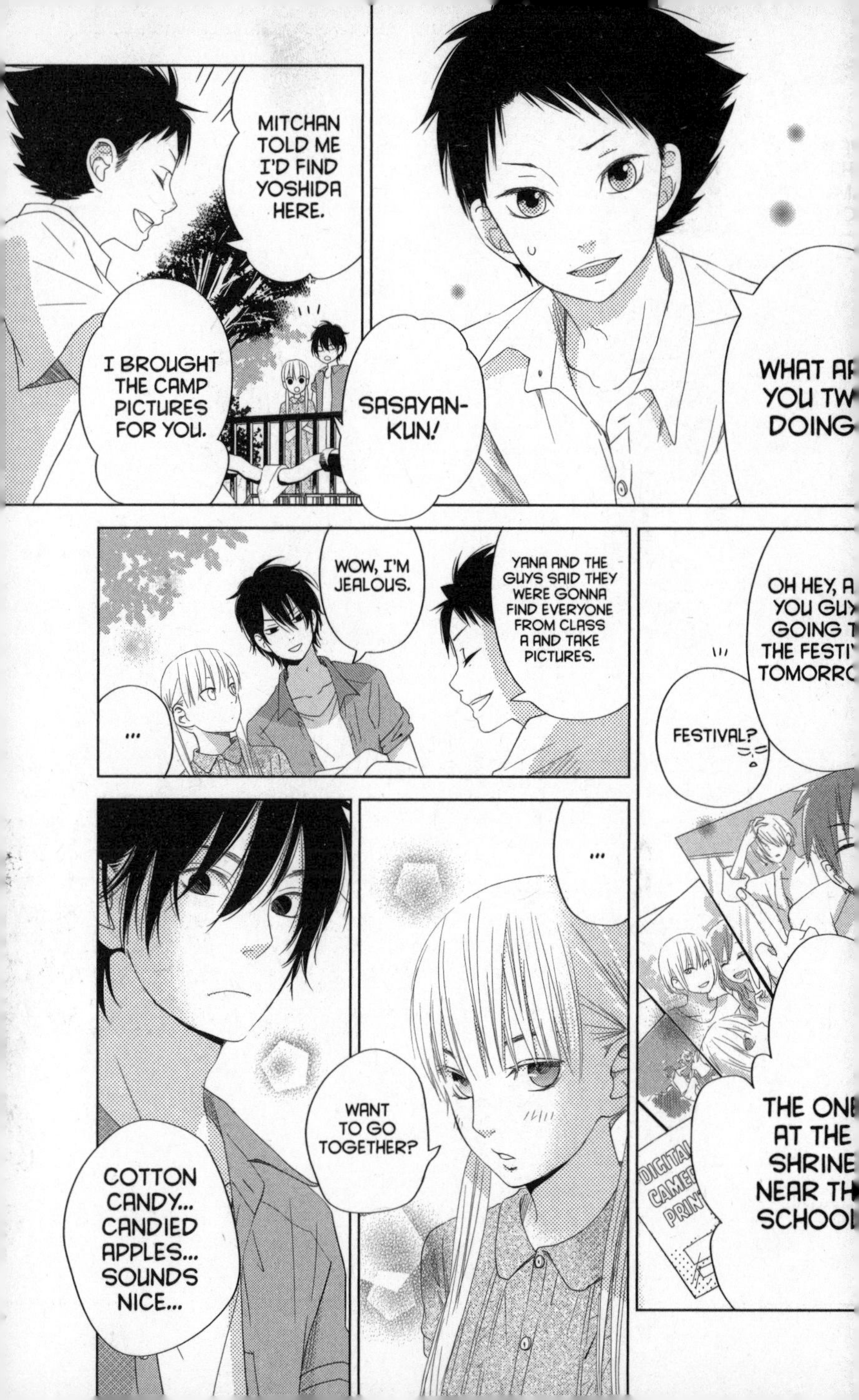
WHAT AR YOU TW DOING
SASAYAN-KUN!
MITCHAN TOLD ME I'D FIND YOSHIDA HERE.
I BROUGHT THE CAMP PICTURES FOR YOU.
OH HEY, A YOU GU GOING T THE FESTI TOMORRO
FESTIVAL?
YANA AND THE GUYS SAID THEY WERE GONNA FIND EVERYONE FROM CLASS A AND TAKE PICTURES.
WOW, I'M JEALOUS.
...
THE ON AT THE SHRINE NEAR TH SCHOO
DIGITAL CAMER PRIN
...
WANT TO GO TOGETHER?
COTTON CANDY... CANDIED APPLES... SOUNDS NICE...

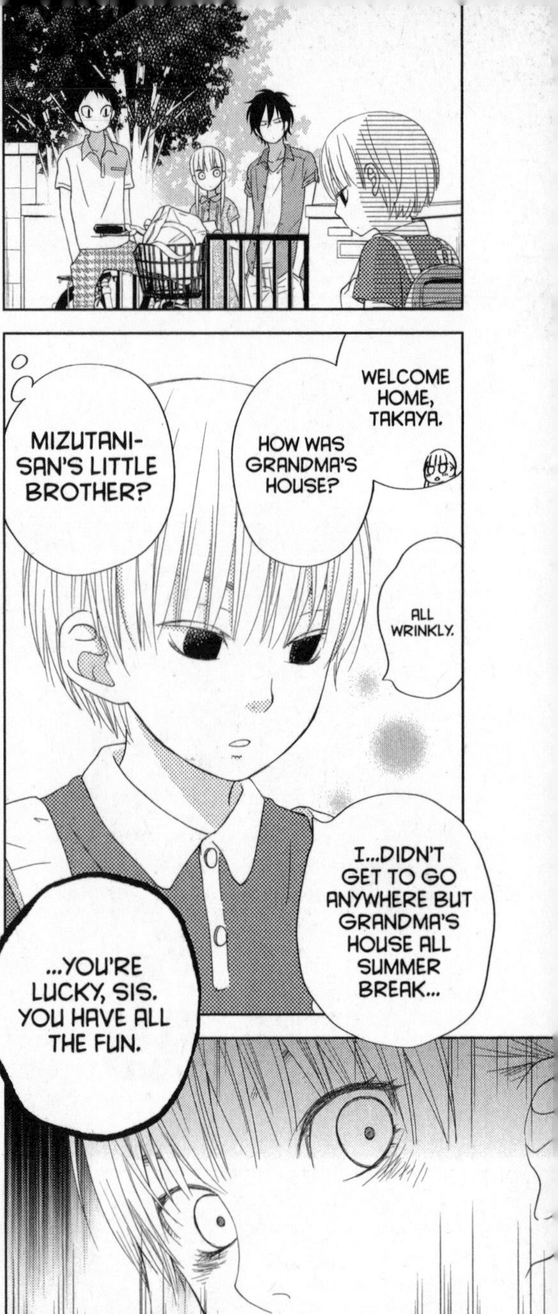
WELCOME HOME, TAKAYA. HOW WAS GRANDMA'S HOUSE?
MIZUTANI-SAN'S LITTLE BROTHER?
ALL WRINKLY.
I...DIDN'T GET TO GO ANYWHERE BUT GRANDMA'S HOUSE ALL SUMMER BREAK...
...YOU'RE LUCKY, SIS. YOU HAVE ALL THE FUN.
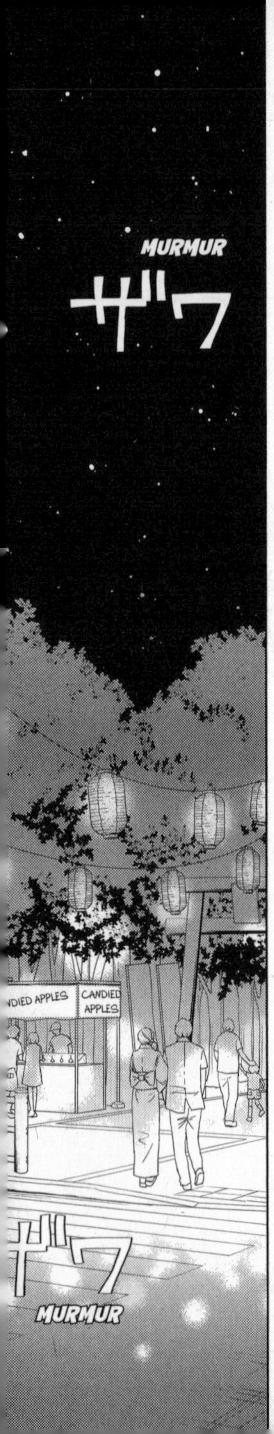
MURMUR
ザワ
CANDIED APPLES
CANDIED APPLES
ザワ
MURMUR

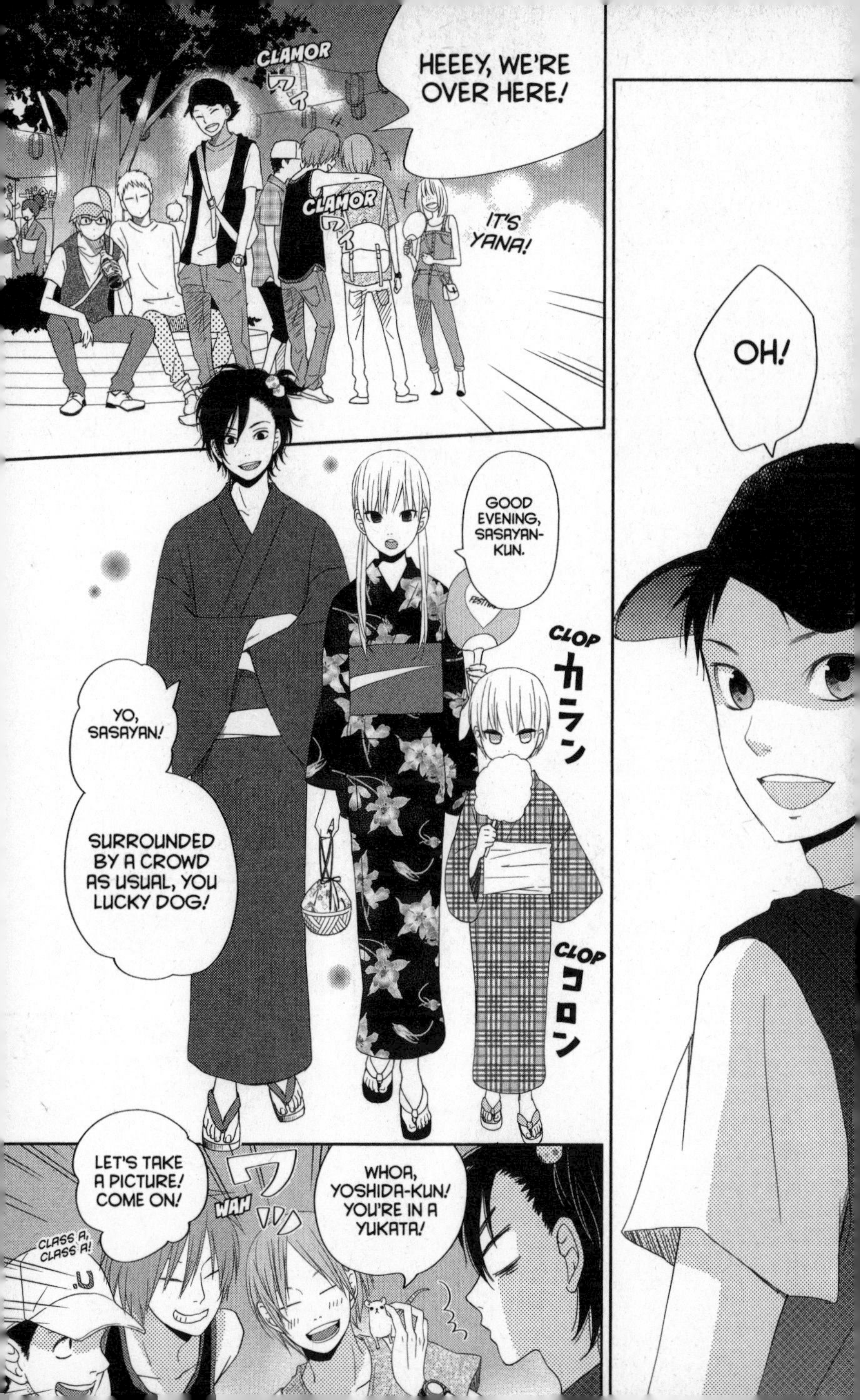
OH!
HEEEY, WE'RE OVER HERE!
IT'S YANA!
CLAMOR ワイ
CLAMOR ワイ
GOOD EVENING, SASAYAN-KUN.
CLOP カラン
YO, SASAYAN!
SURROUNDED BY A CROWD AS USUAL, YOU LUCKY DOG!
CLOP コロン
WHOA, YOSHIDA-KUN! YOU'RE IN A YUKATA!
WAH ワ
LET'S TAKE A PICTURE! COME ON!
CLASS A, CLASS A!

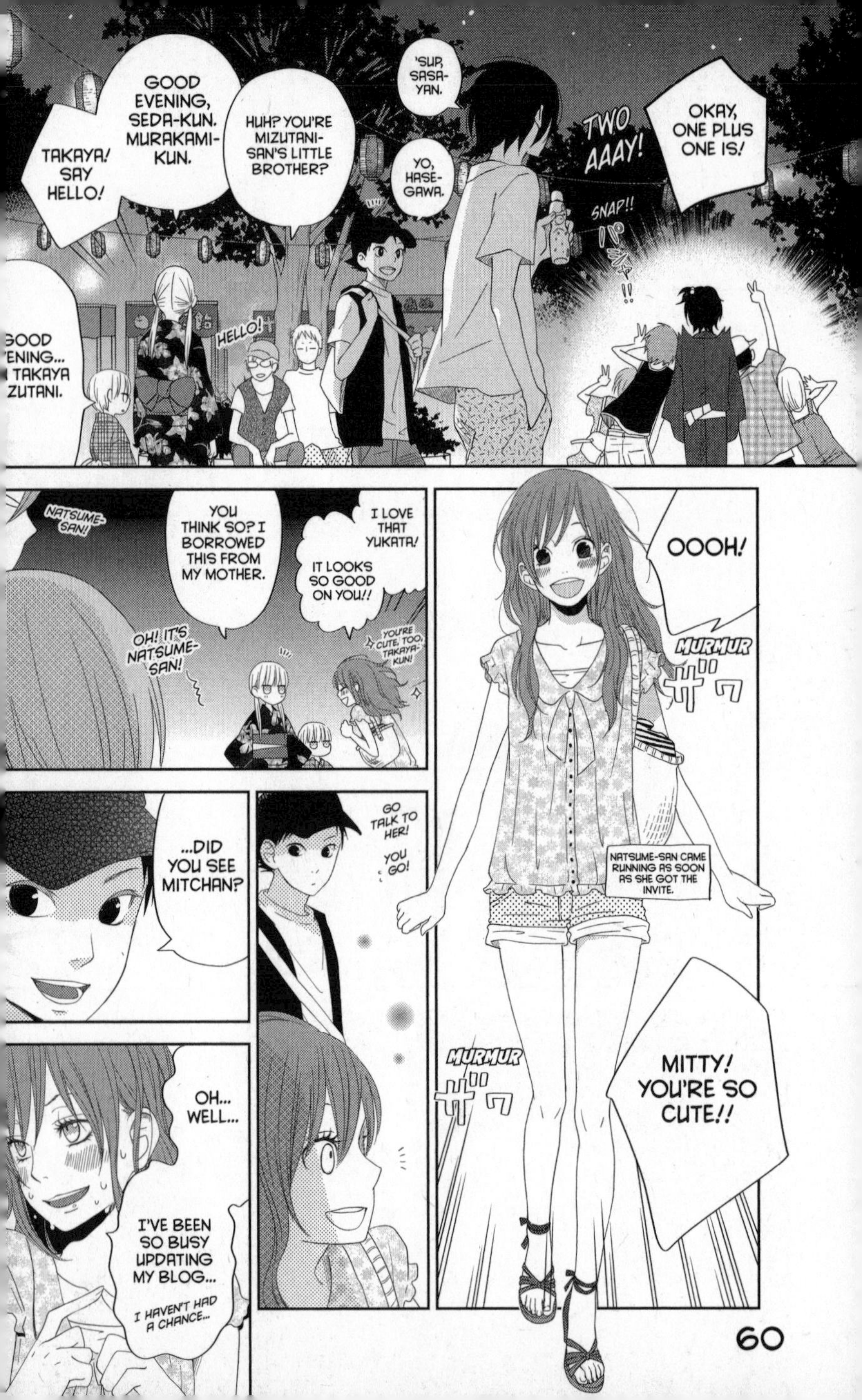
OKAY, ONE PLUS ONE IS!
TWO AAAY!
SNAP!!
'SUP, SASA-YAN.
YO, HASE-GAWA.
HUH? YOU'RE MIZUTANI-SAN'S LITTLE BROTHER?
GOOD EVENING, SEDA-KUN. MURAKAMI-KUN.
TAKAYA! SAY HELLO!
HELLO!
GOOD ENING... TAKAYA ZUTANI.
OOOH!
MURMUR
NATSUME-SAN CAME RUNNING AS SOON AS SHE GOT THE INVITE.
MURMUR
MITTY! YOU'RE SO CUTE!!
I LOVE THAT YUKATA!
IT LOOKS SO GOOD ON YOU!!
YOU THINK SO? I BORROWED THIS FROM MY MOTHER.
YOU'RE CUTE, TOO, TAKAYA-KUN!
OH! IT'S NATSUME-SAN!
NATSUME-SAN!
GO TALK TO HER!
YOU GO!
...DID YOU SEE MITCHAN?
OH... WELL...
I'VE BEEN SO BUSY UPDATING MY BLOG...
I HAVEN'T HAD A CHANCE...

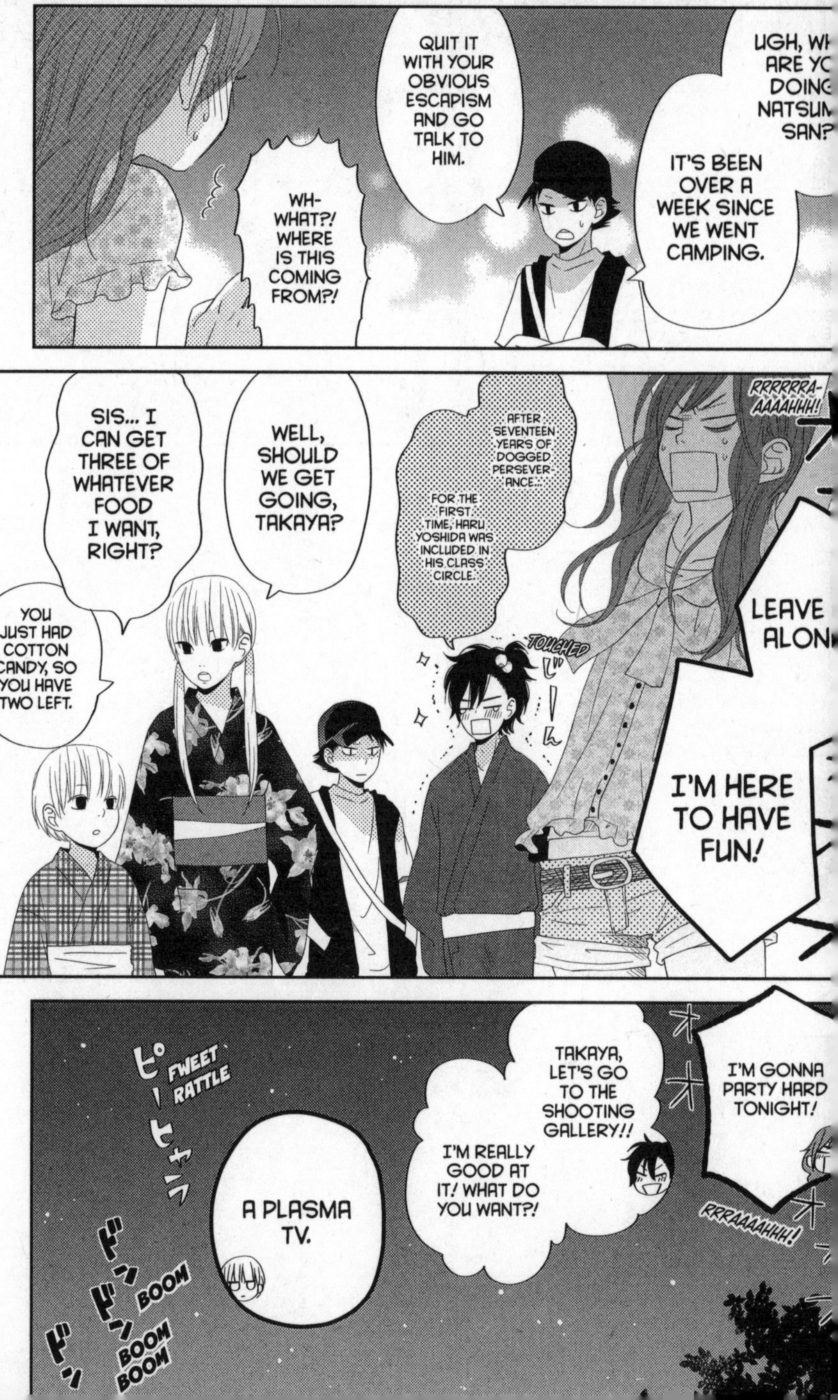
UGH, WH ARE YO DOING NATSUM SAN?
IT'S BEEN OVER A WEEK SINCE WE WENT CAMPING.
QUIT IT WITH YOUR OBVIOUS ESCAPISM AND GO TALK TO HIM.
WH- WHAT?! WHERE IS THIS COMING FROM?!
RRRRRRA- AAAAHHH!
LEAVE ALON
I'M HERE TO HAVE FUN!
AFTER SEVENTEEN YEARS OF DOGGED PERSEVERANCE...
FOR THE FIRST TIME, HARU YOSHIDA WAS INCLUDED IN HIS CLASS CIRCLE.
じーん TOUCHED
WELL, SHOULD WE GET GOING, TAKAYA?
SIS... I CAN GET THREE OF WHATEVER FOOD I WANT, RIGHT?
YOU JUST HAD COTTON CANDY, SO YOU HAVE TWO LEFT.
I'M GONNA PARTY HARD TONIGHT!
RRRAAAAHHH!
TAKAYA, LET'S GO TO THE SHOOTING GALLERY!!
I'M REALLY GOOD AT IT! WHAT DO YOU WANT?!
A PLASMA TV.
ピーヒャラ FWEET RATTLE
ドーンドーンドーン BOOM BOOM BOOM

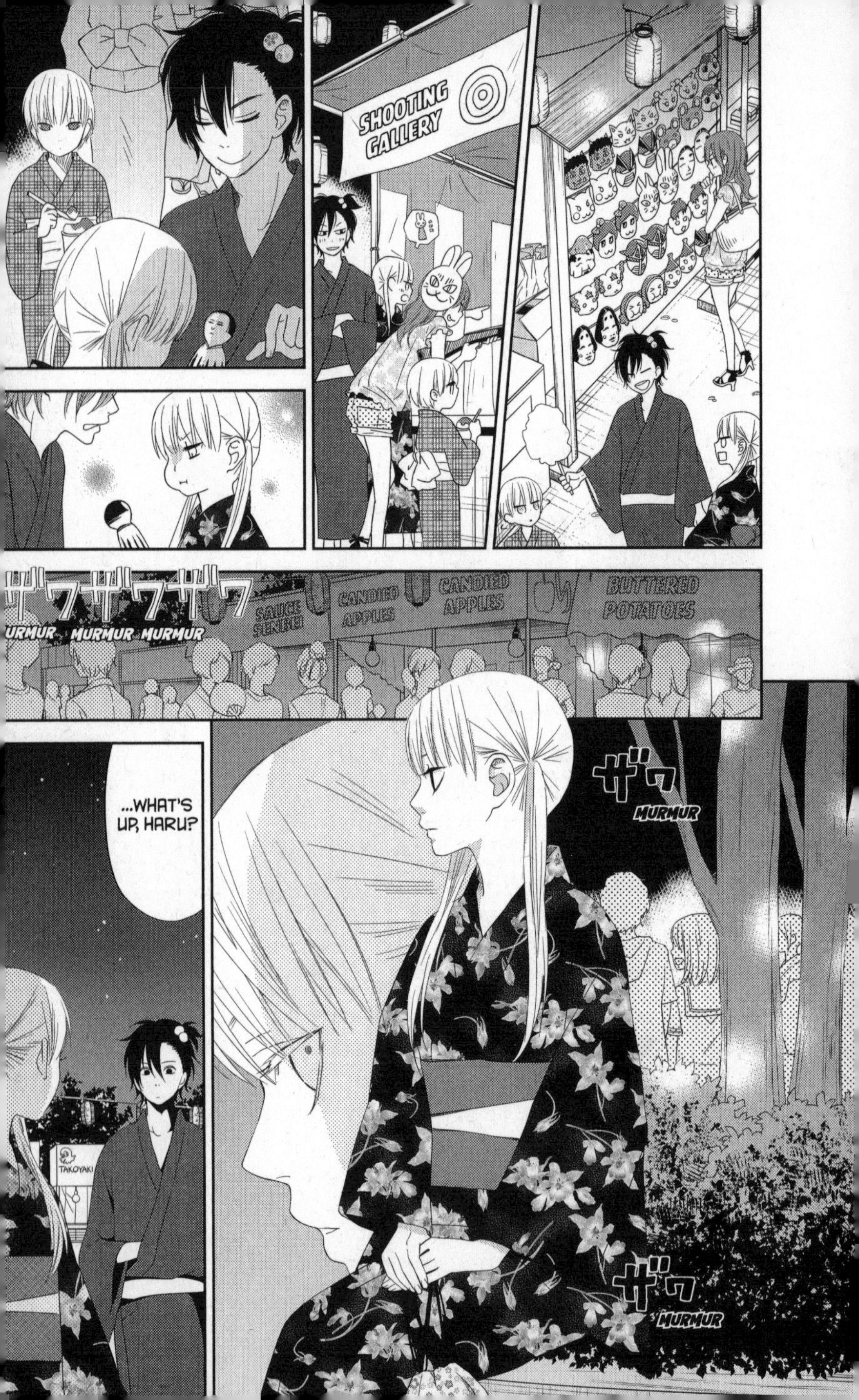
SHOOTING GALLERY
BUTTERED POTATOES
CANDIED APPLES
CANDIED APPLES
SAUCE SENSEI
ザワザワザワ
MURMUR MURMUR MURMUR
ザワ
MURMUR
ザワ
MURMUR
...WHAT'S UP, HARU?
TAKOYAKI

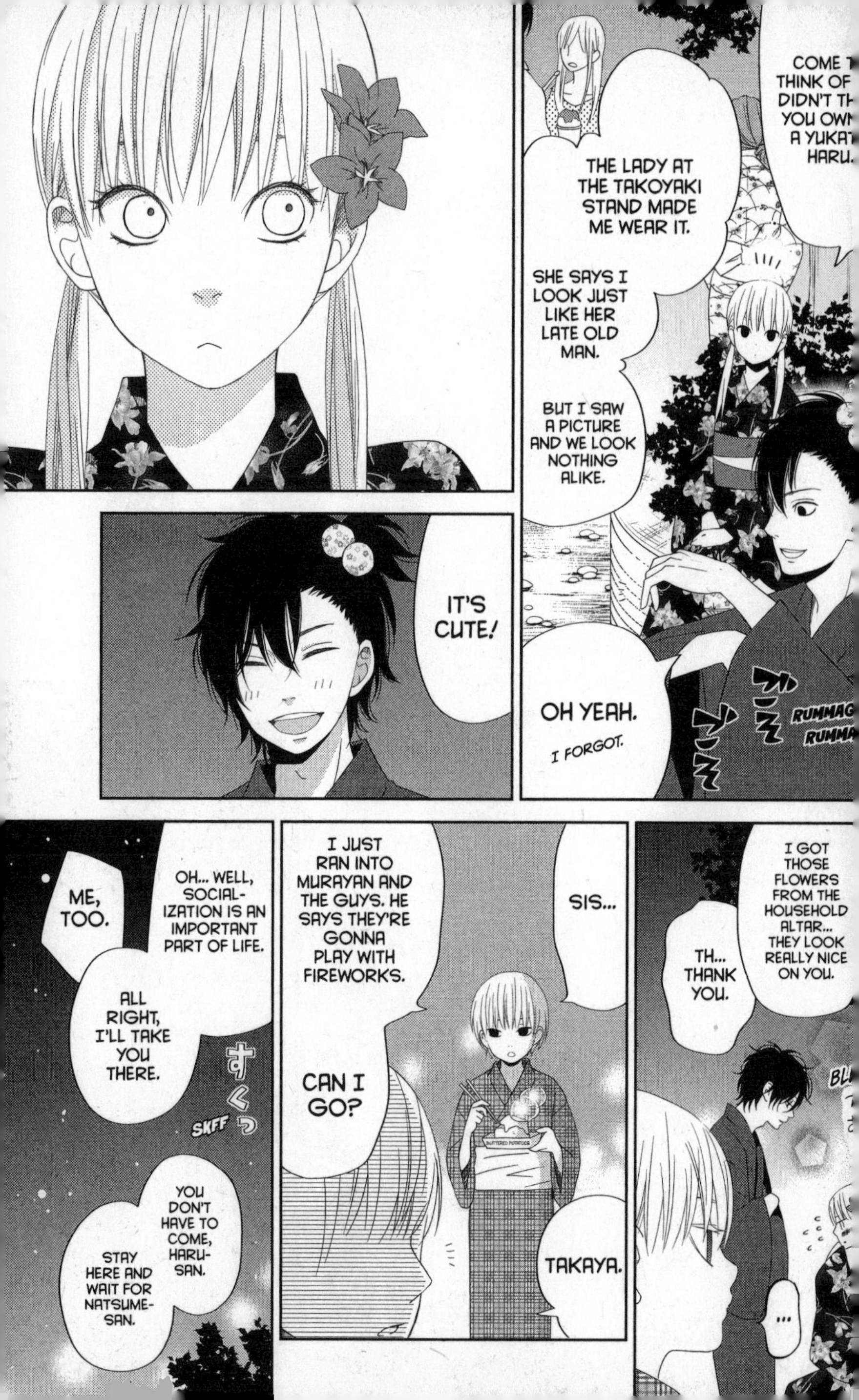
COME T
THINK OF
DIDN'T TH
YOU OWN
A YUKAT
HARU.
THE LADY AT THE TAKOYAKI STAND MADE ME WEAR IT.
SHE SAYS I LOOK JUST LIKE HER LATE OLD MAN.
BUT I SAW A PICTURE AND WE LOOK NOTHING ALIKE.
OH YEAH.
I FORGOT.
ゴソゴソ
RUMMAG
RUMMA
IT'S CUTE!
I GOT THOSE FLOWERS FROM THE HOUSEHOLD ALTAR... THEY LOOK REALLY NICE ON YOU.
TH... THANK YOU.
BL
...
SIS...
I JUST RAN INTO MURAYAN AND THE GUYS. HE SAYS THEY'RE GONNA PLAY WITH FIREWORKS.
CAN I GO?
BUTTERED POTATOES
TAKAYA.
OH... WELL, SOCIAL-IZATION IS AN IMPORTANT PART OF LIFE.
ME, TOO.
ALL RIGHT, I'LL TAKE YOU THERE.
すくっ
SKFF
YOU DON'T HAVE TO COME, HARU-SAN.
STAY HERE AND WAIT FOR NATSUME-SAN.

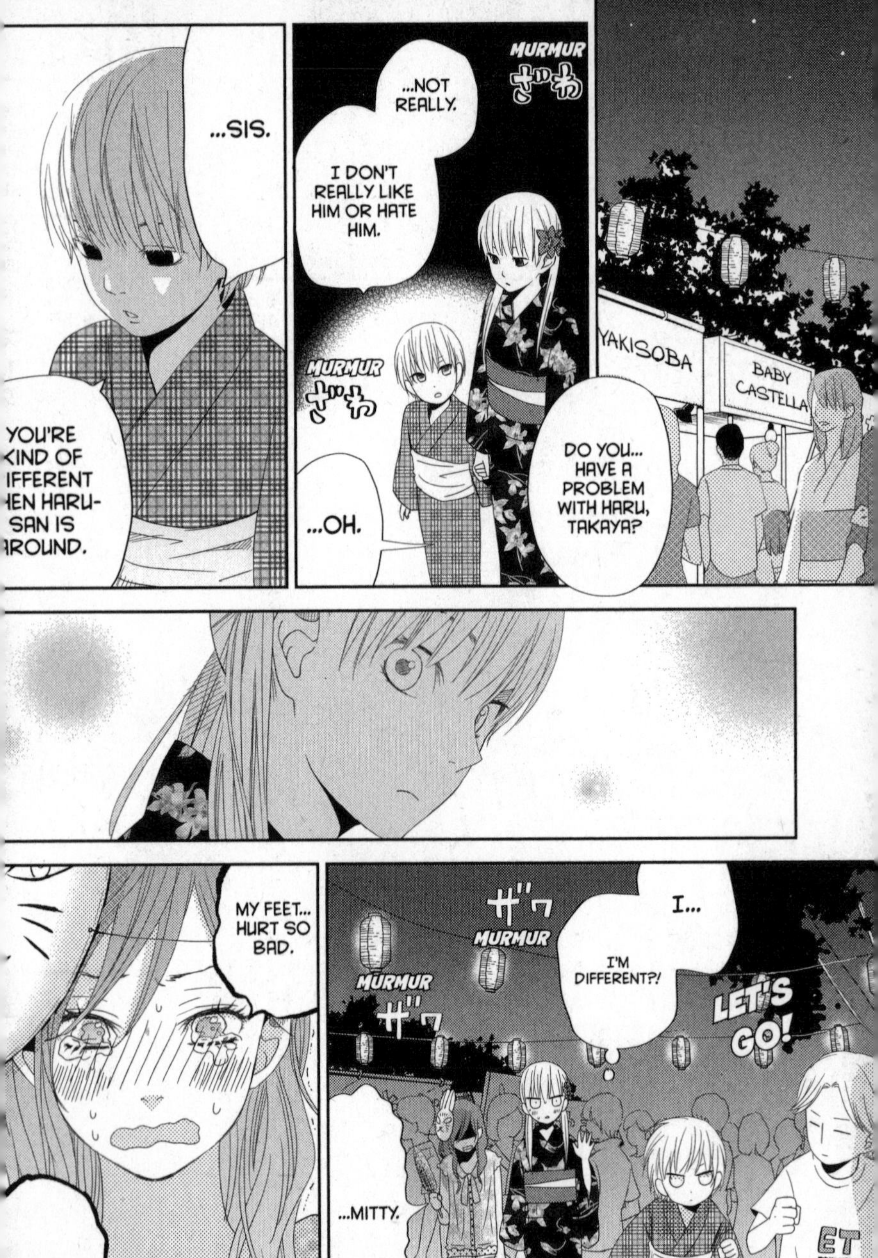
YAKISOBA
BABY CASTELLA
DO YOU... HAVE A PROBLEM WITH HARU, TAKAYA?
MURMUR ざわ
...NOT REALLY.
I DON'T REALLY LIKE HIM OR HATE HIM.
MURMUR ざわ
...OH.
...SIS.
YOU'RE KIND OF IFFERENT HEN HARU-SAN IS AROUND.
I...
I'M DIFFERENT?!
ザワ MURMUR
MURMUR ザワ
LET'S GO!
...MITTY.
ET
MY FEET... HURT SO BAD.
CAN'T WALK!

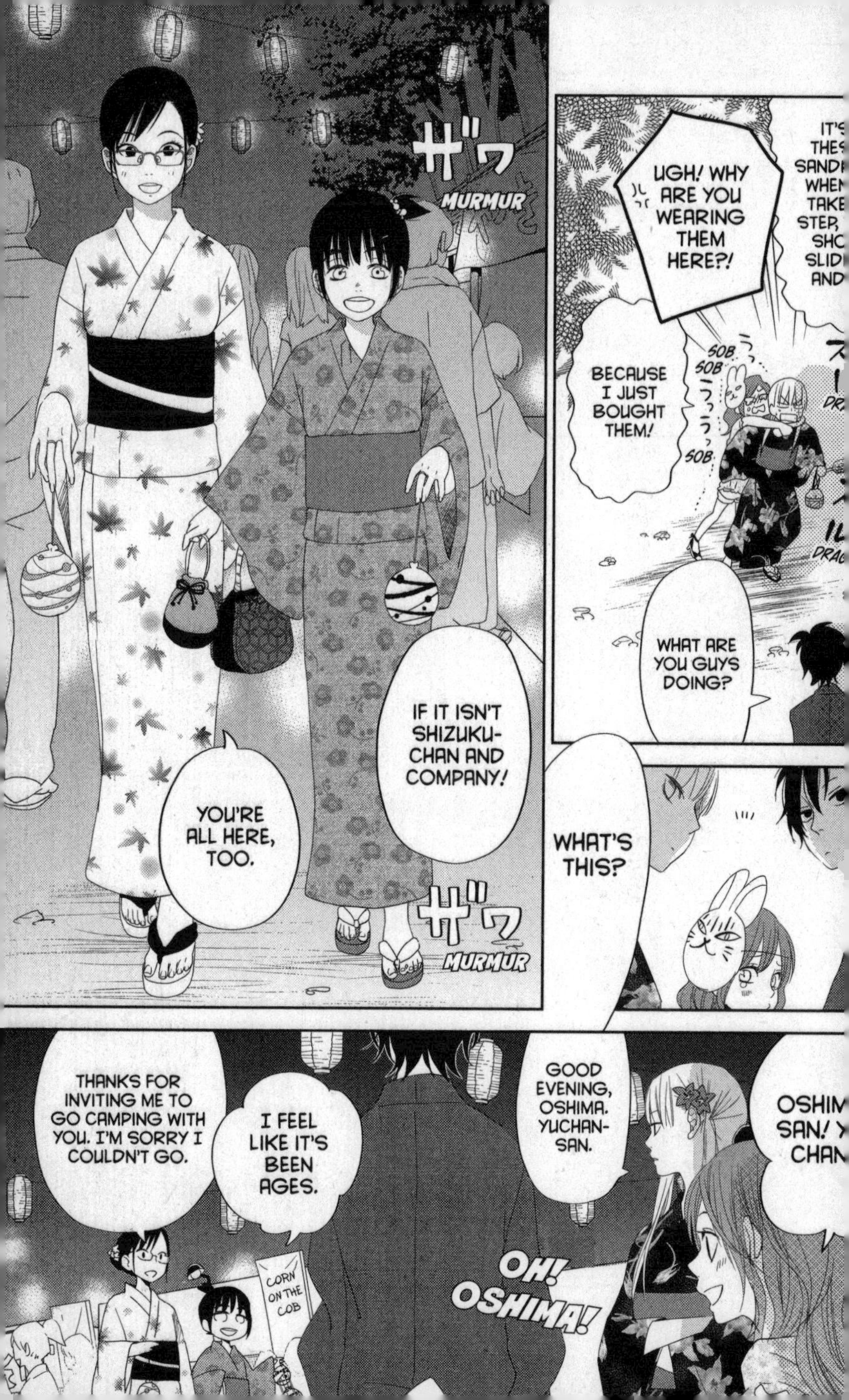
IT'S THES SANDI WHEN TAKE STEP, SHO SLID AND
UGH! WHY ARE YOU WEARING THEM HERE?!
SOB SOB
BECAUSE I JUST BOUGHT THEM!
SOB
DRA
DRAG
WHAT ARE YOU GUYS DOING?
WHAT'S THIS?
MURMUR
IF IT ISN'T SHIZUKU-CHAN AND COMPANY!
YOU'RE ALL HERE, TOO.
MURMUR
OSHIM SAN! Y CHAN
OH! OSHIMA!
GOOD EVENING, OSHIMA. YUCHAN-SAN.
I FEEL LIKE IT'S BEEN AGES.
THANKS FOR INVITING ME TO GO CAMPING WITH YOU. I'M SORRY I COULDN'T GO.
CORN ON THE COB

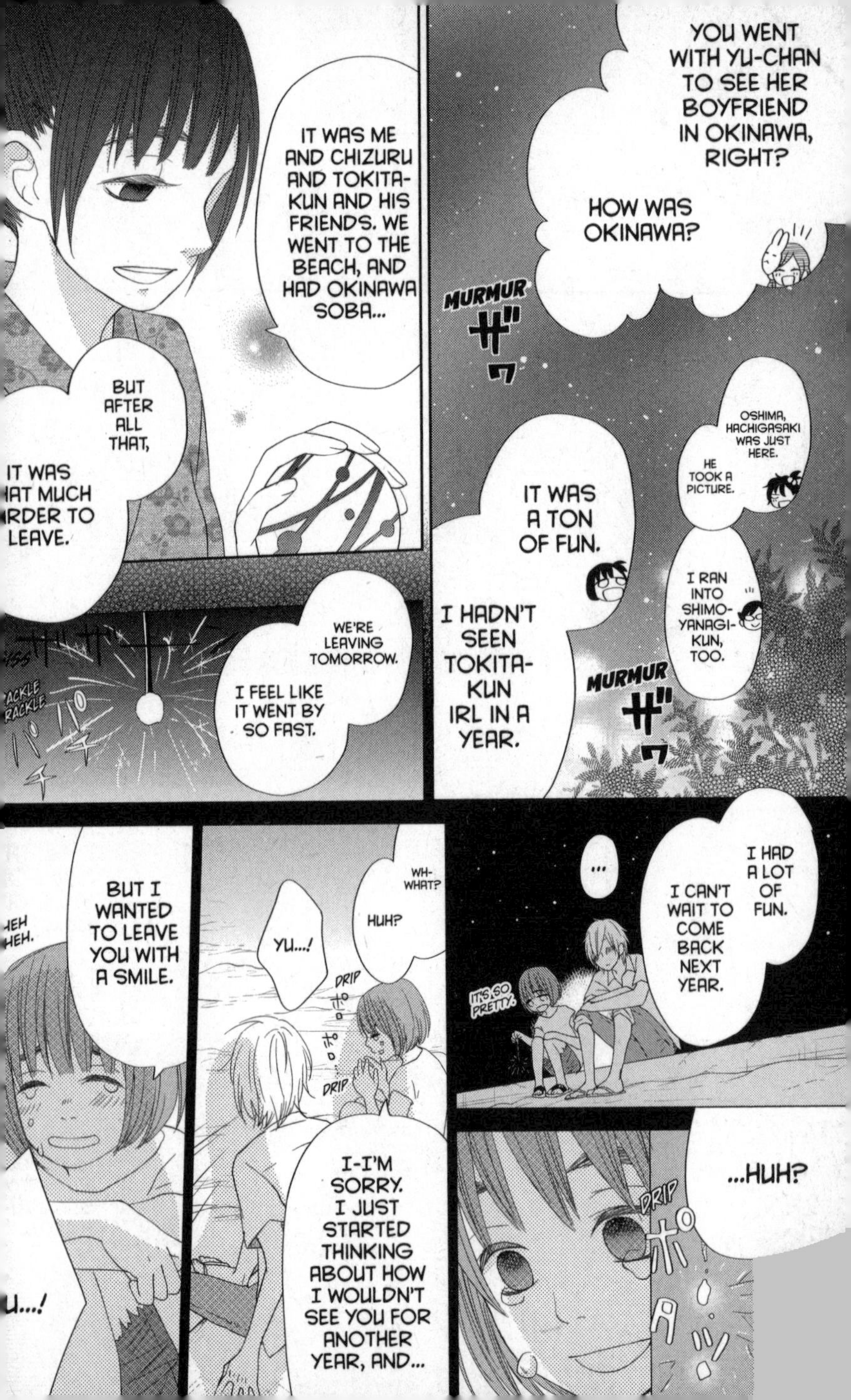
YOU WENT WITH YU-CHAN TO SEE HER BOYFRIEND IN OKINAWA, RIGHT?
HOW WAS OKINAWA?
MURMUR
OSHIMA, HACHIGASAKI WAS JUST HERE.
HE TOOK A PICTURE.
IT WAS A TON OF FUN.
I RAN INTO SHIMO-YANAGI-KUN, TOO.
I HADN'T SEEN TOKITA-KUN IRL IN A YEAR.
MURMUR
IT WAS ME AND CHIZURU AND TOKITA-KUN AND HIS FRIENDS. WE WENT TO THE BEACH, AND HAD OKINAWA SOBA...
BUT AFTER ALL THAT,
IT WAS
AT MUCH
RDER TO
LEAVE.
SS
ACKLE
RACKLE
WE'RE LEAVING TOMORROW.
I FEEL LIKE IT WENT BY SO FAST.
I HAD A LOT OF FUN.
I CAN'T WAIT TO COME BACK NEXT YEAR.
...
IT'S SO PRETTY.
...HUH?
DRIP
WH-WHAT?
HUH?
YU...!
DRIP
DRIP
I-I'M SORRY. I JUST STARTED THINKING ABOUT HOW I WOULDN'T SEE YOU FOR ANOTHER YEAR, AND...
BUT I WANTED TO LEAVE YOU WITH A SMILE.
EH
EH.
U...!

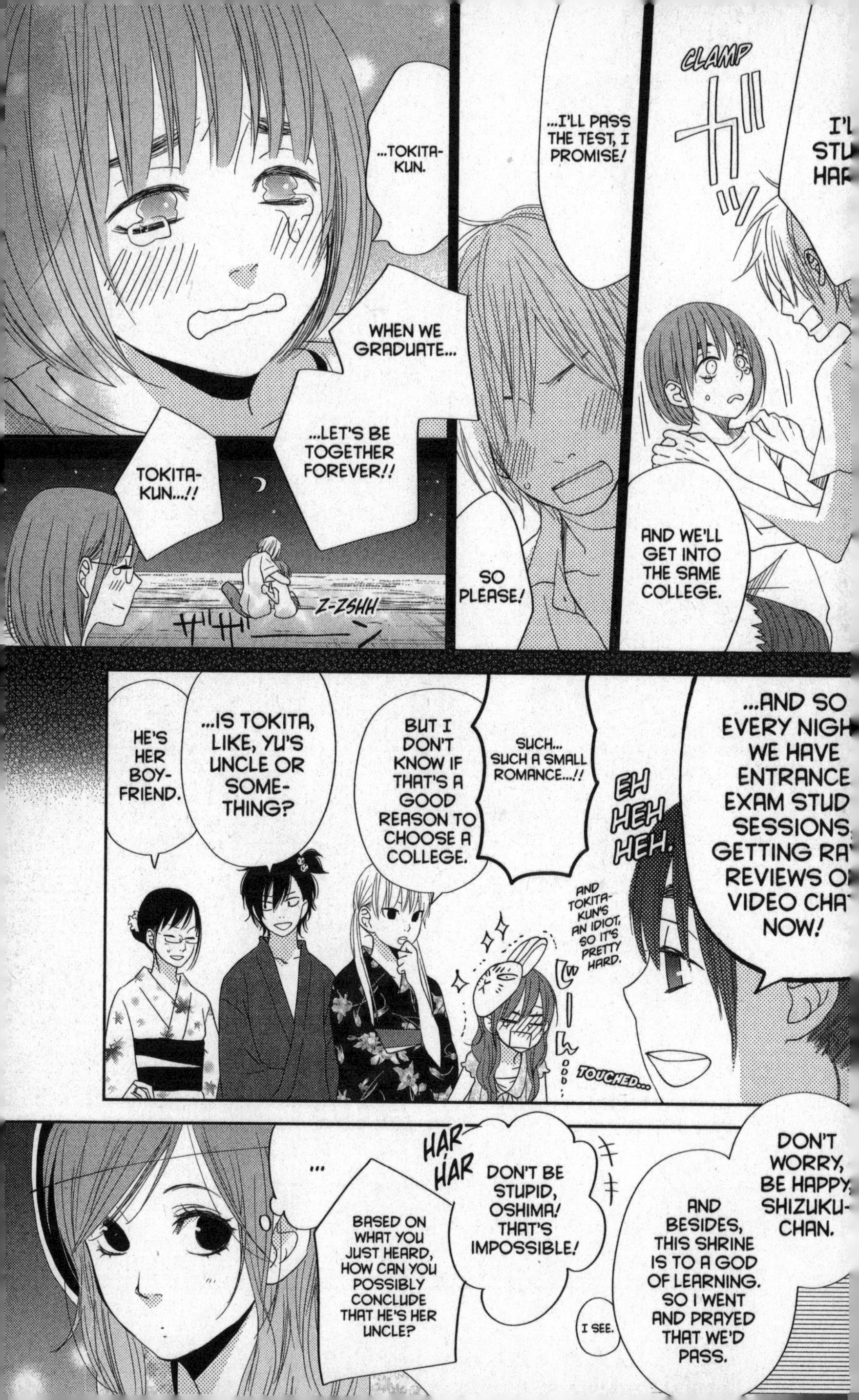
CLAMP
I'L STU HAR
AND WE'LL GET INTO THE SAME COLLEGE.
...I'LL PASS THE TEST, I PROMISE!
SO PLEASE!
...TOKITA-KUN.
WHEN WE GRADUATE...
...LET'S BE TOGETHER FOREVER!!
TOKITA-KUN...!!
Z-ZSHH
...AND SO EVERY NIGH WE HAVE ENTRANCE EXAM STUD SESSIONS. GETTING RA REVIEWS O VIDEO CHA NOW!
EH HEH HEH.
AND TOKITA-KUN'S AN IDIOT, SO IT'S PRETTY HARD.
TOUCHED...
SUCH... SUCH A SMALL ROMANCE...!!
BUT I DON'T KNOW IF THAT'S A GOOD REASON TO CHOOSE A COLLEGE.
...IS TOKITA, LIKE, YU'S UNCLE OR SOMETHING?
HE'S HER BOYFRIEND.
DON'T WORRY, BE HAPPY, SHIZUKU-CHAN.
AND BESIDES, THIS SHRINE IS TO A GOD OF LEARNING. SO I WENT AND PRAYED THAT WE'D PASS.
I SEE.
HAR HAR
DON'T BE STUPID, OSHIMA! THAT'S IMPOSSIBLE!
BASED ON WHAT YOU JUST HEARD, HOW CAN YOU POSSIBLY CONCLUDE THAT HE'S HER UNCLE?
...

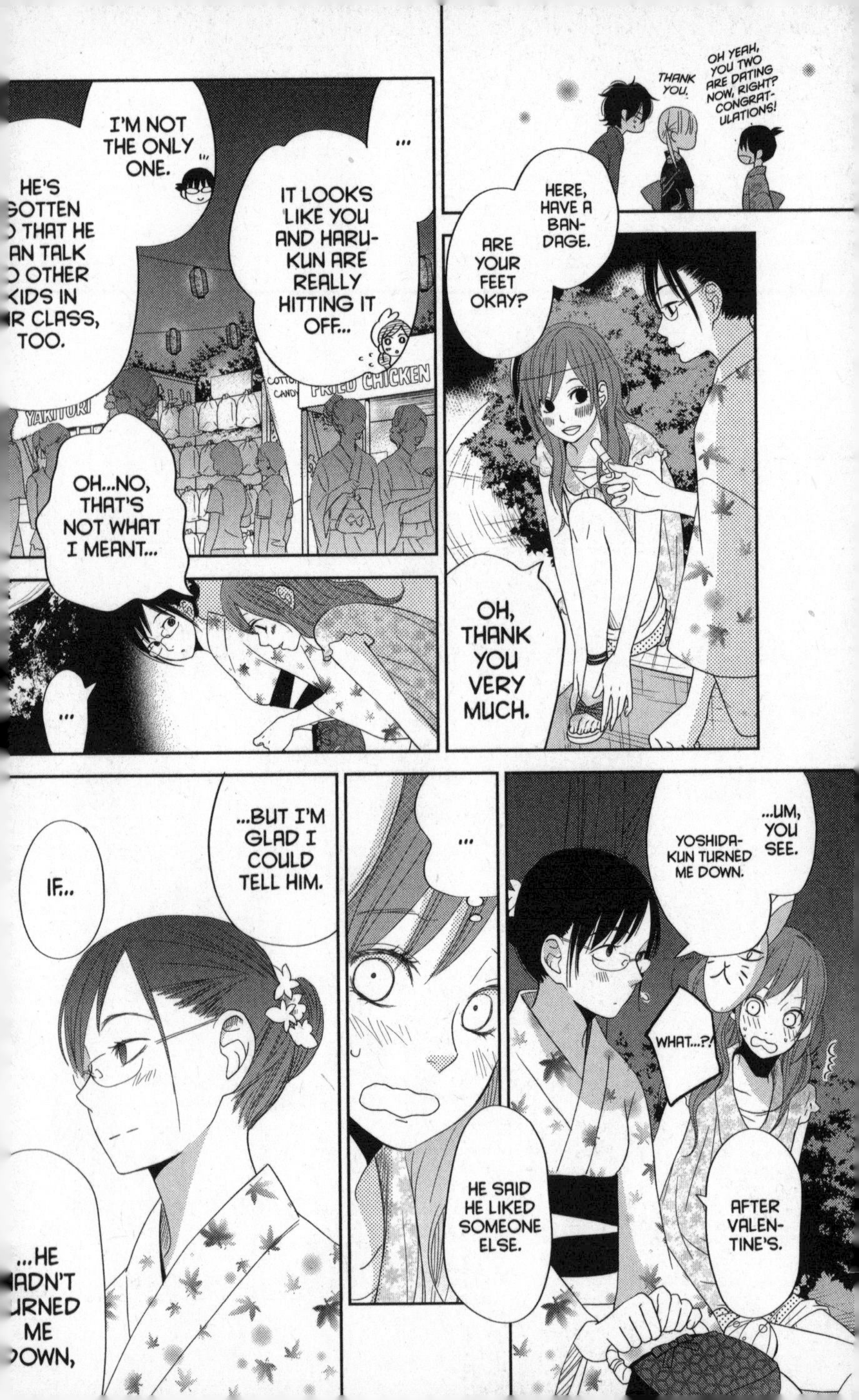

OH YEAH, YOU TWO ARE DATING NOW, RIGHT? CONGRATULATIONS!
THANK YOU.
HERE, HAVE A BAN-DAGE.
ARE YOUR FEET OKAY?
OH, THANK YOU VERY MUCH.
...
IT LOOKS LIKE YOU AND HARU-KUN ARE REALLY HITTING IT OFF...
I'M NOT THE ONLY ONE.
HE'S GOTTEN O THAT HE AN TALK O OTHER KIDS IN R CLASS, TOO.
FRIED CHICKEN
YAKITORI
OH...NO, THAT'S NOT WHAT I MEANT...
...
...UM, YOU SEE.
YOSHIDA-KUN TURNED ME DOWN.
WHAT...?!
AFTER VALEN-TINE'S.
HE SAID HE LIKED SOMEONE ELSE.
...
...BUT I'M GLAD I COULD TELL HIM.
IF...
...HE ADN'T URNED ME OWN,

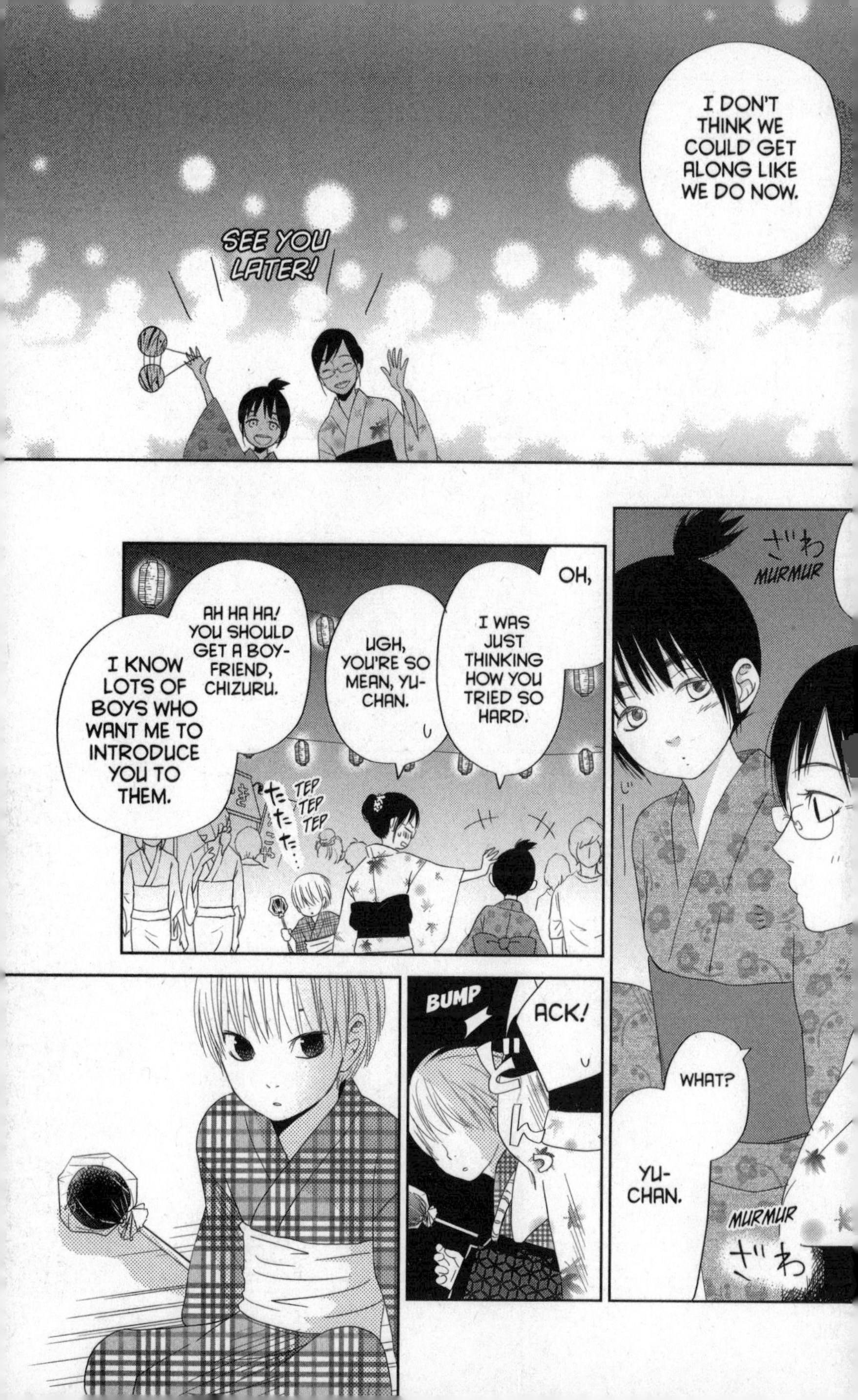
I DON'T THINK WE COULD GET ALONG LIKE WE DO NOW.
SEE YOU LATER!
ざわ
MURMUR
WHAT?
YU-CHAN.
MURMUR
ざわ
OH,
I WAS JUST THINKING HOW YOU TRIED SO HARD.
UGH, YOU'RE SO MEAN, YU-CHAN.
AH HA HA! YOU SHOULD GET A BOY-FRIEND, CHIZURU.
I KNOW LOTS OF BOYS WHO WANT ME TO INTRODUCE YOU TO THEM.
たたた…
TEP TEP TEP
BUMP
ACK!

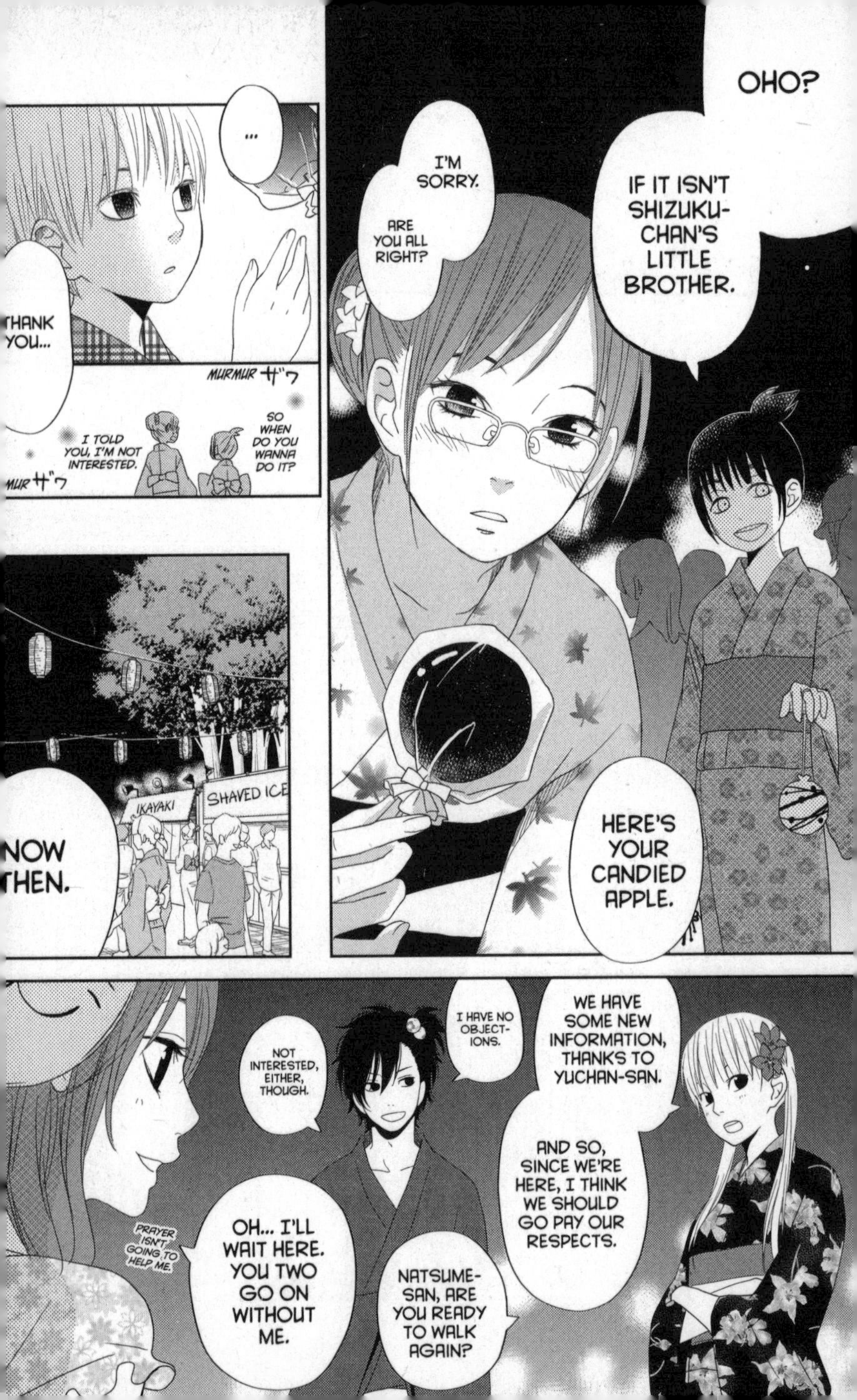
OHO?
IF IT ISN'T SHIZUKU-CHAN'S LITTLE BROTHER.
I'M SORRY.
ARE YOU ALL RIGHT?
HERE'S YOUR CANDIED APPLE.
...
THANK YOU...
MURMUR ザワ
SO WHEN DO YOU WANNA DO IT?
I TOLD YOU, I'M NOT INTERESTED.
MUR ザワ
SHAVED ICE
IKAYAKI
NOW THEN.
WE HAVE SOME NEW INFORMATION, THANKS TO YUCHAN-SAN.
AND SO, SINCE WE'RE HERE, I THINK WE SHOULD GO PAY OUR RESPECTS.
I HAVE NO OBJECTIONS.
NOT INTERESTED, EITHER, THOUGH.
NATSUME-SAN, ARE YOU READY TO WALK AGAIN?
OH... I'LL WAIT HERE. YOU TWO GO ON WITHOUT ME.
PRAYER ISN'T GOING TO HELP ME.

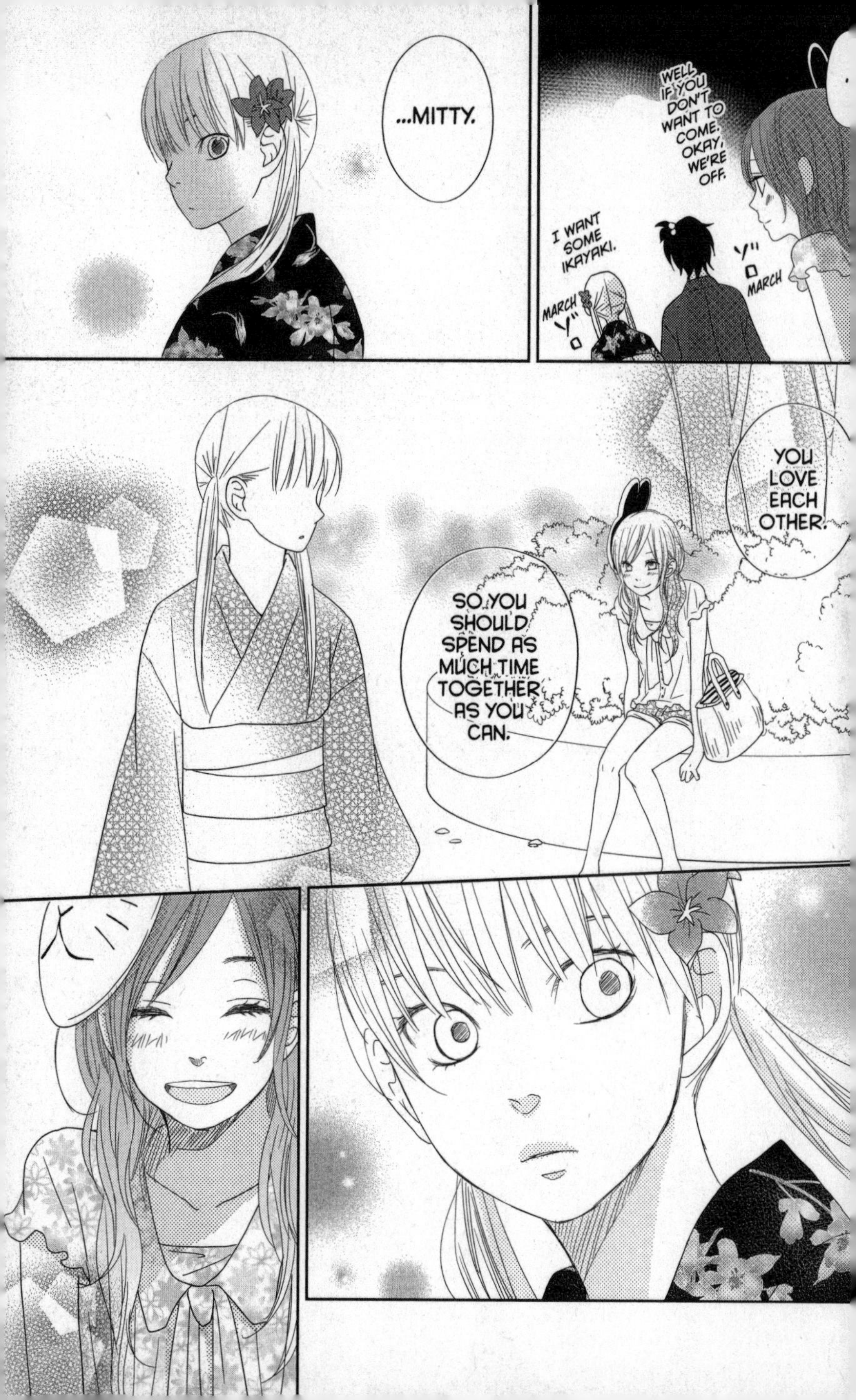
WELL IF YOU DON'T WANT TO COME, OKAY, WE'RE OFF.
MARCH
I WANT SOME IKAYAKI.
MARCH
...MITTY.
YOU LOVE EACH OTHER.
SO YOU SHOULD SPEND AS MUCH TIME TOGETHER AS YOU CAN.

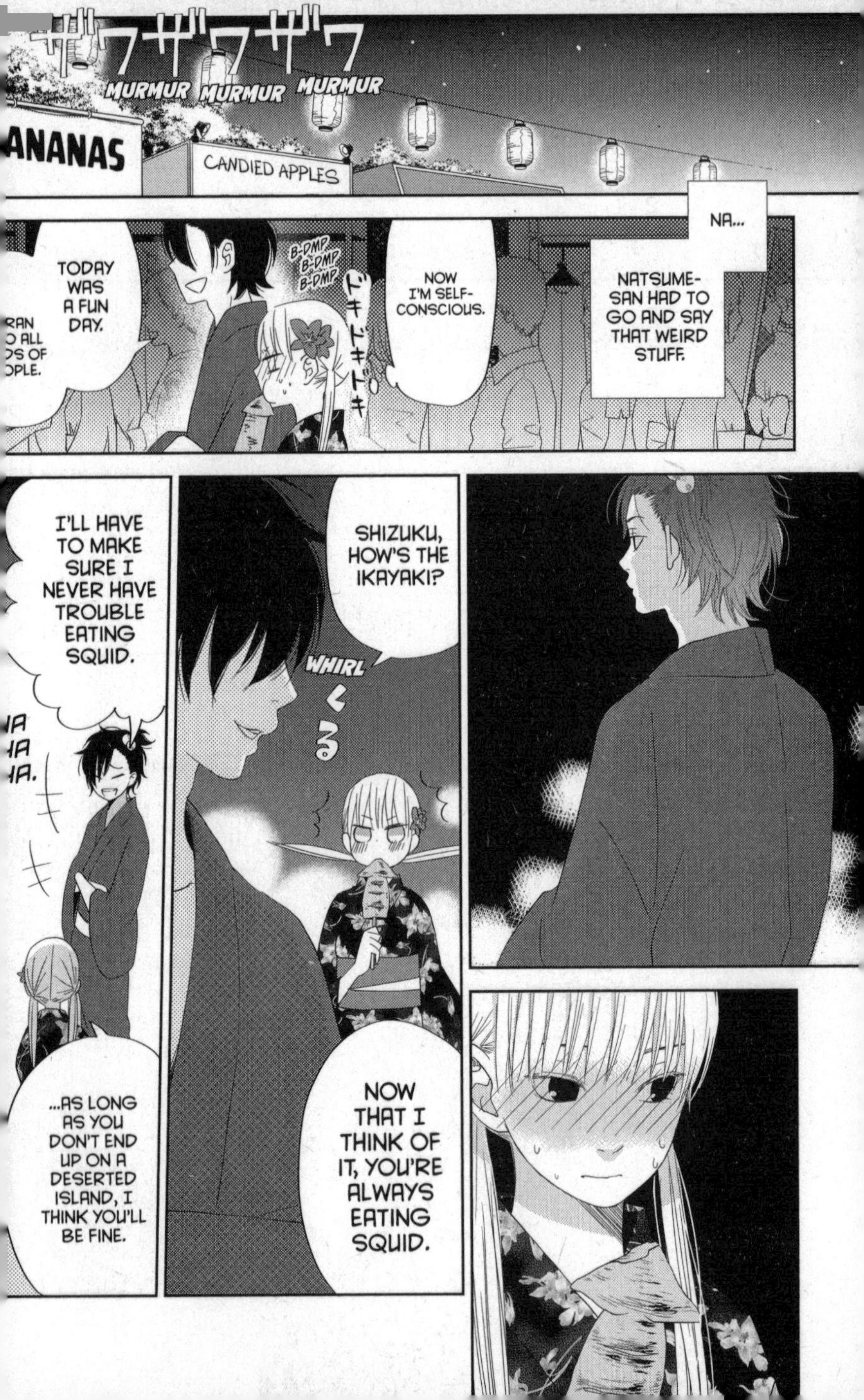
ザワザワザワ
MURMUR MURMUR MURMUR
ANANAS
CANDIED APPLES
NA...
NATSUME-SAN HAD TO GO AND SAY THAT WEIRD STUFF.
B-DMP B-DMP B-DMP
ドキドキドキ
NOW I'M SELF-CONSCIOUS.
TODAY WAS A FUN DAY.
SHIZUKU, HOW'S THE IKAYAKI?
WHIRL
くる
NOW THAT I THINK OF IT, YOU'RE ALWAYS EATING SQUID.
I'LL HAVE TO MAKE SURE I NEVER HAVE TROUBLE EATING SQUID.
...AS LONG AS YOU DON'T END UP ON A DESERTED ISLAND, I THINK YOU'LL BE FINE.

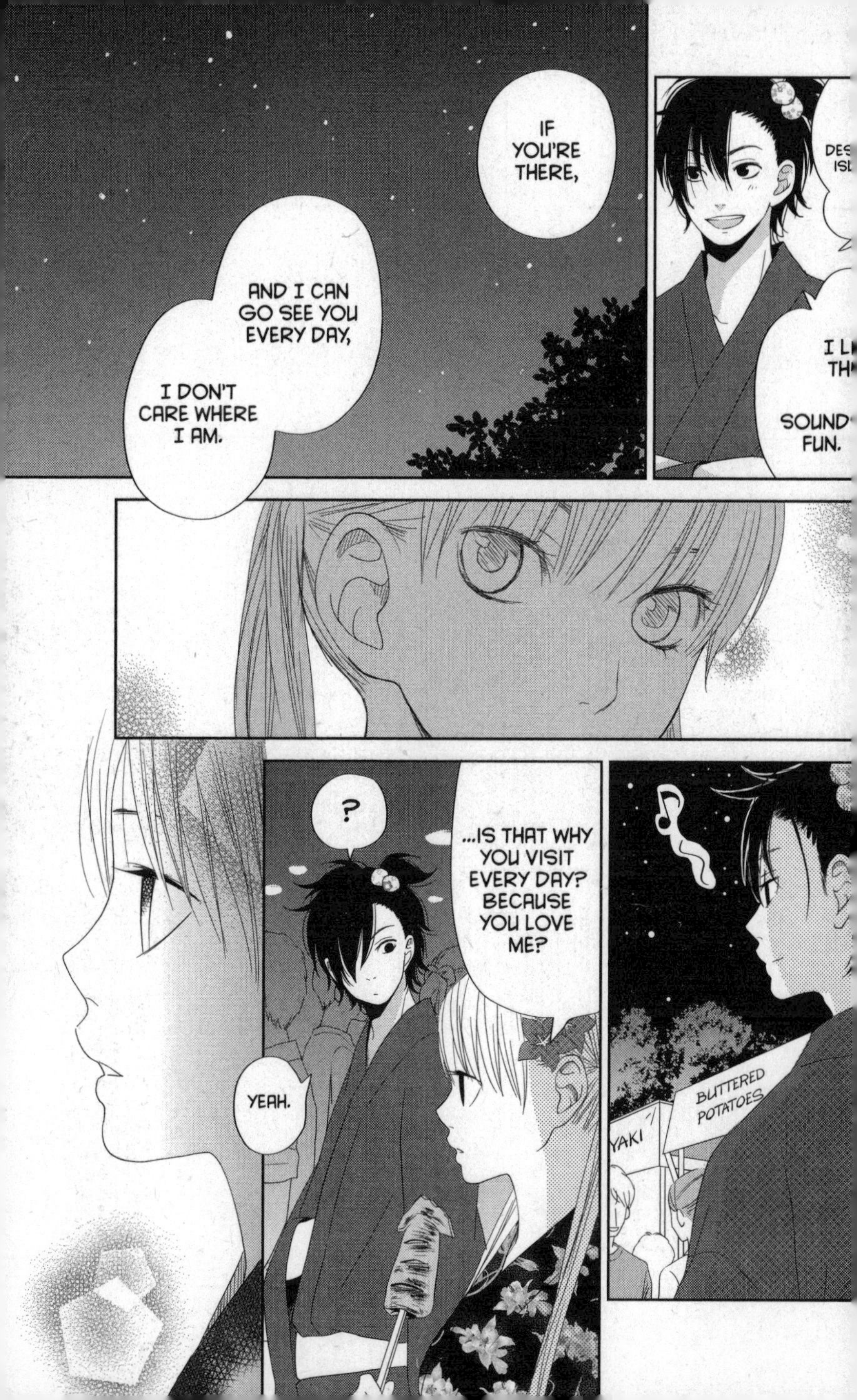
SOUND FUN.
IF YOU'RE THERE,
AND I CAN GO SEE YOU EVERY DAY,
I DON'T CARE WHERE I AM.
BUTTERED POTATOES
YAKI
...IS THAT WHY YOU VISIT EVERY DAY? BECAUSE YOU LOVE ME?
?
YEAH.

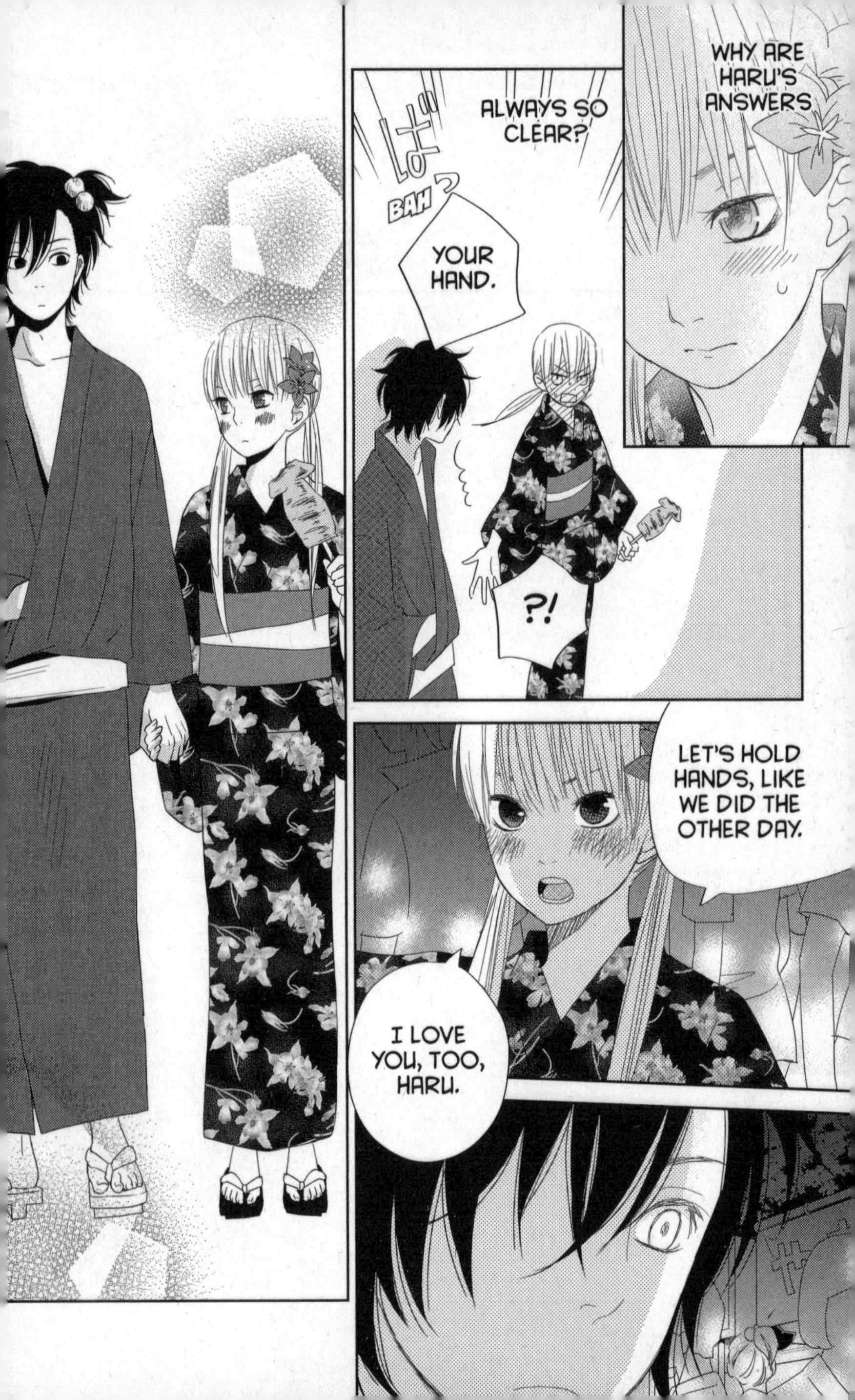
WHY ARE HARU'S ANSWERS
ALWAYS SO CLEAR?
BAH
YOUR HAND.
?!
LET'S HOLD HANDS, LIKE WE DID THE OTHER DAY.
I LOVE YOU, TOO, HARU.

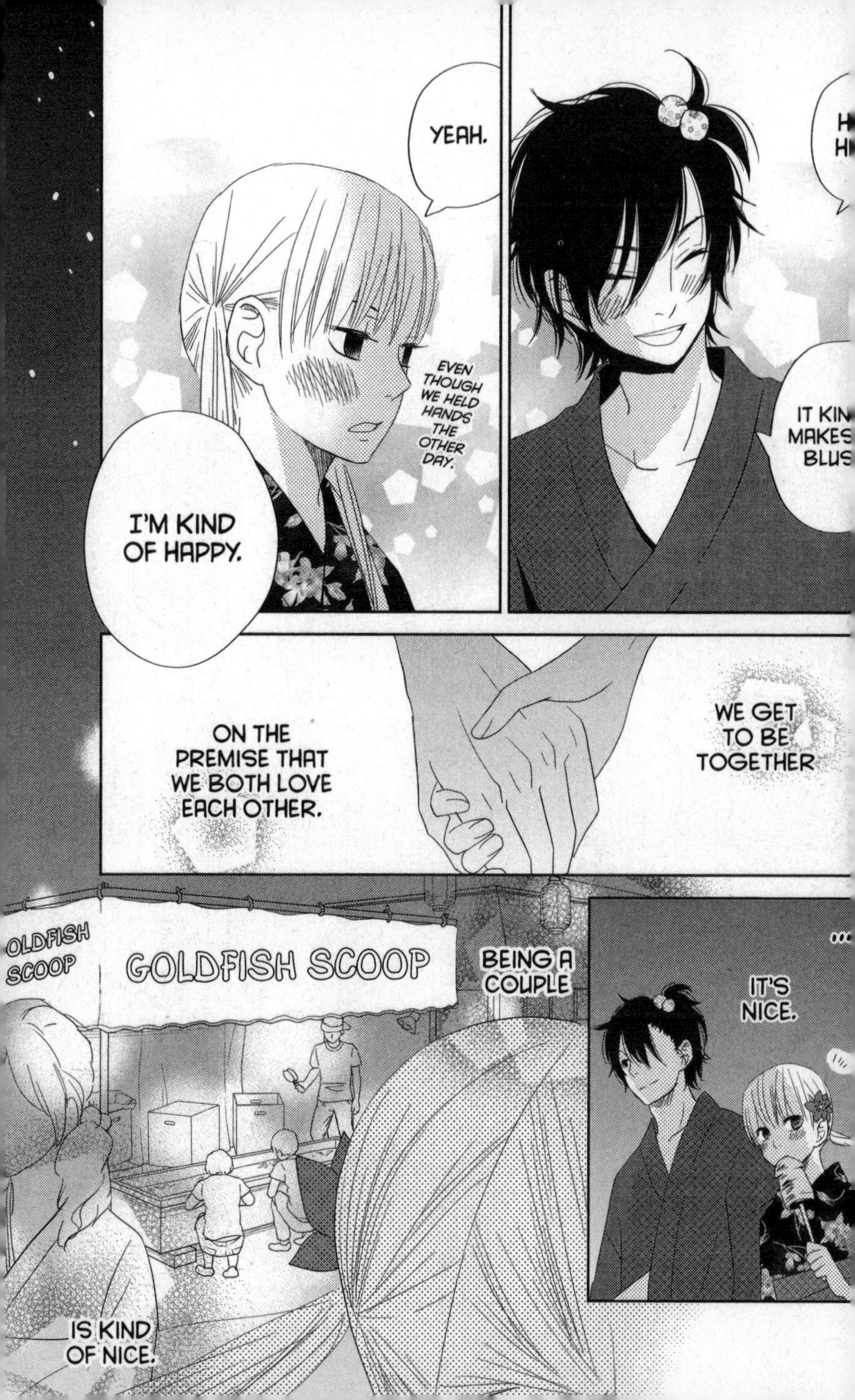
IT KIN MAKES BLUS
YEAH.
EVEN THOUGH WE HELD HANDS THE OTHER DAY.
I'M KIND OF HAPPY.
WE GET TO BE TOGETHER
ON THE PREMISE THAT WE BOTH LOVE EACH OTHER.
...
IT'S NICE.
GOLDFISH SCOOP
GOLDFISH SCOOP
BEING A COUPLE
IS KIND OF NICE.

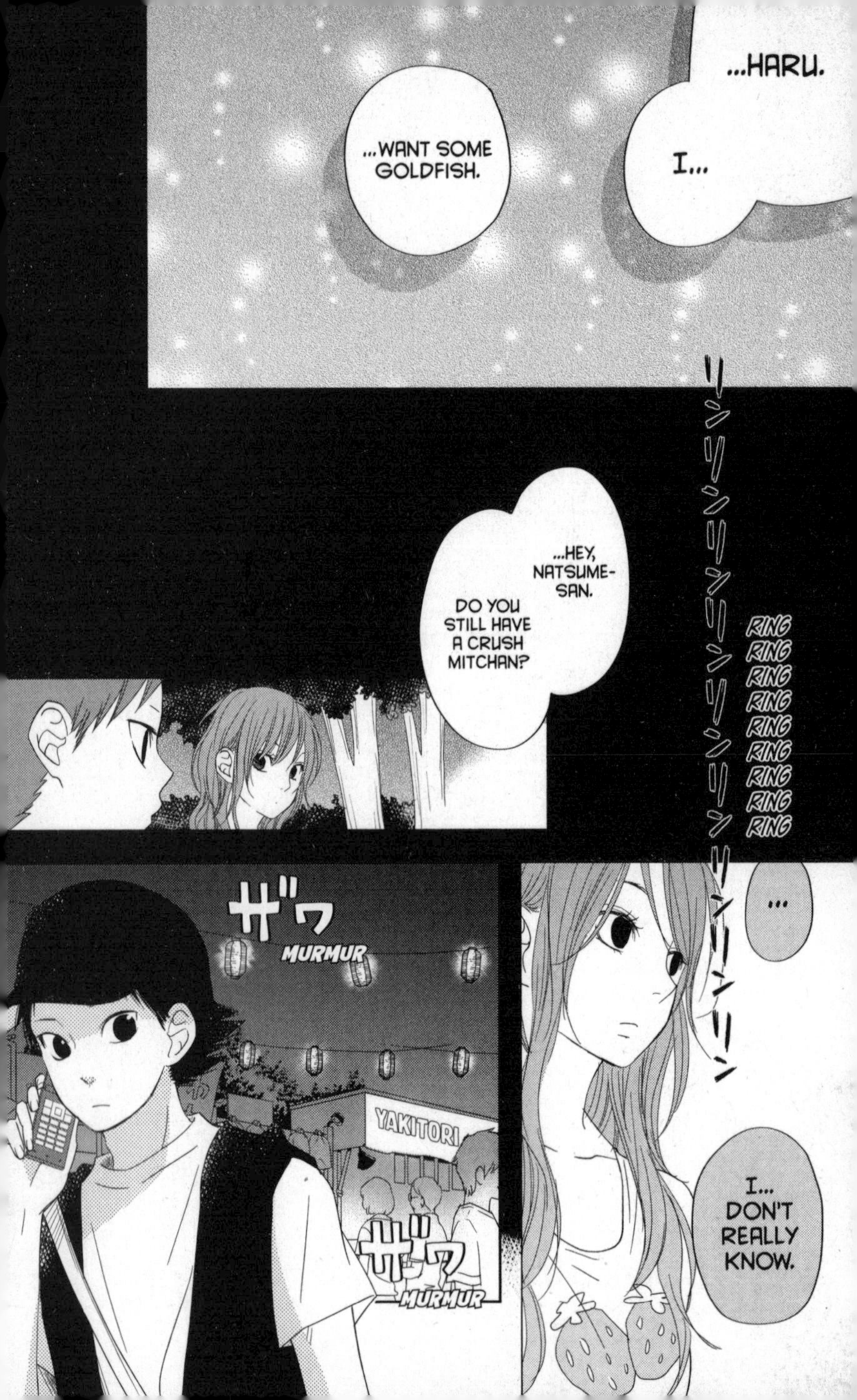
...HARU.
I...
...WANT SOME GOLDFISH.
リンリンリンリンリンリンリンリンリン
RING RING RING RING RING RING RING RING RING
...HEY, NATSUME-SAN.
DO YOU STILL HAVE A CRUSH MITCHAN?
...
I... DON'T REALLY KNOW.
ザワ
MURMUR
YAKITORI
ザワ
MURMUR

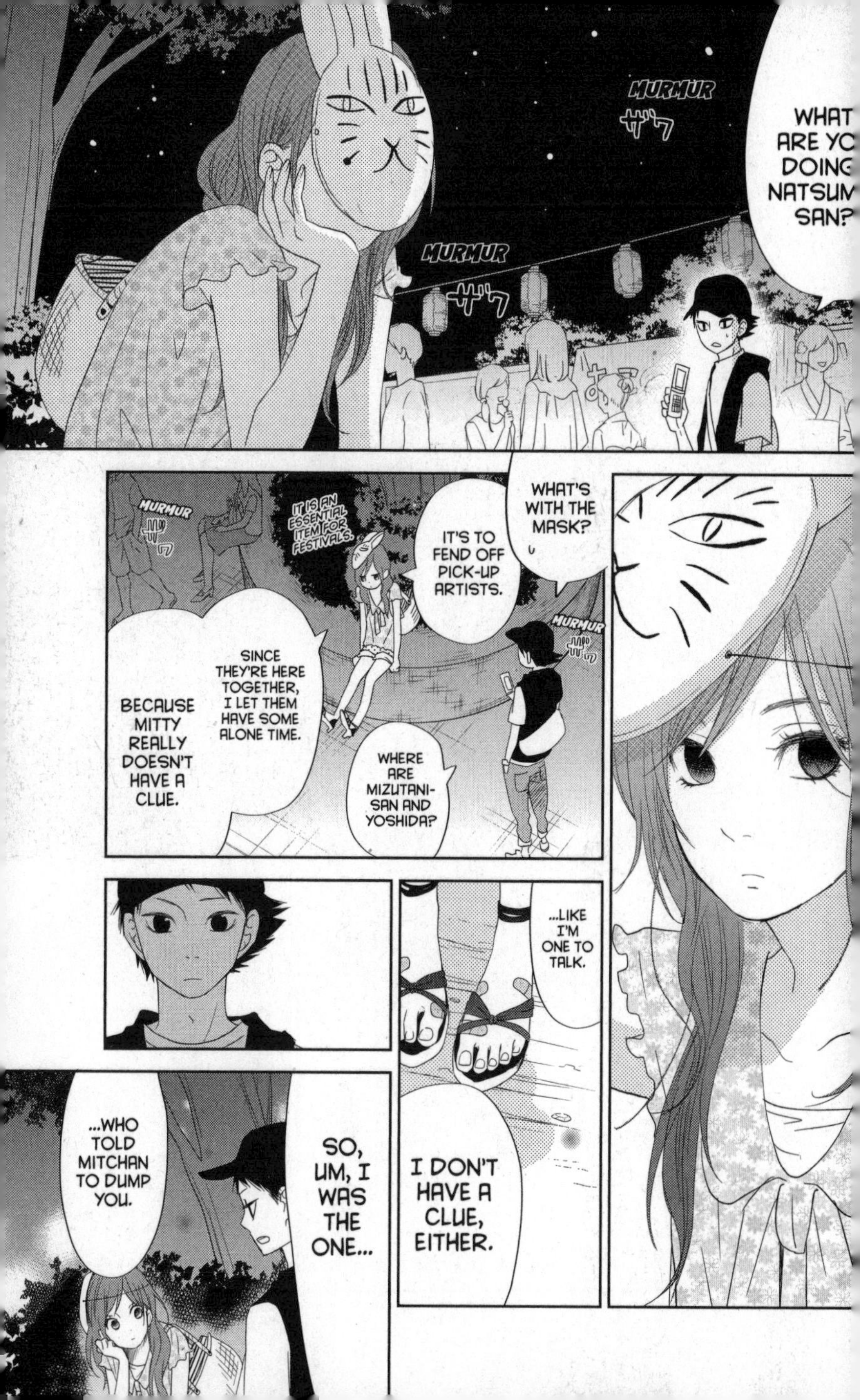
WHAT ARE YO DOING NATSUM SAN?
MURMUR
MURMUR
WHAT'S WITH THE MASK?
IT'S TO FEND OFF PICK-UP ARTISTS.
IT IS AN ESSENTIAL ITEM FOR FESTIVALS.
MURMUR
MURMUR
WHERE ARE MIZUTANI-SAN AND YOSHIDA?
SINCE THEY'RE HERE TOGETHER, I LET THEM HAVE SOME ALONE TIME.
BECAUSE MITTY REALLY DOESN'T HAVE A CLUE.
...LIKE I'M ONE TO TALK.
I DON'T HAVE A CLUE, EITHER.
SO, UM, I WAS THE ONE...
...WHO TOLD MITCHAN TO DUMP YOU.

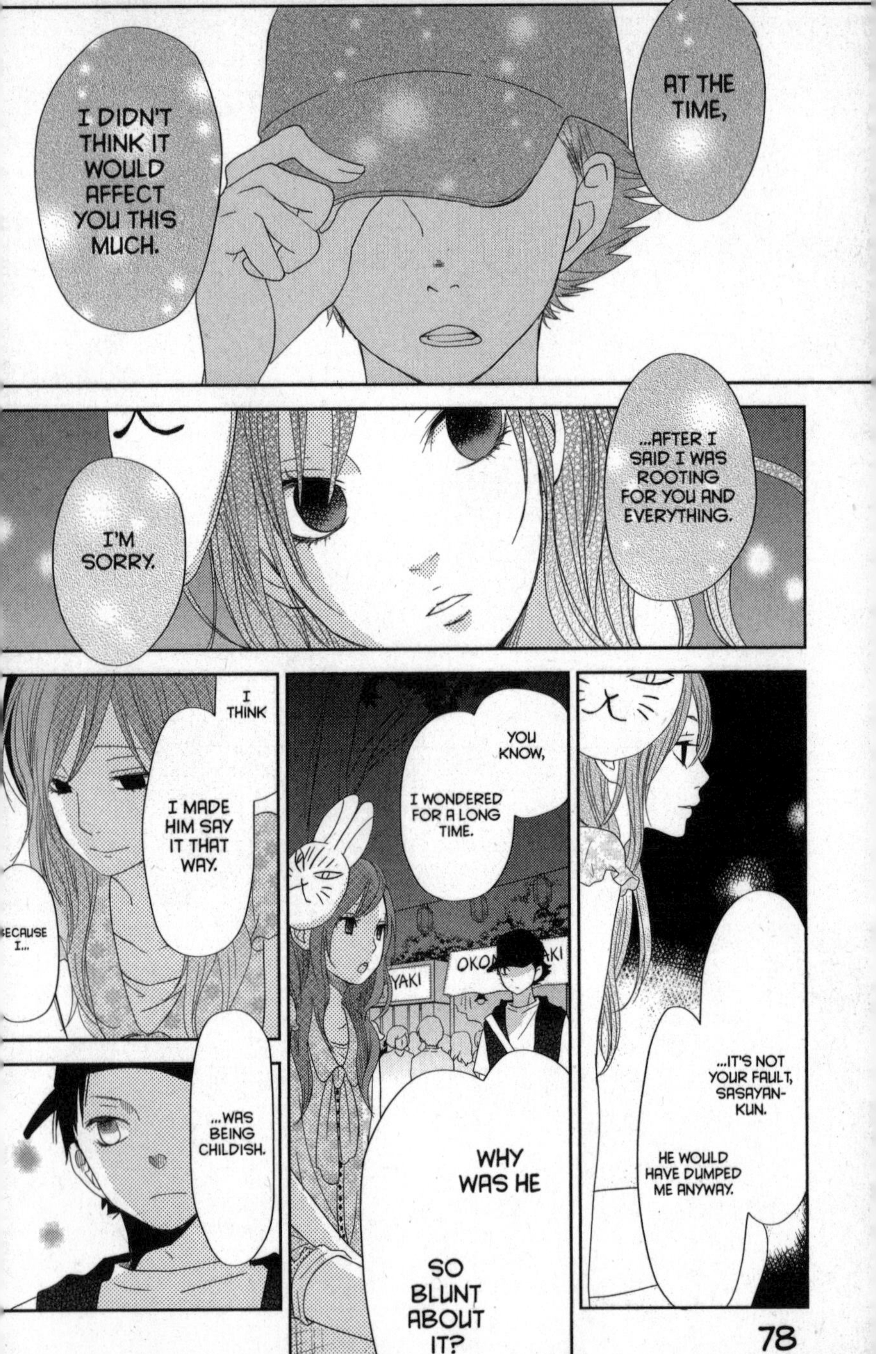
AT THE TIME,
I DIDN'T THINK IT WOULD AFFECT YOU THIS MUCH.
...AFTER I SAID I WAS ROOTING FOR YOU AND EVERYTHING.
I'M SORRY.
...IT'S NOT YOUR FAULT, SASAYAN-KUN.
HE WOULD HAVE DUMPED ME ANYWAY.
YOU KNOW,
I WONDERED FOR A LONG TIME.
WHY WAS HE
SO BLUNT ABOUT IT?
I THINK
I MADE HIM SAY IT THAT WAY.
BECAUSE I...
...WAS BEING CHILDISH.

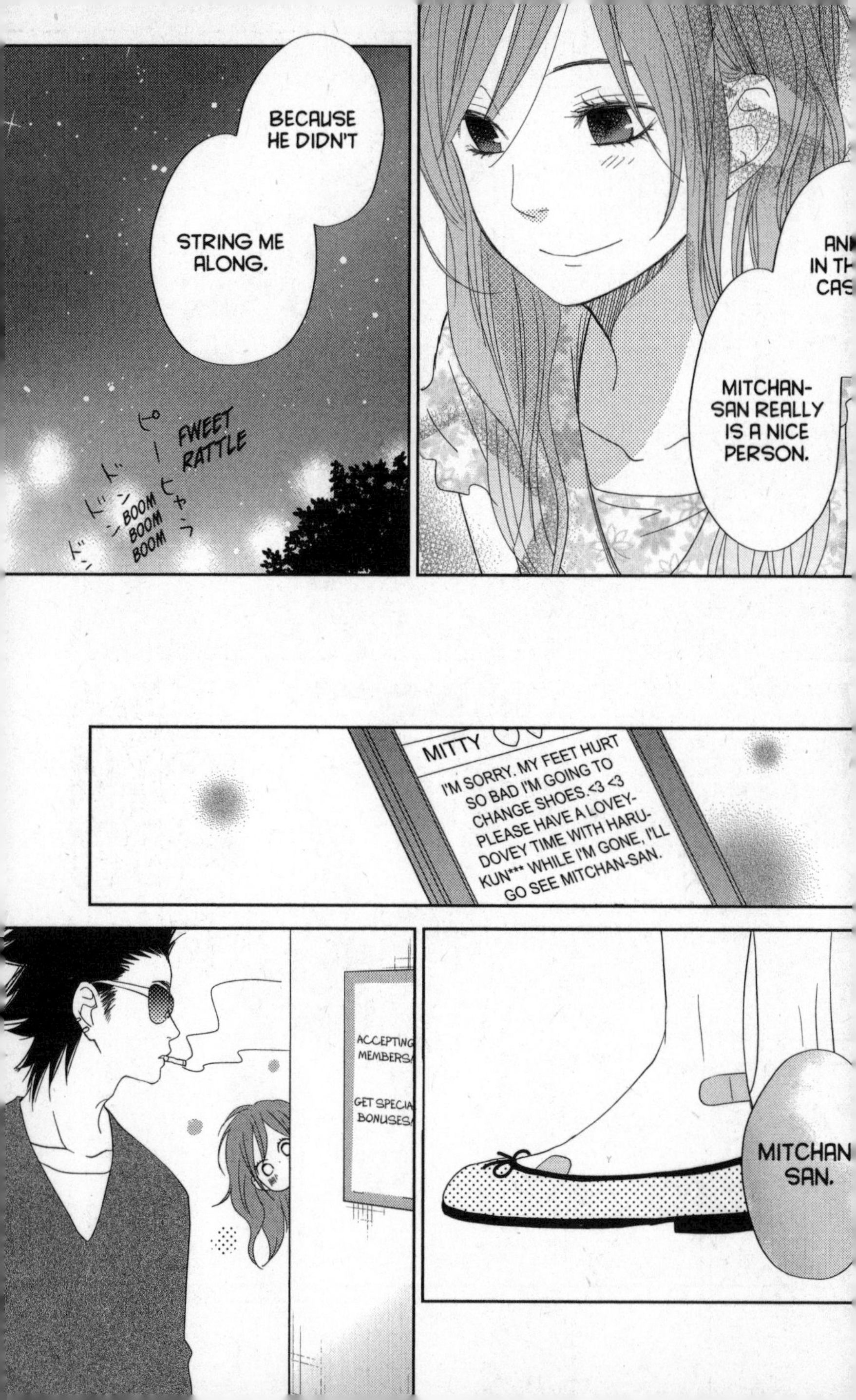
MITCHAN-SAN REALLY IS A NICE PERSON.
BECAUSE HE DIDN'T
STRING ME ALONG.
FWEET RATTLE
ピーヒャラ
BOOM BOOM BOOM
ドンドンドン
MITTY
I'M SORRY. MY FEET HURT SO BAD I'M GOING TO CHANGE SHOES.<3 <3 PLEASE HAVE A LOVEY-DOVEY TIME WITH HARU-KUN*** WHILE I'M GONE, I'LL GO SEE MITCHAN-SAN.
MITCHAN SAN.

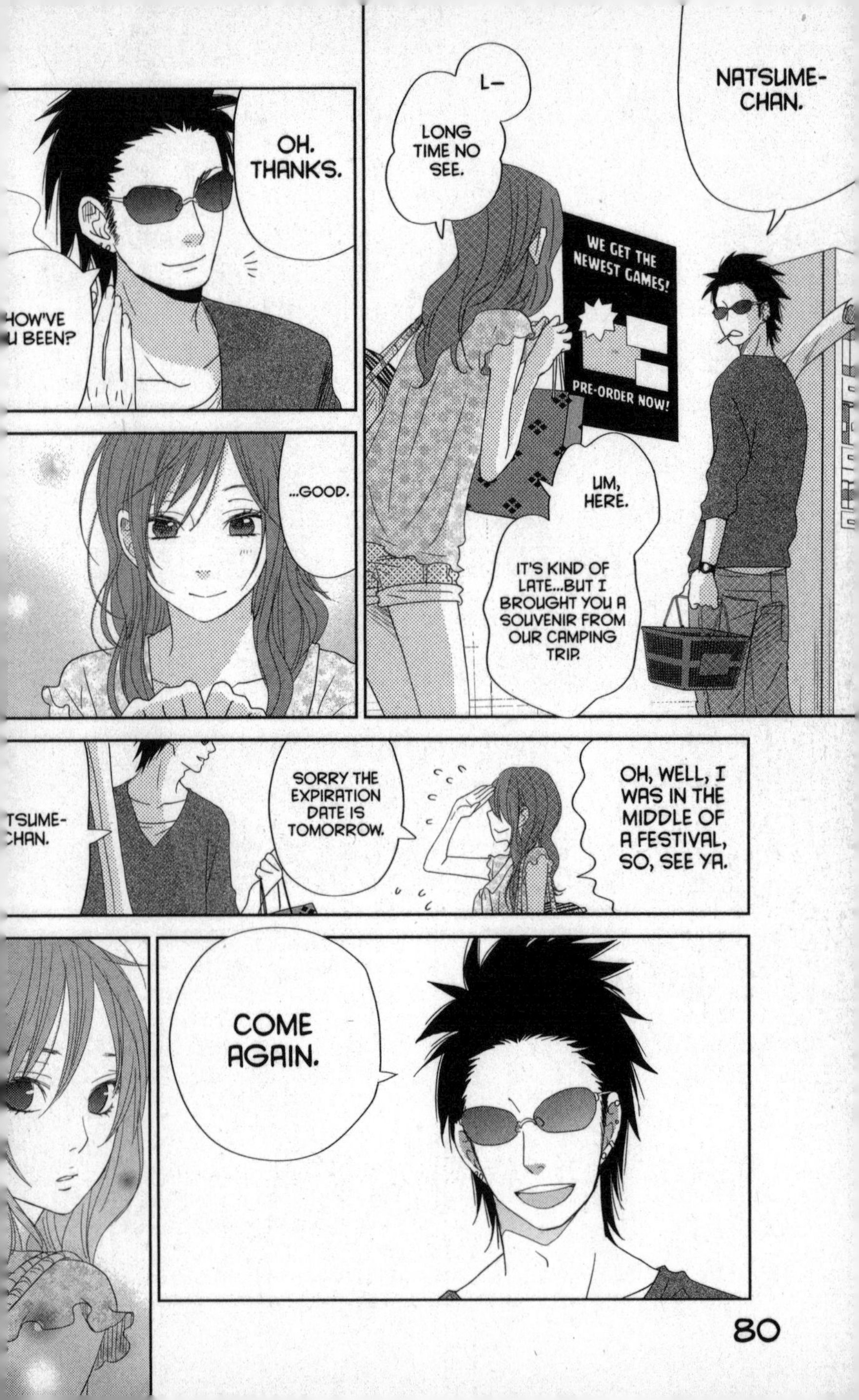
NATSUME-CHAN.
L—
LONG TIME NO SEE.
WE GET THE NEWEST GAMES!
PRE-ORDER NOW!
UM, HERE.
IT'S KIND OF LATE...BUT I BROUGHT YOU A SOUVENIR FROM OUR CAMPING TRIP.
OH. THANKS.
HOW'VE U BEEN?
...GOOD.
OH, WELL, I WAS IN THE MIDDLE OF A FESTIVAL, SO, SEE YA.
SORRY THE EXPIRATION DATE IS TOMORROW.
TSUME-CHAN.
COME AGAIN.

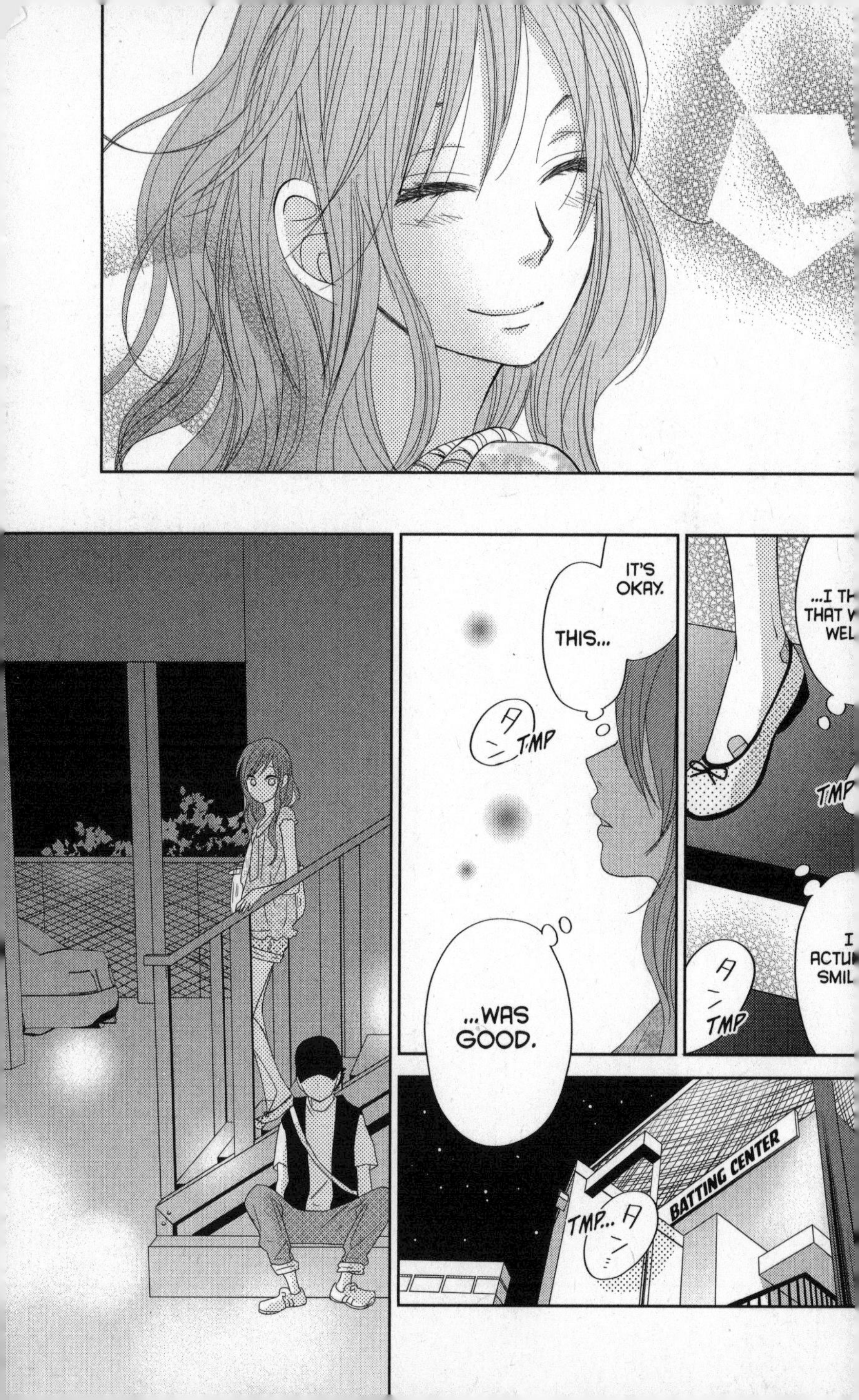
...I TH
THAT W
WEL
TMP
I
ACTU
SMIL
タン TMP
IT'S OKAY.
THIS...
タン TMP
...WAS GOOD.
BATTING CENTER
TMP... タン

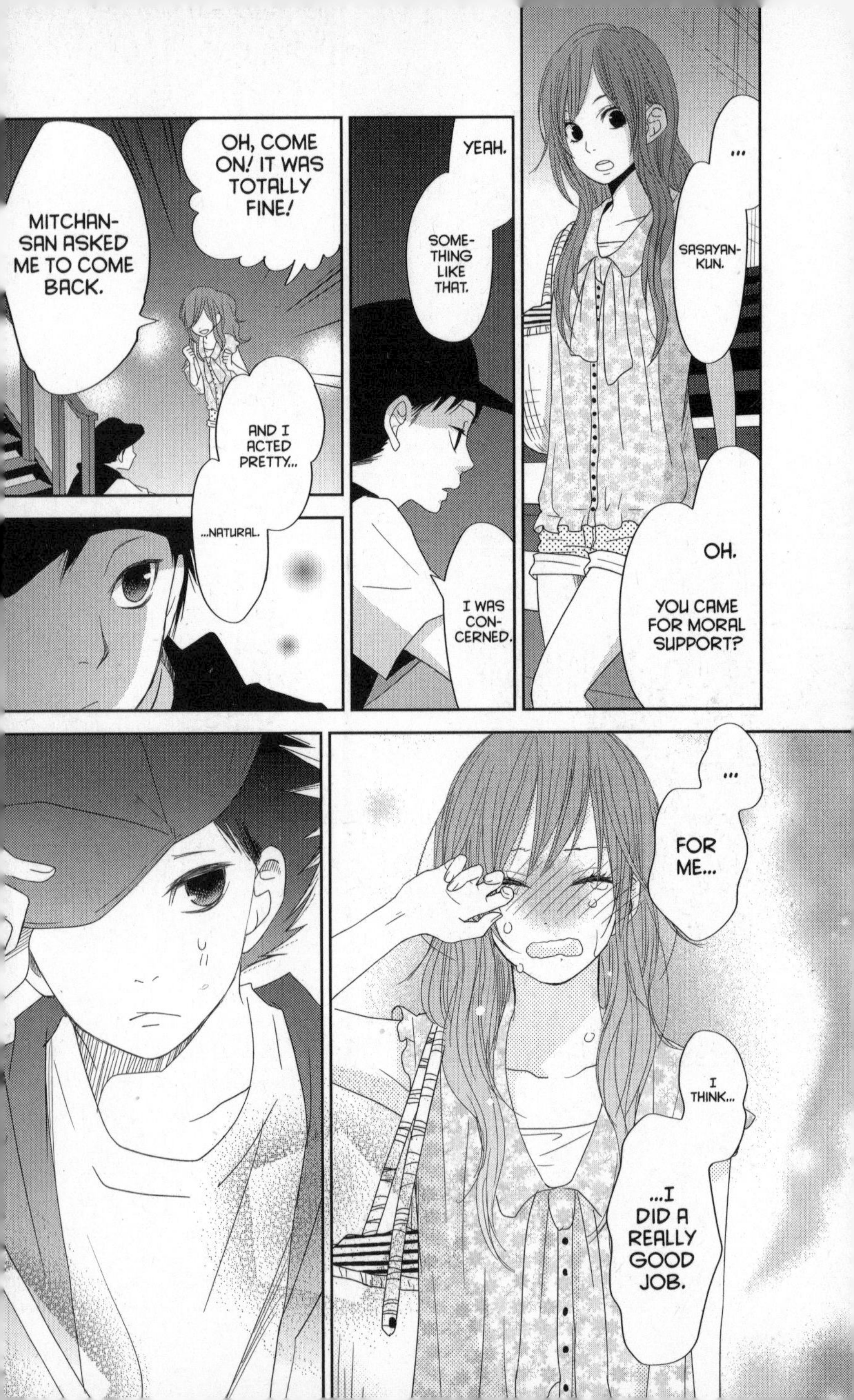
...
SASAYAN-KUN.
OH.
YOU CAME FOR MORAL SUPPORT?
YEAH.
SOME-THING LIKE THAT.
I WAS CON-CERNED.
OH, COME ON! IT WAS TOTALLY FINE!
MITCHAN-SAN ASKED ME TO COME BACK.
AND I ACTED PRETTY...
...NATURAL.
...
FOR ME...
I THINK...
...I DID A REALLY GOOD JOB.

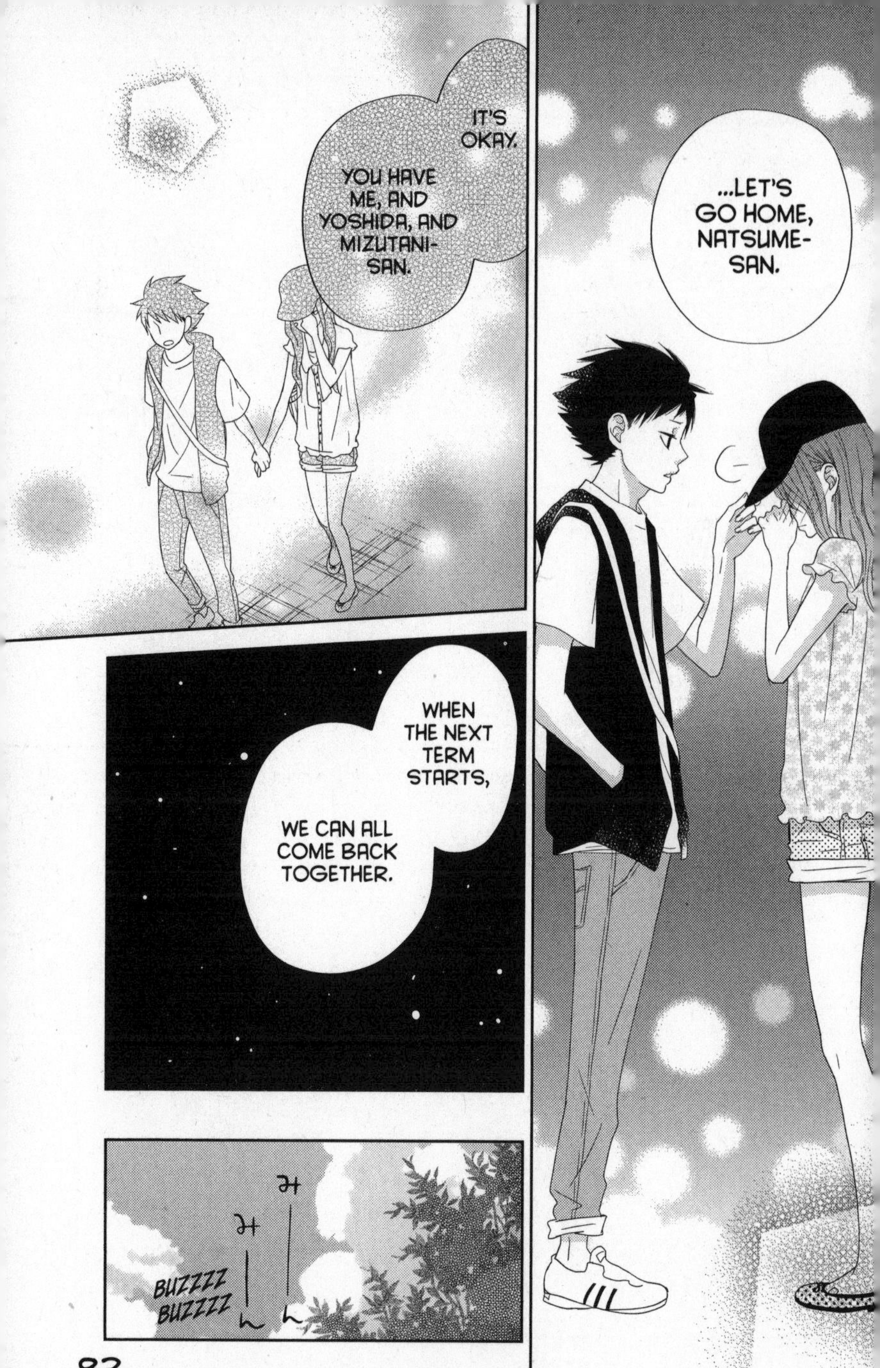
...LET'S GO HOME, NATSUME-SAN.
IT'S OKAY.
YOU HAVE ME, AND YOSHIDA, AND MIZUTANI-SAN.
WHEN THE NEXT TERM STARTS,
WE CAN ALL COME BACK TOGETHER.
みーん
みーん
BUZZZZ BUZZZZ

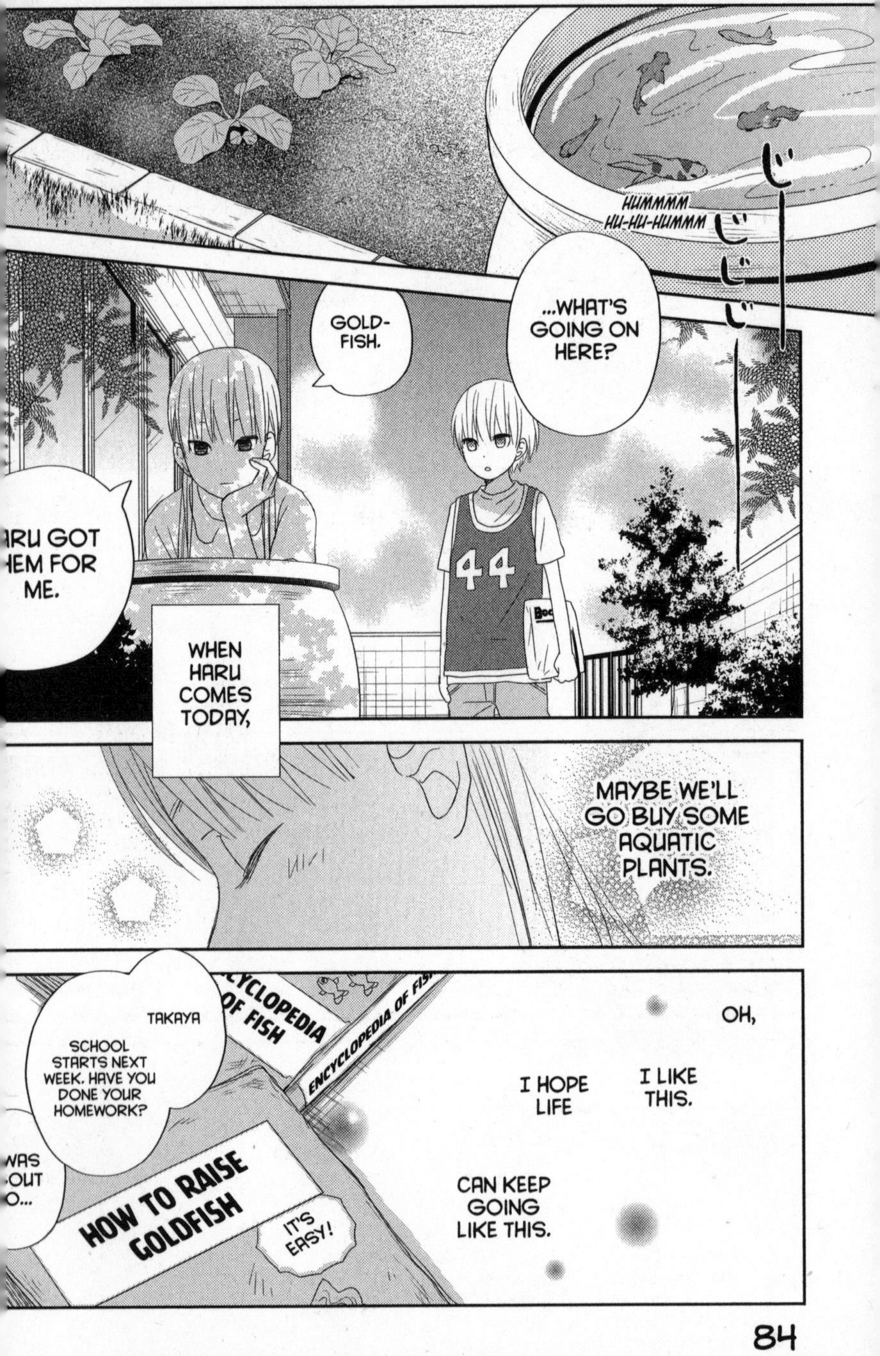
じーじじじ
HUMMMM HU-HU-HUMMM
...WHAT'S GOING ON HERE?
GOLD-FISH.
ARU GOT HEM FOR ME.
WHEN HARU COMES TODAY,
MAYBE WE'LL GO BUY SOME AQUATIC PLANTS.
OH,
I LIKE THIS.
I HOPE LIFE
CAN KEEP GOING LIKE THIS.
ENCYCLOPEDIA OF FISH
ENCYCLOPEDIA OF FISH
HOW TO RAISE GOLDFISH
IT'S EASY!
TAKAYA
SCHOOL STARTS NEXT WEEK. HAVE YOU DONE YOUR HOMEWORK?
WAS OUT O...

WORSHIP

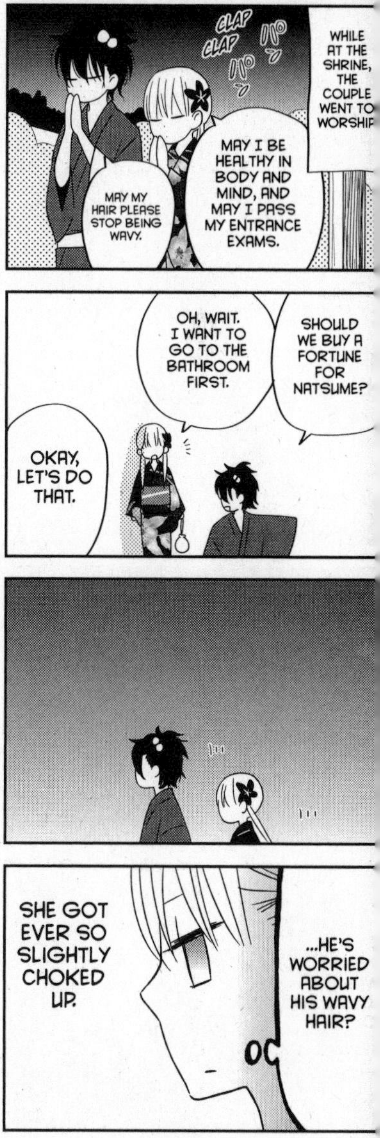
CLAP
CLAP
WHILE AT THE SHRINE, THE COUPLE WENT TO WORSHIP
MAY I BE HEALTHY IN BODY AND MIND, AND MAY I PASS MY ENTRANCE EXAMS.
MAY MY HAIR PLEASE STOP BEING WAVY.
SHOULD WE BUY A FORTUNE FOR NATSUME?
OH, WAIT. I WANT TO GO TO THE BATHROOM FIRST.
OKAY, LET'S DO THAT.
...HE'S WORRIED ABOUT HIS WAVY HAIR?
SHE GOT EVER SO SLIGHTLY CHOKED UP.

CANDIED APPLE

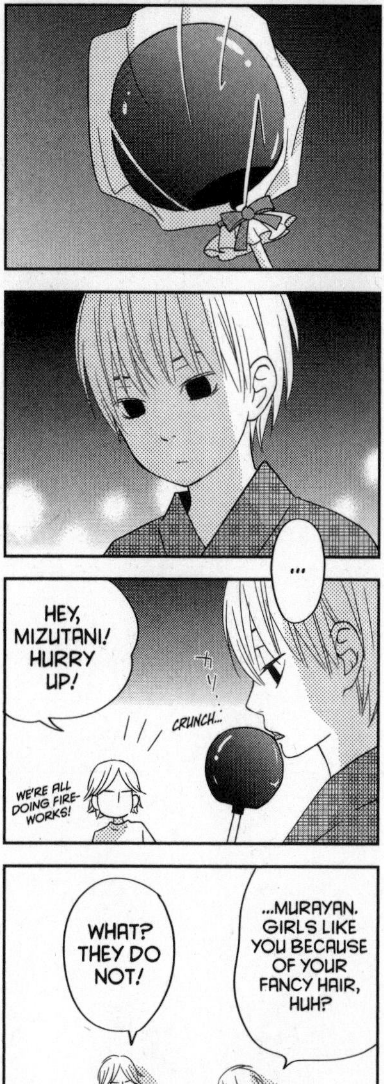
...
HEY, MIZUTANI! HURRY UP!
CRUNCH...
WE'RE ALL DOING FIRE-WORKS!
...MURAYAN. GIRLS LIKE YOU BECAUSE OF YOUR FANCY HAIR, HUH?
WHAT? THEY DO NOT!

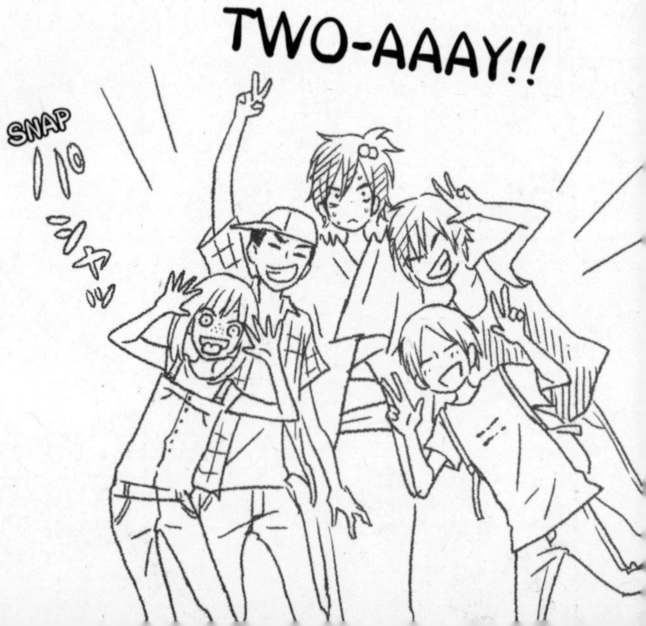
TWO-AAAY!!
SNAP
パシャッ

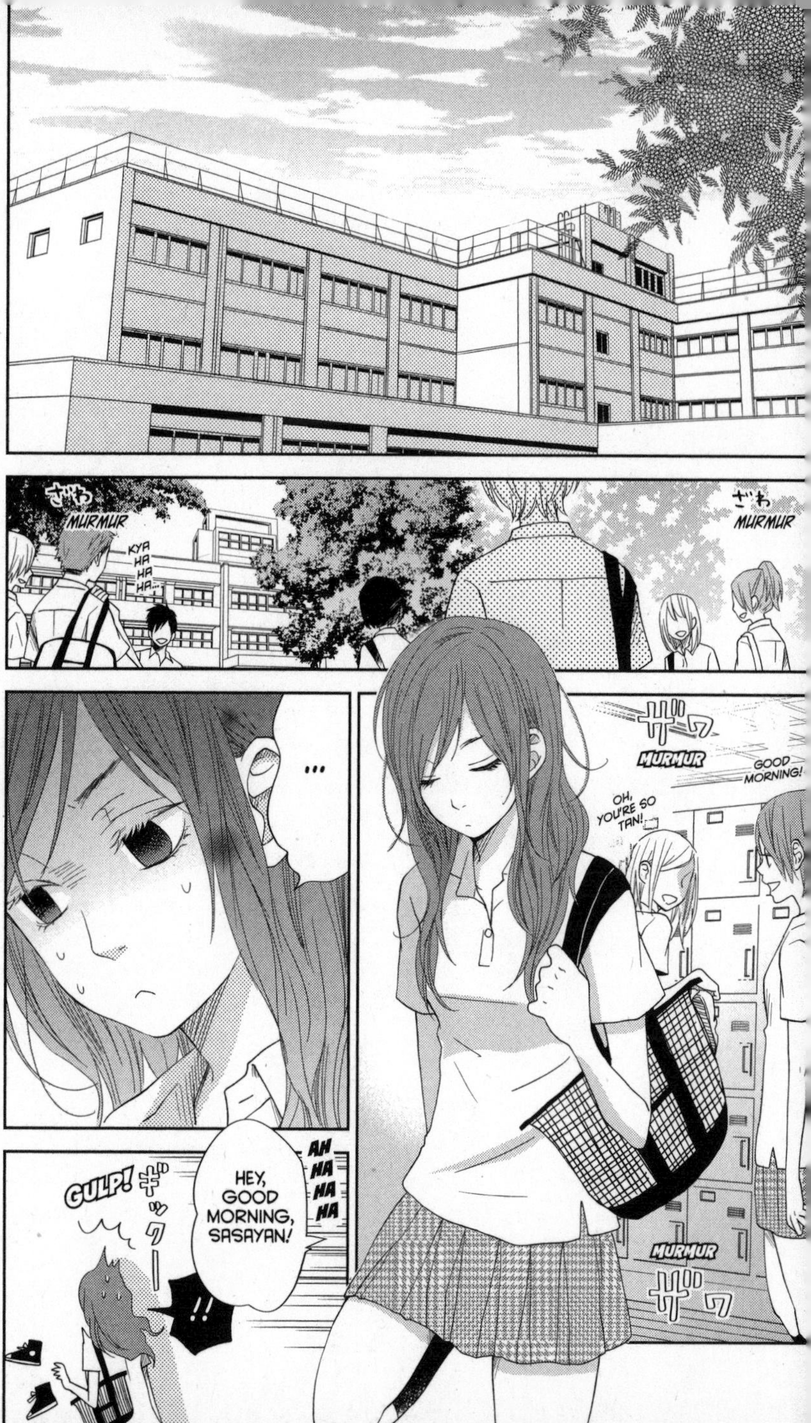
ざわ
MURMUR
ざわ
MURMUR
KYA HA HA HA...
ザワ
MURMUR
GOOD MORNING!
OH, YOU'RE SO TAN!
MURMUR
ザワ
...
HEY, GOOD MORNING, SASAYAN!
AH HA HA HA
GULP!
ギックー
!!

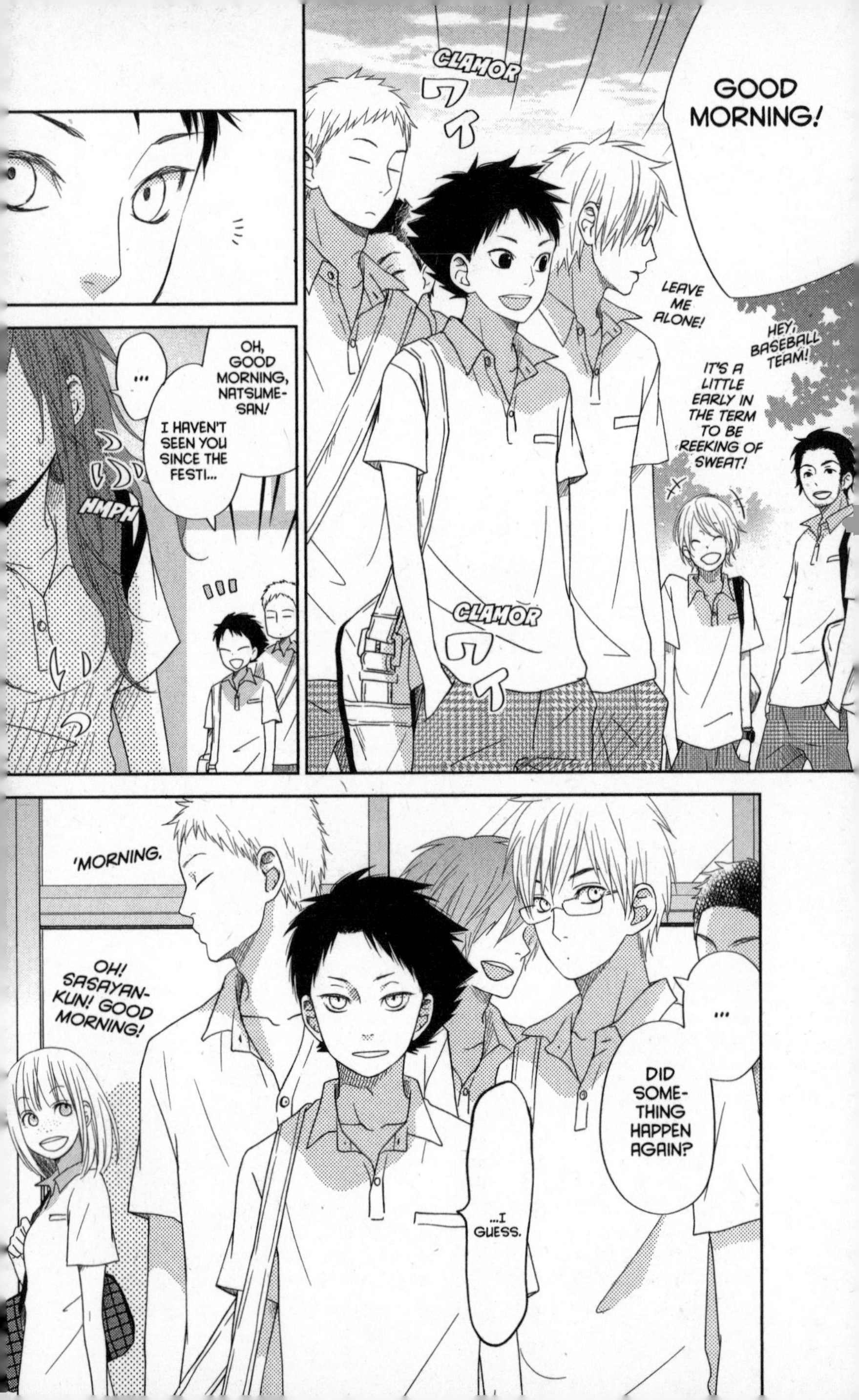
GOOD MORNING!
CLAMOR
ワイ
HEY, BASEBALL TEAM!
IT'S A LITTLE EARLY IN THE TERM TO BE REEKING OF SWEAT!
LEAVE ME ALONE!
CLAMOR
ワイ
OH, GOOD MORNING, NATSUME-SAN!
I HAVEN'T SEEN YOU SINCE THE FESTI...
...
HMPH
OH! SASAYAN-KUN! GOOD MORNING!
'MORNING.
...
DID SOMETHING HAPPEN AGAIN?
...I GUESS.

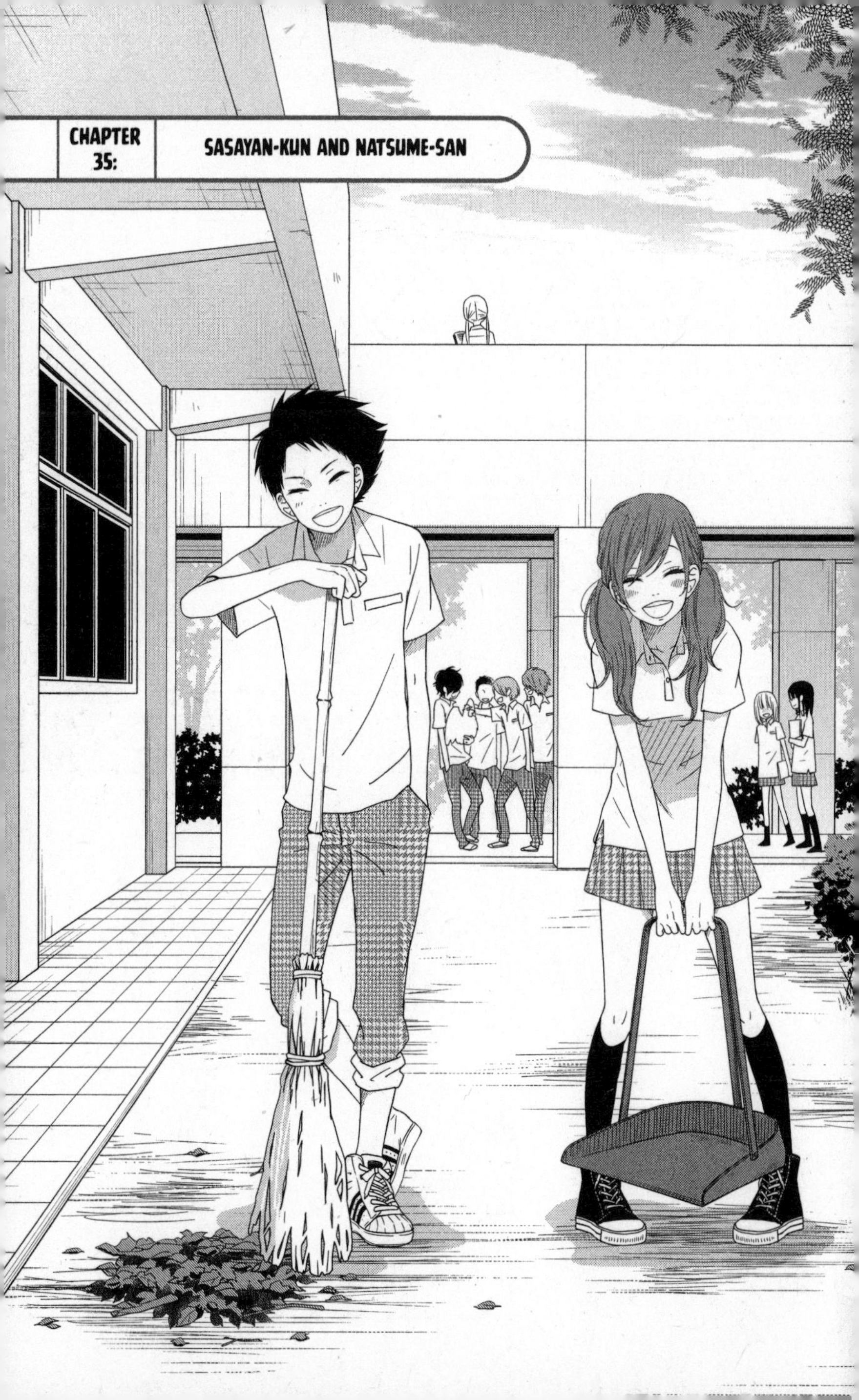
CHAPTER 35:
SASAYAN-KUN AND NATSUME-SAN

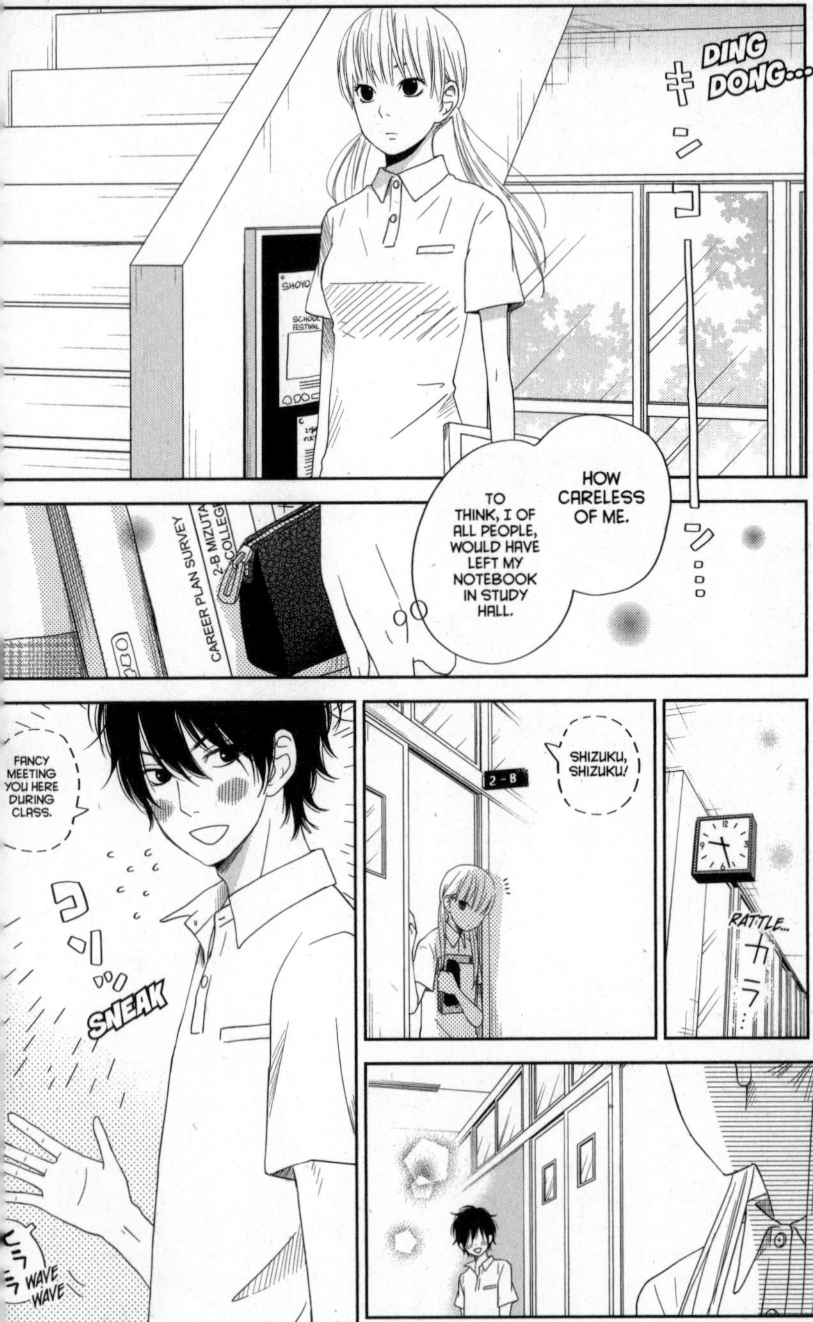
DING DONG...
SHOYO
SCHOOL FESTIVAL
HOW CARELESS OF ME.
TO THINK, I OF ALL PEOPLE, WOULD HAVE LEFT MY NOTEBOOK IN STUDY HALL.
CAREER PLAN SURVEY
RATTLE...
SHIZUKU, SHIZUKU!
2-B
FANCY MEETING YOU HERE DURING CLASS.
SNEAK
WAVE WAVE

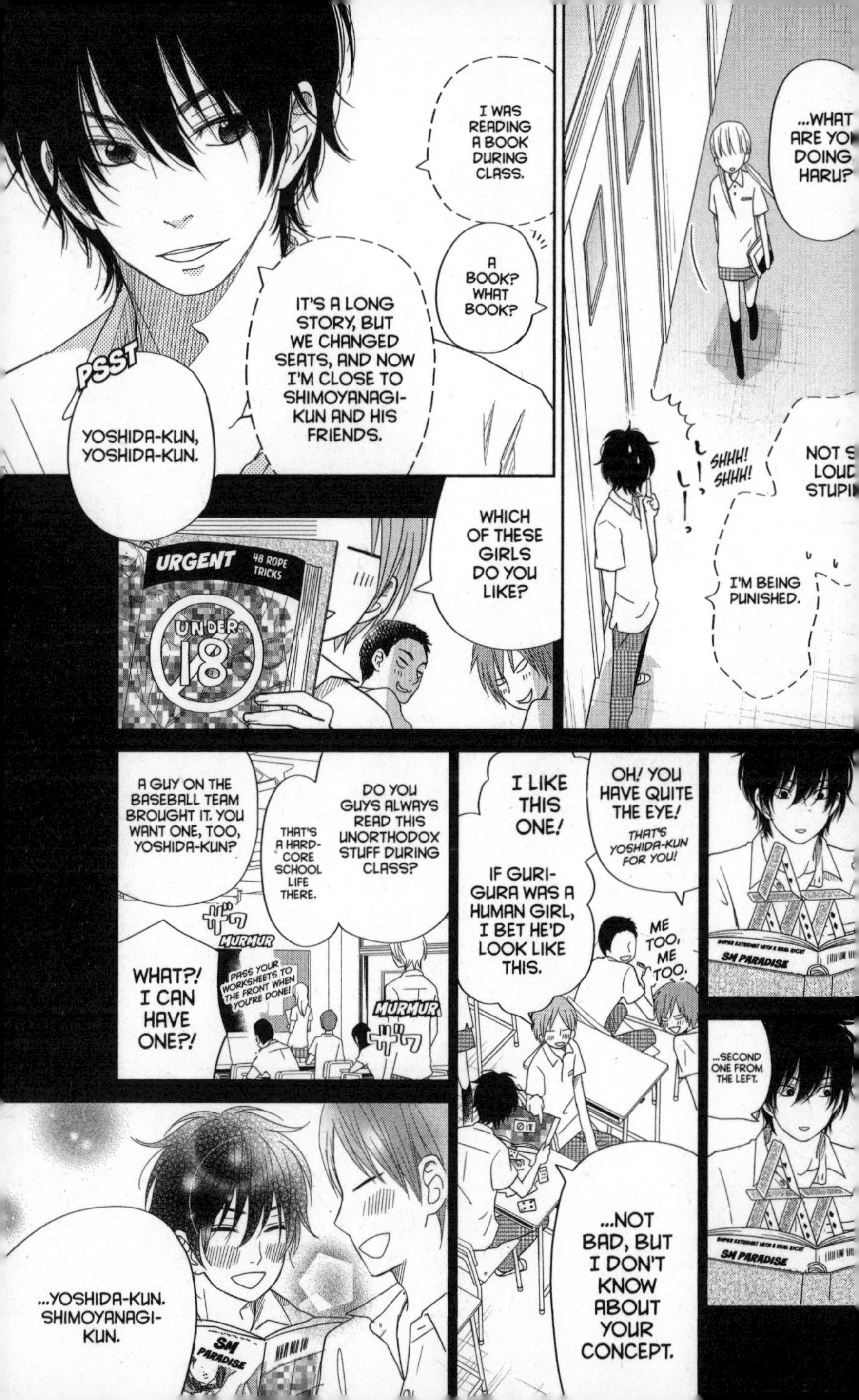
...WHAT ARE YO DOING HARU?
SHHH! SHHH!
NOT S LOUD STUPI
I'M BEING PUNISHED.
I WAS READING A BOOK DURING CLASS.
A BOOK? WHAT BOOK?
IT'S A LONG STORY, BUT WE CHANGED SEATS, AND NOW I'M CLOSE TO SHIMOYANAGI-KUN AND HIS FRIENDS.
PSST
YOSHIDA-KUN, YOSHIDA-KUN.
URGENT
48 ROPE TRICKS
UNDER 18
WHICH OF THESE GIRLS DO YOU LIKE?
SM PARADISE
...SECOND ONE FROM THE LEFT.
SM PARADISE
OH! YOU HAVE QUITE THE EYE!
THAT'S YOSHIDA-KUN FOR YOU!
I LIKE THIS ONE!
IF GURI-GURA WAS A HUMAN GIRL, I BET HE'D LOOK LIKE THIS.
ME TOO, ME TOO.
...NOT BAD, BUT I DON'T KNOW ABOUT YOUR CONCEPT.
DO YOU GUYS ALWAYS READ THIS UNORTHODOX STUFF DURING CLASS?
THAT'S A HARD-CORE SCHOOL LIFE THERE.
A GUY ON THE BASEBALL TEAM BROUGHT IT. YOU WANT ONE, TOO, YOSHIDA-KUN?
ザワ
MURMUR
WHAT?! I CAN HAVE ONE?!
PASS YOUR WORKSHEETS TO THE FRONT WHEN YOU'RE DONE!
MURMUR
ザワ
...YOSHIDA-KUN. SHIMOYANAGI-KUN.
SM PARADISE

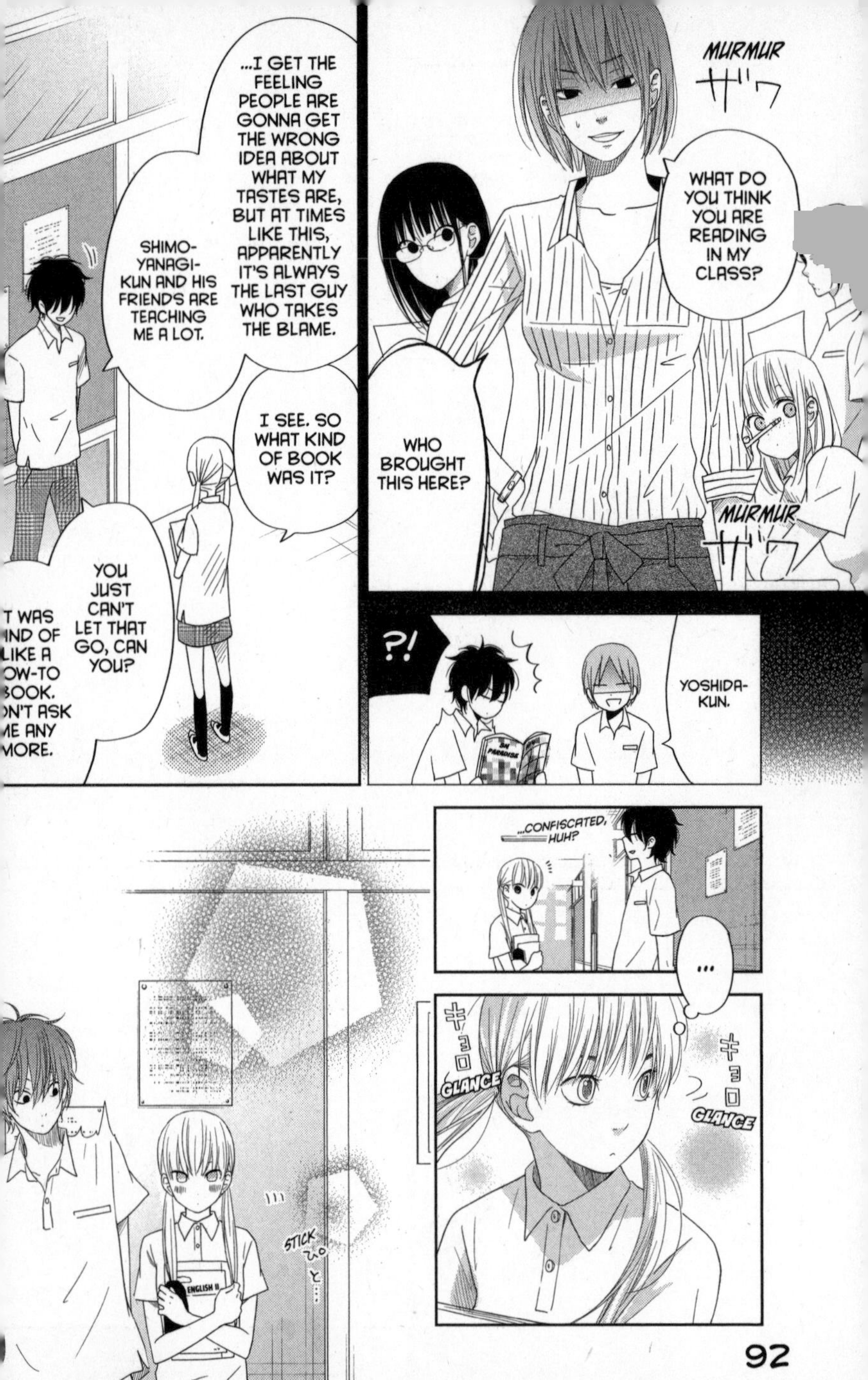
MURMUR
ザワ
WHAT DO YOU THINK YOU ARE READING IN MY CLASS?
WHO BROUGHT THIS HERE?
MURMUR
ザワ
?!
YOSHIDA-KUN.
...I GET THE FEELING PEOPLE ARE GONNA GET THE WRONG IDEA ABOUT WHAT MY TASTES ARE, BUT AT TIMES LIKE THIS, APPARENTLY IT'S ALWAYS THE LAST GUY WHO TAKES THE BLAME.
SHIMO-YANAGI-KUN AND HIS FRIENDS ARE TEACHING ME A LOT.
I SEE. SO WHAT KIND OF BOOK WAS IT?
YOU JUST CAN'T LET THAT GO, CAN YOU?
T WAS IND OF LIKE A OW-TO BOOK. ON'T ASK ME ANY MORE.
...CONFISCATED, HUH?
...
キョロ
GLANCE
キョロ
GLANCE
STICK
ぴと…
ENGLISH II

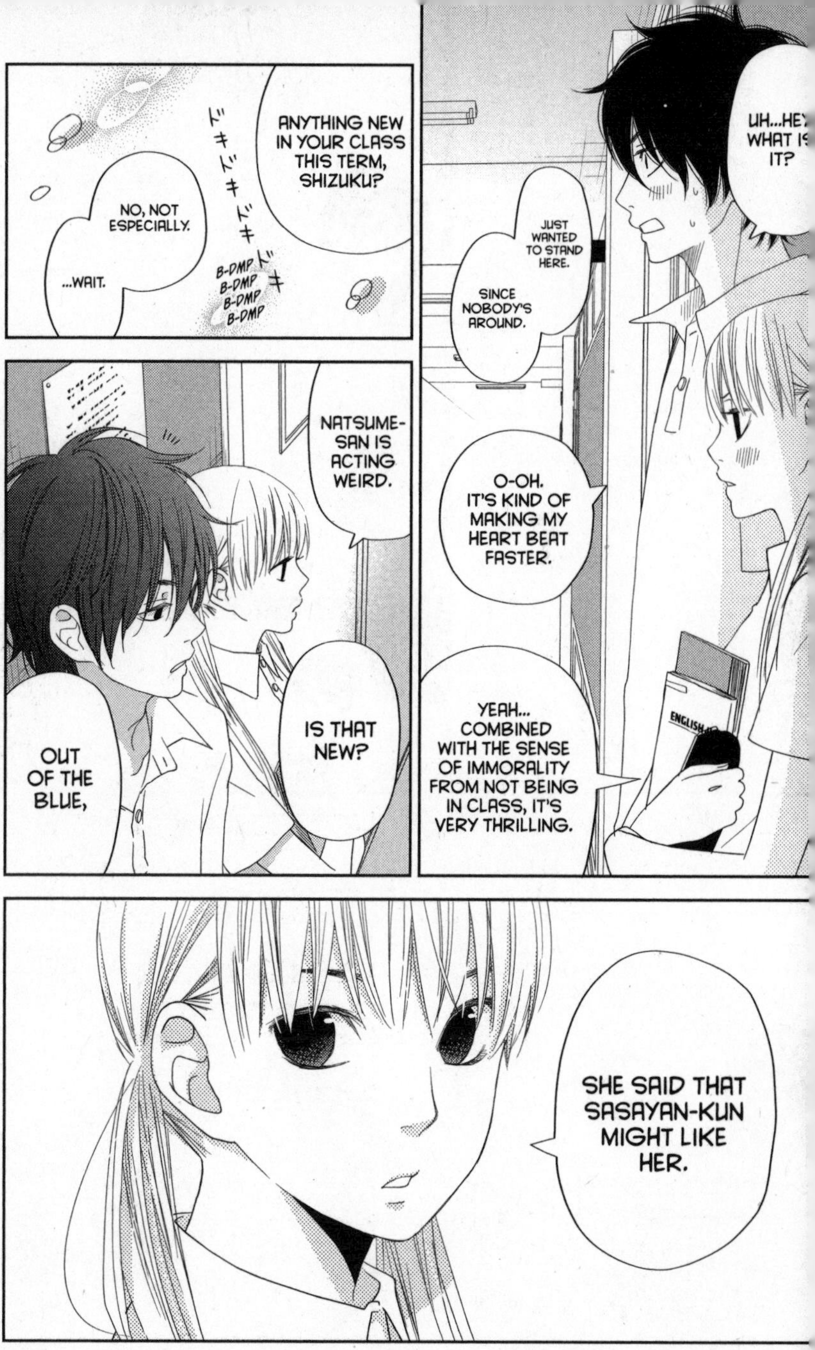
UH...HEY WHAT IS IT?
JUST WANTED TO STAND HERE.
SINCE NOBODY'S AROUND.
O-OH. IT'S KIND OF MAKING MY HEART BEAT FASTER.
YEAH... COMBINED WITH THE SENSE OF IMMORALITY FROM NOT BEING IN CLASS, IT'S VERY THRILLING.
ANYTHING NEW IN YOUR CLASS THIS TERM, SHIZUKU?
ドキドキドキドキ
B-DMP B-DMP B-DMP B-DMP
NO, NOT ESPECIALLY.
...WAIT.
NATSUME-SAN IS ACTING WEIRD.
IS THAT NEW?
OUT OF THE BLUE,
SHE SAID THAT SASAYAN-KUN MIGHT LIKE HER.

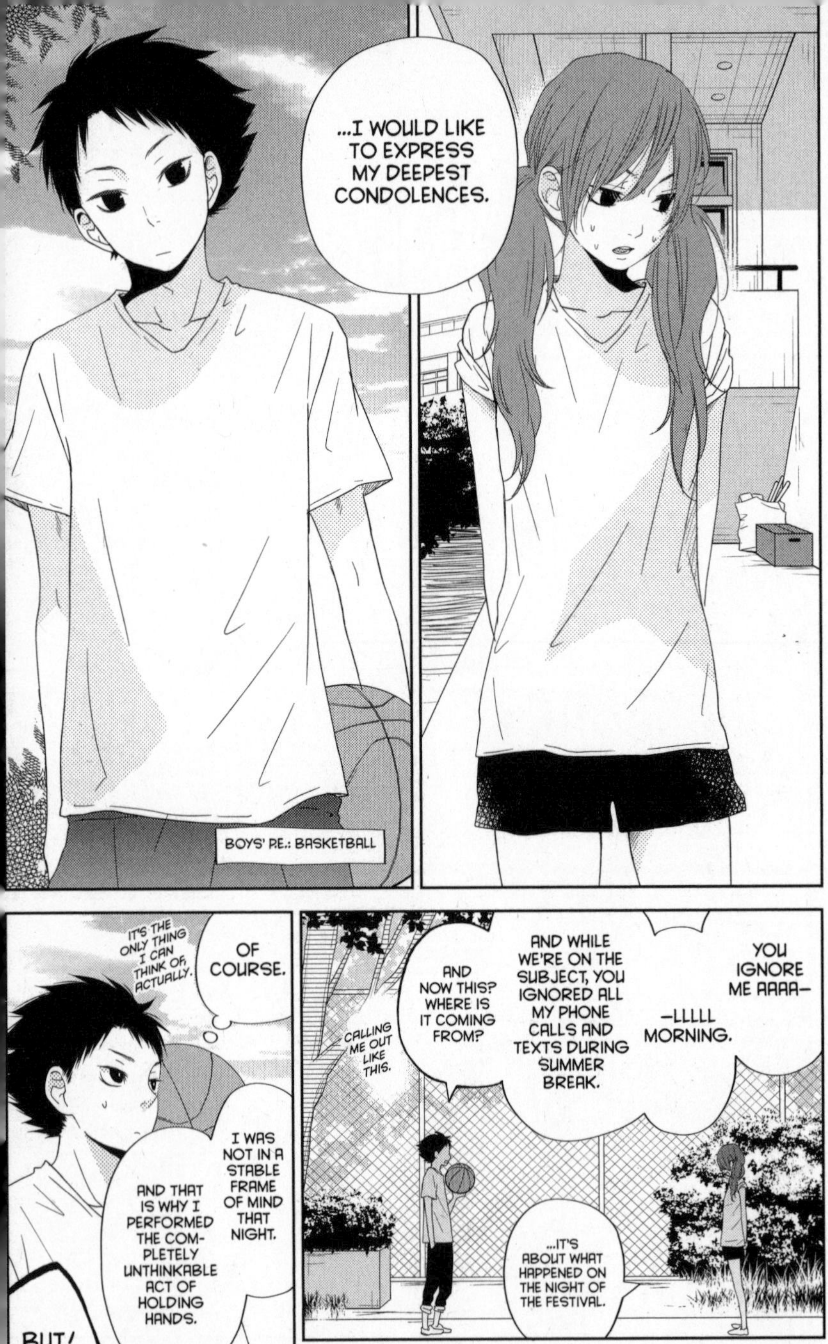
...I WOULD LIKE TO EXPRESS MY DEEPEST CONDOLENCES.
BOYS' P.E.: BASKETBALL
YOU IGNORE ME AAAA—
—LLLLL MORNING.
AND WHILE WE'RE ON THE SUBJECT, YOU IGNORED ALL MY PHONE CALLS AND TEXTS DURING SUMMER BREAK.
AND NOW THIS? WHERE IS IT COMING FROM?
CALLING ME OUT LIKE THIS.
...IT'S ABOUT WHAT HAPPENED ON THE NIGHT OF THE FESTIVAL.
OF COURSE.
IT'S THE ONLY THING I CAN THINK OF, ACTUALLY.
I WAS NOT IN A STABLE FRAME OF MIND THAT NIGHT.
AND THAT IS WHY I PERFORMED THE COM-PLETELY UNTHINKABLE ACT OF HOLDING HANDS.
BUT!

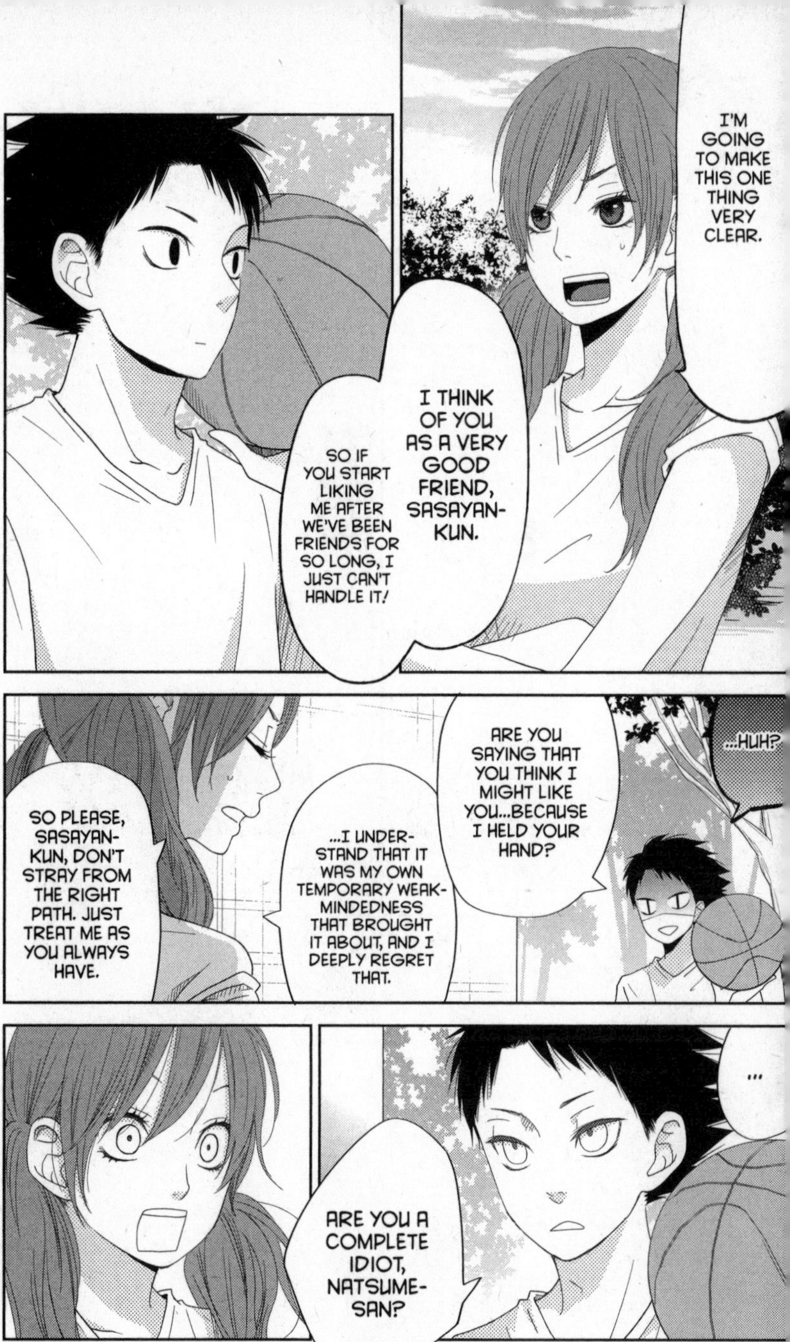
I'M GOING TO MAKE THIS ONE THING VERY CLEAR.
I THINK OF YOU AS A VERY GOOD FRIEND, SASAYAN-KUN.
SO IF YOU START LIKING ME AFTER WE'VE BEEN FRIENDS FOR SO LONG, I JUST CAN'T HANDLE IT!
...HUH?
ARE YOU SAYING THAT YOU THINK I MIGHT LIKE YOU...BECAUSE I HELD YOUR HAND?
...I UNDERSTAND THAT IT WAS MY OWN TEMPORARY WEAK-MINDEDNESS THAT BROUGHT IT ABOUT, AND I DEEPLY REGRET THAT.
SO PLEASE, SASAYAN-KUN, DON'T STRAY FROM THE RIGHT PATH. JUST TREAT ME AS YOU ALWAYS HAVE.
...
ARE YOU A COMPLETE IDIOT, NATSUME-SAN?

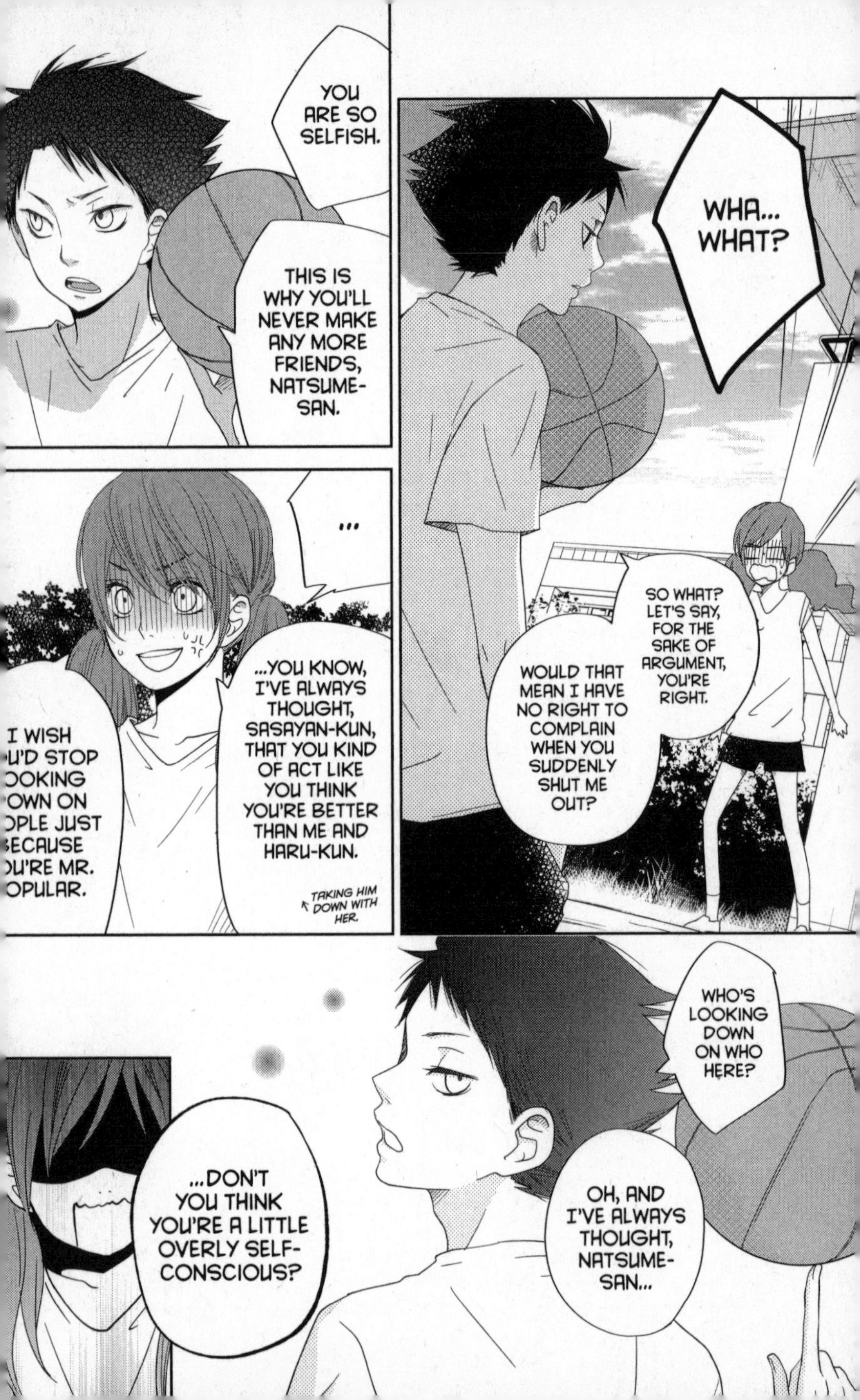
WHA... WHAT?
SO WHAT? LET'S SAY, FOR THE SAKE OF ARGUMENT, YOU'RE RIGHT.
WOULD THAT MEAN I HAVE NO RIGHT TO COMPLAIN WHEN YOU SUDDENLY SHUT ME OUT?
YOU ARE SO SELFISH.
THIS IS WHY YOU'LL NEVER MAKE ANY MORE FRIENDS, NATSUME-SAN.
...
...YOU KNOW, I'VE ALWAYS THOUGHT, SASAYAN-KUN, THAT YOU KIND OF ACT LIKE YOU THINK YOU'RE BETTER THAN ME AND HARU-KUN.
TAKING HIM DOWN WITH HER.
I WISH U'D STOP OOKING OWN ON OPLE JUST ECAUSE U'RE MR. OPULAR.
WHO'S LOOKING DOWN ON WHO HERE?
OH, AND I'VE ALWAYS THOUGHT, NATSUME-SAN...
...DON'T YOU THINK YOU'RE A LITTLE OVERLY SELF-CONSCIOUS?

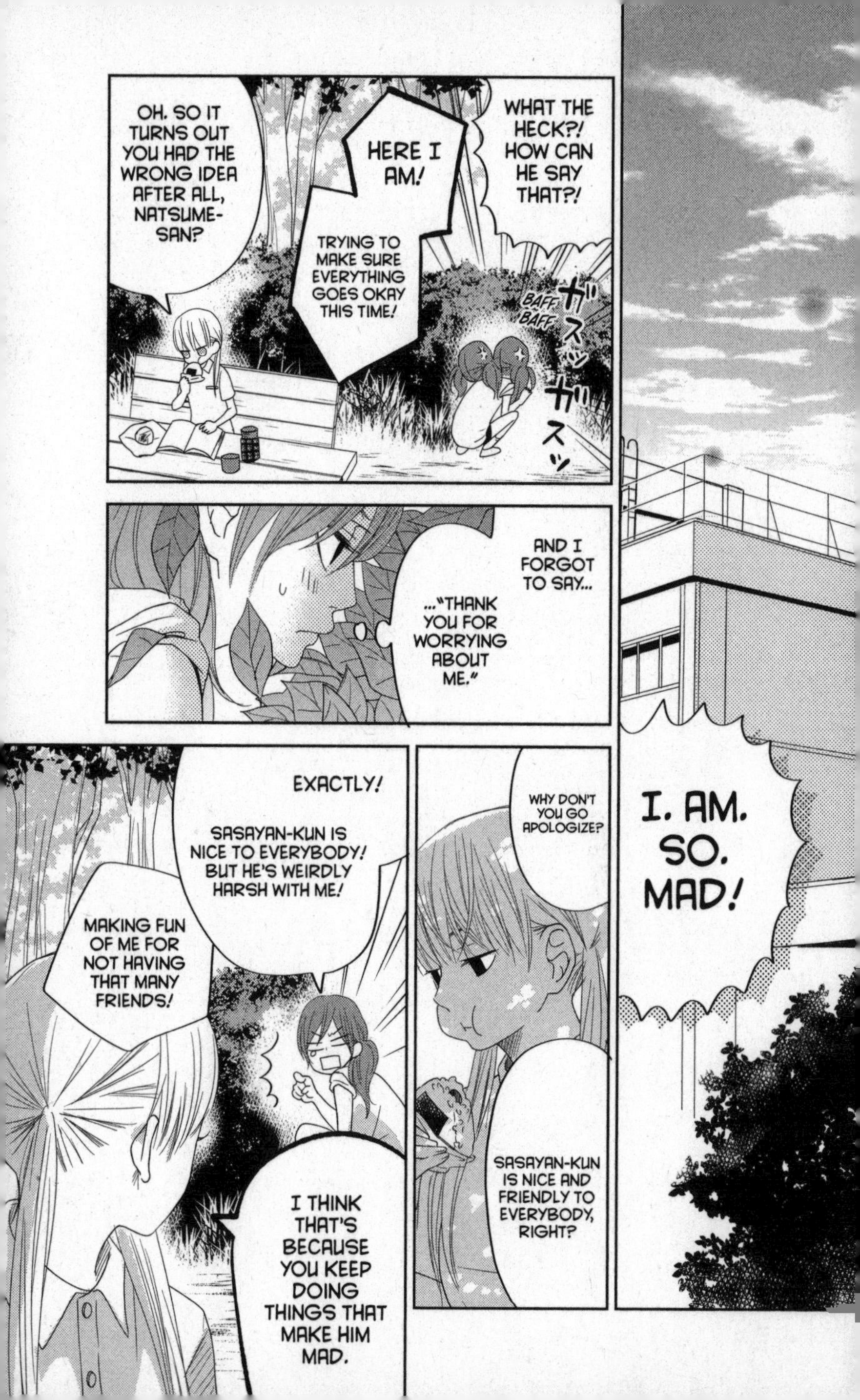
I. AM. SO. MAD!
WHAT THE HECK?! HOW CAN HE SAY THAT?!
HERE I AM!
TRYING TO MAKE SURE EVERYTHING GOES OKAY THIS TIME!
ガスッ BAFF
ガスッ BAFF
OH. SO IT TURNS OUT YOU HAD THE WRONG IDEA AFTER ALL, NATSUME-SAN?
AND I FORGOT TO SAY...
..."THANK YOU FOR WORRYING ABOUT ME."
WHY DON'T YOU GO APOLOGIZE?
SASAYAN-KUN IS NICE AND FRIENDLY TO EVERYBODY, RIGHT?
EXACTLY!
SASAYAN-KUN IS NICE TO EVERYBODY! BUT HE'S WEIRDLY HARSH WITH ME!
MAKING FUN OF ME FOR NOT HAVING THAT MANY FRIENDS!
I THINK THAT'S BECAUSE YOU KEEP DOING THINGS THAT MAKE HIM MAD.

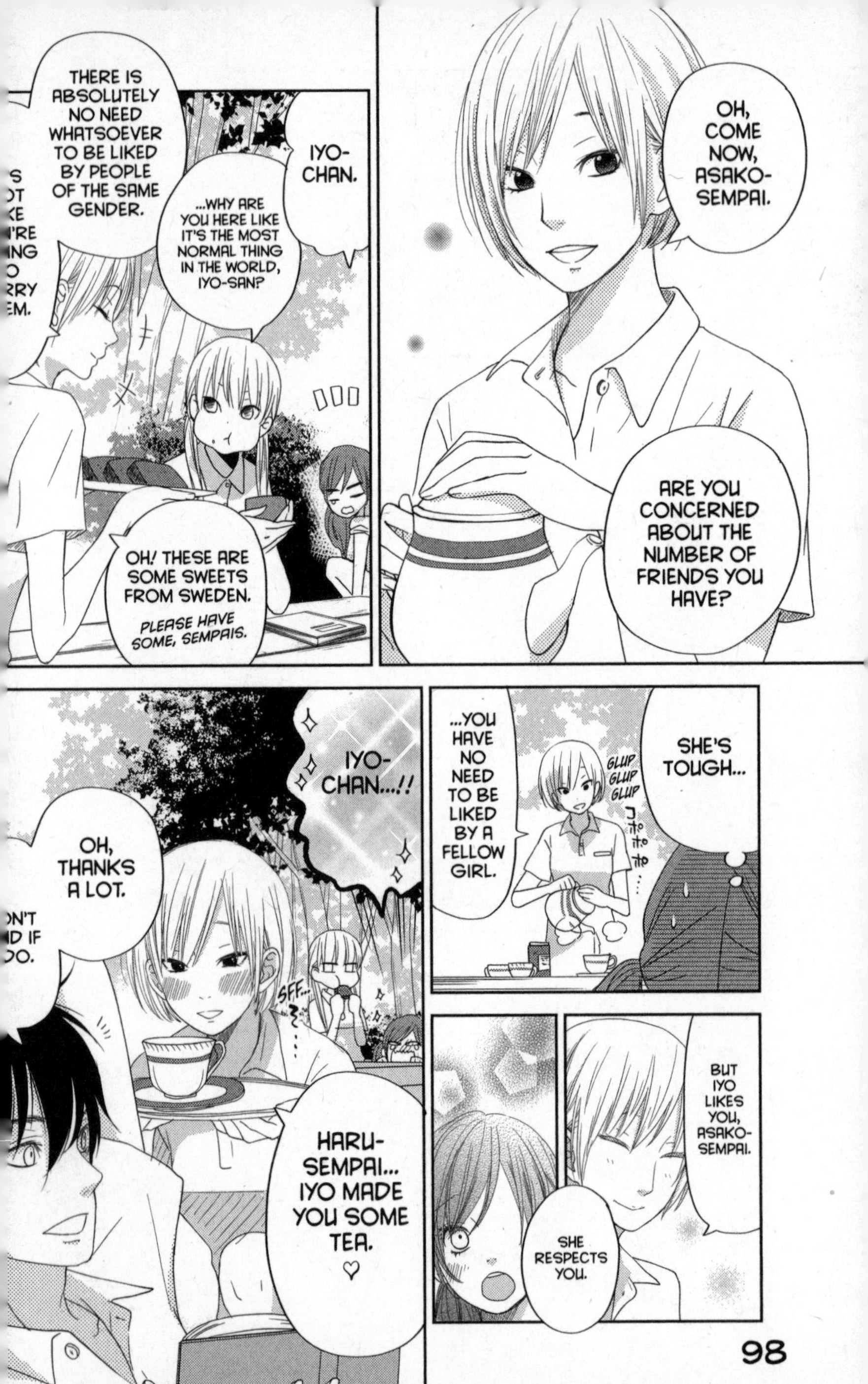
OH, COME NOW, ASAKO-SEMPAI.
ARE YOU CONCERNED ABOUT THE NUMBER OF FRIENDS YOU HAVE?
THERE IS ABSOLUTELY NO NEED WHATSOEVER TO BE LIKED BY PEOPLE OF THE SAME GENDER.
IYO-CHAN.
...WHY ARE YOU HERE LIKE IT'S THE MOST NORMAL THING IN THE WORLD, IYO-SAN?
OH! THESE ARE SOME SWEETS FROM SWEDEN.
PLEASE HAVE SOME, SEMPAIS.
SHE'S TOUGH...
...YOU HAVE NO NEED TO BE LIKED BY A FELLOW GIRL.
GLUP GLUP GLUP
BUT IYO LIKES YOU, ASAKO-SEMPAI.
SHE RESPECTS YOU.
IYO-CHAN...!!
OH, THANKS A LOT.
SFF...
HARU-SEMPAI... IYO MADE YOU SOME TEA. ♡

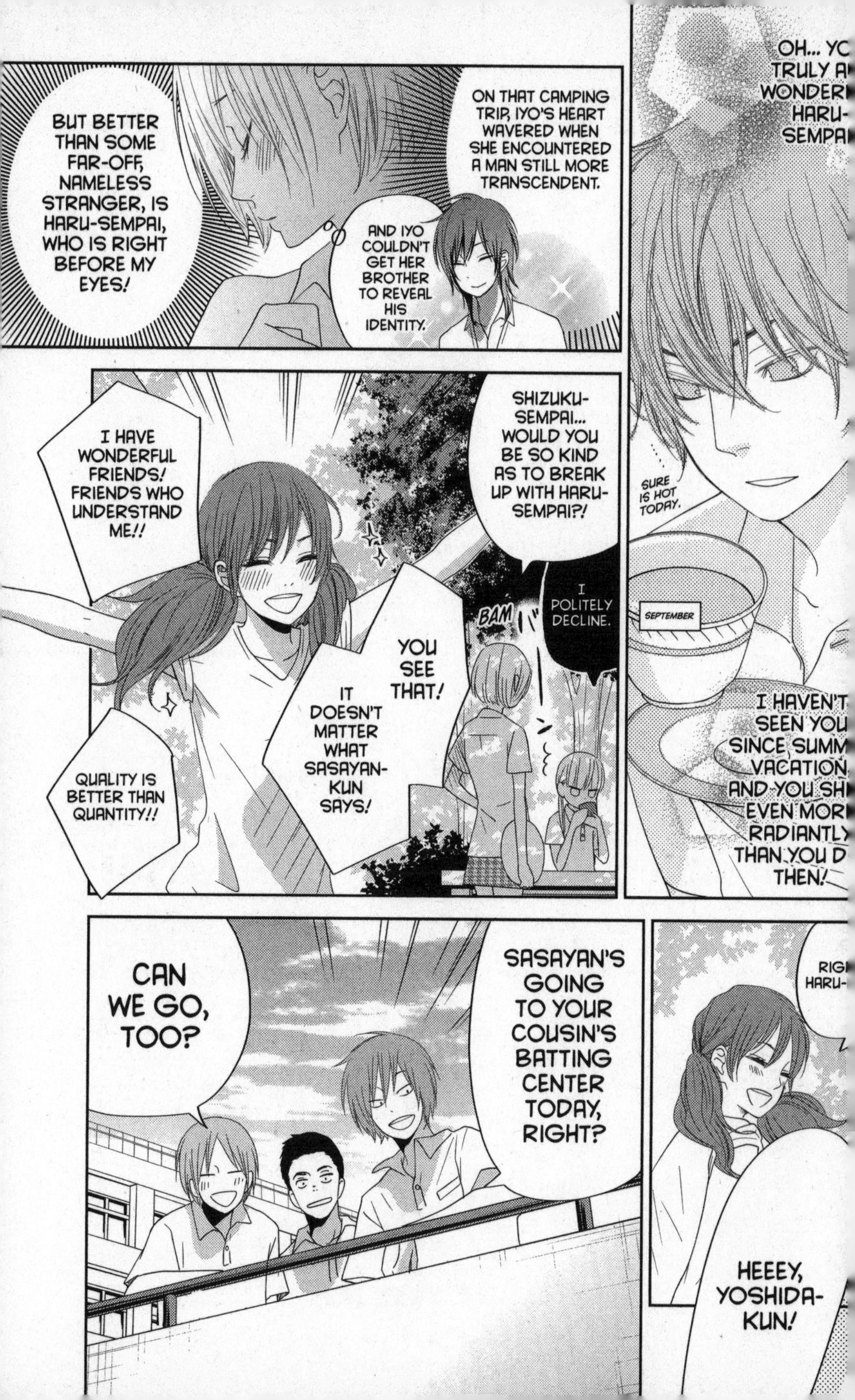
OH... YO TRULY A WONDER HARU- SEMPA
SURE IS HOT TODAY.
SEPTEMBER
I HAVEN'T SEEN YOU SINCE SUMM VACATION, AND YOU SH EVEN MOR RADIANTLY THAN YOU D THEN!
RIG HARU-
HEEEY, YOSHIDA-KUN!
ON THAT CAMPING TRIP, IYO'S HEART WAVERED WHEN SHE ENCOUNTERED A MAN STILL MORE TRANSCENDENT.
AND IYO COULDN'T GET HER BROTHER TO REVEAL HIS IDENTITY.
BUT BETTER THAN SOME FAR-OFF, NAMELESS STRANGER, IS HARU-SEMPAI, WHO IS RIGHT BEFORE MY EYES!
SHIZUKU-SEMPAI... WOULD YOU BE SO KIND AS TO BREAK UP WITH HARU-SEMPAI?!
I POLITELY DECLINE.
BAM
YOU SEE THAT!
I HAVE WONDERFUL FRIENDS! FRIENDS WHO UNDERSTAND ME!!
IT DOESN'T MATTER WHAT SASAYAN-KUN SAYS!
QUALITY IS BETTER THAN QUANTITY!!
SASAYAN'S GOING TO YOUR COUSIN'S BATTING CENTER TODAY, RIGHT?
CAN WE GO, TOO?

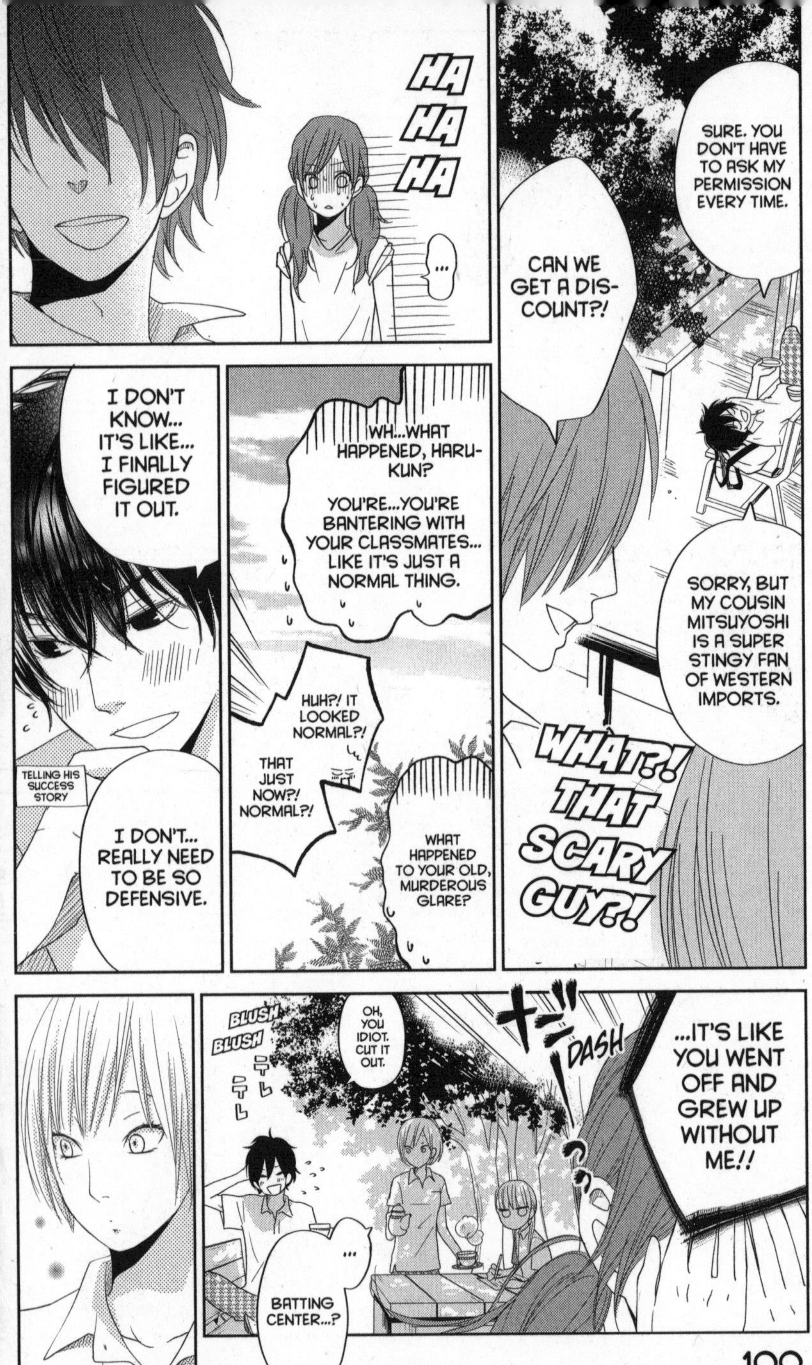
SURE. YOU DON'T HAVE TO ASK MY PERMISSION EVERY TIME.
CAN WE GET A DIS-COUNT?!
SORRY, BUT MY COUSIN MITSUYOSHI IS A SUPER STINGY FAN OF WESTERN IMPORTS.
WHAT?! THAT SCARY GUY?!
HA HA HA
...
WH...WHAT HAPPENED, HARU-KUN?
YOU'RE...YOU'RE BANTERING WITH YOUR CLASSMATES... LIKE IT'S JUST A NORMAL THING.
HUH?! IT LOOKED NORMAL?!
THAT JUST NOW?! NORMAL?!
WHAT HAPPENED TO YOUR OLD, MURDEROUS GLARE?
I DON'T KNOW... IT'S LIKE... I FINALLY FIGURED IT OUT.
TELLING HIS SUCCESS STORY
I DON'T... REALLY NEED TO BE SO DEFENSIVE.
...IT'S LIKE YOU WENT OFF AND GREW UP WITHOUT ME!!
DASH
OH, YOU IDIOT. CUT IT OUT.
BLUSH BLUSH
...
BATTING CENTER...?

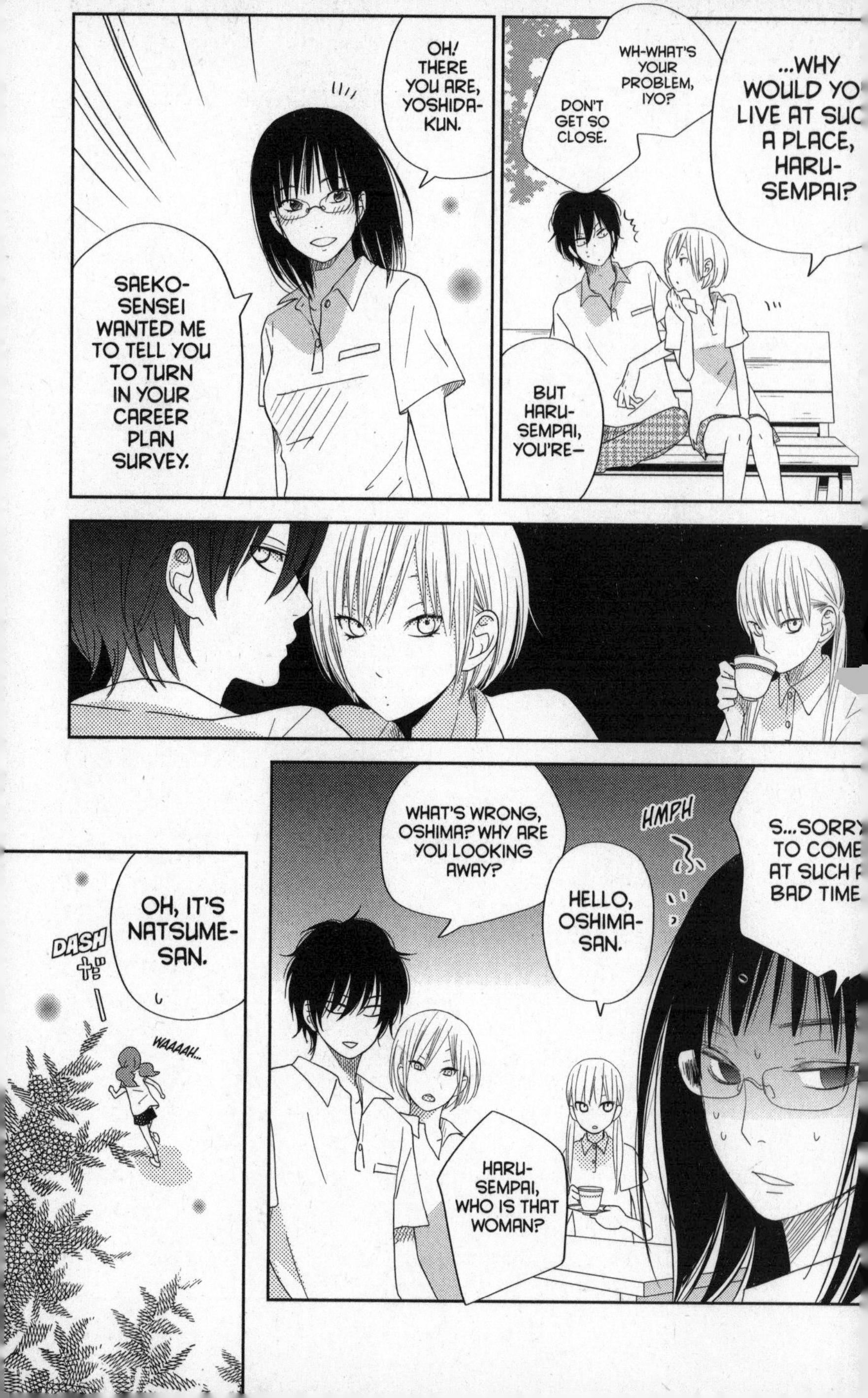
...WHY WOULD YO LIVE AT SUC A PLACE, HARU-SEMPAI?
WH-WHAT'S YOUR PROBLEM, IYO?
DON'T GET SO CLOSE.
BUT HARU-SEMPAI, YOU'RE—
OH! THERE YOU ARE, YOSHIDA-KUN.
SAEKO-SENSEI WANTED ME TO TELL YOU TO TURN IN YOUR CAREER PLAN SURVEY.
S...SORR TO COME AT SUCH BAD TIME
HMPH
WHAT'S WRONG, OSHIMA? WHY ARE YOU LOOKING AWAY?
HELLO, OSHIMA-SAN.
HARU-SEMPAI, WHO IS THAT WOMAN?
OH, IT'S NATSUME-SAN.
DASH
WAAAAH...

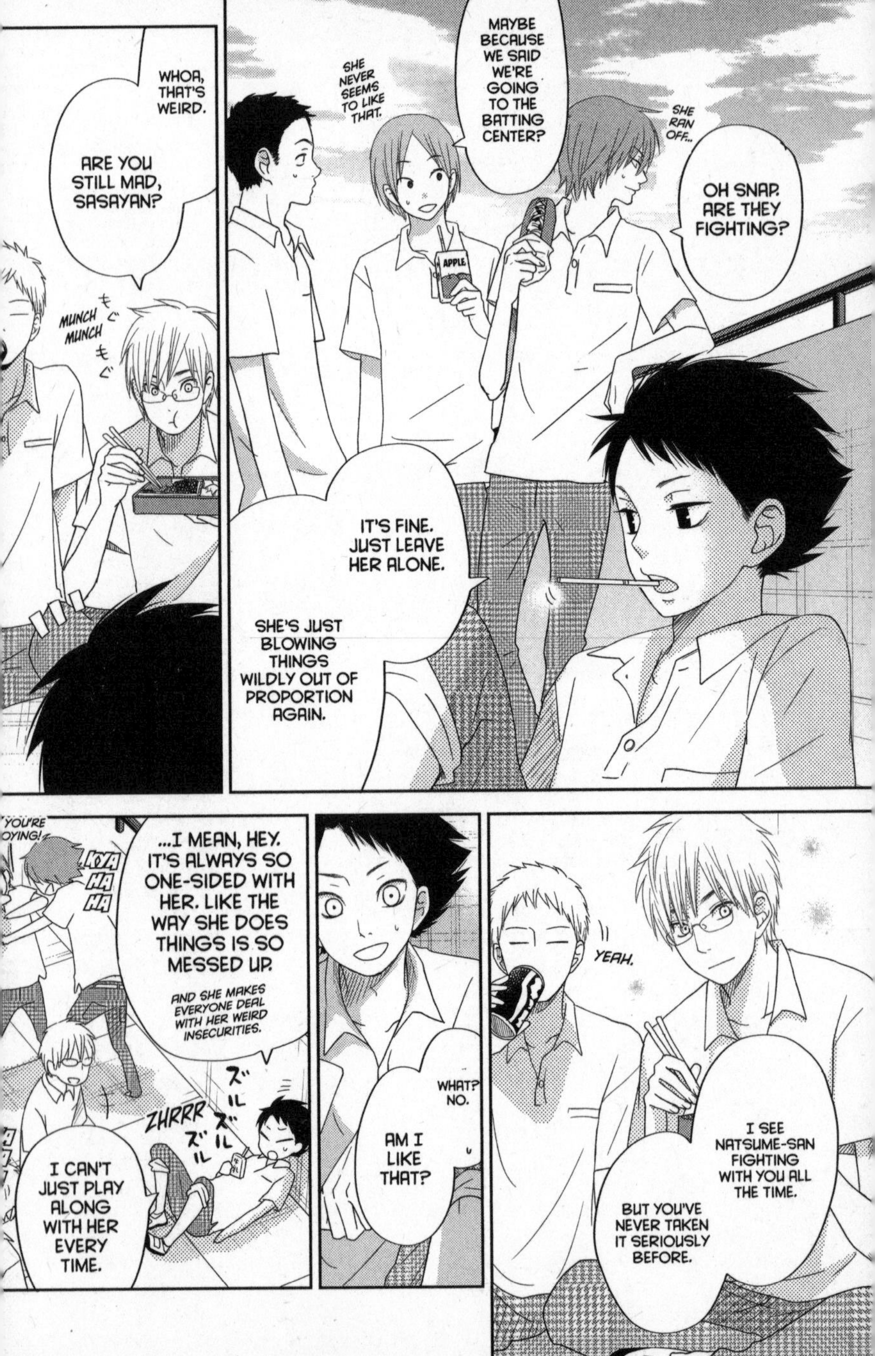
SHE RAN OFF...
OH SNAP. ARE THEY FIGHTING?
MAYBE BECAUSE WE SAID WE'RE GOING TO THE BATTING CENTER?
SHE NEVER SEEMS TO LIKE THAT.
APPLE
IT'S FINE. JUST LEAVE HER ALONE.
SHE'S JUST BLOWING THINGS WILDLY OUT OF PROPORTION AGAIN.
WHOA, THAT'S WEIRD.
ARE YOU STILL MAD, SASAYAN?
MUNCH MUNCH
もぐもぐ
YEAH.
I SEE NATSUME-SAN FIGHTING WITH YOU ALL THE TIME.
BUT YOU'VE NEVER TAKEN IT SERIOUSLY BEFORE.
WHAT? NO.
AM I LIKE THAT?
...I MEAN, HEY. IT'S ALWAYS SO ONE-SIDED WITH HER. LIKE THE WAY SHE DOES THINGS IS SO MESSED UP.
AND SHE MAKES EVERYONE DEAL WITH HER WEIRD INSECURITIES.
YOU'RE
OYING!
KYA HA HA
ZHRRR
ズルズルズル
I CAN'T JUST PLAY ALONG WITH HER EVERY TIME.

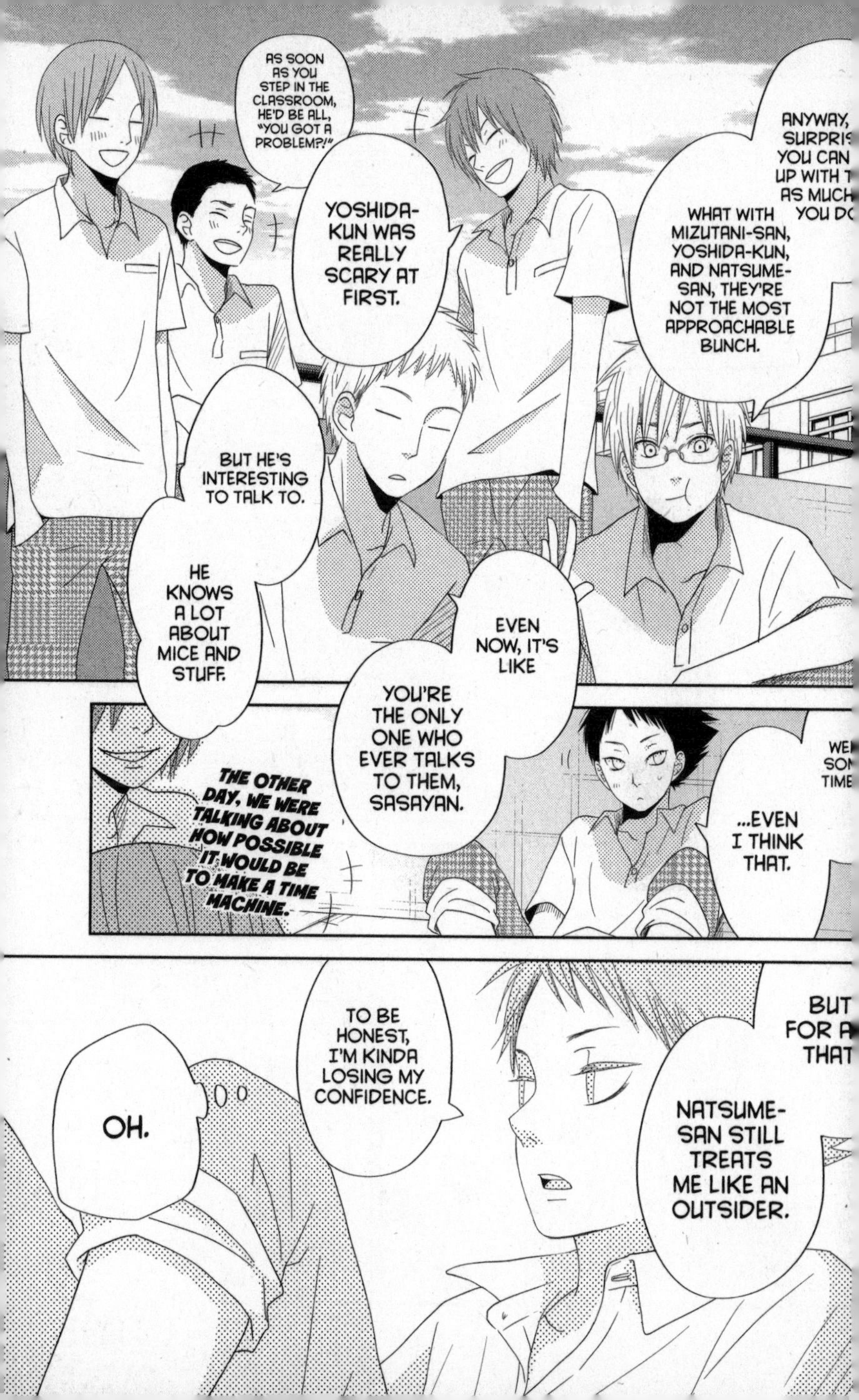
ANYWAY, SURPRIS YOU CAN UP WITH T AS MUCH YOU D
WHAT WITH MIZUTANI-SAN, YOSHIDA-KUN, AND NATSUME-SAN, THEY'RE NOT THE MOST APPROACHABLE BUNCH.
YOSHIDA-KUN WAS REALLY SCARY AT FIRST.
AS SOON AS YOU STEP IN THE CLASSROOM, HE'D BE ALL, "YOU GOT A PROBLEM?!"
BUT HE'S INTERESTING TO TALK TO.
HE KNOWS A LOT ABOUT MICE AND STUFF.
EVEN NOW, IT'S LIKE
YOU'RE THE ONLY ONE WHO EVER TALKS TO THEM, SASAYAN.
WE SON TIME
...EVEN I THINK THAT.
THE OTHER DAY, WE WERE TALKING ABOUT HOW POSSIBLE IT WOULD BE TO MAKE A TIME MACHINE.
BUT FOR A THAT
NATSUME-SAN STILL TREATS ME LIKE AN OUTSIDER.
TO BE HONEST, I'M KINDA LOSING MY CONFIDENCE.
OH.

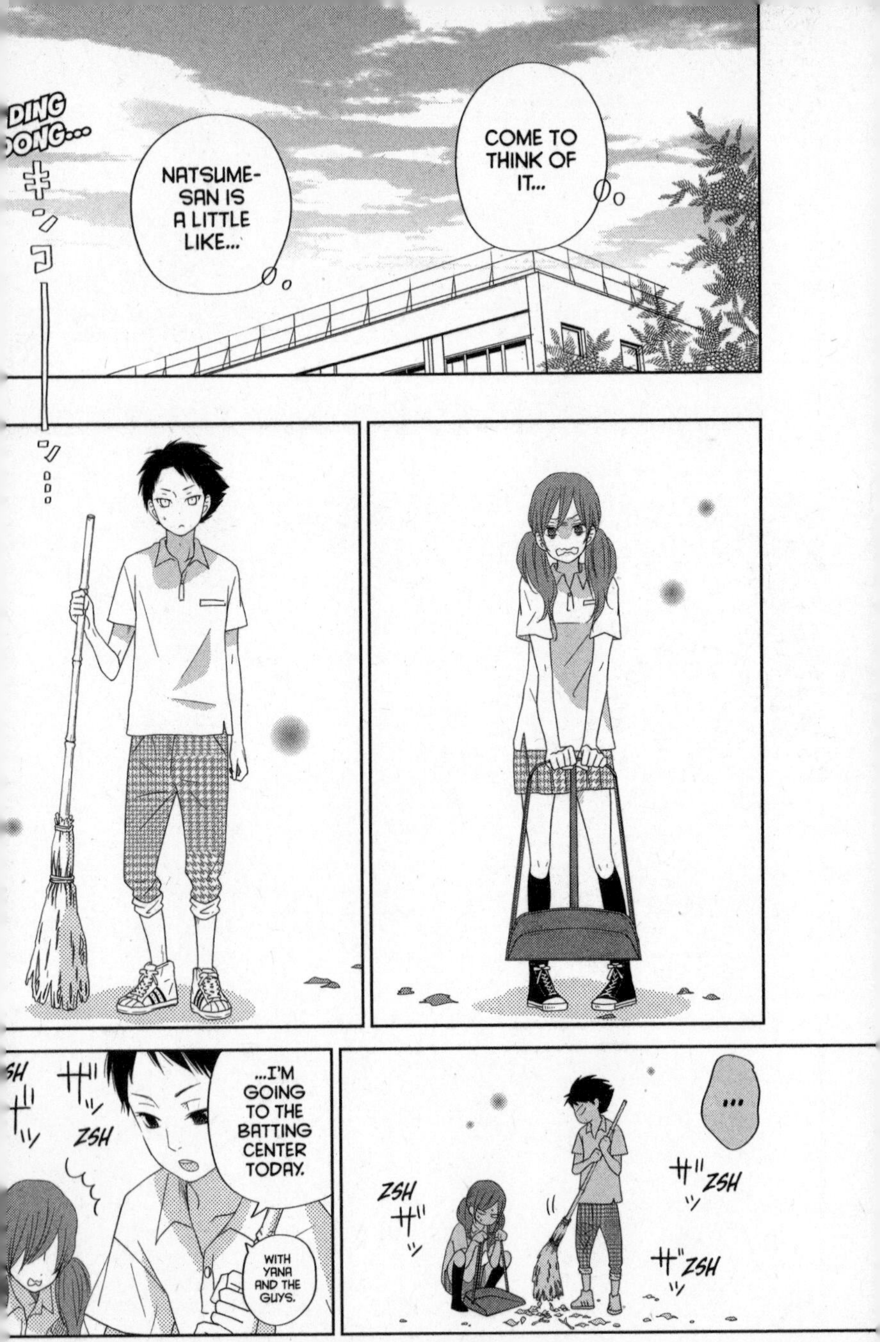
COME TO THINK OF IT...
NATSUME-SAN IS A LITTLE LIKE...
DING DONG...
キンコーン…
...
ザッ ZSH
ザッ ZSH
ZSH ザッ
...I'M GOING TO THE BATTING CENTER TODAY.
WITH YANA AND THE GUYS.
ザッ ZSH
ZSH ザッ

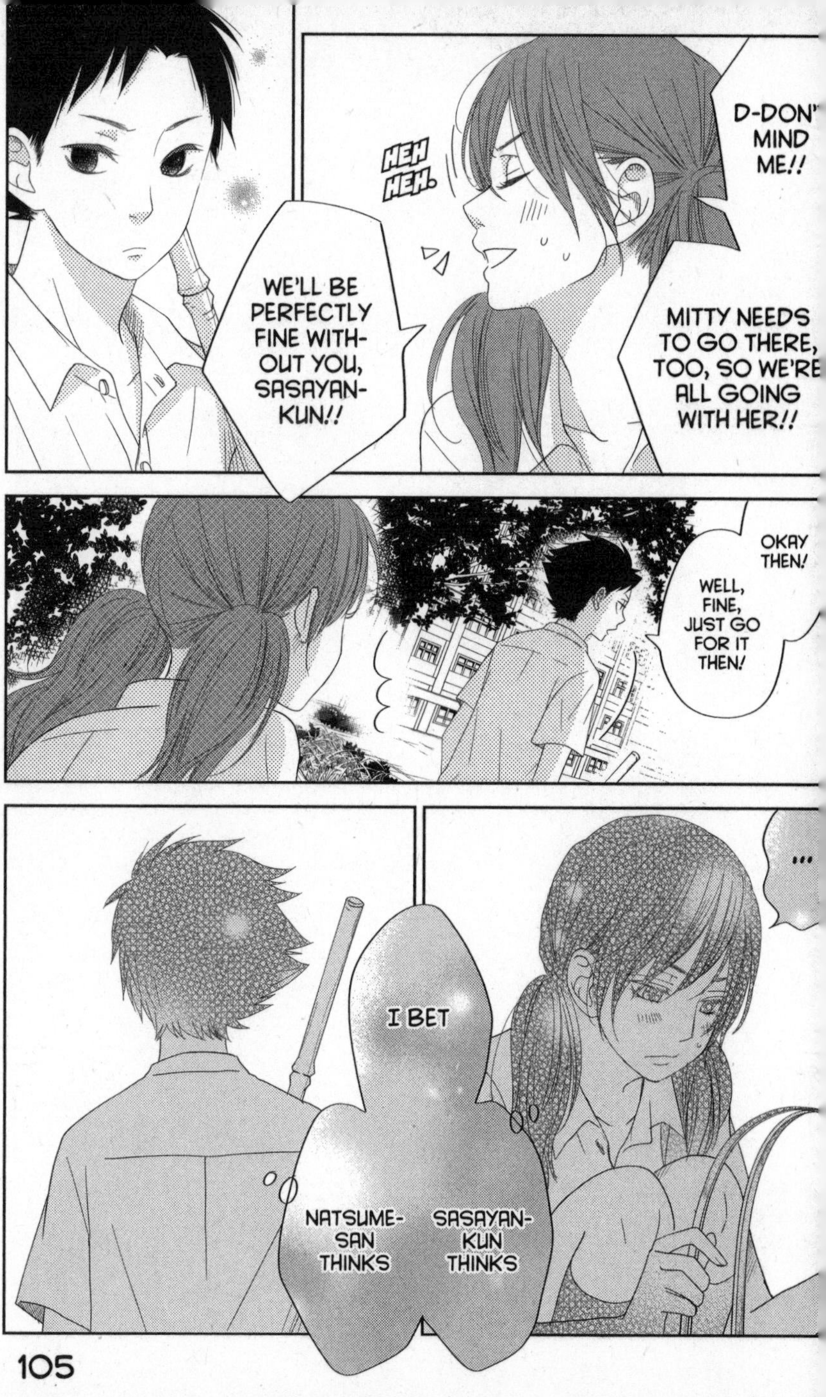
D-DON' MIND ME!!
HEH HEH.
MITTY NEEDS TO GO THERE, TOO, SO WE'RE ALL GOING WITH HER!!
WE'LL BE PERFECTLY FINE WITH-OUT YOU, SASAYAN-KUN!!
OKAY THEN!
WELL, FINE, JUST GO FOR IT THEN!
...
I BET
SASAYAN-KUN THINKS
NATSUME-SAN THINKS

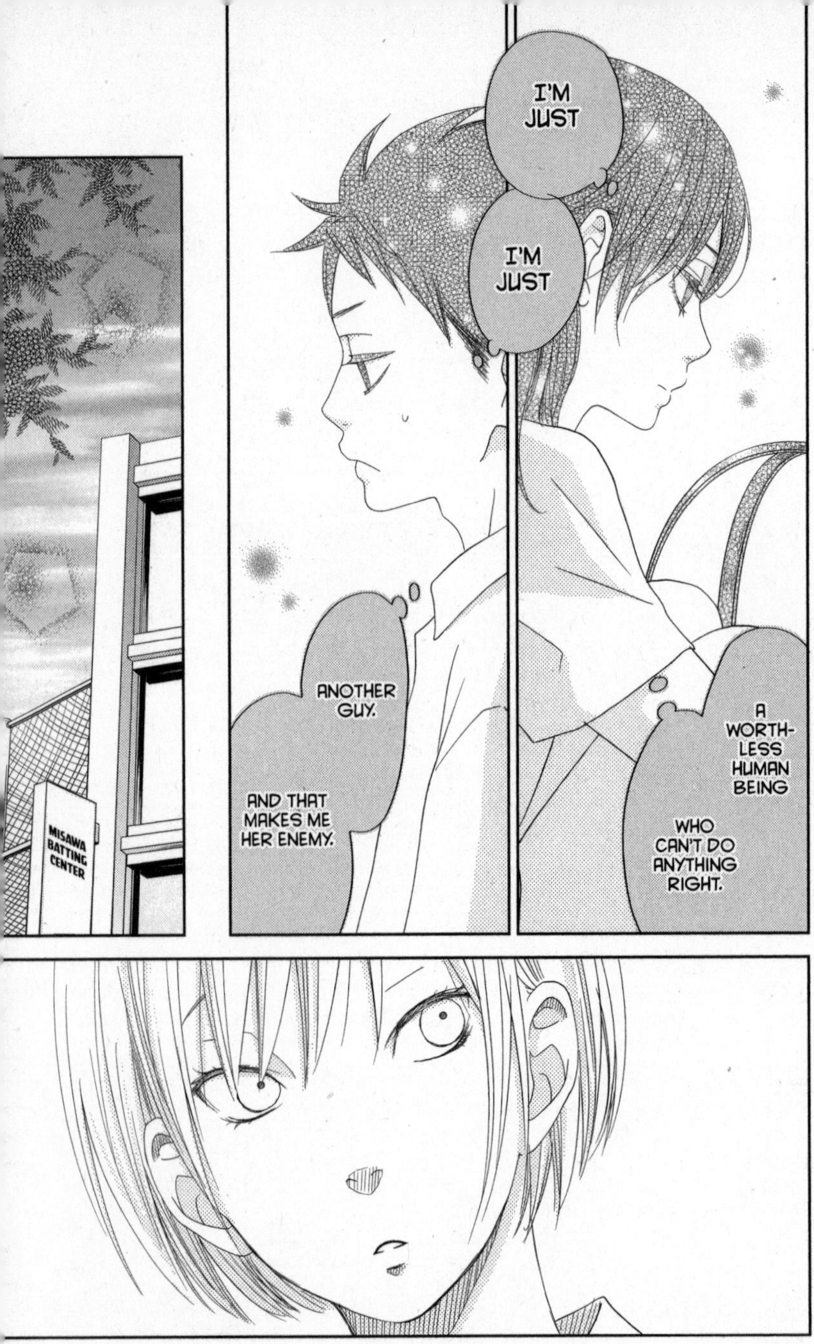
I'M JUST
A WORTH-LESS HUMAN BEING
WHO CAN'T DO ANYTHING RIGHT.
I'M JUST
ANOTHER GUY.
AND THAT MAKES ME HER ENEMY.
MISAWA BATTING CENTER

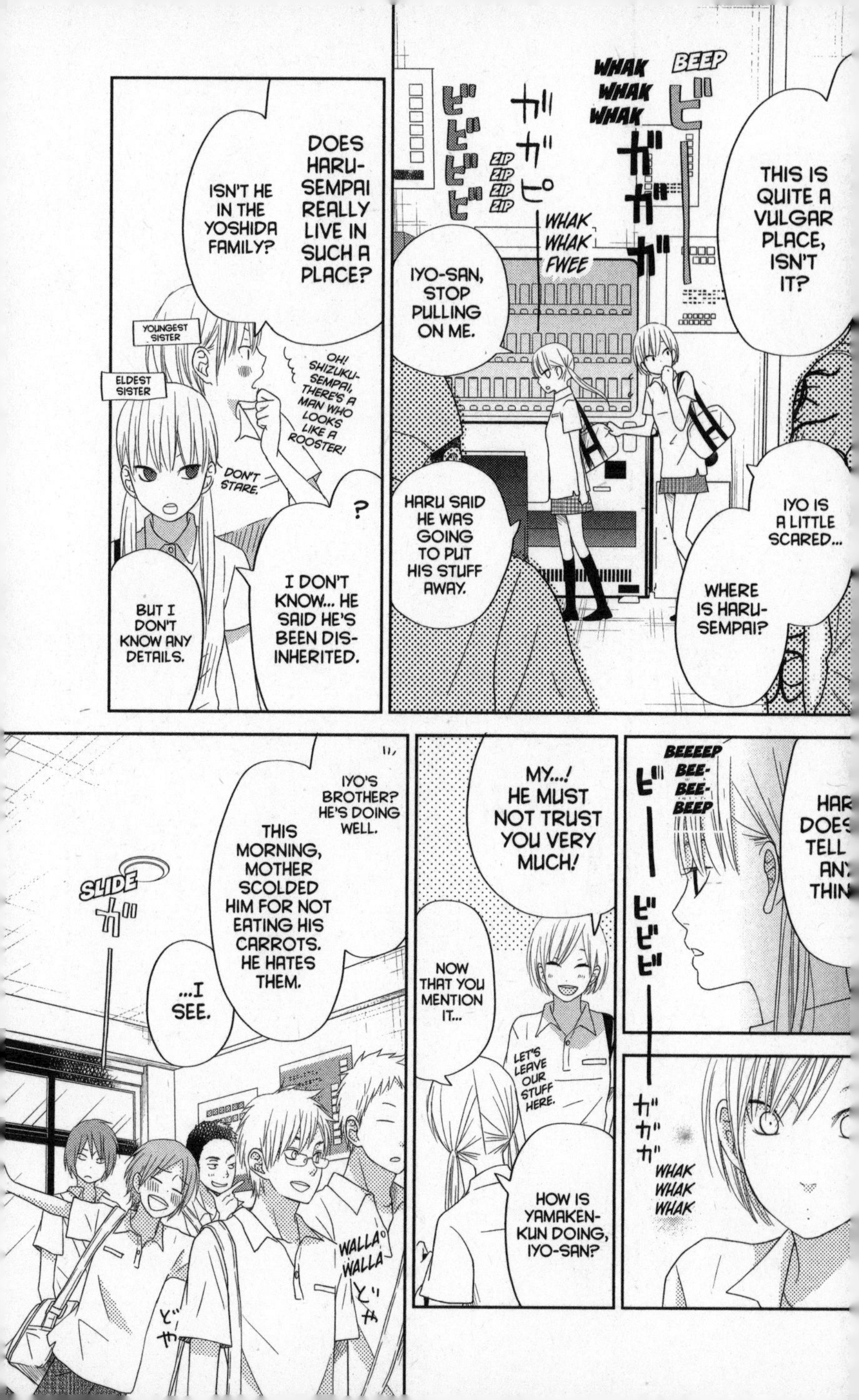

THIS IS QUITE A VULGAR PLACE, ISN'T IT?
BEEP
WHAK WHAK WHAK
ZIP ZIP ZIP ZIP
WHAK WHAK FWEE
IYO-SAN, STOP PULLING ON ME.
IYO IS A LITTLE SCARED...
WHERE IS HARU-SEMPAI?
HARU SAID HE WAS GOING TO PUT HIS STUFF AWAY.
DOES HARU-SEMPAI REALLY LIVE IN SUCH A PLACE?
ISN'T HE IN THE YOSHIDA FAMILY?
YOUNGEST SISTER
ELDEST SISTER
OH! SHIZUKU-SEMPAI, THERE'S A MAN WHO LOOKS LIKE A ROOSTER!
DON'T STARE.
?
I DON'T KNOW... HE SAID HE'S BEEN DIS-INHERITED.
BUT I DON'T KNOW ANY DETAILS.
BEEEEP BEE-BEE-BEEP
HAR DOES TELL AN THIN
WHAK WHAK WHAK
MY...! HE MUST NOT TRUST YOU VERY MUCH!
NOW THAT YOU MENTION IT...
LET'S LEAVE OUR STUFF HERE.
HOW IS YAMAKEN-KUN DOING, IYO-SAN?
IYO'S BROTHER? HE'S DOING WELL.
THIS MORNING, MOTHER SCOLDED HIM FOR NOT EATING HIS CARROTS. HE HATES THEM.
...I SEE.
SLIDE
WALLA WALLA

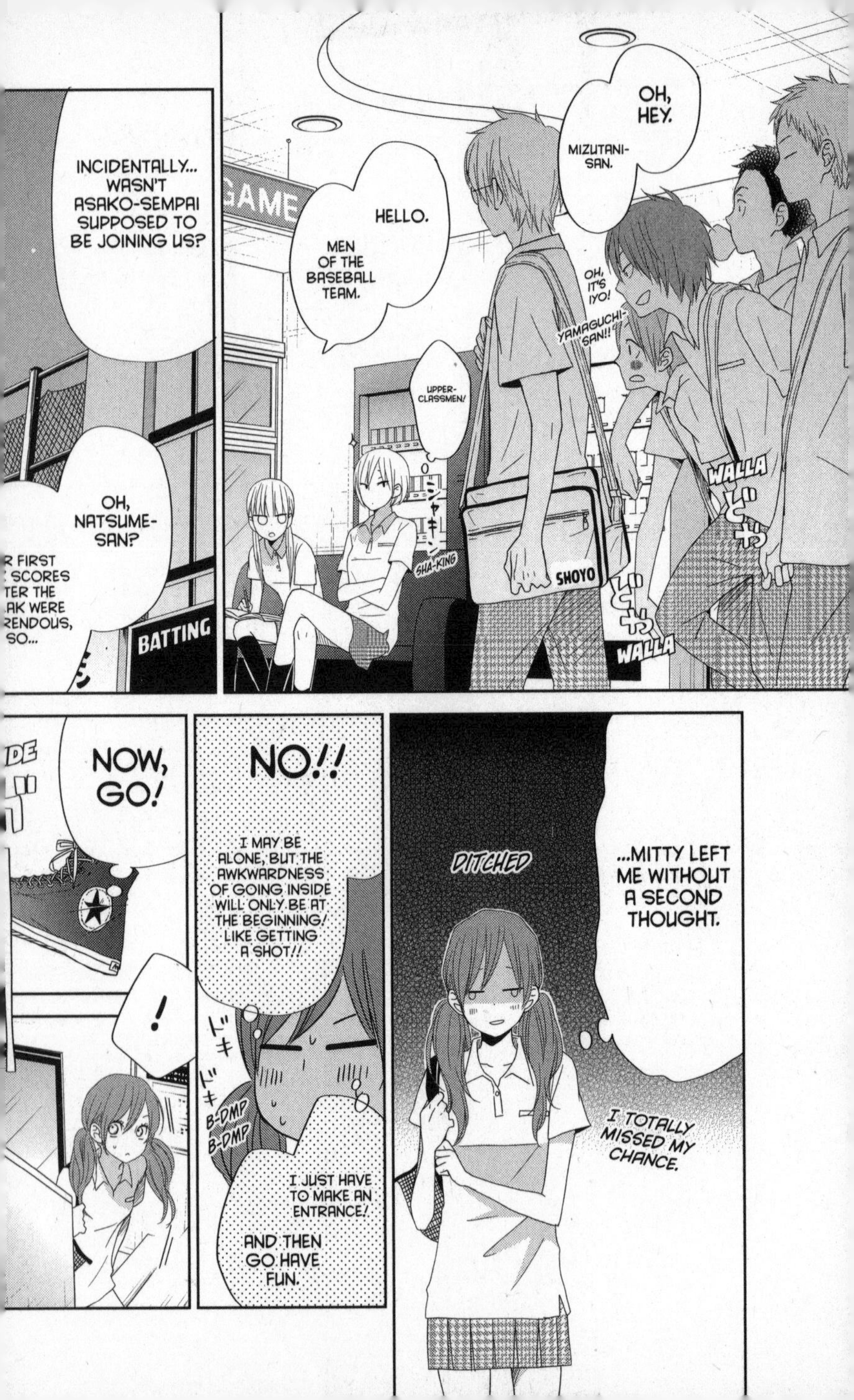
OH, HEY.
MIZUTANI-SAN.
OH, IT'S IYO!
YAMAGUCHI-SAN!!
HELLO.
MEN OF THE BASEBALL TEAM.
GAME
UPPER-CLASSMEN!
SHA-KING
WALLA
SHOYO
WALLA
BATTING
INCIDENTALLY... WASN'T ASAKO-SEMPAI SUPPOSED TO BE JOINING US?
OH, NATSUME-SAN?
R FIRST
SCORES
TER THE
AK WERE
RENDOUS,
SO...
...MITTY LEFT ME WITHOUT A SECOND THOUGHT.
DITCHED
I TOTALLY MISSED MY CHANCE.
NO!!
I MAY BE ALONE, BUT THE AWKWARDNESS OF GOING INSIDE WILL ONLY BE AT THE BEGINNING! LIKE GETTING A SHOT!!
B-DMP B-DMP
I JUST HAVE TO MAKE AN ENTRANCE!
AND THEN GO HAVE FUN.
NOW, GO!
IDE
!

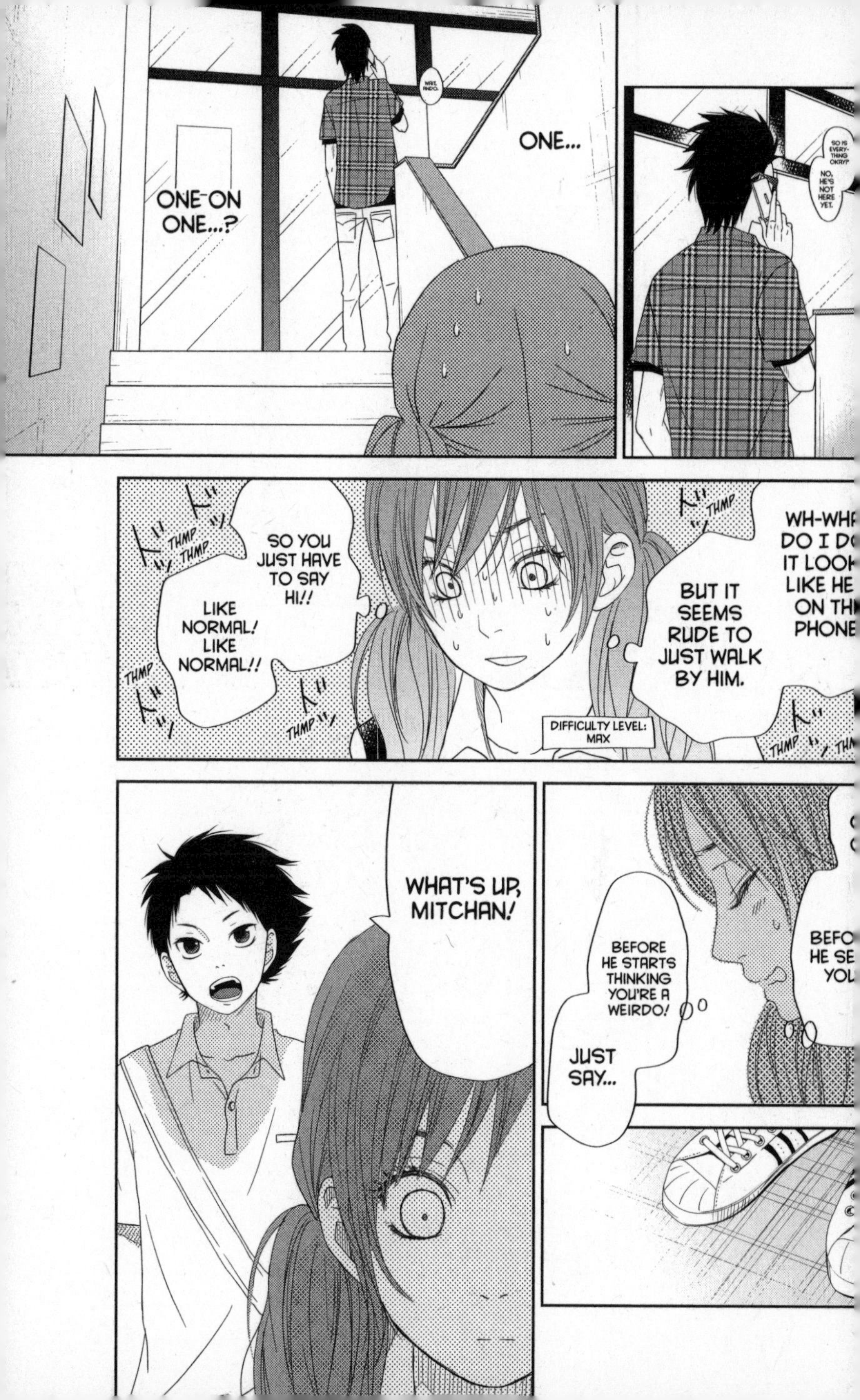
SO IS EVERYTHING OKAY?
NO, HE'S NOT HERE YET.
WAIT, ANDO.
ONE...
ONE-ON ONE...?
WH-WHA DO I D IT LOOK LIKE HE ON TH PHONE
THMP
BUT IT SEEMS RUDE TO JUST WALK BY HIM.
THMP
SO YOU JUST HAVE TO SAY HI!!
LIKE NORMAL! LIKE NORMAL!!
THMP THMP
THMP
THMP
DIFFICULTY LEVEL: MAX
BEFO HE SE YOU
BEFORE HE STARTS THINKING YOU'RE A WEIRDO!
JUST SAY...
WHAT'S UP, MITCHAN!

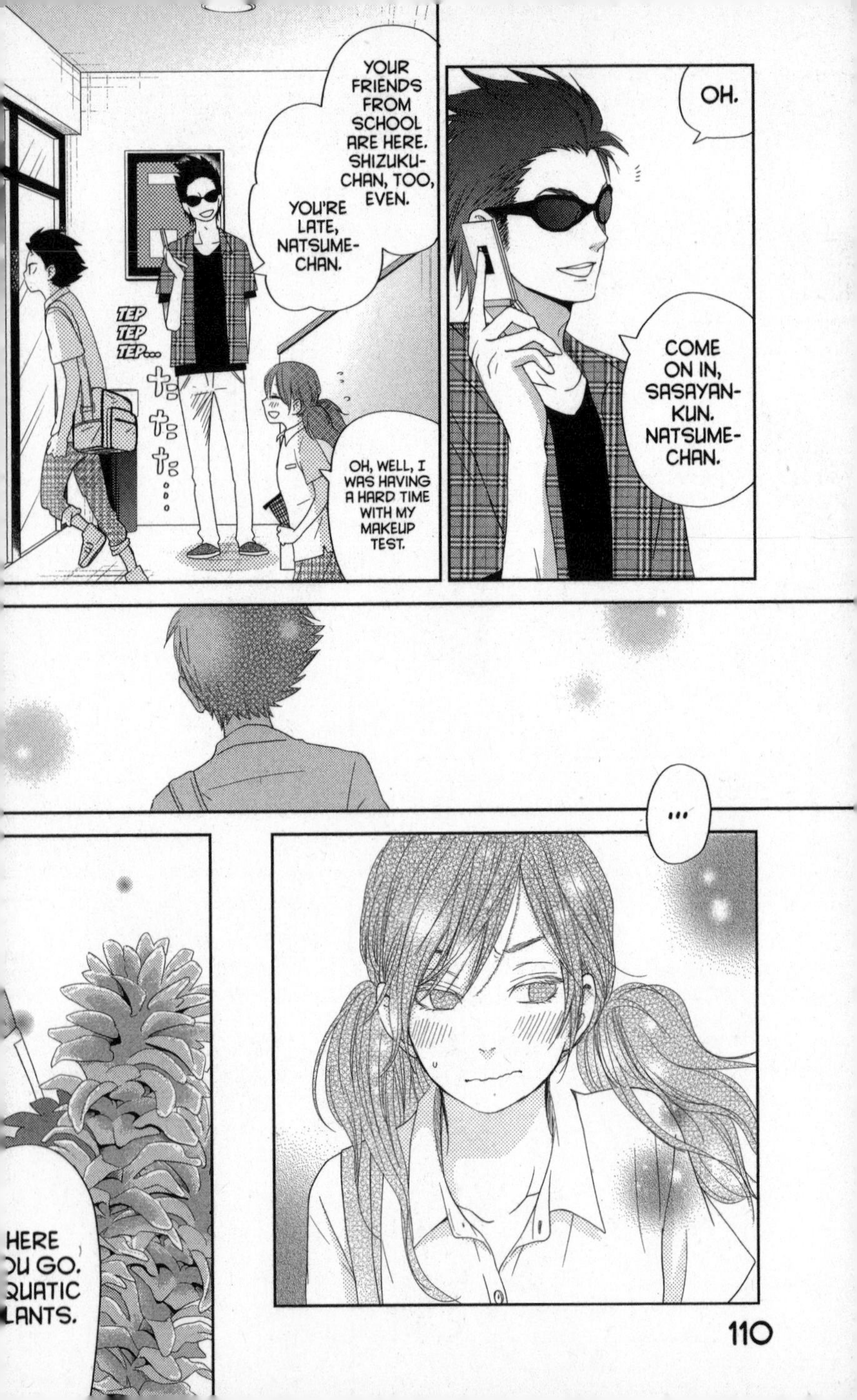
OH.
COME ON IN, SASAYAN-KUN. NATSUME-CHAN.
YOUR FRIENDS FROM SCHOOL ARE HERE. SHIZUKU-CHAN, TOO, EVEN.
YOU'RE LATE, NATSUME-CHAN.
OH, WELL, I WAS HAVING A HARD TIME WITH MY MAKEUP TEST.
TEP TEP TEP...
...
HERE OU GO. QUATIC LANTS.

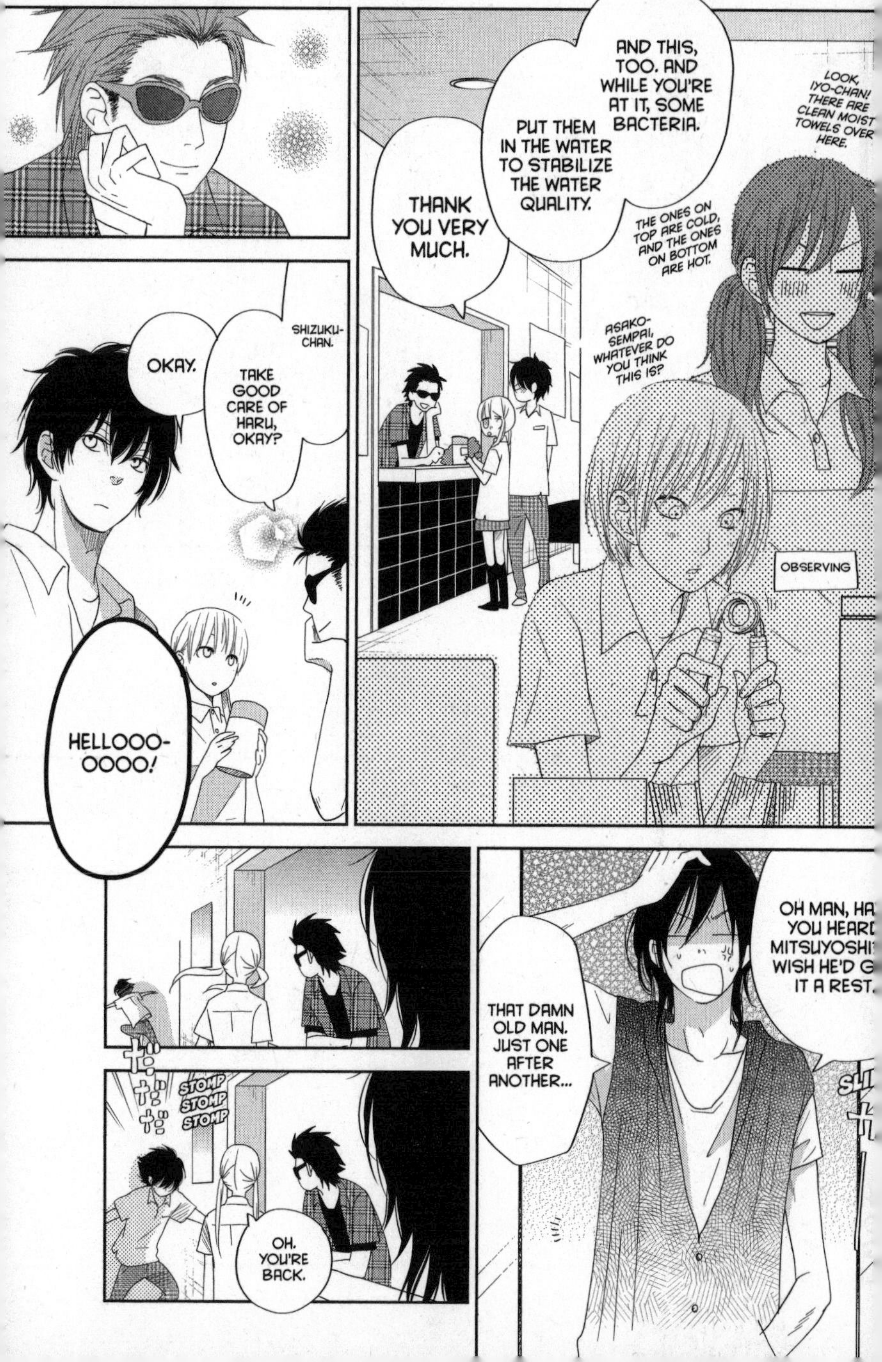
LOOK, IYO-CHAN! THERE ARE CLEAN MOIST TOWELS OVER HERE.
AND THIS, TOO. AND WHILE YOU'RE AT IT, SOME BACTERIA.
PUT THEM IN THE WATER TO STABILIZE THE WATER QUALITY.
THE ONES ON TOP ARE COLD, AND THE ONES ON BOTTOM ARE HOT.
THANK YOU VERY MUCH.
ASAKO-SEMPAI, WHATEVER DO YOU THINK THIS IS?
OBSERVING
SHIZUKU-CHAN.
TAKE GOOD CARE OF HARU, OKAY?
OKAY.
HELLOOO-OOOO!
OH MAN, HA
YOU HEARD
MITSUYOSHI
WISH HE'D G
IT A REST.
THAT DAMN OLD MAN. JUST ONE AFTER ANOTHER...
STOMP STOMP STOMP
OH. YOU'RE BACK.

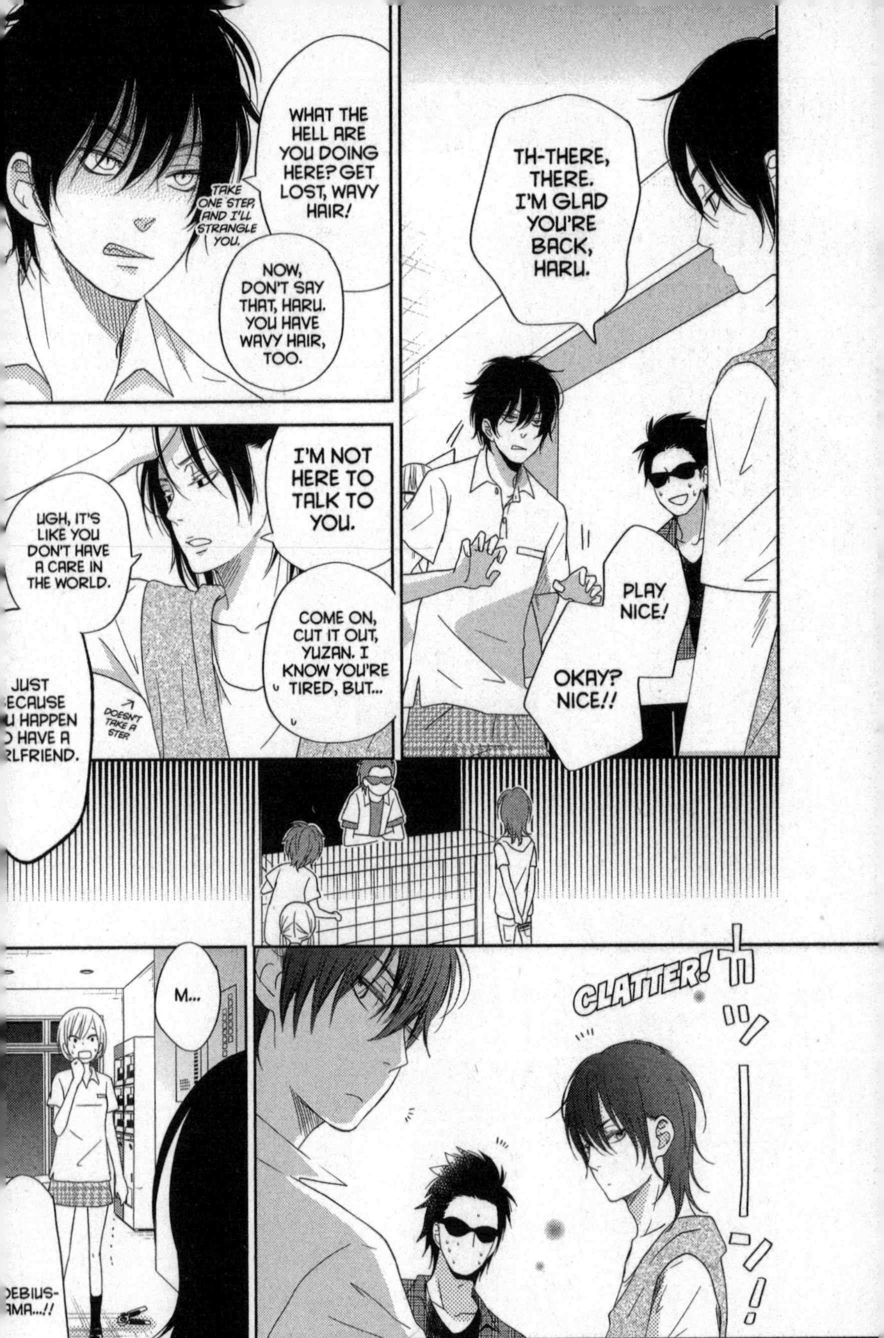
TH-THERE, THERE. I'M GLAD YOU'RE BACK, HARU.
PLAY NICE!
OKAY? NICE!!
WHAT THE HELL ARE YOU DOING HERE? GET LOST, WAVY HAIR!
TAKE ONE STEP, AND I'LL STRANGLE YOU.
NOW, DON'T SAY THAT, HARU. YOU HAVE WAVY HAIR, TOO.
I'M NOT HERE TO TALK TO YOU.
UGH, IT'S LIKE YOU DON'T HAVE A CARE IN THE WORLD.
COME ON, CUT IT OUT, YUZAN. I KNOW YOU'RE TIRED, BUT...
DOESN'T TAKE A STEP
JUST ECAUSE U HAPPEN O HAVE A RLFRIEND.
CLATTER!
M...
DEBIUS-AMA...!!

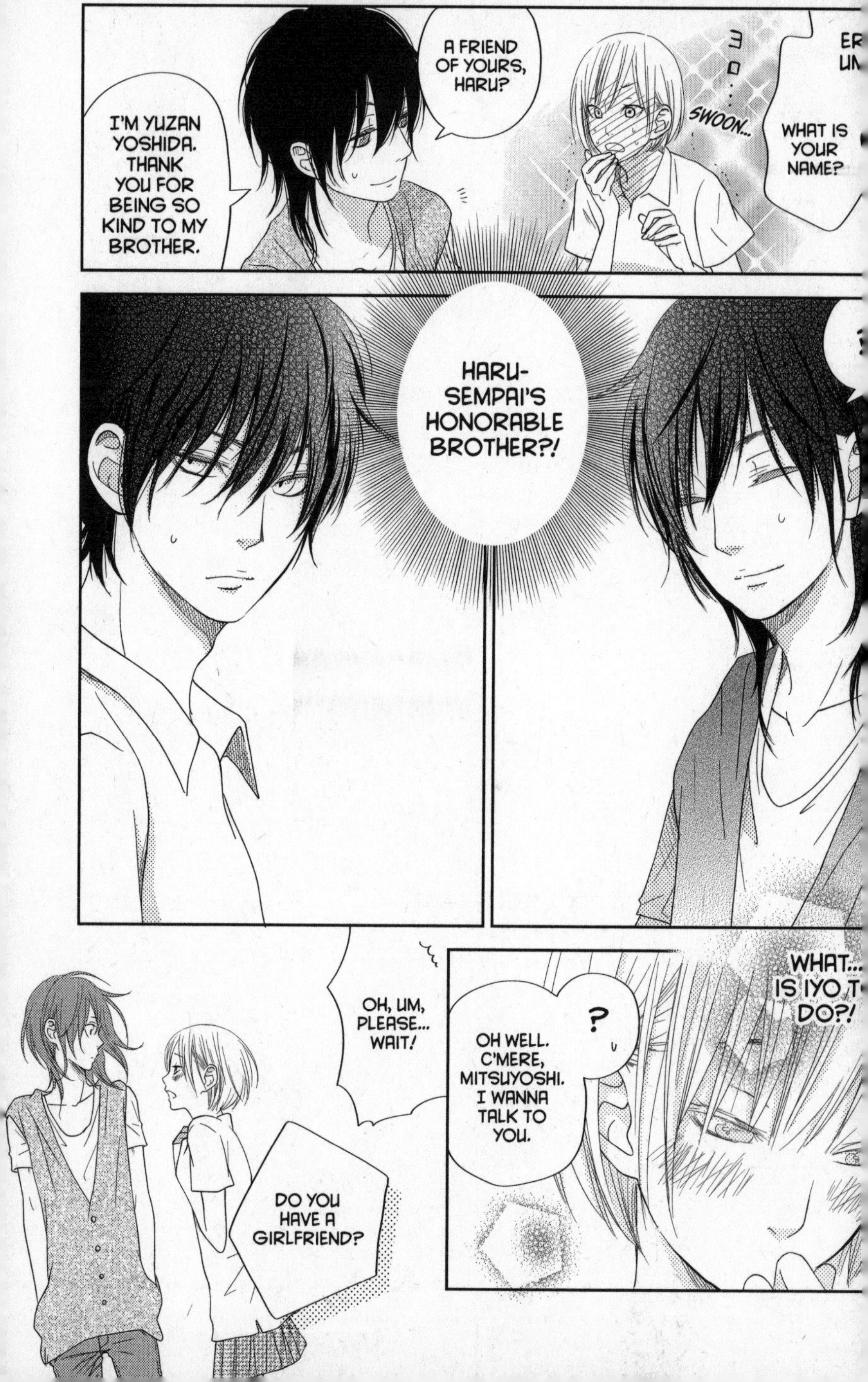
WHAT IS YOUR NAME?
ヨロ…
SWOON...
A FRIEND OF YOURS, HARU?
I'M YUZAN YOSHIDA. THANK YOU FOR BEING SO KIND TO MY BROTHER.
HARU-SEMPAI'S HONORABLE BROTHER?!
WHAT... IS IYO
DO?!
?
OH WELL. C'MERE, MITSUYOSHI. I WANNA TALK TO YOU.
OH, UM, PLEASE... WAIT!
DO YOU HAVE A GIRLFRIEND?

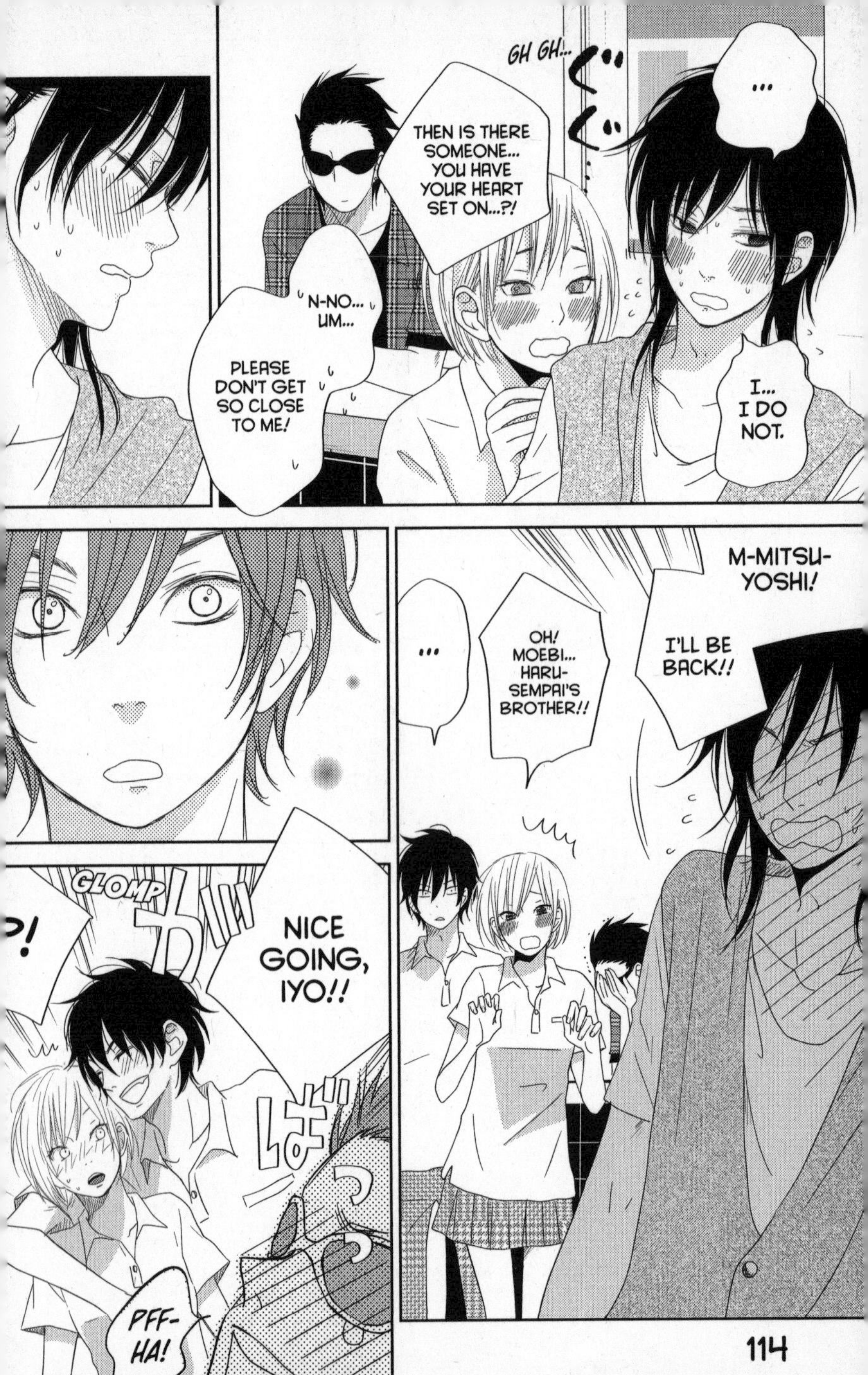
...
GH GH...
THEN IS THERE SOMEONE... YOU HAVE YOUR HEART SET ON...?!
I... I DO NOT.
N-NO... UM...
PLEASE DON'T GET SO CLOSE TO ME!
M-MITSU-YOSHI!
I'LL BE BACK!!
OH! MOEBI... HARU-SEMPAI'S BROTHER!!
...
GLOMP
NICE GOING, IYO!!
?!
PFF-HA!

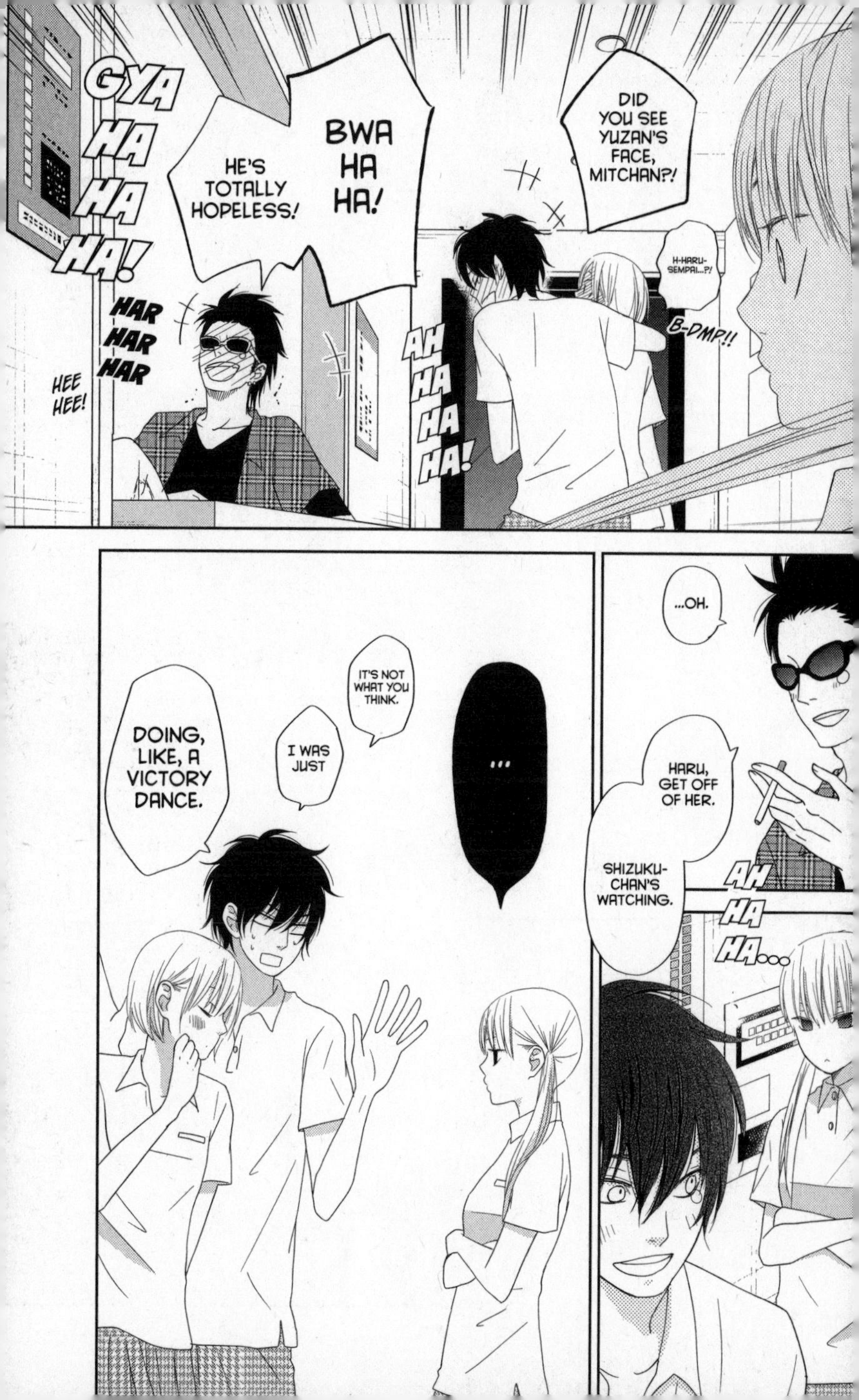
DID YOU SEE YUZAN'S FACE, MITCHAN?!
H-HARU-SEMPAI...?!
B-DMP!!
AH HA HA HA HA!
BWA HA HA!
HE'S TOTALLY HOPELESS!
GYA HA HA HA!
HAR HAR HAR
HEE HEE!
...OH.
HARU, GET OFF OF HER.
SHIZUKU-CHAN'S WATCHING.
AH HA HA...
...
IT'S NOT WHAT YOU THINK.
I WAS JUST
DOING, LIKE, A VICTORY DANCE.

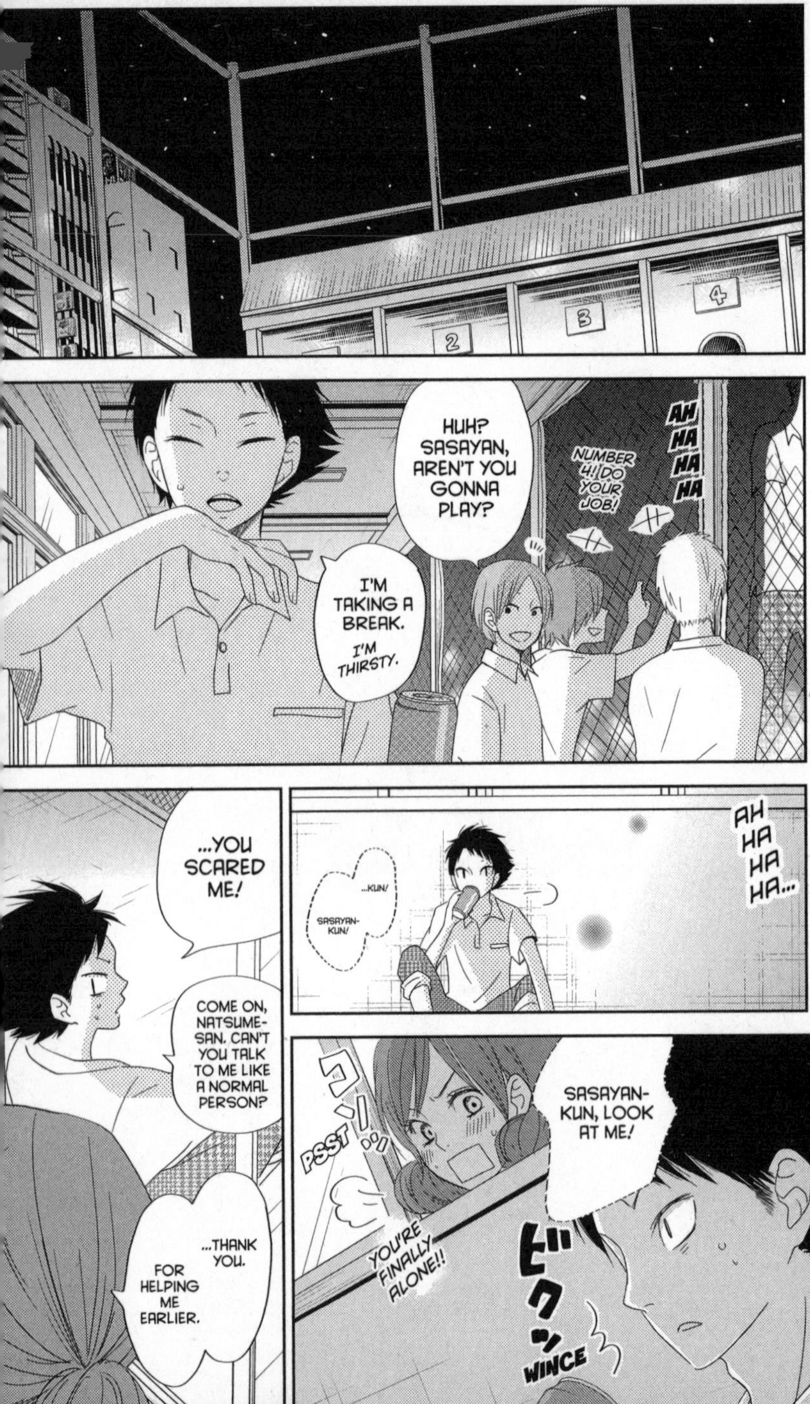
2
3
4
AH HA HA HA
NUMBER 4! DO YOUR JOB!
HUH? SASAYAN, AREN'T YOU GONNA PLAY?
I'M TAKING A BREAK.
I'M THIRSTY.
AH HA HA HA...
...KUN!
SASAYAN-KUN!
SASAYAN-KUN, LOOK AT ME!
WINCE
PSST
YOU'RE FINALLY ALONE!!
...YOU SCARED ME!
COME ON, NATSUME-SAN. CAN'T YOU TALK TO ME LIKE A NORMAL PERSON?
...THANK YOU.
FOR HELPING ME EARLIER.

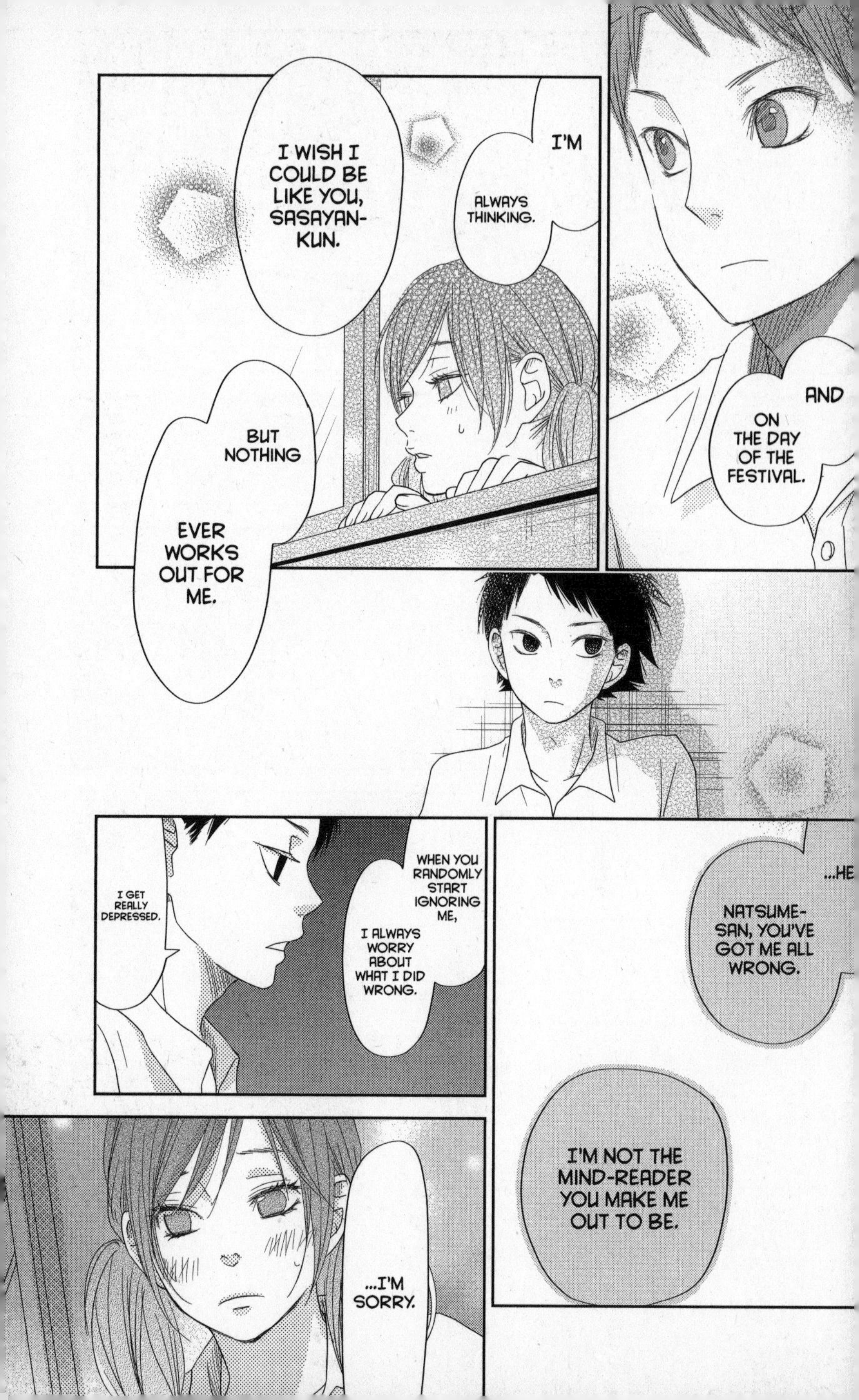
AND ON THE DAY OF THE FESTIVAL.
I'M ALWAYS THINKING.
I WISH I COULD BE LIKE YOU, SASAYAN-KUN.
BUT NOTHING EVER WORKS OUT FOR ME.
...HE
NATSUME-SAN, YOU'VE GOT ME ALL WRONG.
I'M NOT THE MIND-READER YOU MAKE ME OUT TO BE.
WHEN YOU RANDOMLY START IGNORING ME,
I ALWAYS WORRY ABOUT WHAT I DID WRONG.
I GET REALLY DEPRESSED.
...I'M SORRY.

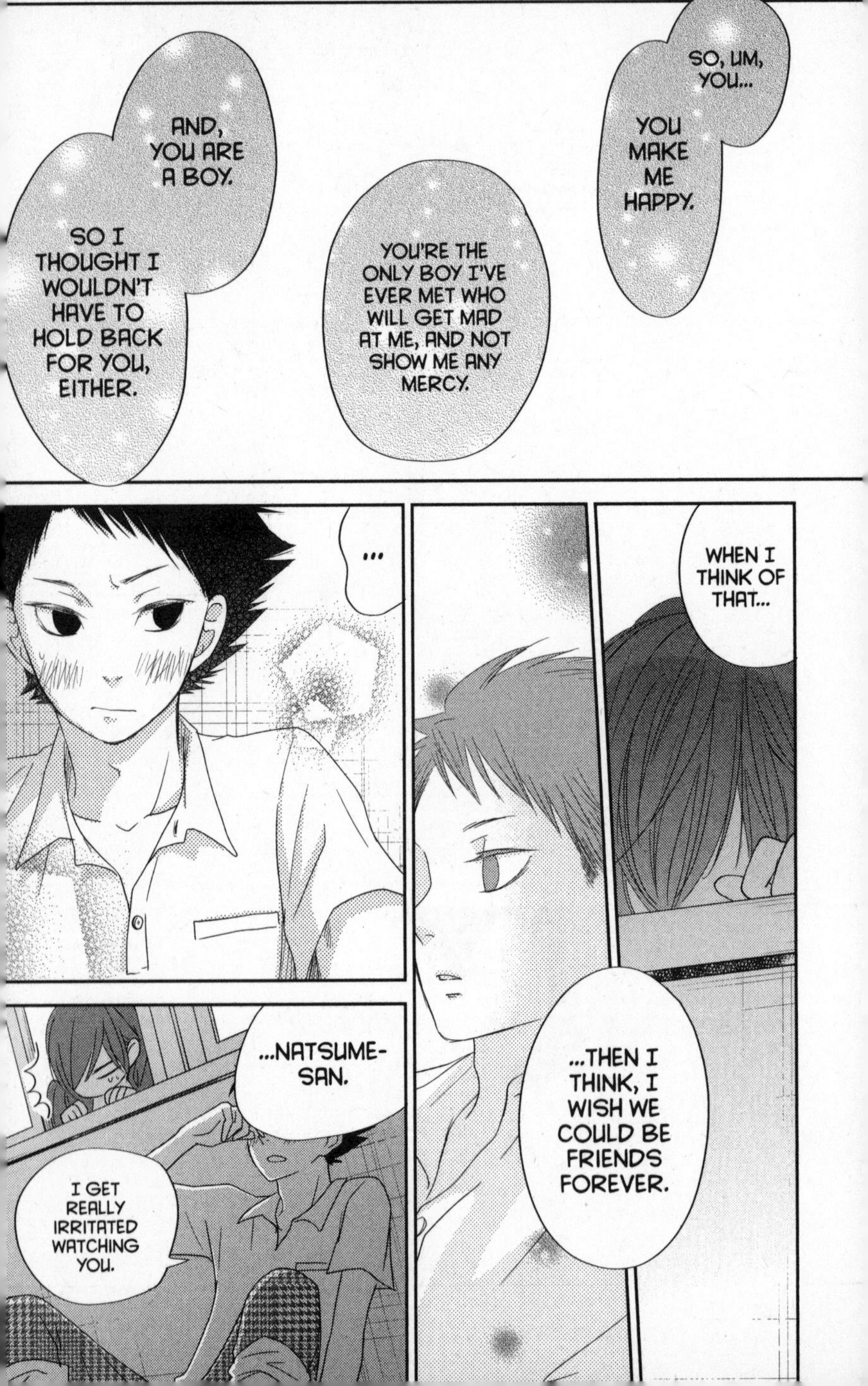
SO, UM, YOU...
YOU MAKE ME HAPPY.
YOU'RE THE ONLY BOY I'VE EVER MET WHO WILL GET MAD AT ME, AND NOT SHOW ME ANY MERCY.
AND, YOU ARE A BOY.
SO I THOUGHT I WOULDN'T HAVE TO HOLD BACK FOR YOU, EITHER.
WHEN I THINK OF THAT...
...THEN I THINK, I WISH WE COULD BE FRIENDS FOREVER.
...
...NATSUME-SAN.
I GET REALLY IRRITATED WATCHING YOU.

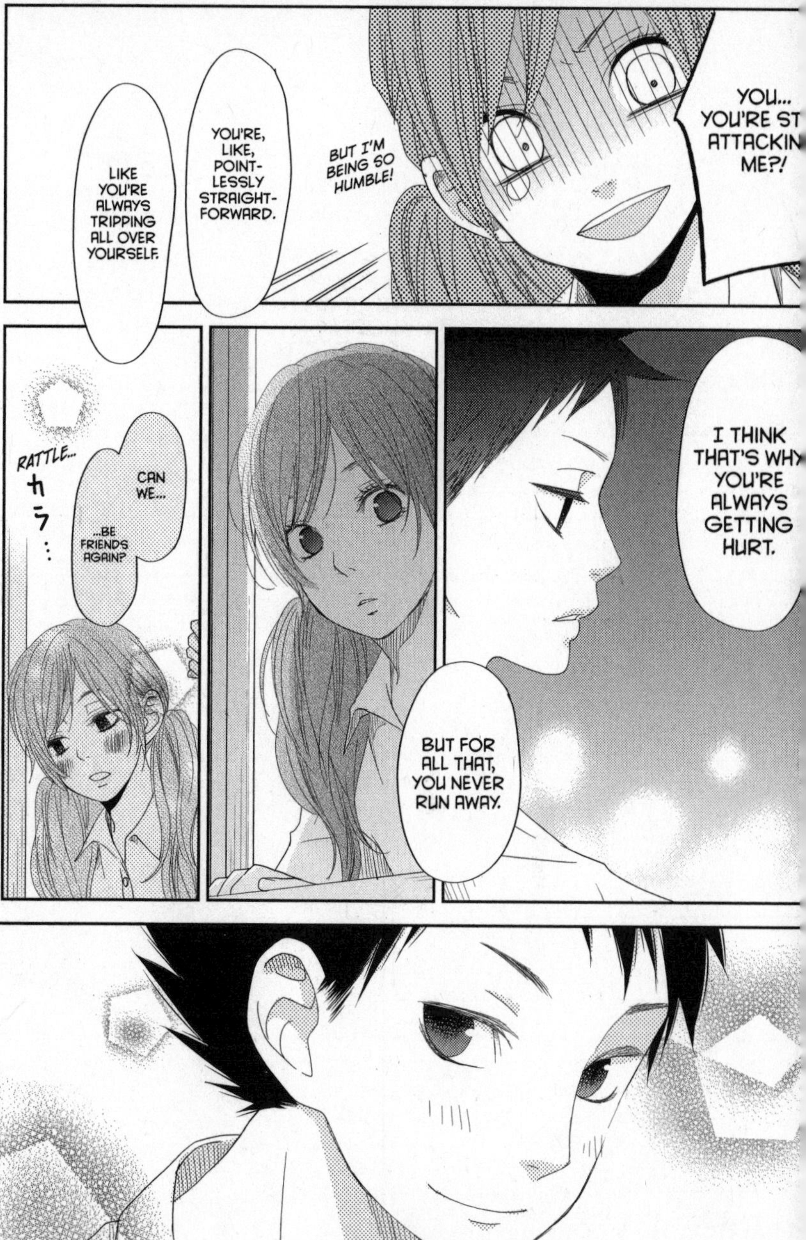
YOU... YOU'RE ST ATTACKIN ME?!
BUT I'M BEING SO HUMBLE!
YOU'RE, LIKE, POINTLESSLY STRAIGHTFORWARD.
LIKE YOU'RE ALWAYS TRIPPING ALL OVER YOURSELF.
I THINK THAT'S WHY YOU'RE ALWAYS GETTING HURT.
BUT FOR ALL THAT, YOU NEVER RUN AWAY.
CAN WE...
...BE FRIENDS AGAIN?
RATTLE...
カラ…

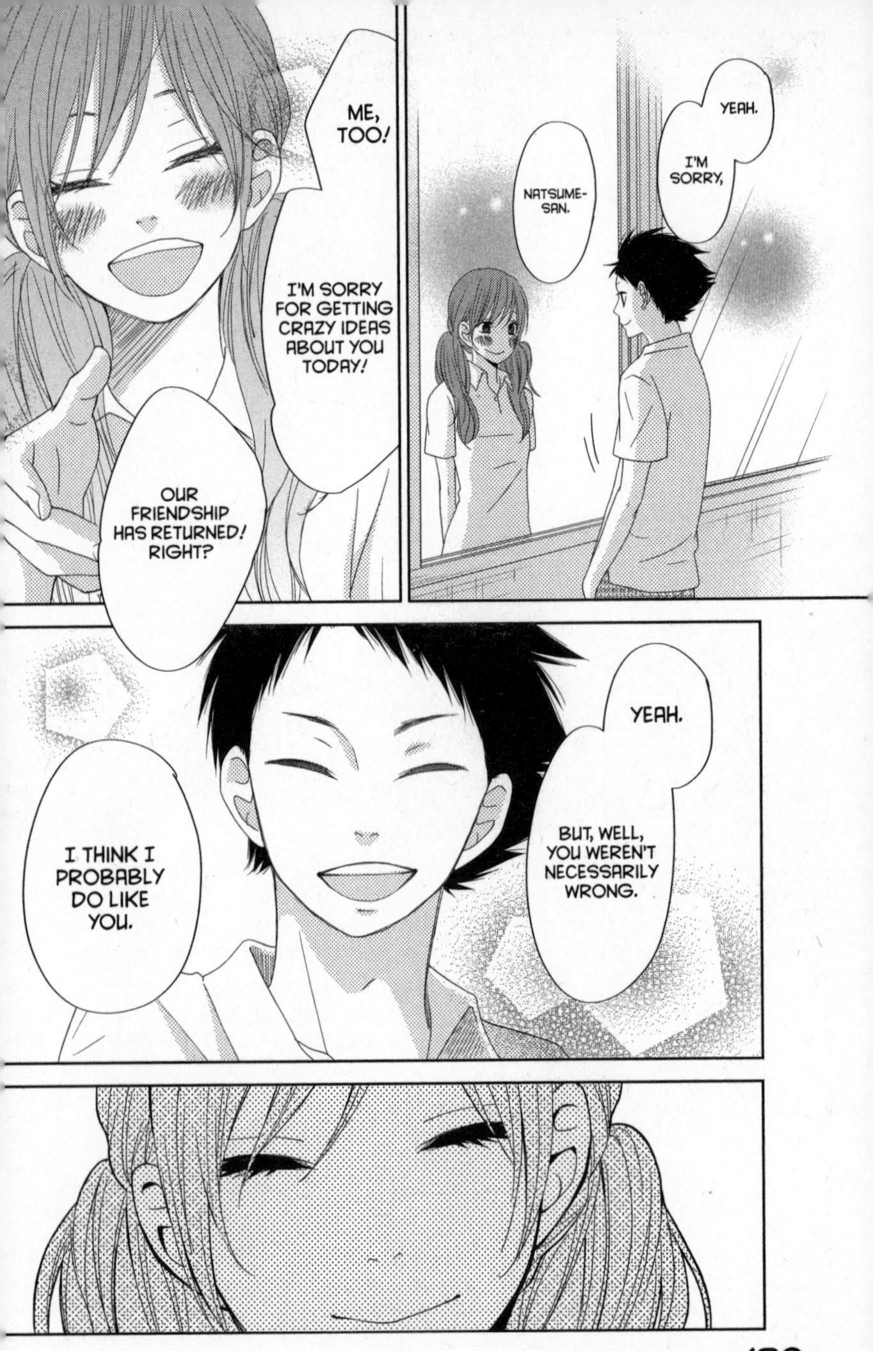
YEAH.
I'M SORRY,
NATSUME-SAN.
ME, TOO!
I'M SORRY FOR GETTING CRAZY IDEAS ABOUT YOU TODAY!
OUR FRIENDSHIP HAS RETURNED! RIGHT?
YEAH.
BUT, WELL, YOU WEREN'T NECESSARILY WRONG.
I THINK I PROBABLY DO LIKE YOU.

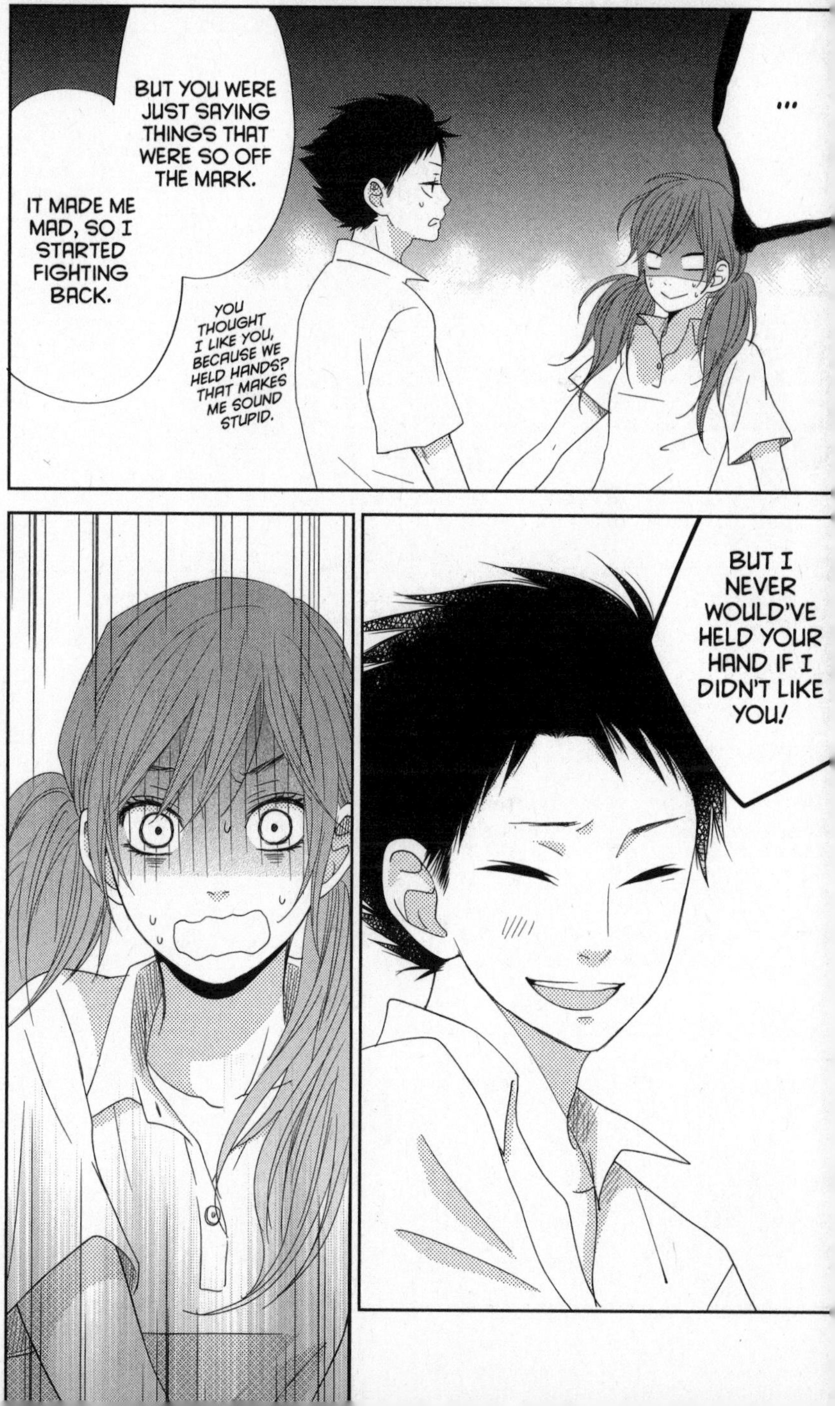
...
BUT YOU WERE JUST SAYING THINGS THAT WERE SO OFF THE MARK.
IT MADE ME MAD, SO I STARTED FIGHTING BACK.
YOU THOUGHT I LIKE YOU, BECAUSE WE HELD HANDS? THAT MAKES ME SOUND STUPID.
BUT I NEVER WOULD'VE HELD YOUR HAND IF I DIDN'T LIKE YOU!

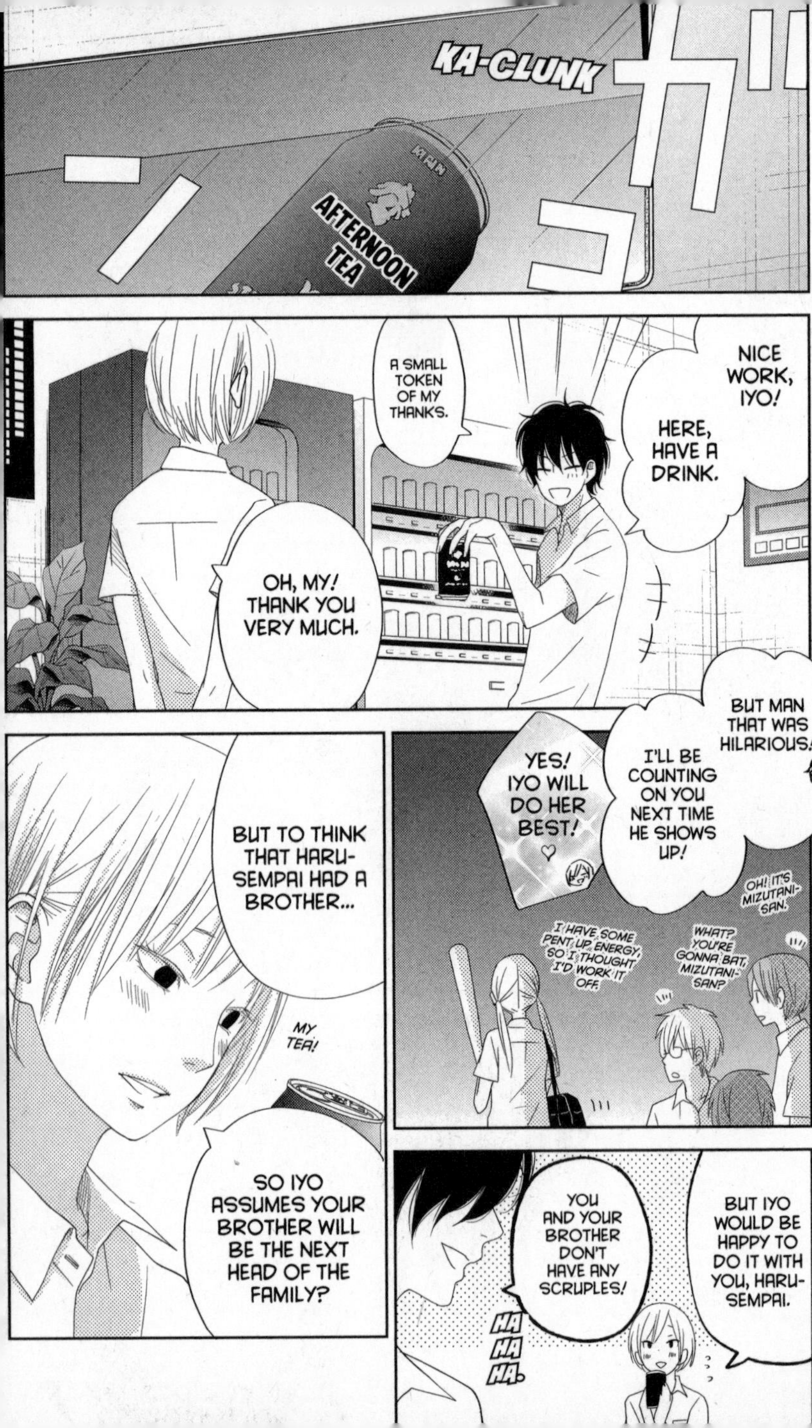
KA-CLUNK
AFTERNOON TEA
NICE WORK, IYO!
HERE, HAVE A DRINK.
A SMALL TOKEN OF MY THANKS.
OH, MY! THANK YOU VERY MUCH.
BUT MAN THAT WAS HILARIOUS!
I'LL BE COUNTING ON YOU NEXT TIME HE SHOWS UP!
YES! IYO WILL DO HER BEST! ♡
OH! IT'S MIZUTANI-SAN.
WHAT? YOU'RE GONNA BAT, MIZUTANI-SAN?
I HAVE SOME PENT UP ENERGY, SO I THOUGHT I'D WORK IT OFF.
BUT IYO WOULD BE HAPPY TO DO IT WITH YOU, HARU-SEMPAI.
YOU AND YOUR BROTHER DON'T HAVE ANY SCRUPLES!
HA HA HA.
BUT TO THINK THAT HARU-SEMPAI HAD A BROTHER...
MY TEA!
SO IYO ASSUMES YOUR BROTHER WILL BE THE NEXT HEAD OF THE FAMILY?

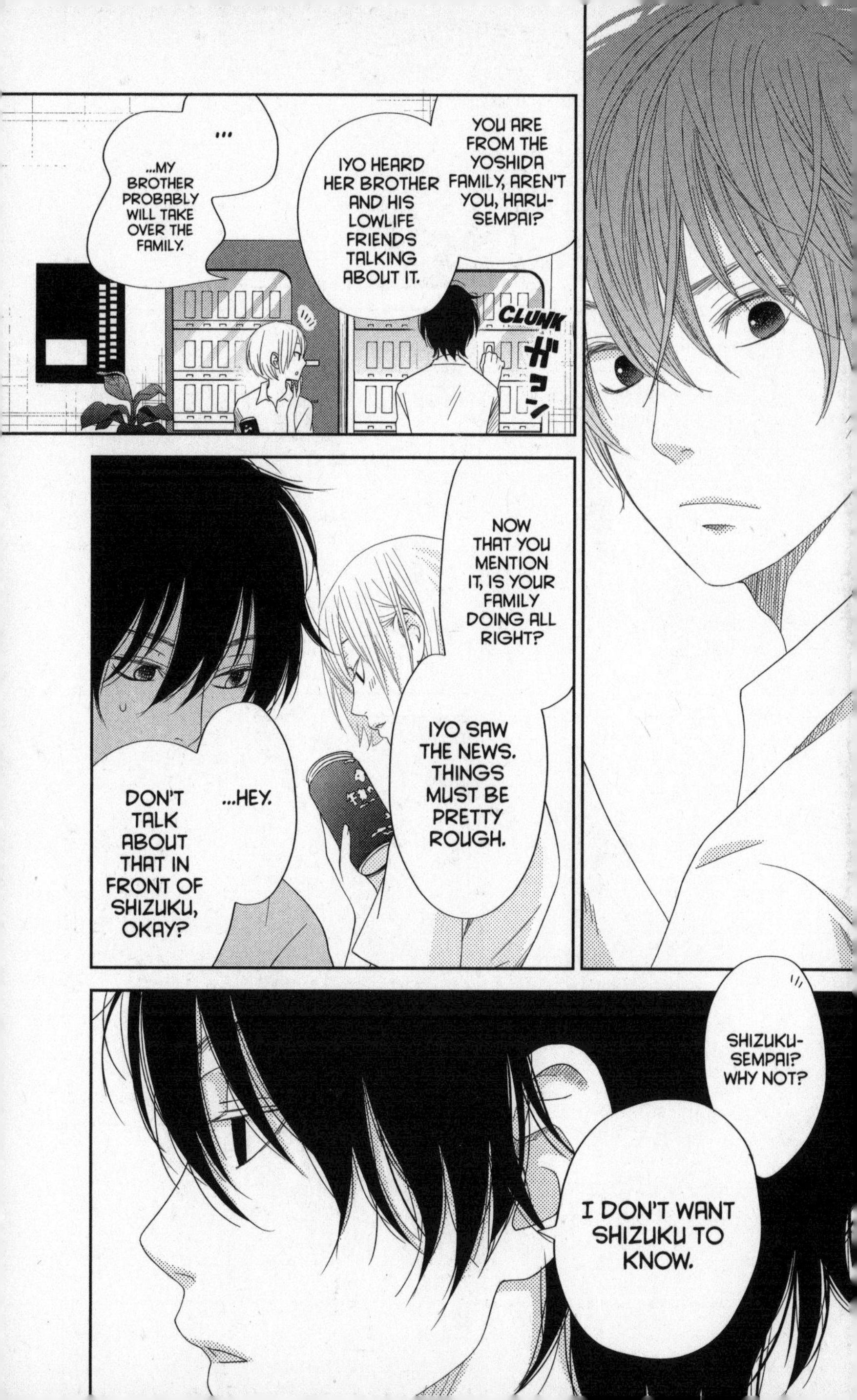
YOU ARE FROM THE YOSHIDA FAMILY, AREN'T YOU, HARU-SEMPAI?
IYO HEARD HER BROTHER AND HIS LOWLIFE FRIENDS TALKING ABOUT IT.
...
...MY BROTHER PROBABLY WILL TAKE OVER THE FAMILY.
CLUNK
ガコン
NOW THAT YOU MENTION IT, IS YOUR FAMILY DOING ALL RIGHT?
IYO SAW THE NEWS. THINGS MUST BE PRETTY ROUGH.
...HEY.
DON'T TALK ABOUT THAT IN FRONT OF SHIZUKU, OKAY?
SHIZUKU-SEMPAI? WHY NOT?
I DON'T WANT SHIZUKU TO KNOW.

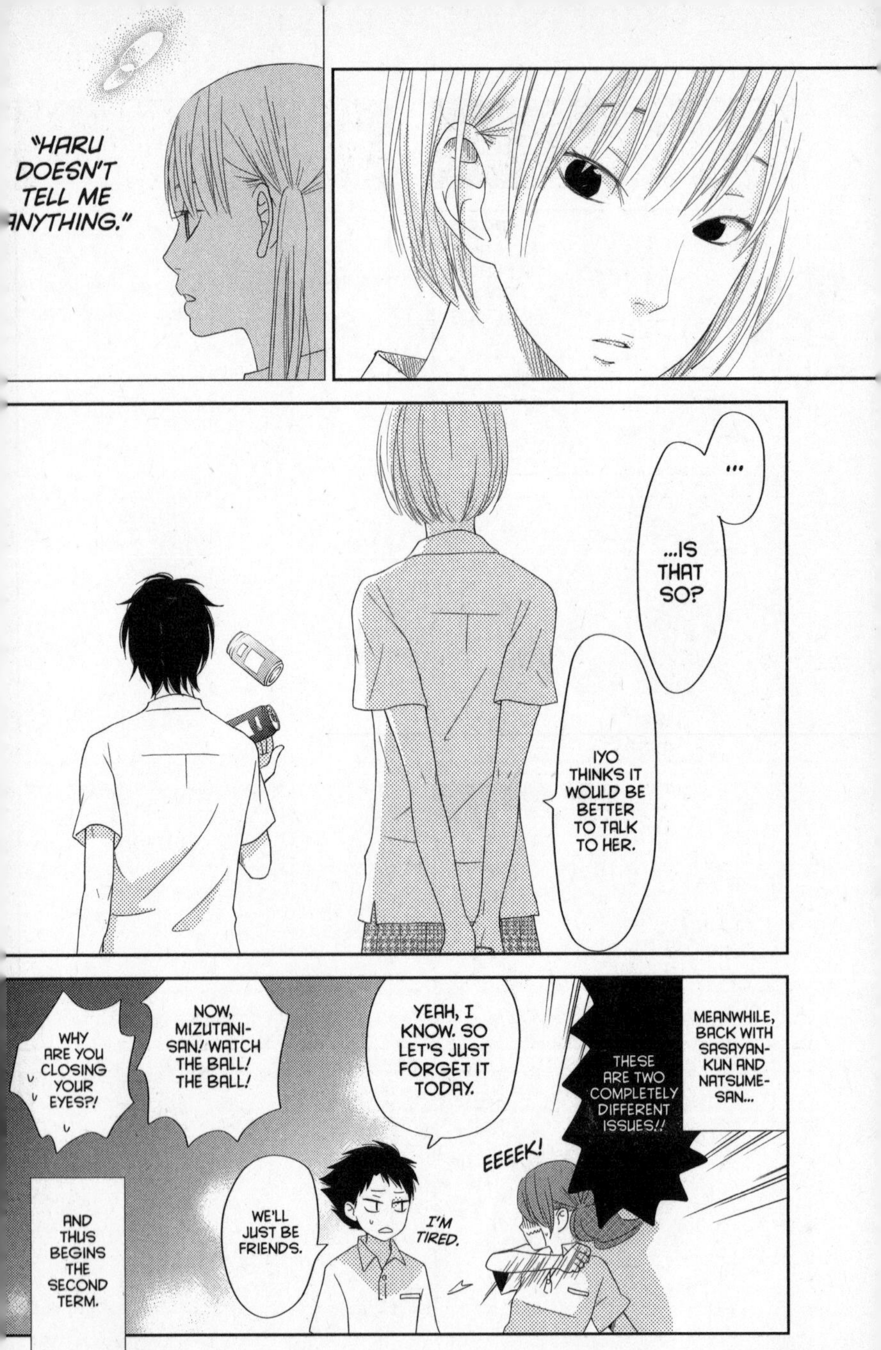
"HARU DOESN'T TELL ME ANYTHING."
...
...IS THAT SO?
IYO THINKS IT WOULD BE BETTER TO TALK TO HER.
MEANWHILE, BACK WITH SASAYAN-KUN AND NATSUME-SAN...
THESE ARE TWO COMPLETELY DIFFERENT ISSUES!!
EEEEK!
YEAH, I KNOW. SO LET'S JUST FORGET IT TODAY.
I'M TIRED.
WE'LL JUST BE FRIENDS.
NOW, MIZUTANI-SAN! WATCH THE BALL! THE BALL!
WHY ARE YOU CLOSING YOUR EYES?!
AND THUS BEGINS THE SECOND TERM.

CLASS A BOYS

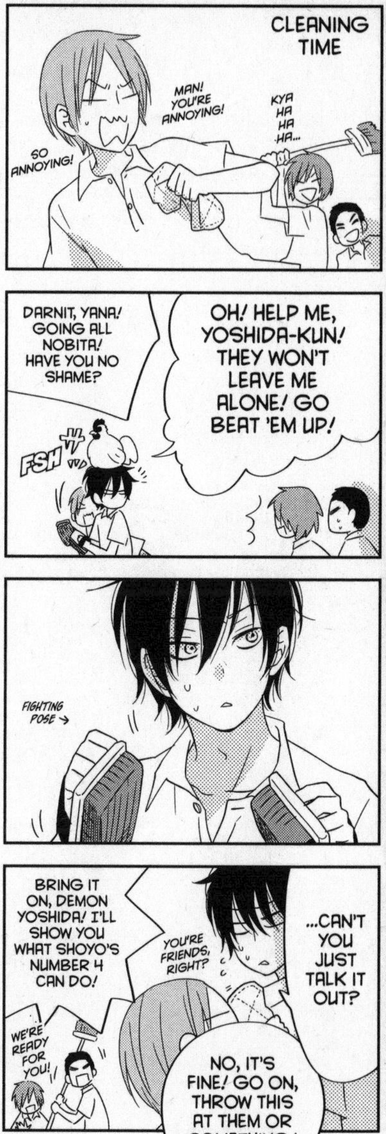
CLEANING TIME
KYA HA HA HA...
MAN! YOU'RE ANNOYING!
SO ANNOYING!
OH! HELP ME, YOSHIDA-KUN! THEY WON'T LEAVE ME ALONE! GO BEAT 'EM UP!
DARNIT, YANA! GOING ALL NOBITA! HAVE YOU NO SHAME?
FSH
FIGHTING POSE →
...CAN'T YOU JUST TALK IT OUT?
YOU'RE FRIENDS, RIGHT?
BRING IT ON, DEMON YOSHIDA! I'LL SHOW YOU WHAT SHOYO'S NUMBER 4 CAN DO!
NO, IT'S FINE! GO ON, THROW THIS AT THEM OR SOMETHING!
WE'RE READY FOR YOU!

COLD WAR

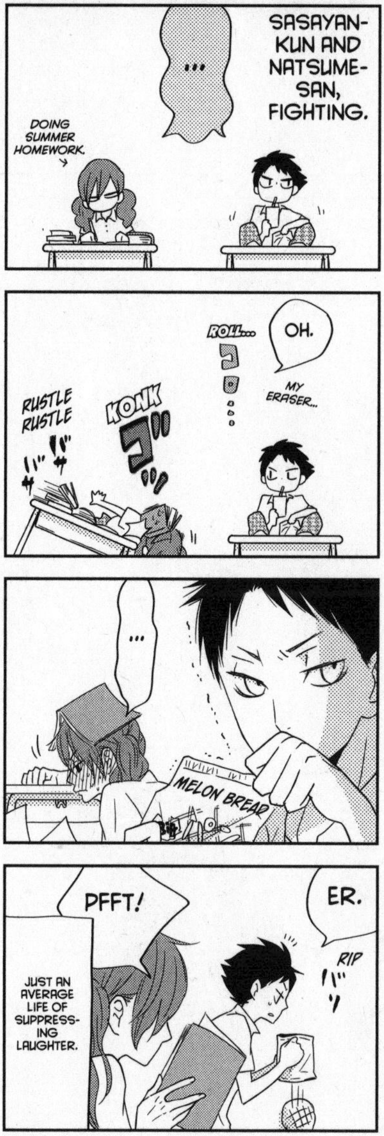
SASAYAN-KUN AND NATSUME-SAN, FIGHTING.
...
DOING SUMMER HOMEWORK. →
OH.
MY ERASER...
ROLL...
KONK
RUSTLE RUSTLE
...
MELON BREAD
ER.
RIP
PFFT!
JUST AN AVERAGE LIFE OF SUPPRESSING LAUGHTER.

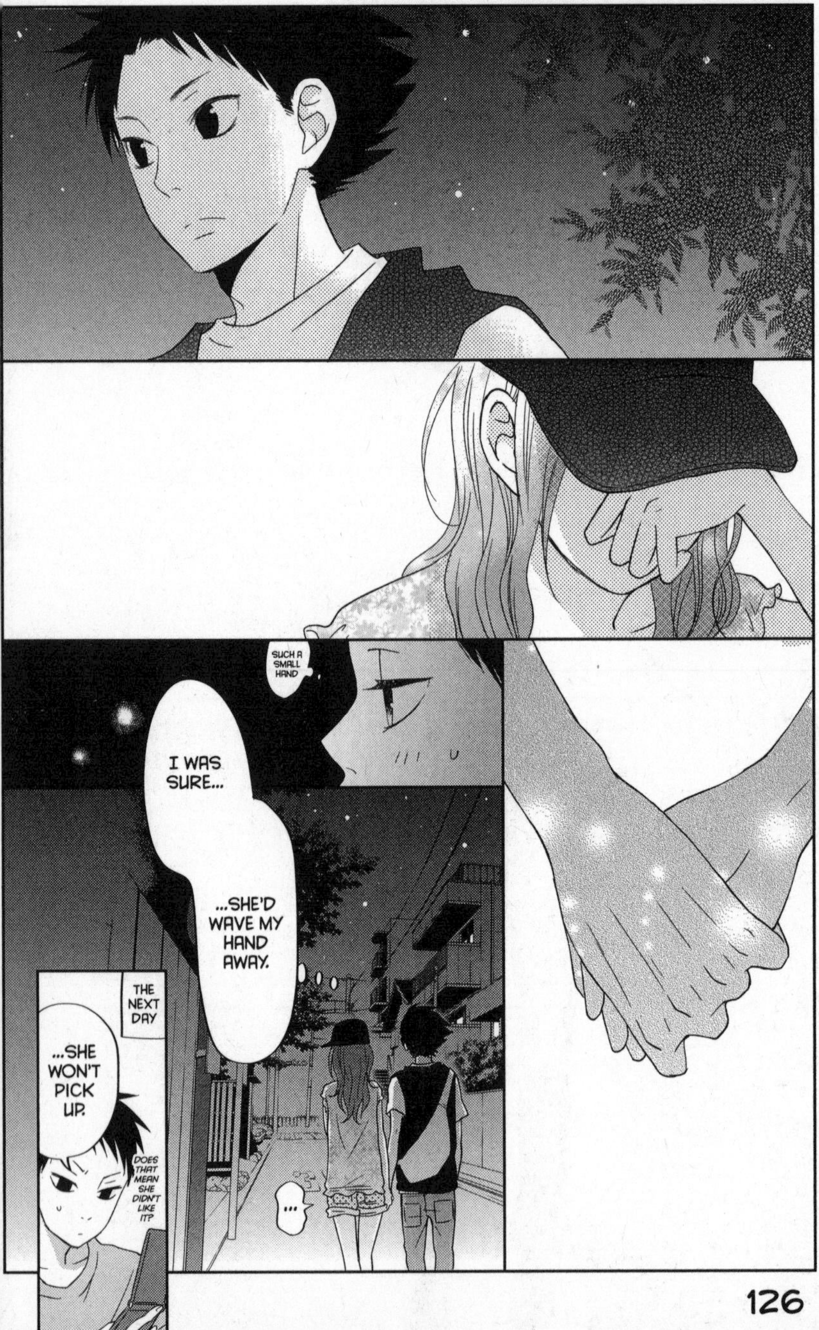
SUCH A SMALL HAND
I WAS SURE...
...SHE'D WAVE MY HAND AWAY.
...
THE NEXT DAY
...SHE WON'T PICK UP.
DOES THAT MEAN SHE DIDN'T LIKE IT?

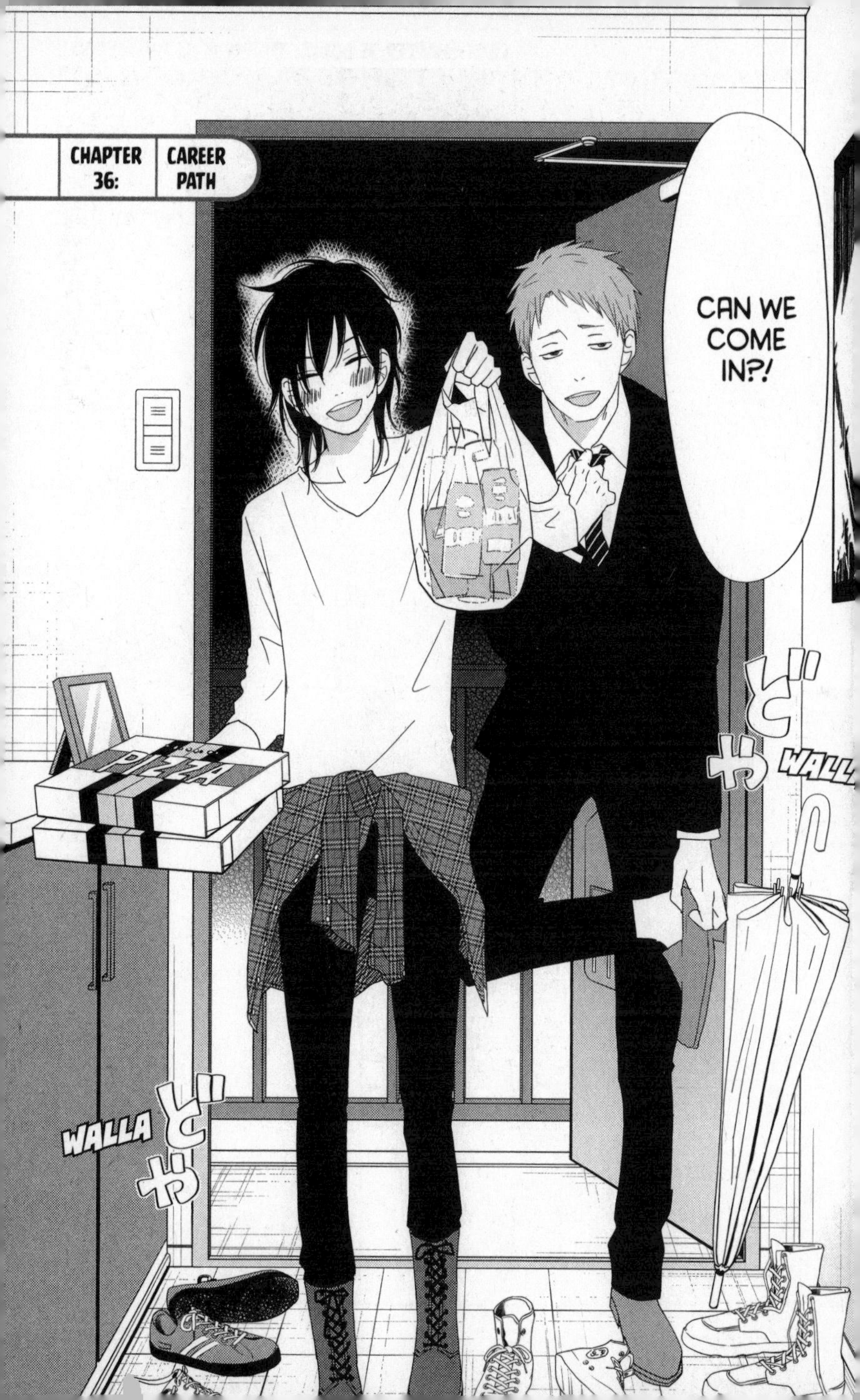
CAN WE COME IN?!
CHAPTER 36: CAREER PATH
どや WALLA
どや WALLA

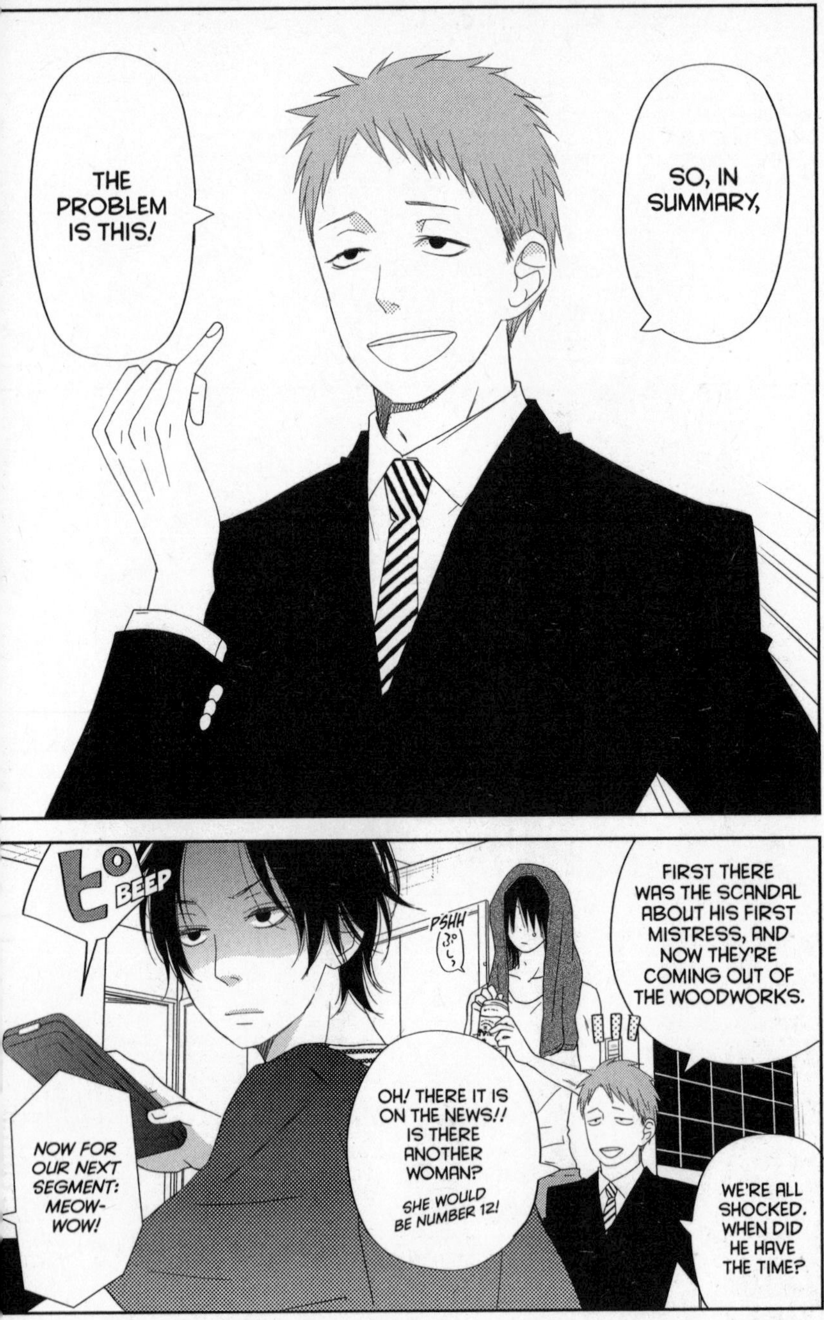
SO, IN SUMMARY,
THE PROBLEM IS THIS!
FIRST THERE WAS THE SCANDAL ABOUT HIS FIRST MISTRESS, AND NOW THEY'RE COMING OUT OF THE WOODWORKS.
WE'RE ALL SHOCKED. WHEN DID HE HAVE THE TIME?
PSHH ぷしっ
OH! THERE IT IS ON THE NEWS!! IS THERE ANOTHER WOMAN?
SHE WOULD BE NUMBER 12!
ピッ BEEP
NOW FOR OUR NEXT SEGMENT: MEOW-WOW!

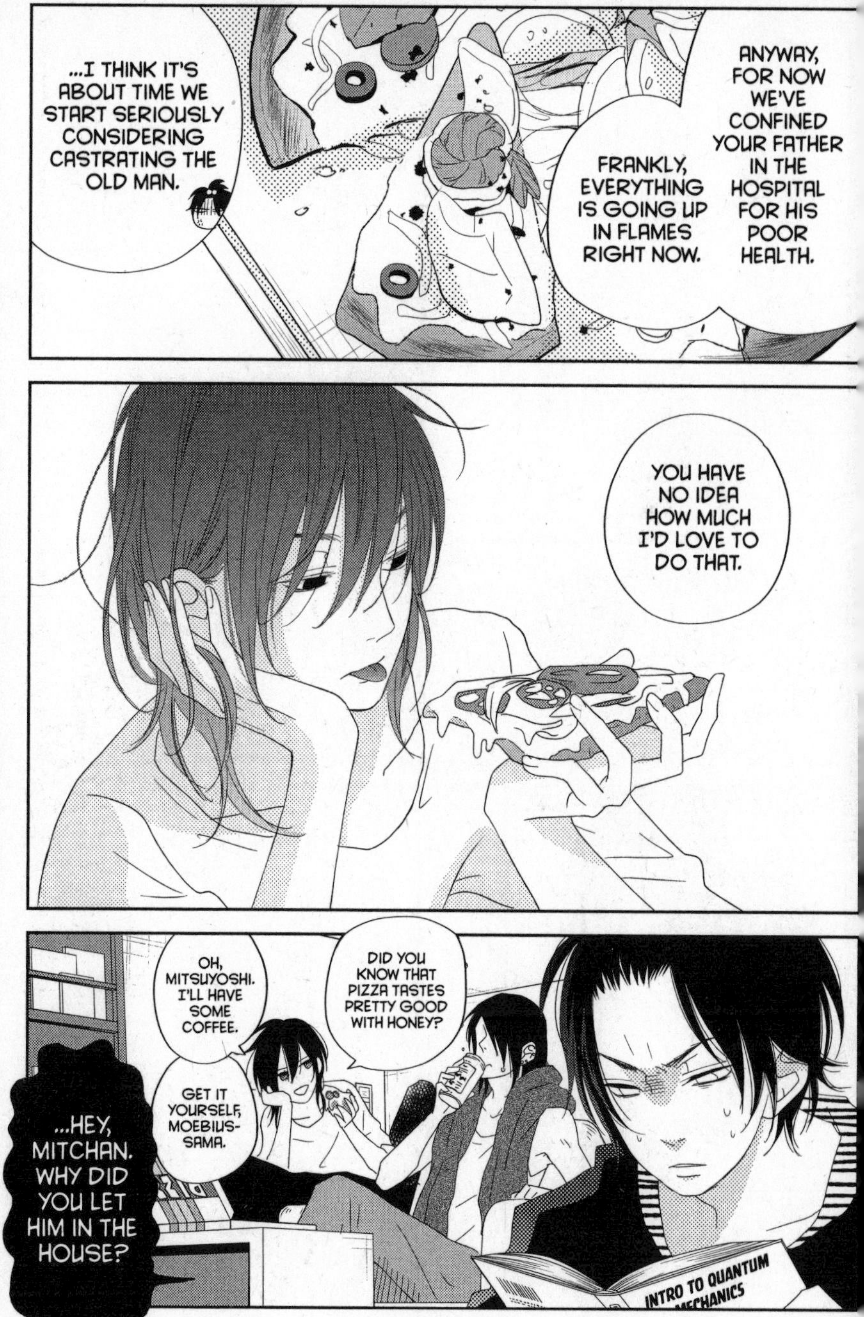
ANYWAY, FOR NOW WE'VE CONFINED YOUR FATHER IN THE HOSPITAL FOR HIS POOR HEALTH.
FRANKLY, EVERYTHING IS GOING UP IN FLAMES RIGHT NOW.
...I THINK IT'S ABOUT TIME WE START SERIOUSLY CONSIDERING CASTRATING THE OLD MAN.
YOU HAVE NO IDEA HOW MUCH I'D LOVE TO DO THAT.
DID YOU KNOW THAT PIZZA TASTES PRETTY GOOD WITH HONEY?
OH, MITSUYOSHI. I'LL HAVE SOME COFFEE.
GET IT YOURSELF, MOEBIUS-SAMA.
INTRO TO QUANTUM MECHANICS
...HEY, MITCHAN. WHY DID YOU LET HIM IN THE HOUSE?

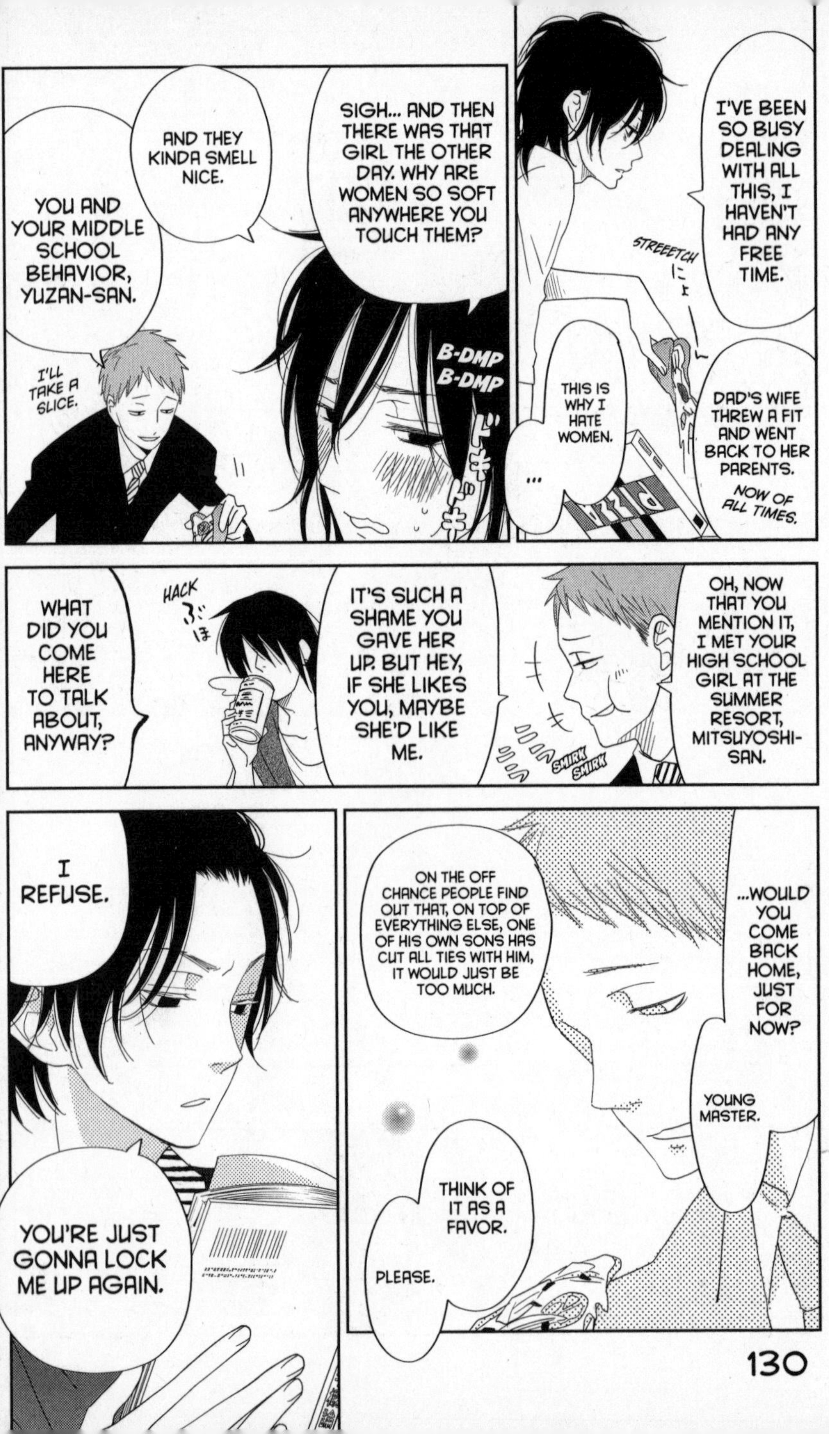
I'VE BEEN SO BUSY DEALING WITH ALL THIS, I HAVEN'T HAD ANY FREE TIME.
STREEETCH
にょ
DAD'S WIFE THREW A FIT AND WENT BACK TO HER PARENTS.
NOW OF ALL TIMES.
THIS IS WHY I HATE WOMEN.
...
SIGH... AND THEN THERE WAS THAT GIRL THE OTHER DAY. WHY ARE WOMEN SO SOFT ANYWHERE YOU TOUCH THEM?
B-DMP B-DMP
ドキドキ
AND THEY KINDA SMELL NICE.
YOU AND YOUR MIDDLE SCHOOL BEHAVIOR, YUZAN-SAN.
I'LL TAKE A SLICE.
OH, NOW THAT YOU MENTION IT, I MET YOUR HIGH SCHOOL GIRL AT THE SUMMER RESORT, MITSUYOSHI-SAN.
SMIRK SMIRK
IT'S SUCH A SHAME YOU GAVE HER UP. BUT HEY, IF SHE LIKES YOU, MAYBE SHE'D LIKE ME.
HACK
ぶほ
WHAT DID YOU COME HERE TO TALK ABOUT, ANYWAY?
...WOULD YOU COME BACK HOME, JUST FOR NOW?
YOUNG MASTER.
ON THE OFF CHANCE PEOPLE FIND OUT THAT, ON TOP OF EVERYTHING ELSE, ONE OF HIS OWN SONS HAS CUT ALL TIES WITH HIM, IT WOULD JUST BE TOO MUCH.
THINK OF IT AS A FAVOR.
PLEASE.
I REFUSE.
YOU'RE JUST GONNA LOCK ME UP AGAIN.

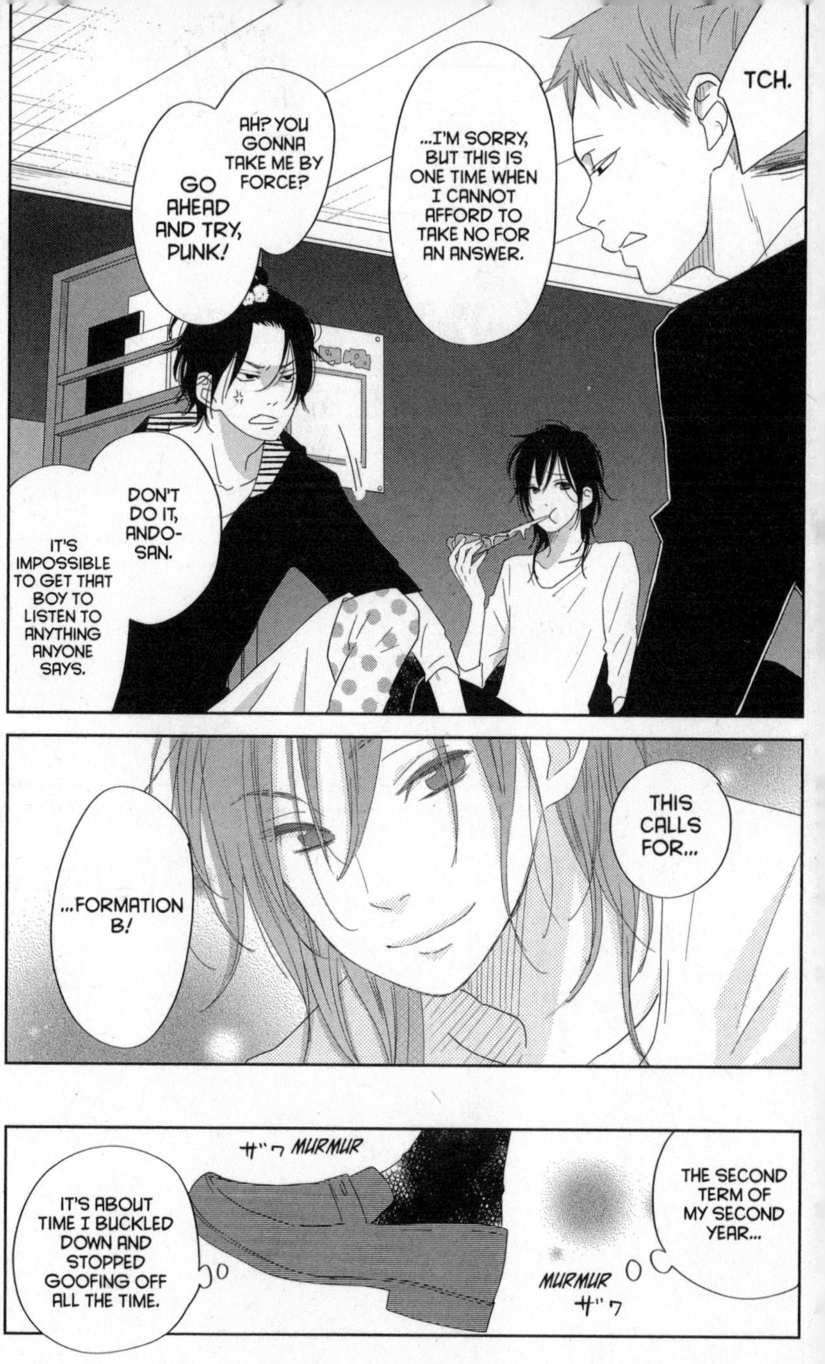
TCH.
...I'M SORRY, BUT THIS IS ONE TIME WHEN I CANNOT AFFORD TO TAKE NO FOR AN ANSWER.
AH? YOU GONNA TAKE ME BY FORCE?
GO AHEAD AND TRY, PUNK!
DON'T DO IT, ANDO-SAN.
IT'S IMPOSSIBLE TO GET THAT BOY TO LISTEN TO ANYTHING ANYONE SAYS.
THIS CALLS FOR...
...FORMATION B!
THE SECOND TERM OF MY SECOND YEAR...
MURMUR ザワ
ザワ MURMUR
IT'S ABOUT TIME I BUCKLED DOWN AND STOPPED GOOFING OFF ALL THE TIME.

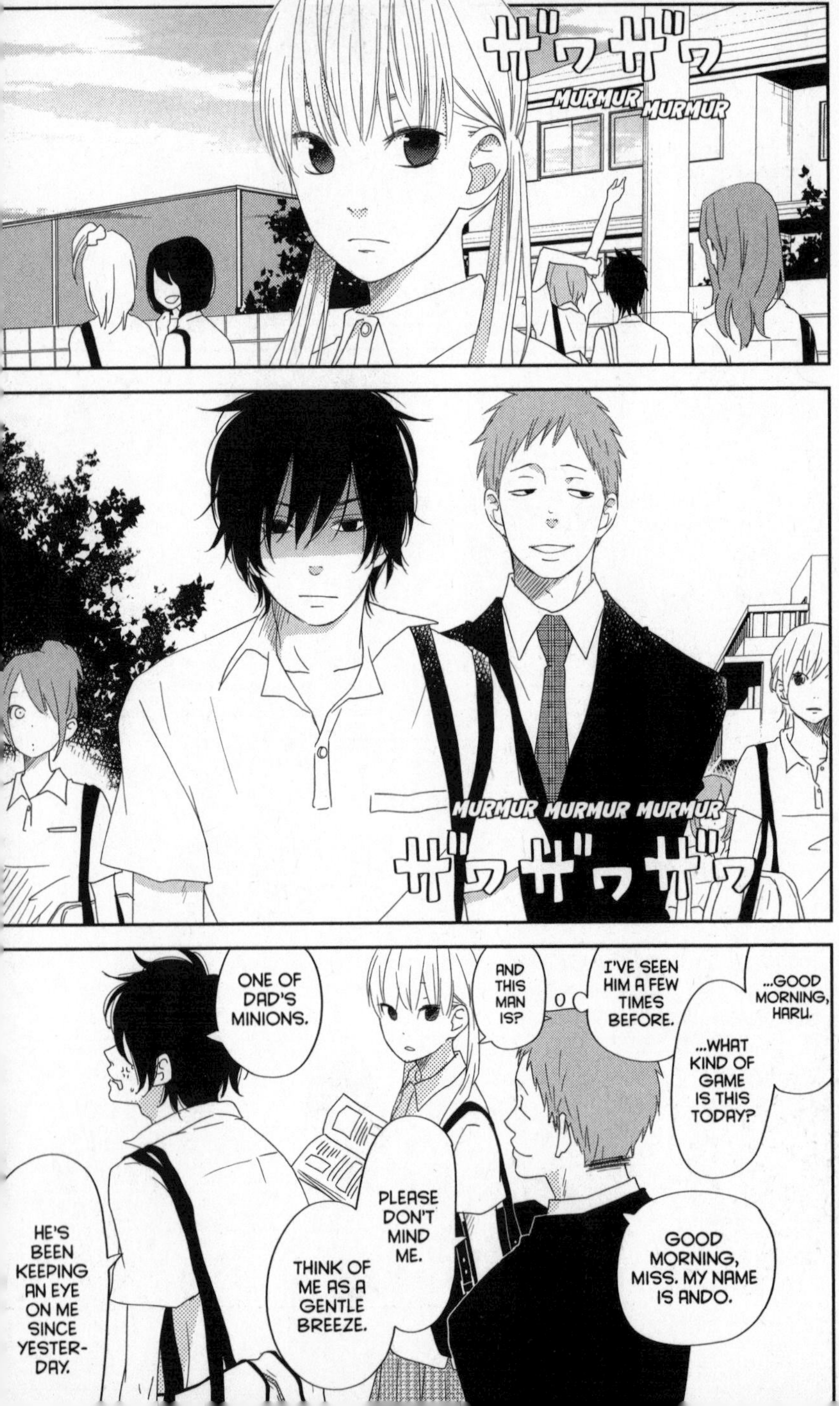
ザワザワ
MURMUR MURMUR
MURMUR MURMUR MURMUR
ザヮザヮザワ
...GOOD MORNING, HARU.
...WHAT KIND OF GAME IS THIS TODAY?
I'VE SEEN HIM A FEW TIMES BEFORE.
AND THIS MAN IS?
ONE OF DAD'S MINIONS.
GOOD MORNING, MISS. MY NAME IS ANDO.
PLEASE DON'T MIND ME.
THINK OF ME AS A GENTLE BREEZE.
HE'S BEEN KEEPING AN EYE ON ME SINCE YESTER-DAY.

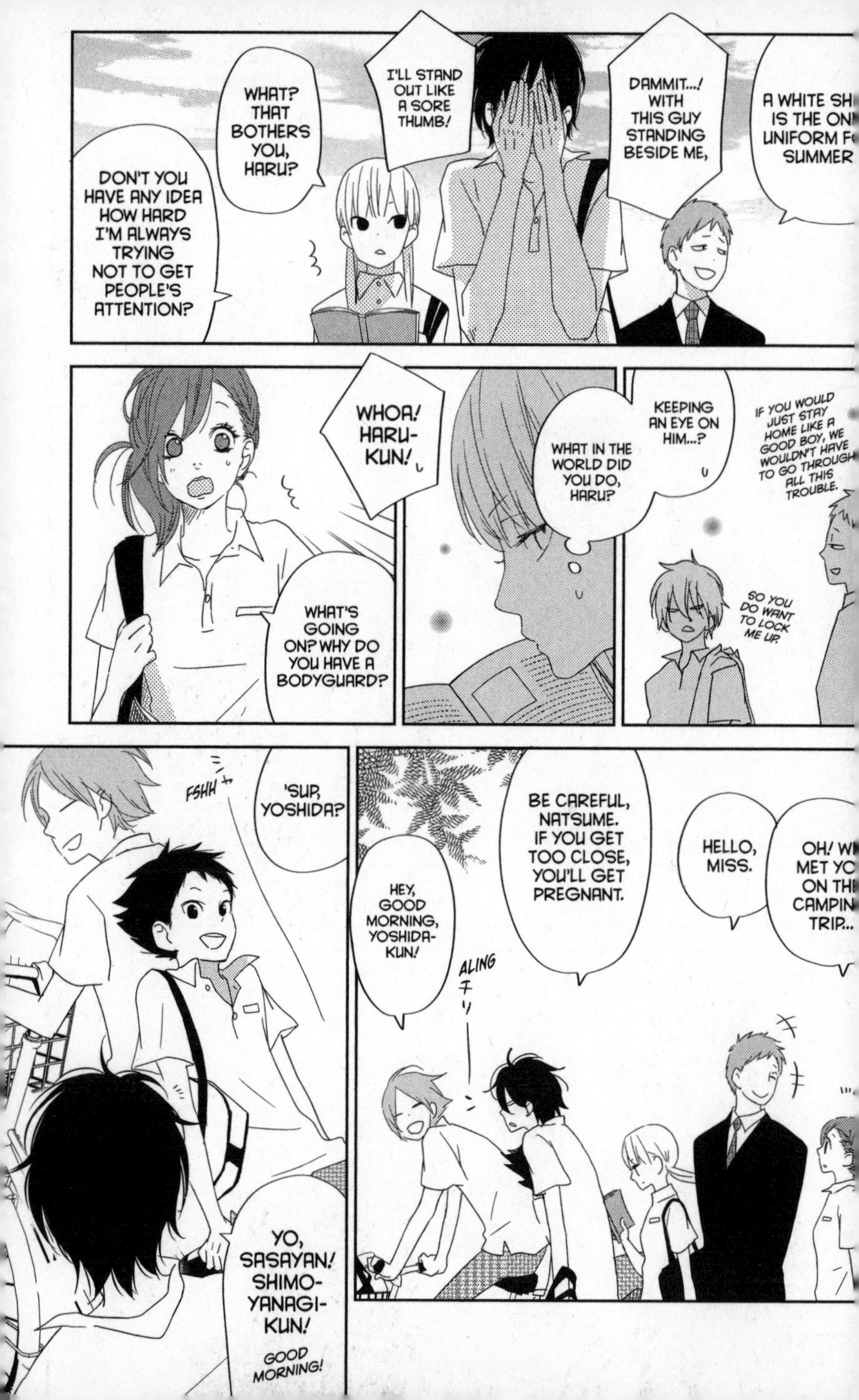
A WHITE SH IS THE ON UNIFORM F SUMMER
DAMMIT...! WITH THIS GUY STANDING BESIDE ME,
I'LL STAND OUT LIKE A SORE THUMB!
WHAT? THAT BOTHERS YOU, HARU?
DON'T YOU HAVE ANY IDEA HOW HARD I'M ALWAYS TRYING NOT TO GET PEOPLE'S ATTENTION?
IF YOU WOULD JUST STAY HOME LIKE A GOOD BOY, WE WOULDN'T HAVE TO GO THROUGH ALL THIS TROUBLE.
SO YOU DO WANT TO LOCK ME UP.
KEEPING AN EYE ON HIM...?
WHAT IN THE WORLD DID YOU DO, HARU?
WHOA! HARU-KUN!
WHAT'S GOING ON? WHY DO YOU HAVE A BODYGUARD?
OH! W MET YO ON TH CAMPIN TRIP...
HELLO, MISS.
BE CAREFUL, NATSUME. IF YOU GET TOO CLOSE, YOU'LL GET PREGNANT.
HEY, GOOD MORNING, YOSHIDA-KUN!
ALING
'SUP, YOSHIDA?
FSHH
YO, SASAYAN! SHIMO-YANAGI-KUN!
GOOD MORNING!

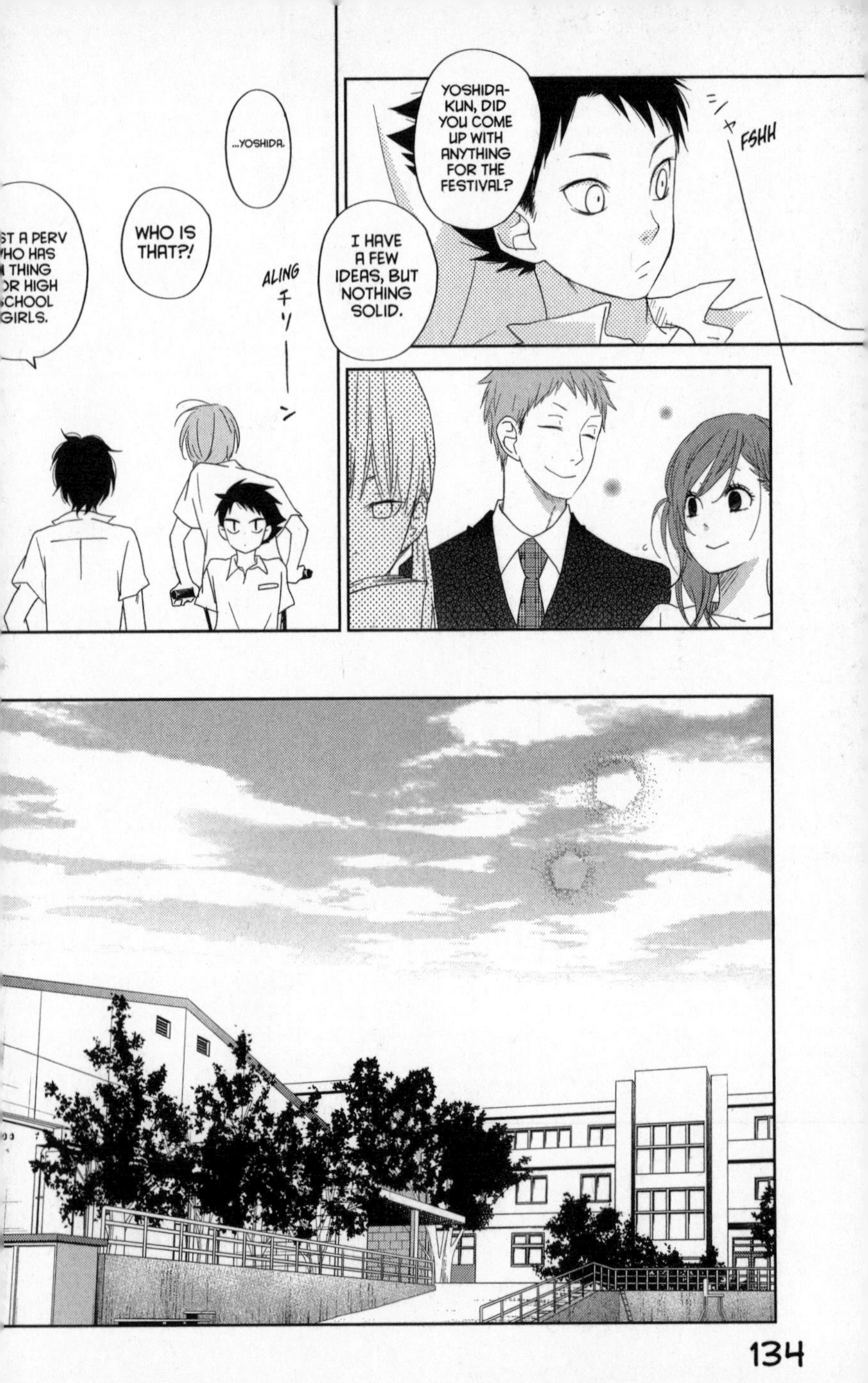
YOSHIDA-KUN, DID YOU COME UP WITH ANYTHING FOR THE FESTIVAL?
シャ
FSHH
I HAVE A FEW IDEAS, BUT NOTHING SOLID.
...YOSHIDA.
WHO IS THAT?!
ST A PERV HO HAS THING OR HIGH SCHOOL GIRLS.
ALING
チリーン

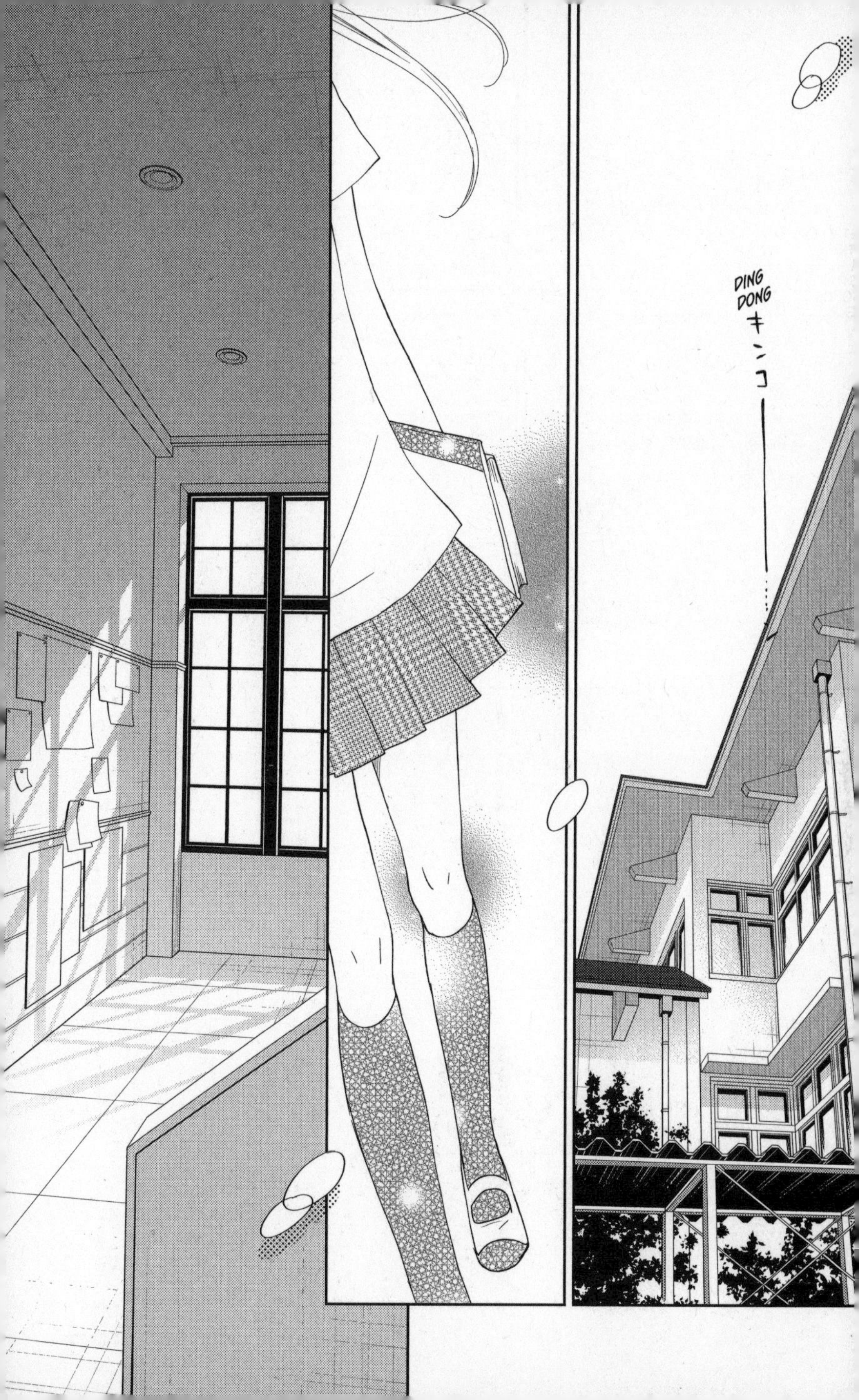
DING DONG
キンコ——

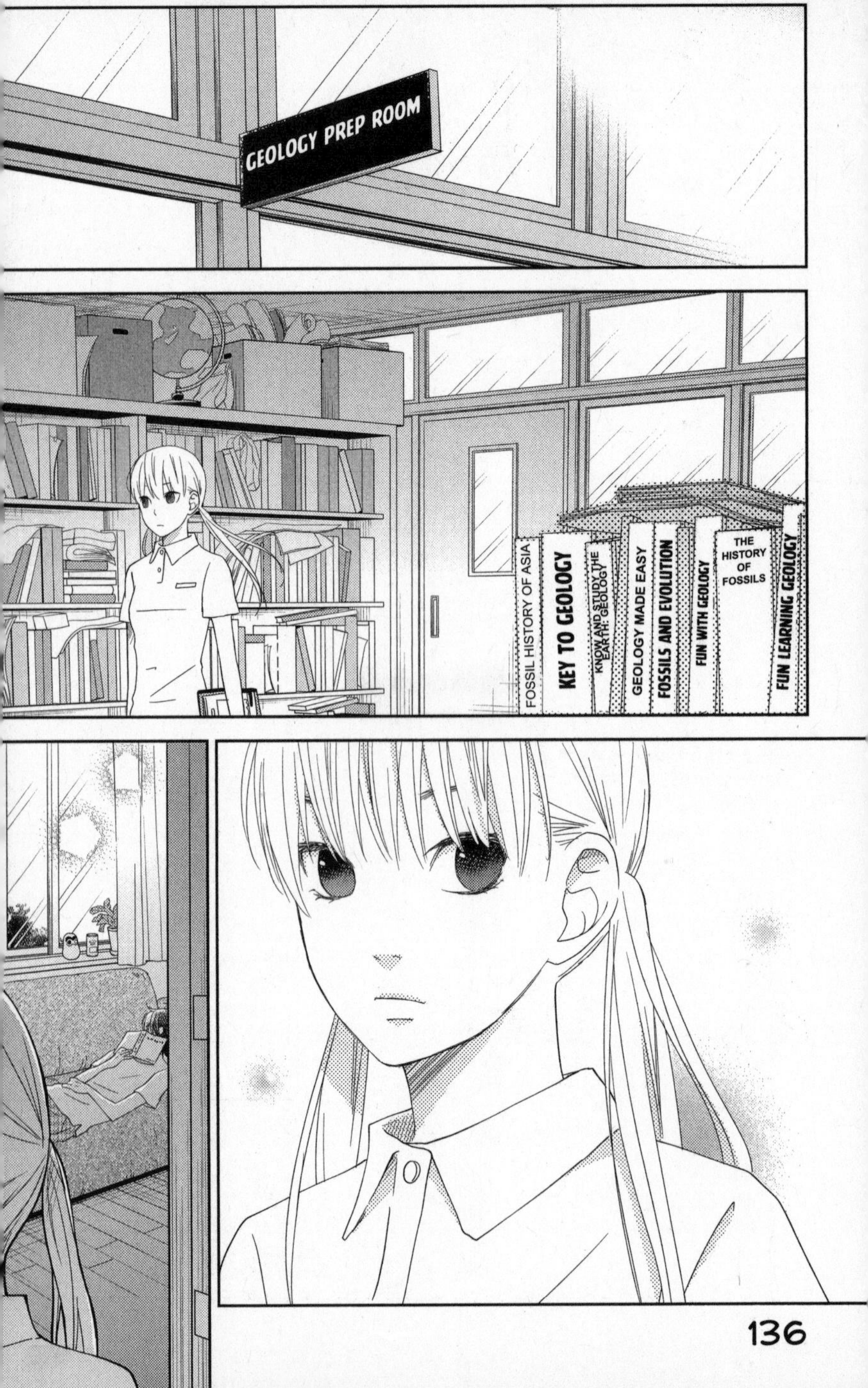
GEOLOGY PREP ROOM
FUN LEARNING GEOLOGY
THE HISTORY OF FOSSILS
FUN WITH GEOLOGY
FOSSILS AND EVOLUTION
GEOLOGY MADE EASY
KNOW AND STUDY THE EARTH: GEOLOGY
KEY TO GEOLOGY
FOSSIL HISTORY OF ASIA

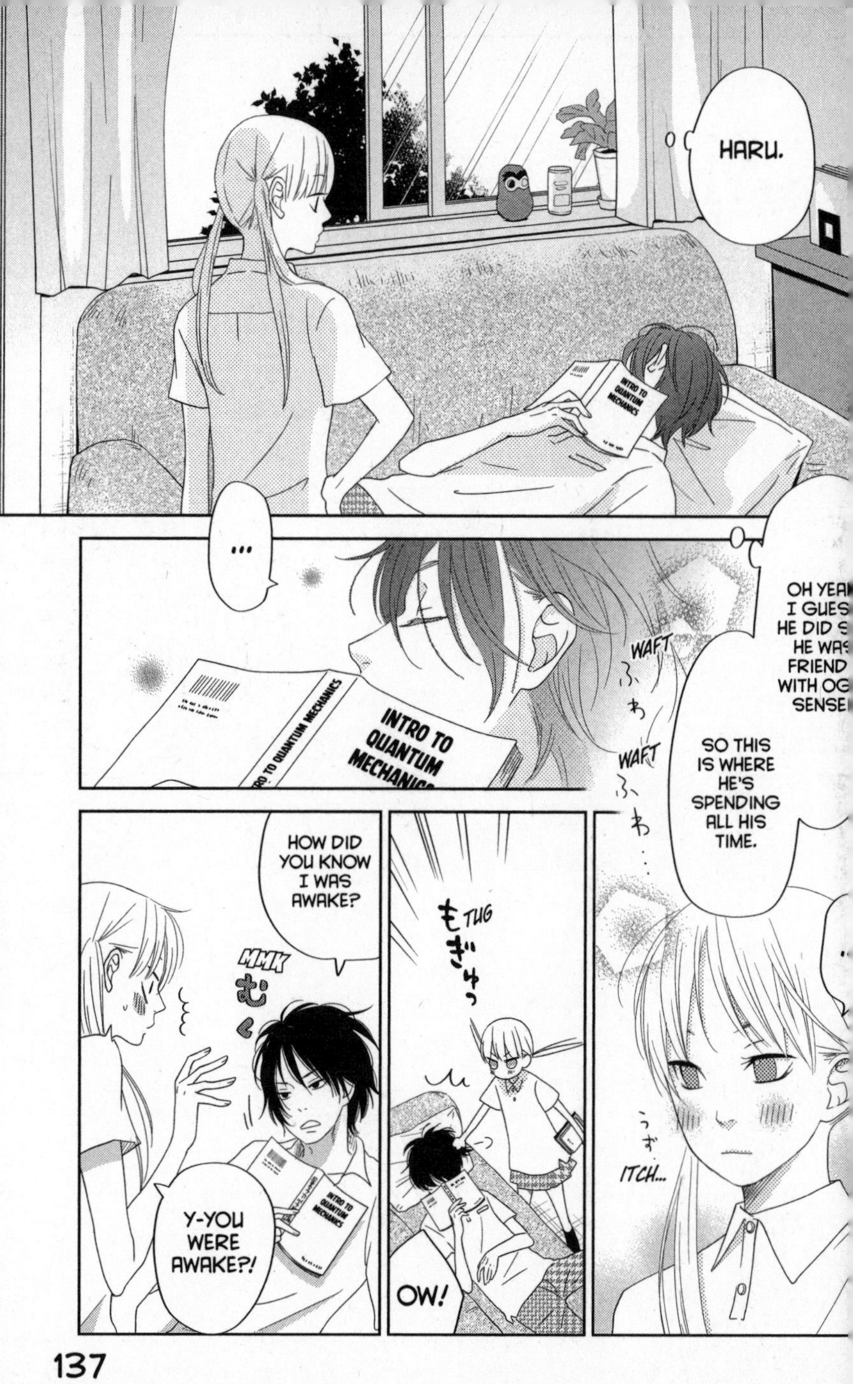
HARU.
OH YEA I GUES HE DID S HE WAS FRIEND WITH OG SENSE
SO THIS IS WHERE HE'S SPENDING ALL HIS TIME.
WAFT ふわ
WAFT ふわ...
ITCH... うず
...
TUG もぎゅっ
OW!
HOW DID YOU KNOW I WAS AWAKE?
MMK むく
Y-YOU WERE AWAKE?!

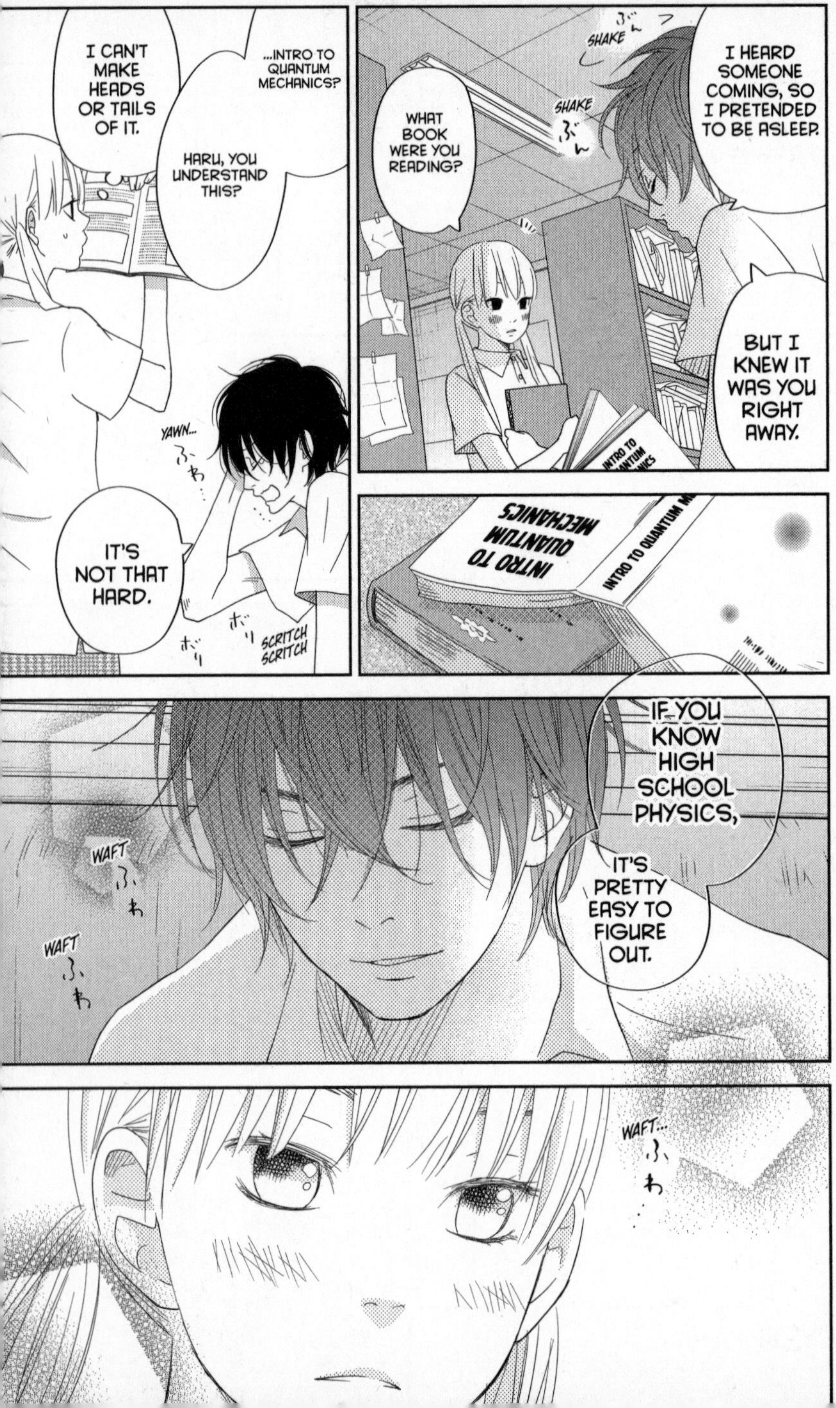
SHAKE ぶん
SHAKE ぶん
I HEARD SOMEONE COMING, SO I PRETENDED TO BE ASLEEP.
WHAT BOOK WERE YOU READING?
BUT I KNEW IT WAS YOU RIGHT AWAY.
INTRO TO QUANTUM MECHANICS
INTRO TO QUANTUM
...INTRO TO QUANTUM MECHANICS?
I CAN'T MAKE HEADS OR TAILS OF IT.
HARU, YOU UNDERSTAND THIS?
YAWN... ふわ...
IT'S NOT THAT HARD.
SCRITCH SCRITCH ボリ ボリ
IF YOU KNOW HIGH SCHOOL PHYSICS,
IT'S PRETTY EASY TO FIGURE OUT.
WAFT ふわ
WAFT ふわ
WAFT... ふわ...

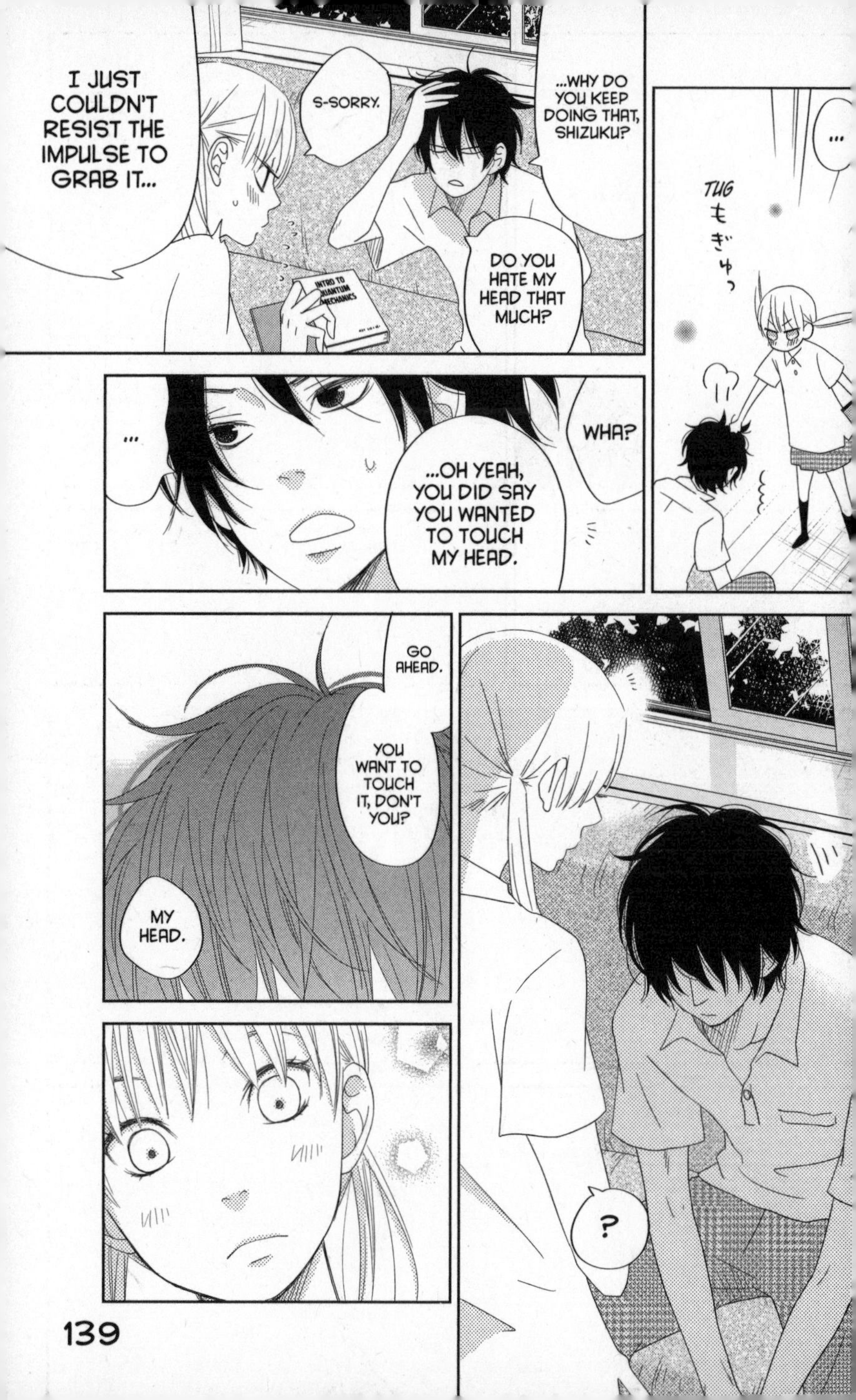
...
TUG もぎゅっ
...WHY DO YOU KEEP DOING THAT, SHIZUKU?
DO YOU HATE MY HEAD THAT MUCH?
S-SORRY.
I JUST COULDN'T RESIST THE IMPULSE TO GRAB IT...
INTRO TO QUANTUM MECHANICS
WHA?
...OH YEAH, YOU DID SAY YOU WANTED TO TOUCH MY HEAD.
...
?
GO AHEAD.
YOU WANT TO TOUCH IT, DON'T YOU?
MY HEAD.

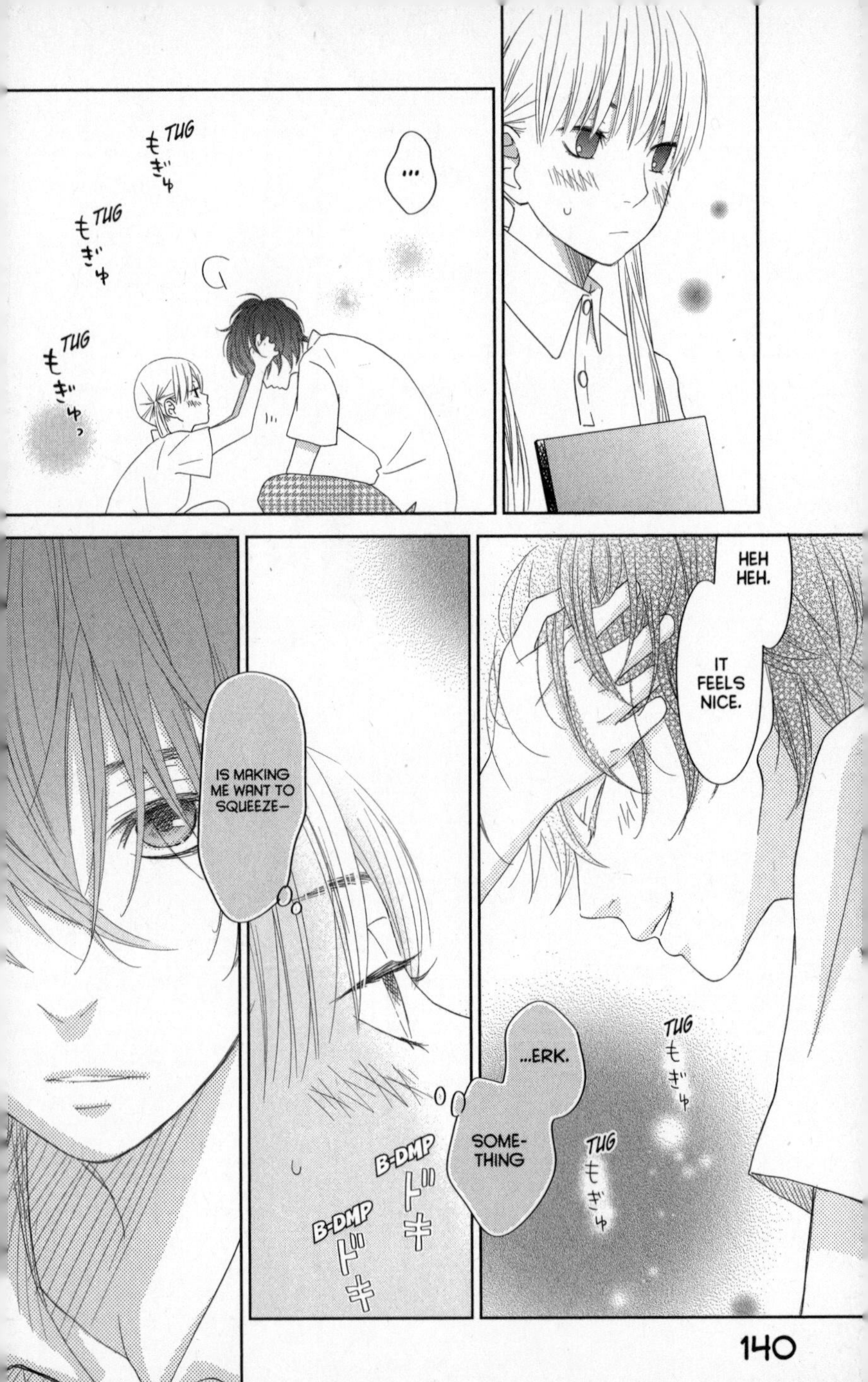
...
TUG もぎゅ
TUG もぎゅ
TUG もぎゅっ
HEH HEH.
IT FEELS NICE.
TUG もぎゅ
TUG もぎゅ
...ERK.
SOME-THING
B-DMP ドキ
B-DMP ドキ
IS MAKING ME WANT TO SQUEEZE—

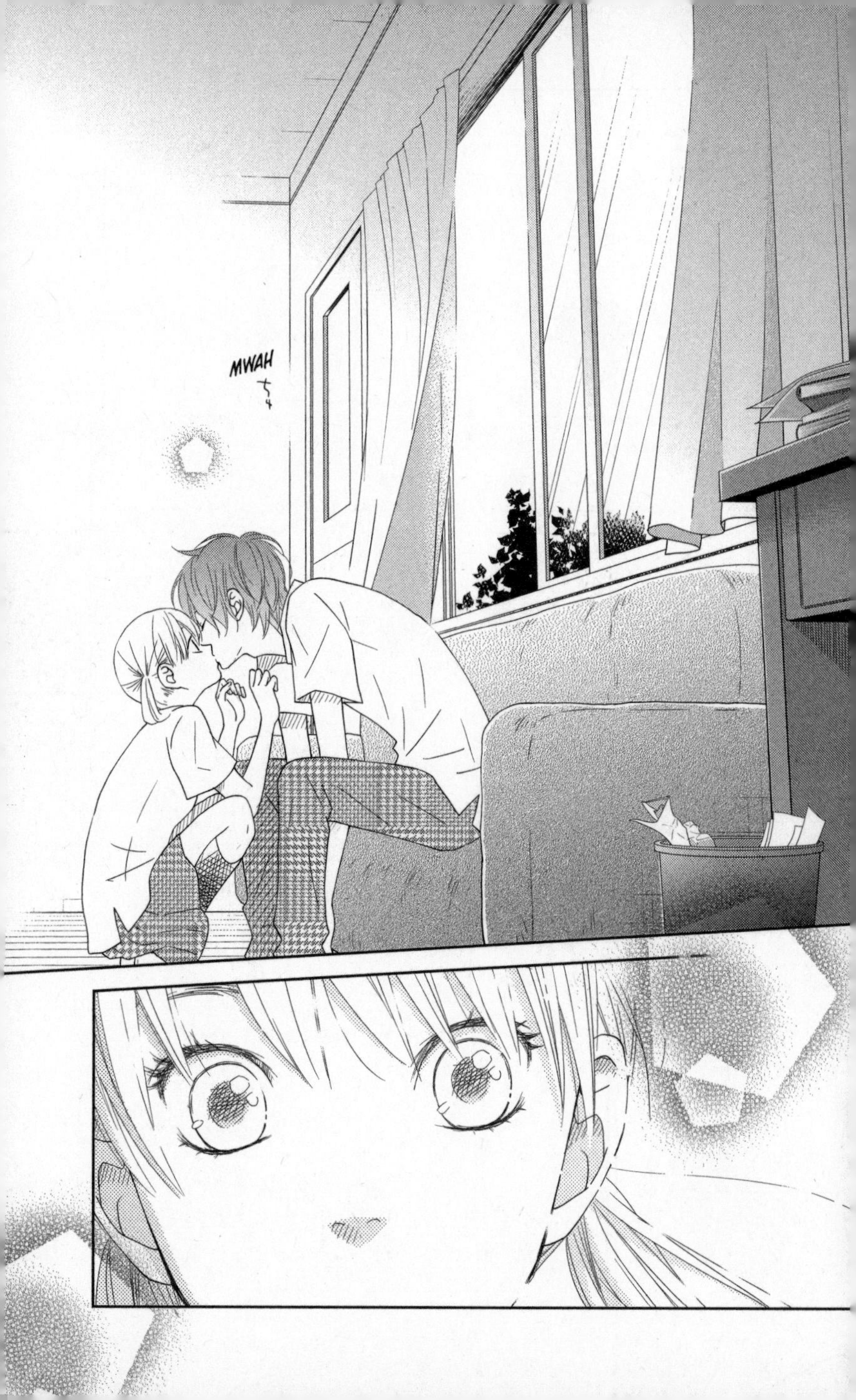
MWAH
ちゅ

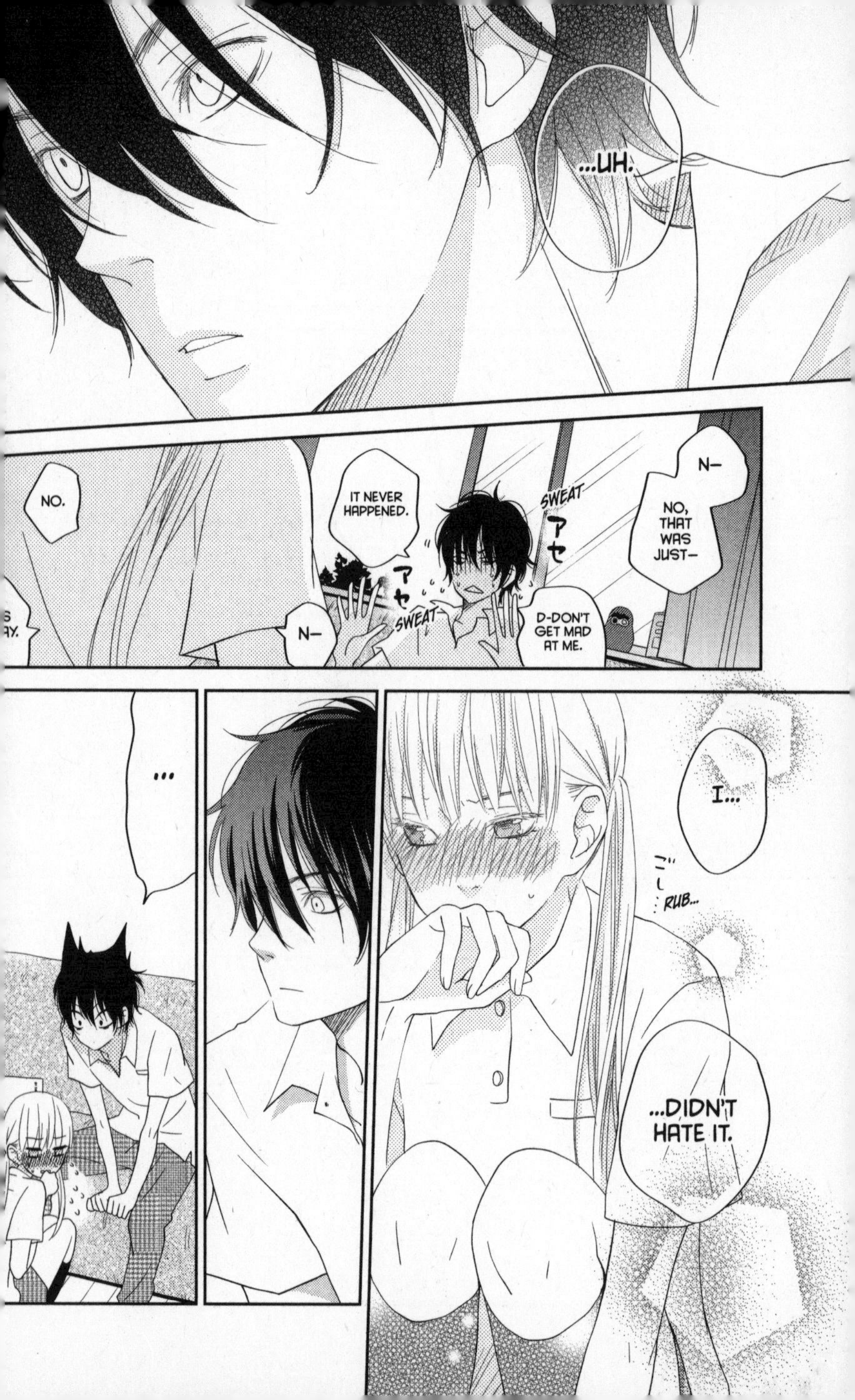

...UH.
N—
NO, THAT WAS JUST—
SWEAT アセ
D-DON'T GET MAD AT ME.
IT NEVER HAPPENED.
アセ SWEAT
N—
NO.
I...
ごし RUB...
...DIDN'T HATE IT.
...

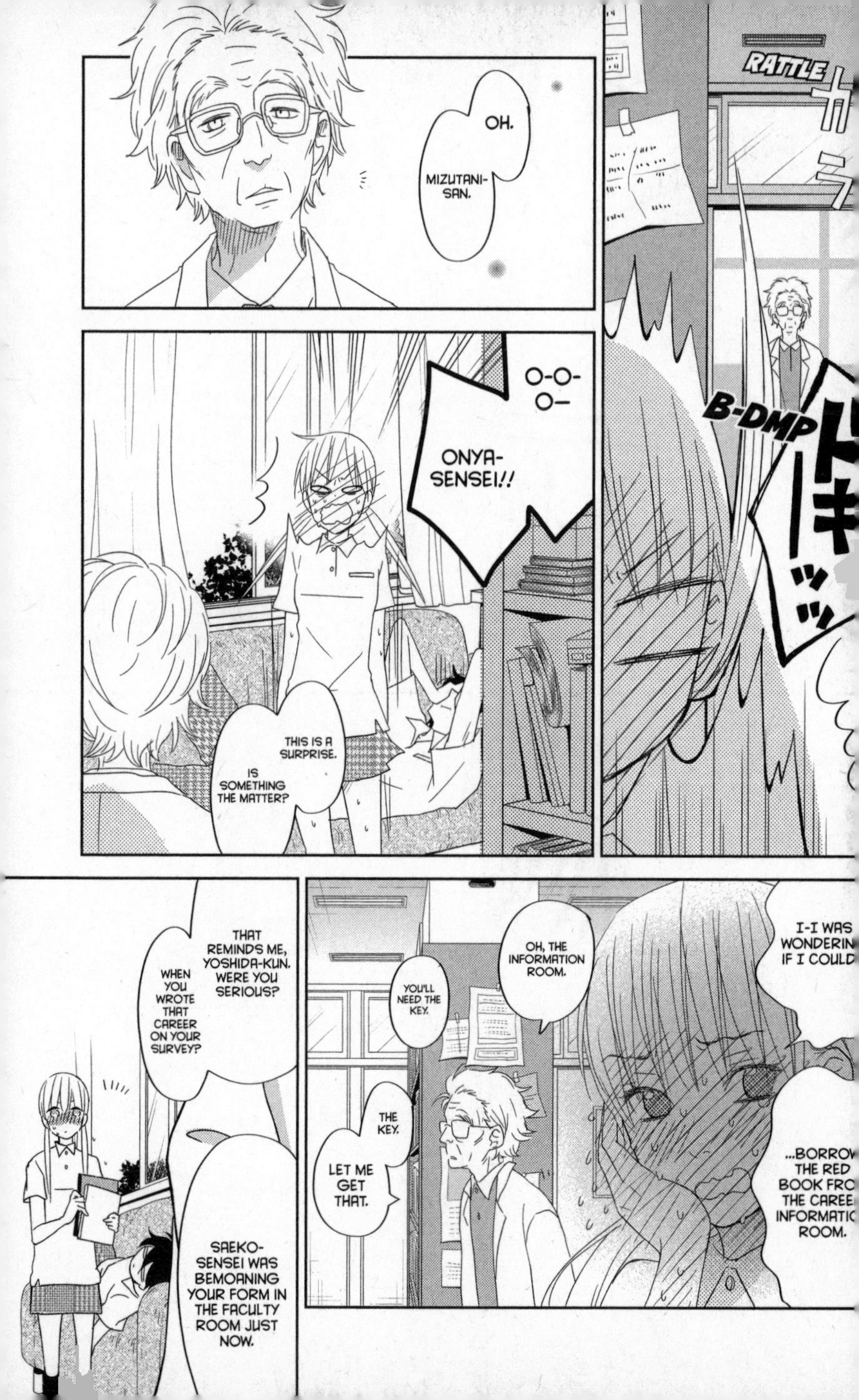
RATTLE
B-DMP
OH.
MIZUTANI-SAN.
O-O-O–
ONYA-SENSEI!!
THIS IS A SURPRISE.
IS SOMETHING THE MATTER?
I-I WAS WONDERIN IF I COULD
...BORROW THE RED BOOK FRO THE CAREE INFORMATIO ROOM.
OH, THE INFORMATION ROOM.
YOU'LL NEED THE KEY.
THE KEY.
LET ME GET THAT.
THAT REMINDS ME, YOSHIDA-KUN. WERE YOU SERIOUS?
WHEN YOU WROTE THAT CAREER ON YOUR SURVEY?
SAEKO-SENSEI WAS BEMOANING YOUR FORM IN THE FACULTY ROOM JUST NOW.

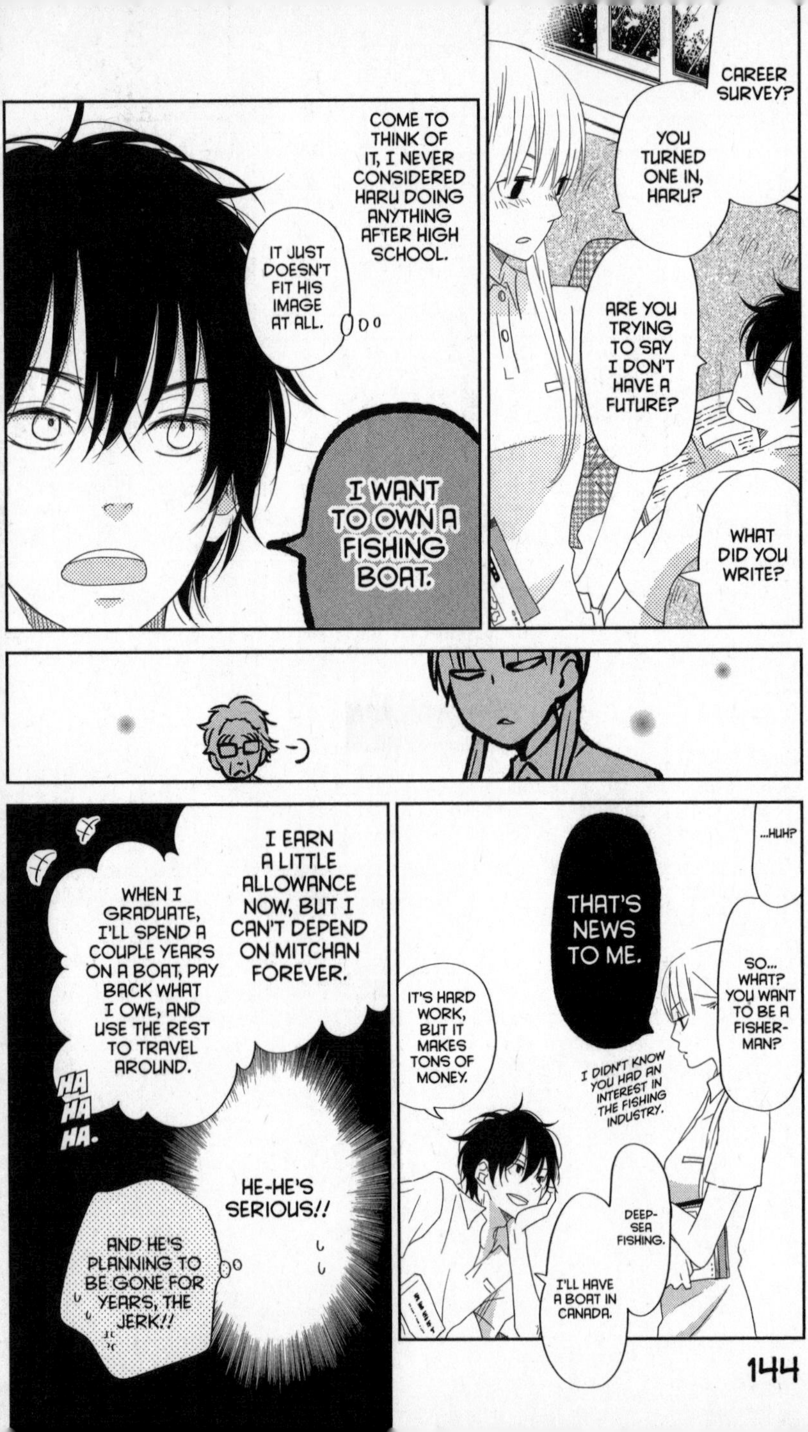
CAREER SURVEY?
YOU TURNED ONE IN, HARU?
ARE YOU TRYING TO SAY I DON'T HAVE A FUTURE?
WHAT DID YOU WRITE?
COME TO THINK OF IT, I NEVER CONSIDERED HARU DOING ANYTHING AFTER HIGH SCHOOL.
IT JUST DOESN'T FIT HIS IMAGE AT ALL.
I WANT TO OWN A FISHING BOAT.
...HUH?
THAT'S NEWS TO ME.
SO... WHAT? YOU WANT TO BE A FISHER-MAN?
I DIDN'T KNOW YOU HAD AN INTEREST IN THE FISHING INDUSTRY.
IT'S HARD WORK, BUT IT MAKES TONS OF MONEY.
DEEP-SEA FISHING.
I'LL HAVE A BOAT IN CANADA.
I EARN A LITTLE ALLOWANCE NOW, BUT I CAN'T DEPEND ON MITCHAN FOREVER.
WHEN I GRADUATE, I'LL SPEND A COUPLE YEARS ON A BOAT, PAY BACK WHAT I OWE, AND USE THE REST TO TRAVEL AROUND.
HA HA HA.
HE-HE'S SERIOUS!!
AND HE'S PLANNING TO BE GONE FOR YEARS, THE JERK!!

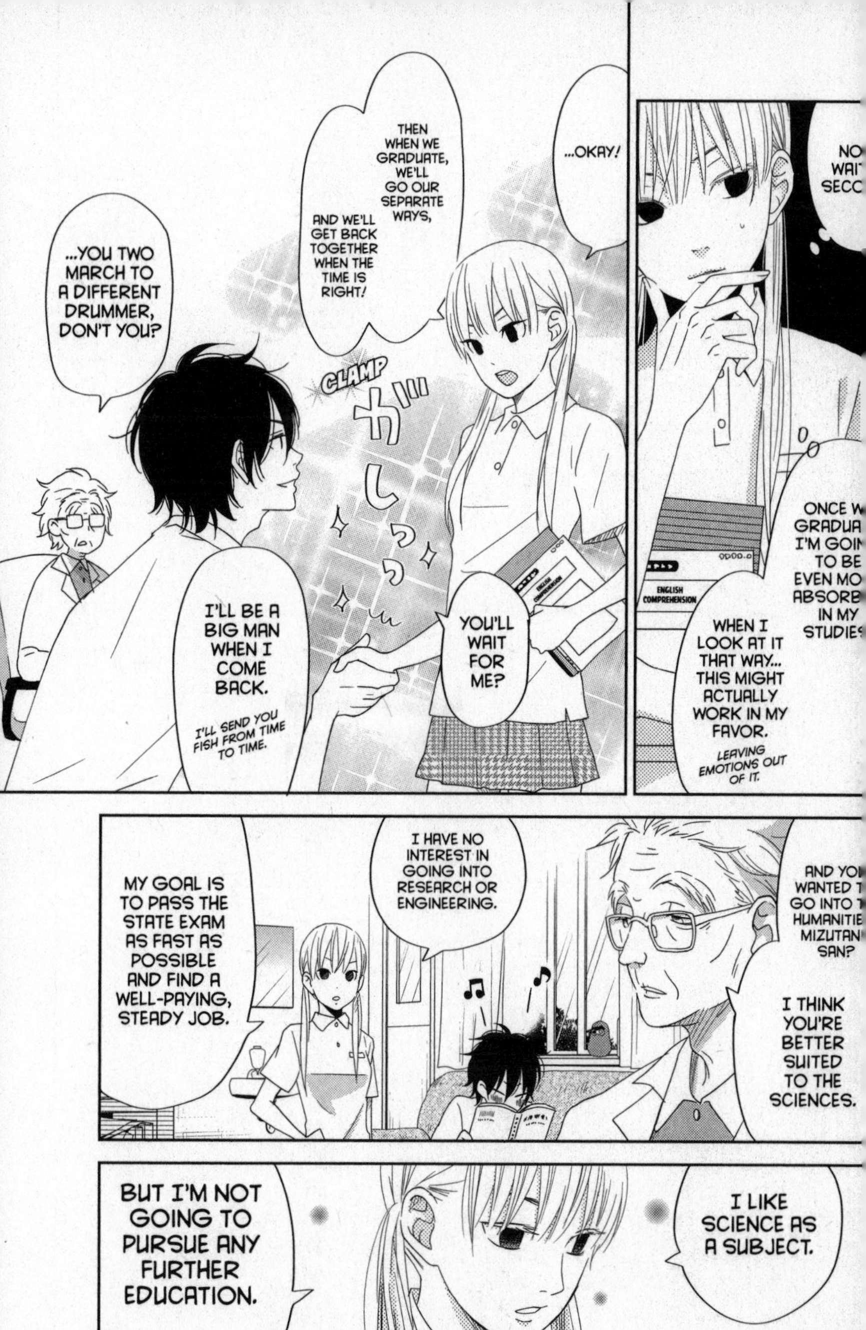
NO WAI SECO
ONCE W GRADUA I'M GOIN TO BE EVEN MO ABSORB IN MY STUDIES
WHEN I LOOK AT IT THAT WAY... THIS MIGHT ACTUALLY WORK IN MY FAVOR.
LEAVING EMOTIONS OUT OF IT.
ENGLISH COMPREHENSION
...OKAY!
THEN WHEN WE GRADUATE, WE'LL GO OUR SEPARATE WAYS,
AND WE'LL GET BACK TOGETHER WHEN THE TIME IS RIGHT!
...YOU TWO MARCH TO A DIFFERENT DRUMMER, DON'T YOU?
CLAMP
かしっ
YOU'LL WAIT FOR ME?
I'LL BE A BIG MAN WHEN I COME BACK.
I'LL SEND YOU FISH FROM TIME TO TIME.
AND YO WANTED T GO INTO T HUMANITIE MIZUTAN SAN?
I THINK YOU'RE BETTER SUITED TO THE SCIENCES.
I HAVE NO INTEREST IN GOING INTO RESEARCH OR ENGINEERING.
MY GOAL IS TO PASS THE STATE EXAM AS FAST AS POSSIBLE AND FIND A WELL-PAYING, STEADY JOB.
I LIKE SCIENCE AS A SUBJECT.
BUT I'M NOT GOING TO PURSUE ANY FURTHER EDUCATION.

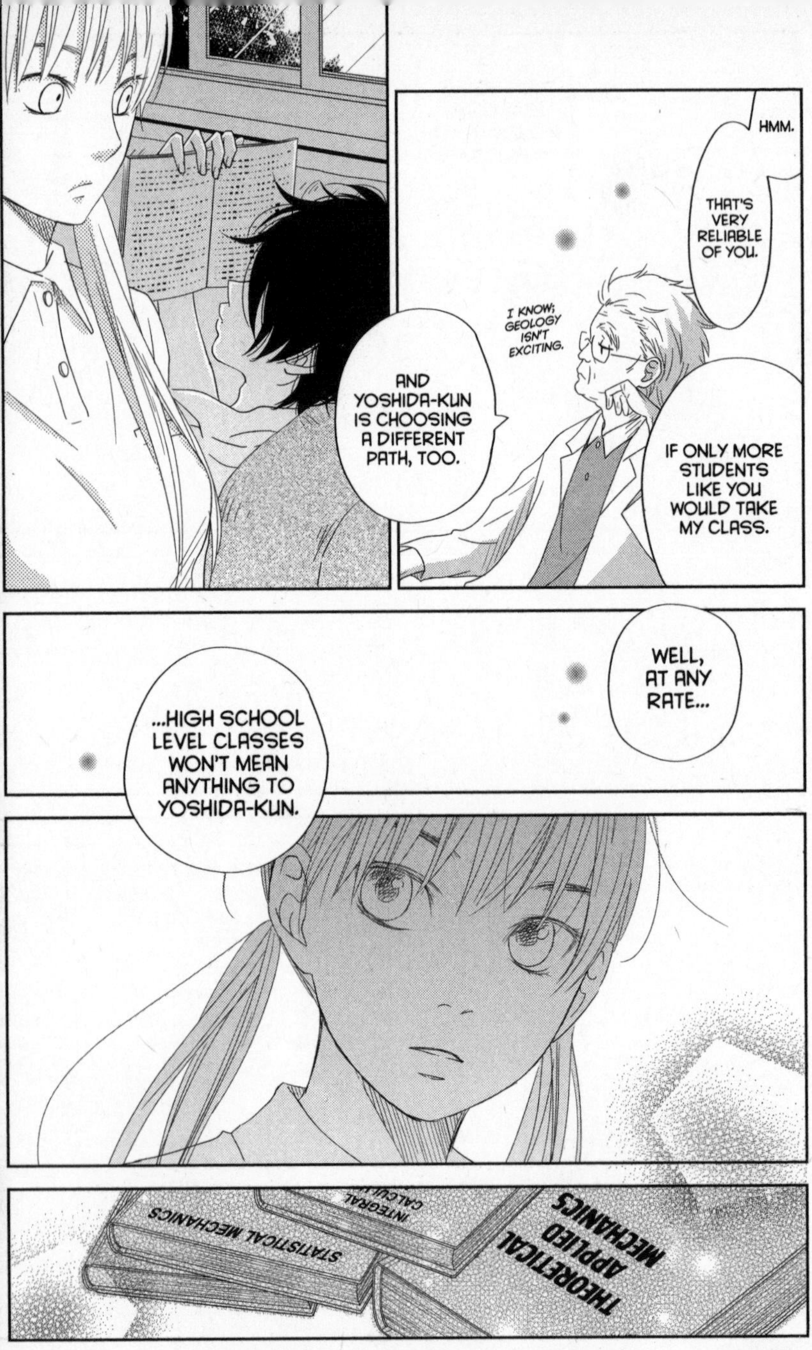
HMM.
THAT'S VERY RELIABLE OF YOU.
IF ONLY MORE STUDENTS LIKE YOU WOULD TAKE MY CLASS.
I KNOW; GEOLOGY ISN'T EXCITING.
AND YOSHIDA-KUN IS CHOOSING A DIFFERENT PATH, TOO.
WELL, AT ANY RATE...
...HIGH SCHOOL LEVEL CLASSES WON'T MEAN ANYTHING TO YOSHIDA-KUN.
THEORETICAL APPLIED MECHANICS
INTEGRAL
STATISTICAL MECHANICS

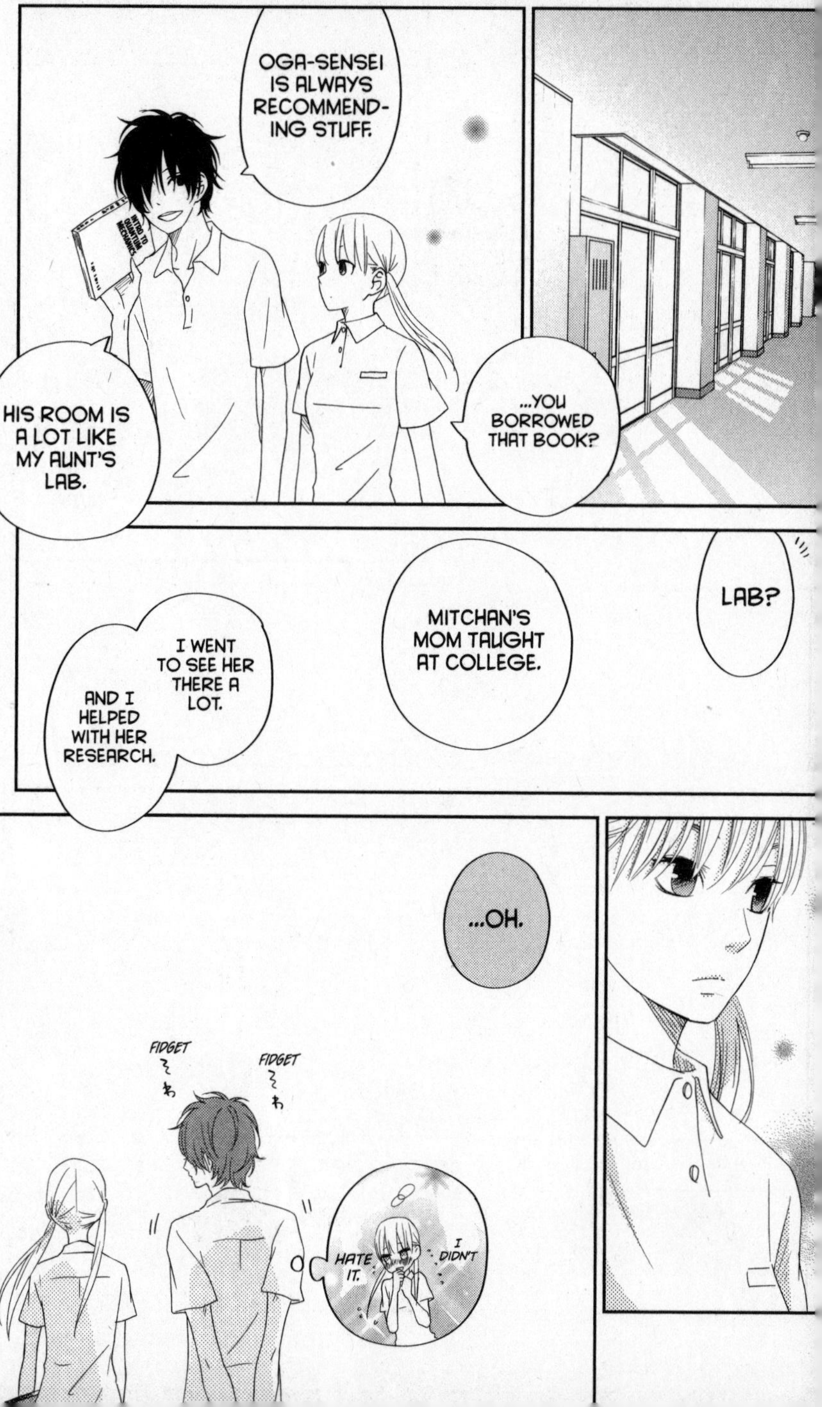
...YOU BORROWED THAT BOOK?
OGA-SENSEI IS ALWAYS RECOMMENDING STUFF.
INTRO TO QUANTUM MECHANICS
HIS ROOM IS A LOT LIKE MY AUNT'S LAB.
LAB?
MITCHAN'S MOM TAUGHT AT COLLEGE.
I WENT TO SEE HER THERE A LOT.
AND I HELPED WITH HER RESEARCH.
...OH.
FIDGET
FIDGET
I DIDN'T
HATE IT.

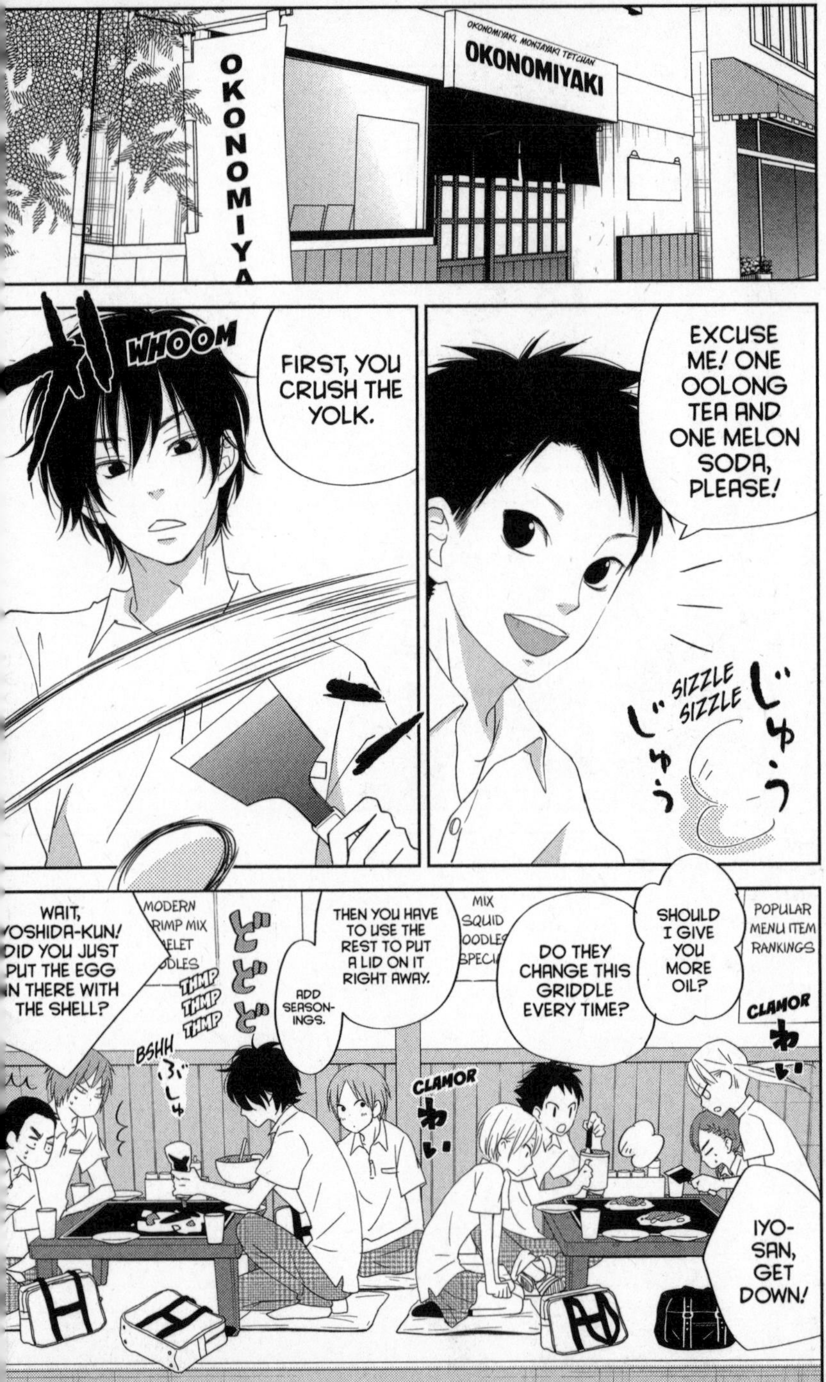
OKONOMIYAKI, MONJAYAKI TETCHAN
OKONOMIYAKI
OKONOMIYA
EXCUSE ME! ONE OOLONG TEA AND ONE MELON SODA, PLEASE!
SIZZLE SIZZLE
じゅうじゅう
WHOOM
FIRST, YOU CRUSH THE YOLK.
POPULAR MENU ITEM RANKINGS
CLAMOR
わー
SHOULD I GIVE YOU MORE OIL?
IYO-SAN, GET DOWN!
DO THEY CHANGE THIS GRIDDLE EVERY TIME?
MIX
SQUID
CLAMOR
わー
THEN YOU HAVE TO USE THE REST TO PUT A LID ON IT RIGHT AWAY.
ADD SEASONINGS.
どどど
THMP THMP THMP
BSHH
ぶしゅ
MODERN
WAIT, YOSHIDA-KUN! DID YOU JUST PUT THE EGG IN THERE WITH THE SHELL?

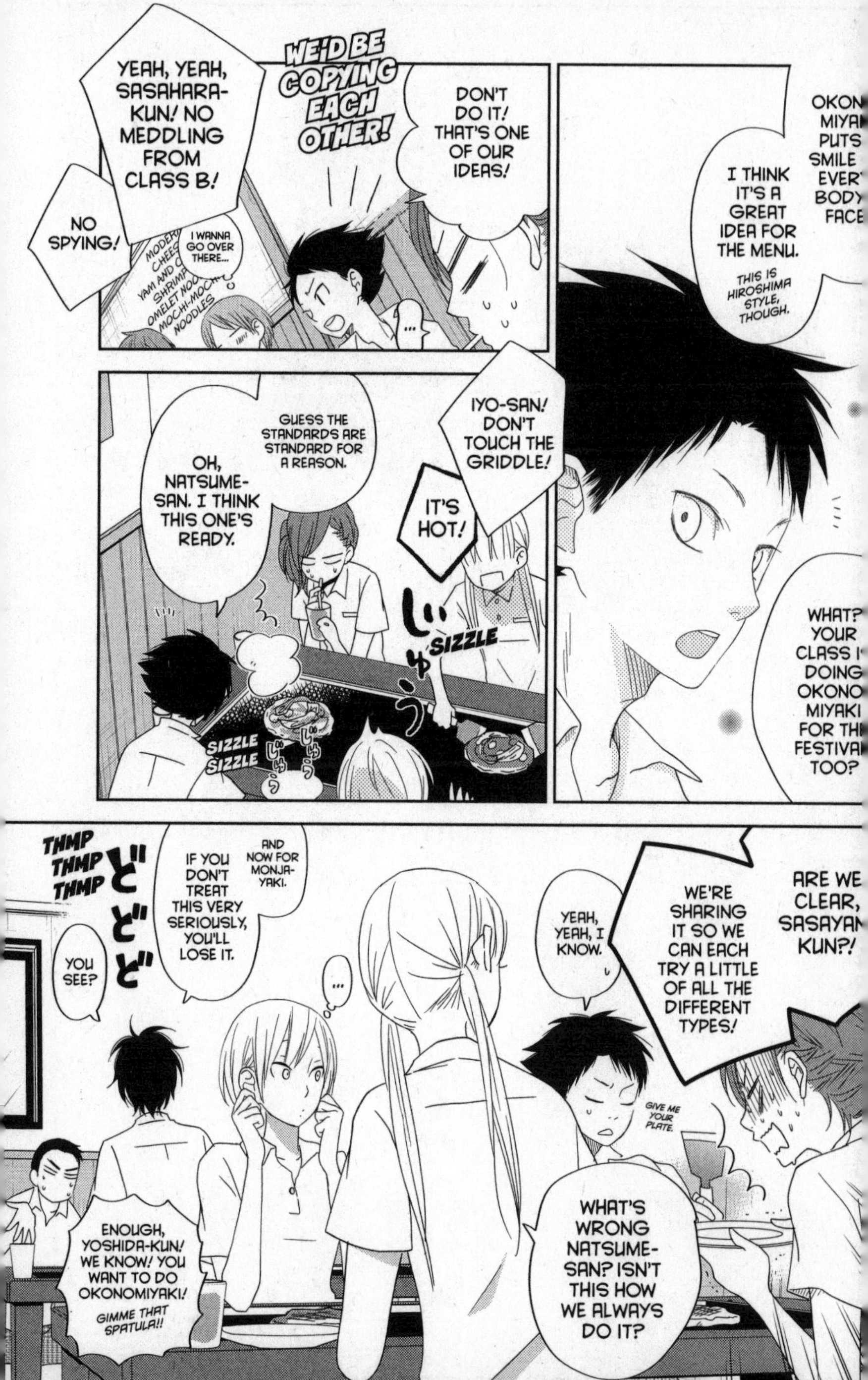
OKON MIYA PUTS SMILE EVER BODY FACE
I THINK IT'S A GREAT IDEA FOR THE MENU.
THIS IS HIROSHIMA STYLE, THOUGH.
WHAT? YOUR CLASS I DOING OKONO MIYAKI FOR TH FESTIVA TOO?
DON'T DO IT! THAT'S ONE OF OUR IDEAS!
WE'D BE COPYING EACH OTHER!
YEAH, YEAH, SASAHARA-KUN! NO MEDDLING FROM CLASS B!
NO SPYING!
I WANNA GO OVER THERE...
...
IYO-SAN! DON'T TOUCH THE GRIDDLE!
IT'S HOT!
GUESS THE STANDARDS ARE STANDARD FOR A REASON.
OH, NATSUME-SAN. I THINK THIS ONE'S READY.
じゅう SIZZLE
じゅう じゅう SIZZLE SIZZLE
ARE WE CLEAR, SASAYAN KUN?!
WE'RE SHARING IT SO WE CAN EACH TRY A LITTLE OF ALL THE DIFFERENT TYPES!
YEAH, YEAH, I KNOW.
GIVE ME YOUR PLATE.
AND NOW FOR MONJA-YAKI.
IF YOU DON'T TREAT THIS VERY SERIOUSLY, YOU'LL LOSE IT.
YOU SEE?
THMP THMP THMP どどど
...
WHAT'S WRONG NATSUME-SAN? ISN'T THIS HOW WE ALWAYS DO IT?
ENOUGH, YOSHIDA-KUN! WE KNOW! YOU WANT TO DO OKONOMIYAKI!
GIMME THAT SPATULA!!

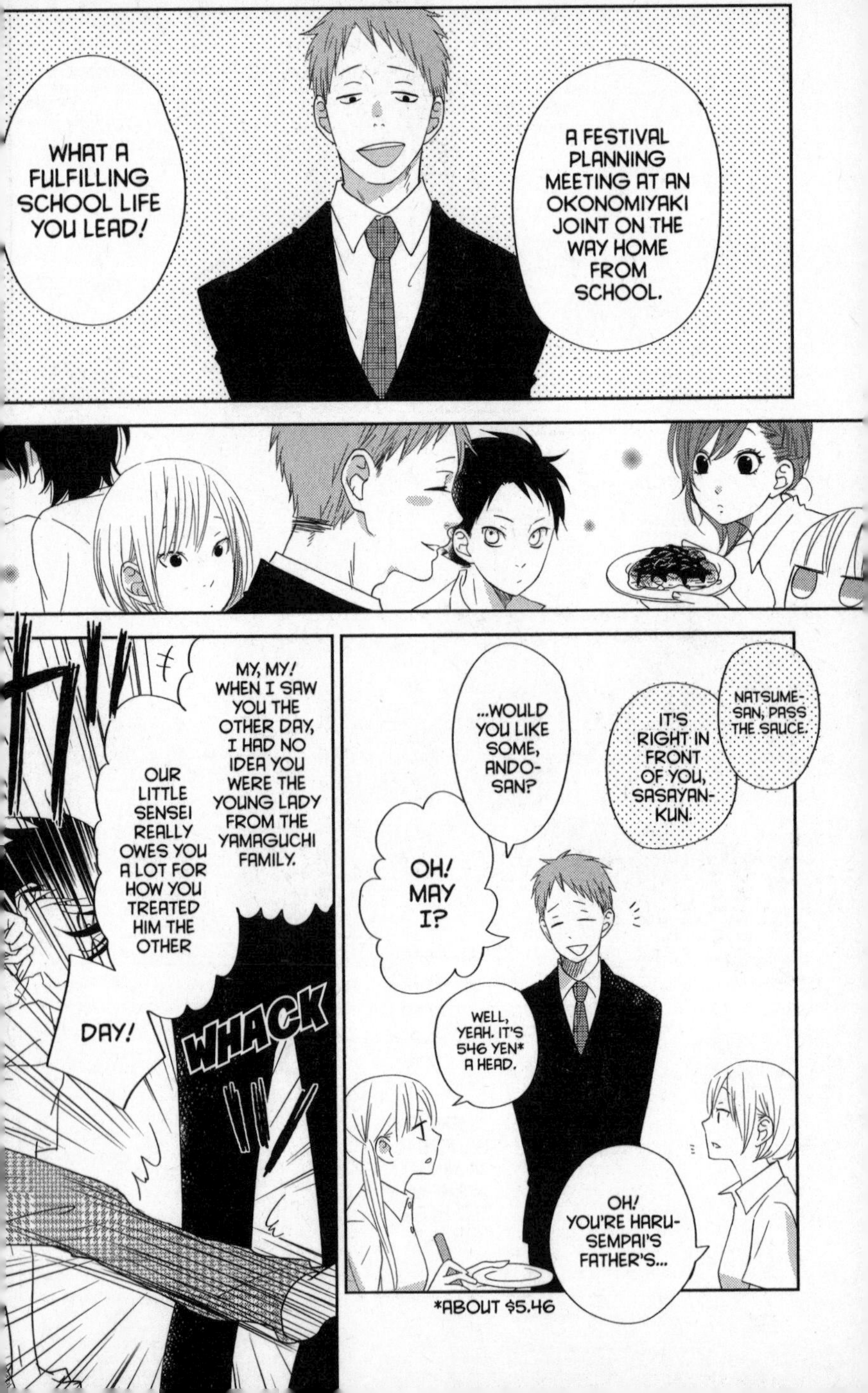
A FESTIVAL PLANNING MEETING AT AN OKONOMIYAKI JOINT ON THE WAY HOME FROM SCHOOL.
WHAT A FULFILLING SCHOOL LIFE YOU LEAD!
NATSUME-SAN, PASS THE SAUCE.
IT'S RIGHT IN FRONT OF YOU, SASAYAN-KUN.
...WOULD YOU LIKE SOME, ANDO-SAN?
OH! MAY I?
WELL, YEAH. IT'S 546 YEN* A HEAD.
OH! YOU'RE HARU-SEMPAI'S FATHER'S...
MY, MY! WHEN I SAW YOU THE OTHER DAY, I HAD NO IDEA YOU WERE THE YOUNG LADY FROM THE YAMAGUCHI FAMILY.
OUR LITTLE SENSEI REALLY OWES YOU A LOT FOR HOW YOU TREATED HIM THE OTHER
DAY!
WHACK

*ABOUT $5.46

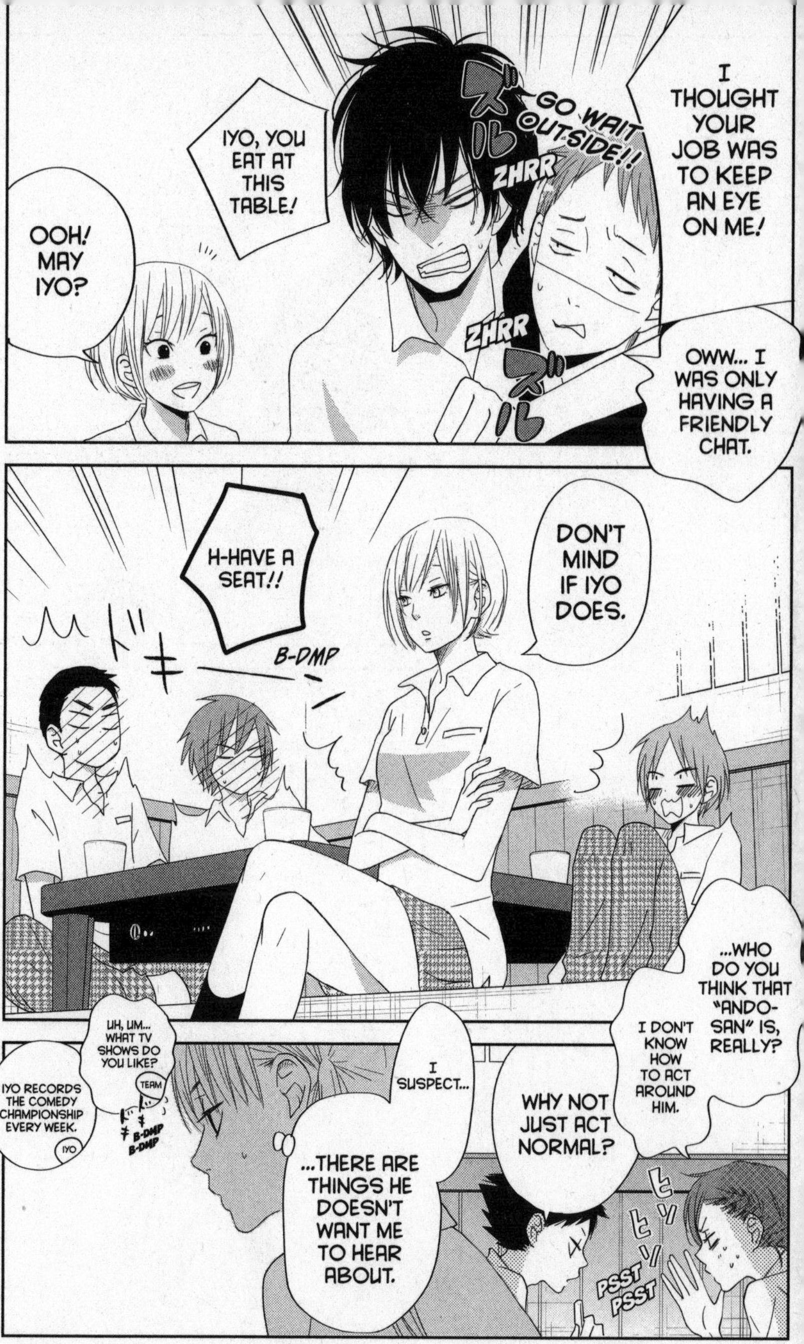
I THOUGHT YOUR JOB WAS TO KEEP AN EYE ON ME!
GO WAIT OUTSIDE!!
ZHRR
IYO, YOU EAT AT THIS TABLE!
ZHRR
OWW... I WAS ONLY HAVING A FRIENDLY CHAT.
OOH! MAY IYO?
DON'T MIND IF IYO DOES.
H-HAVE A SEAT!!
B-DMP
...WHO DO YOU THINK THAT "ANDO-SAN" IS, REALLY?
I DON'T KNOW HOW TO ACT AROUND HIM.
WHY NOT JUST ACT NORMAL?
PSST PSST
I SUSPECT...
...THERE ARE THINGS HE DOESN'T WANT ME TO HEAR ABOUT.
UH, UM... WHAT TV SHOWS DO YOU LIKE?
TEAM
B-DMP B-DMP
IYO RECORDS THE COMEDY CHAMPIONSHIP EVERY WEEK.
IYO

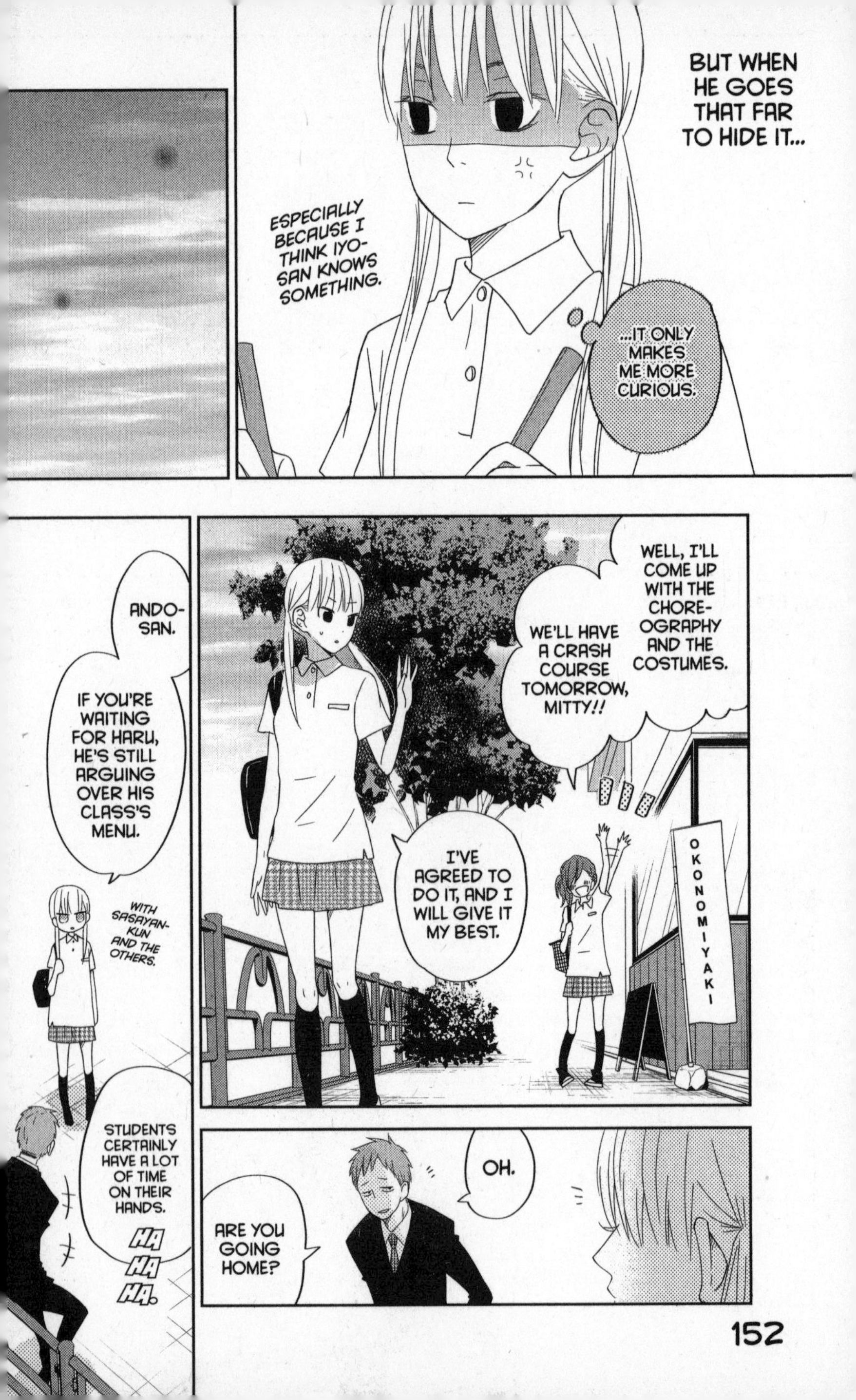
BUT WHEN HE GOES THAT FAR TO HIDE IT...
...IT ONLY MAKES ME MORE CURIOUS.
ESPECIALLY BECAUSE I THINK IYO-SAN KNOWS SOMETHING.
WELL, I'LL COME UP WITH THE CHORE-OGRAPHY AND THE COSTUMES.
WE'LL HAVE A CRASH COURSE TOMORROW, MITTY!!
I'VE AGREED TO DO IT, AND I WILL GIVE IT MY BEST.
OKONOMIYAKI
OH.
ARE YOU GOING HOME?
ANDO-SAN.
IF YOU'RE WAITING FOR HARU, HE'S STILL ARGUING OVER HIS CLASS'S MENU.
WITH SASAYAN-KUN AND THE OTHERS.
STUDENTS CERTAINLY HAVE A LOT OF TIME ON THEIR HANDS.
HA HA HA.

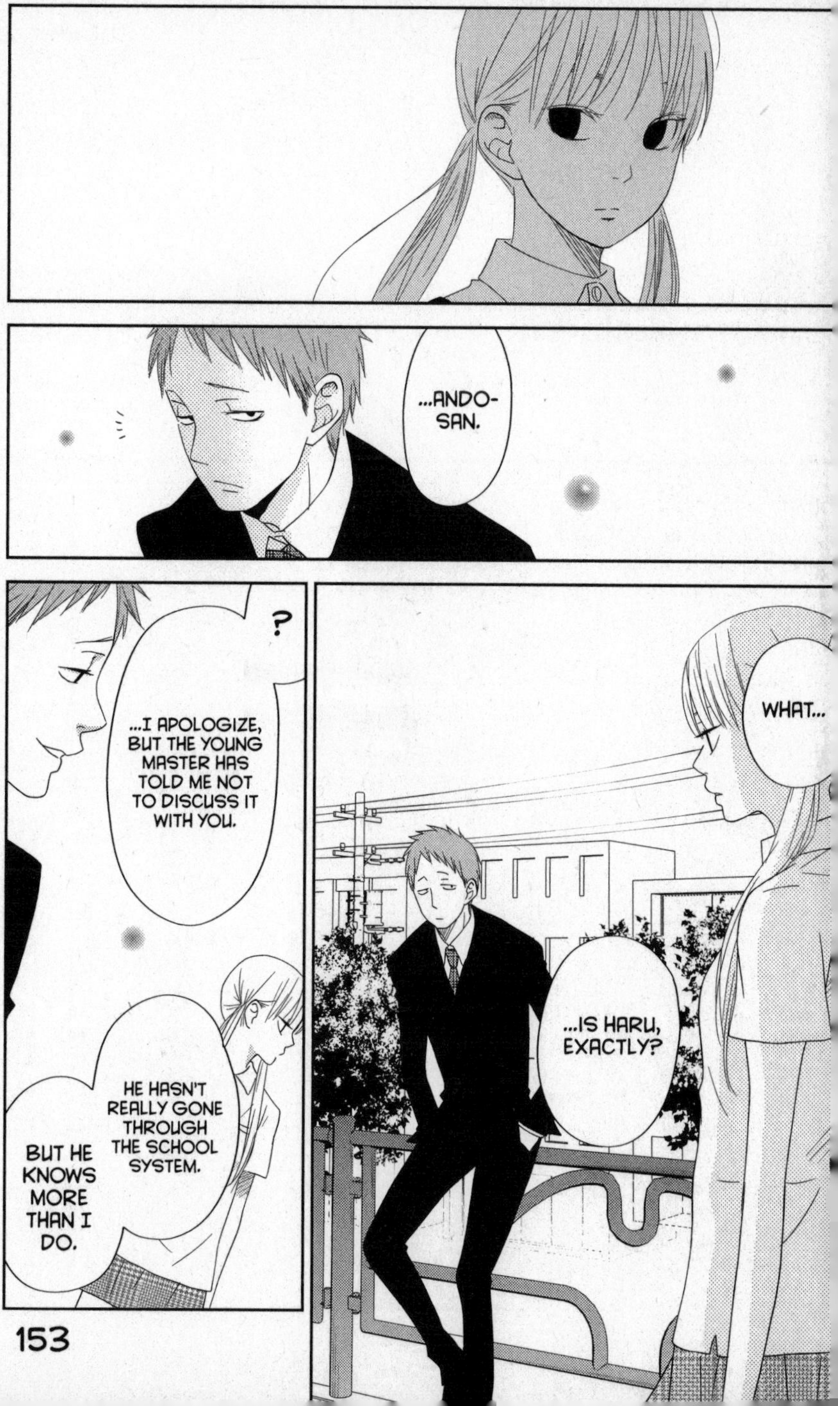
...ANDO-SAN.
WHAT...
...IS HARU, EXACTLY?
?
...I APOLOGIZE, BUT THE YOUNG MASTER HAS TOLD ME NOT TO DISCUSS IT WITH YOU.
HE HASN'T REALLY GONE THROUGH THE SCHOOL SYSTEM.
BUT HE KNOWS MORE THAN I DO.

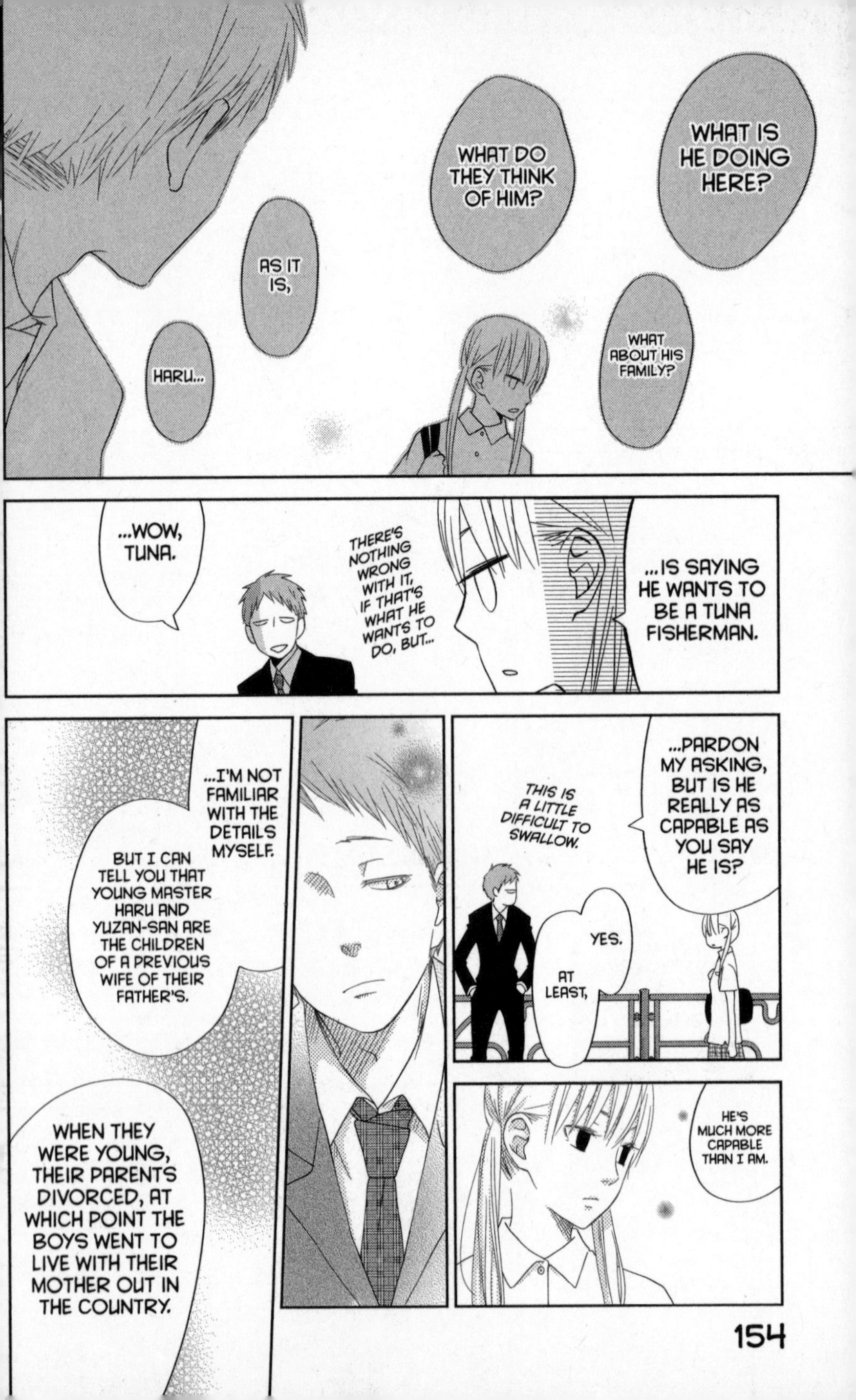
WHAT IS HE DOING HERE?
WHAT DO THEY THINK OF HIM?
WHAT ABOUT HIS FAMILY?
AS IT IS,
HARU...
...IS SAYING HE WANTS TO BE A TUNA FISHERMAN.
THERE'S NOTHING WRONG WITH IT, IF THAT'S WHAT HE WANTS TO DO, BUT...
...WOW, TUNA.
...PARDON MY ASKING, BUT IS HE REALLY AS CAPABLE AS YOU SAY HE IS?
THIS IS A LITTLE DIFFICULT TO SWALLOW.
YES.
AT LEAST,
HE'S MUCH MORE CAPABLE THAN I AM.
...I'M NOT FAMILIAR WITH THE DETAILS MYSELF.
BUT I CAN TELL YOU THAT YOUNG MASTER HARU AND YUZAN-SAN ARE THE CHILDREN OF A PREVIOUS WIFE OF THEIR FATHER'S.
WHEN THEY WERE YOUNG, THEIR PARENTS DIVORCED, AT WHICH POINT THE BOYS WENT TO LIVE WITH THEIR MOTHER OUT IN THE COUNTRY.

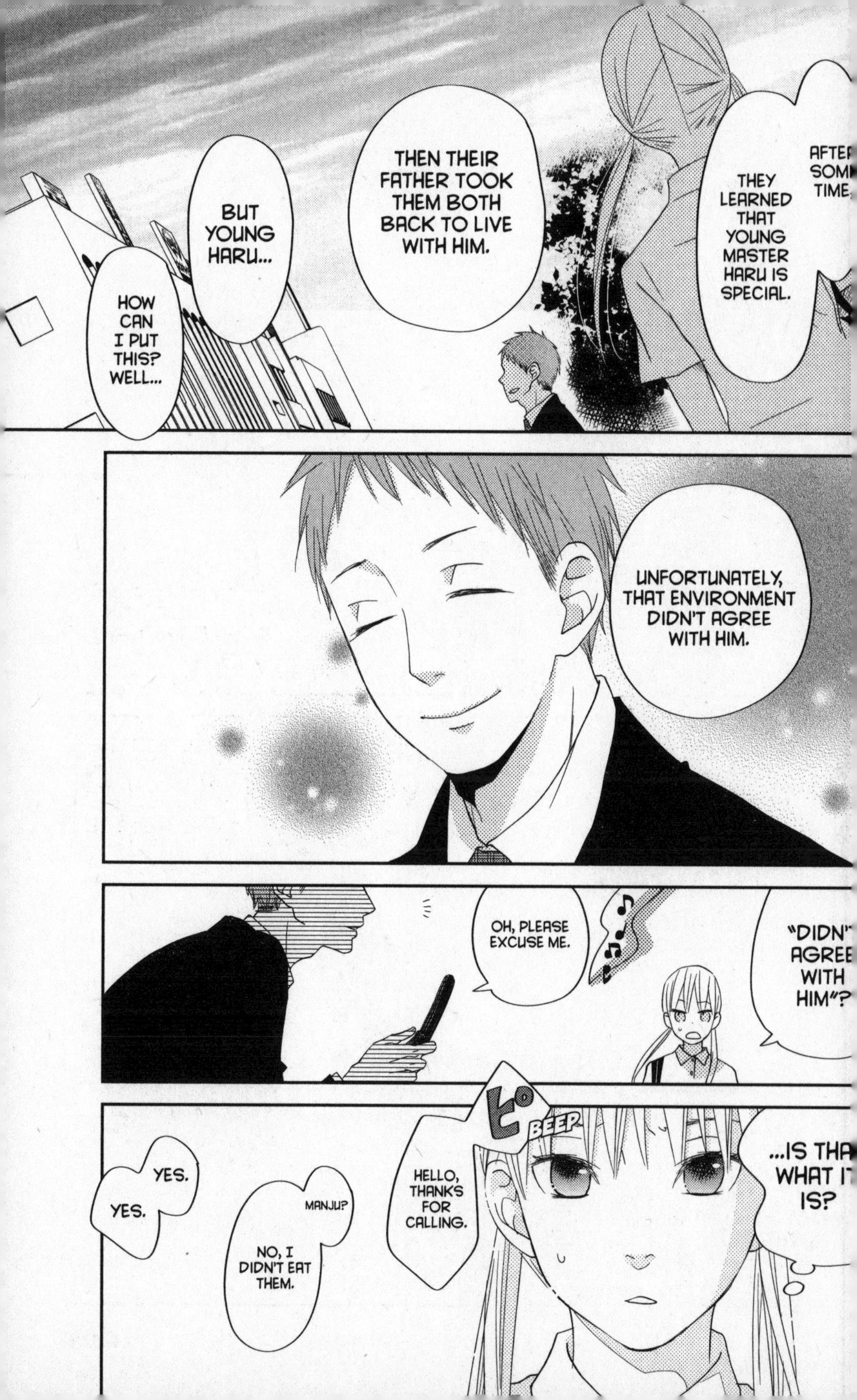
AFTE SOM TIME,
THEY LEARNED THAT YOUNG MASTER HARU IS SPECIAL.
THEN THEIR FATHER TOOK THEM BOTH BACK TO LIVE WITH HIM.
BUT YOUNG HARU...
HOW CAN I PUT THIS? WELL...
UNFORTUNATELY, THAT ENVIRONMENT DIDN'T AGREE WITH HIM.
"DIDN' AGREE WITH HIM"?
OH, PLEASE EXCUSE ME.
...IS THA WHAT IT IS?
BEEP
HELLO, THANKS FOR CALLING.
MANJU?
NO, I DIDN'T EAT THEM.
YES.
YES.

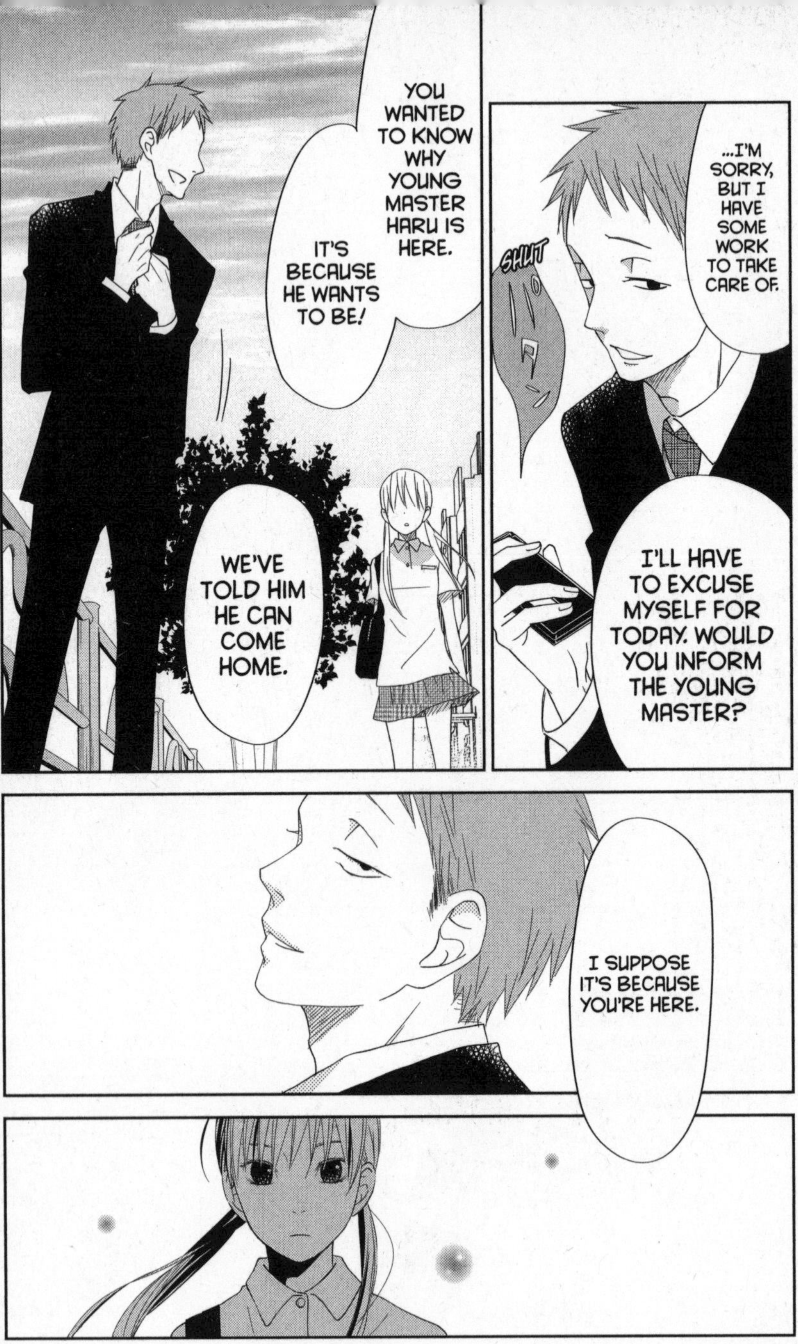
...I'M SORRY, BUT I HAVE SOME WORK TO TAKE CARE OF.
SHUT
I'LL HAVE TO EXCUSE MYSELF FOR TODAY. WOULD YOU INFORM THE YOUNG MASTER?
YOU WANTED TO KNOW WHY YOUNG MASTER HARU IS HERE.
IT'S BECAUSE HE WANTS TO BE!
WE'VE TOLD HIM HE CAN COME HOME.
I SUPPOSE IT'S BECAUSE YOU'RE HERE.

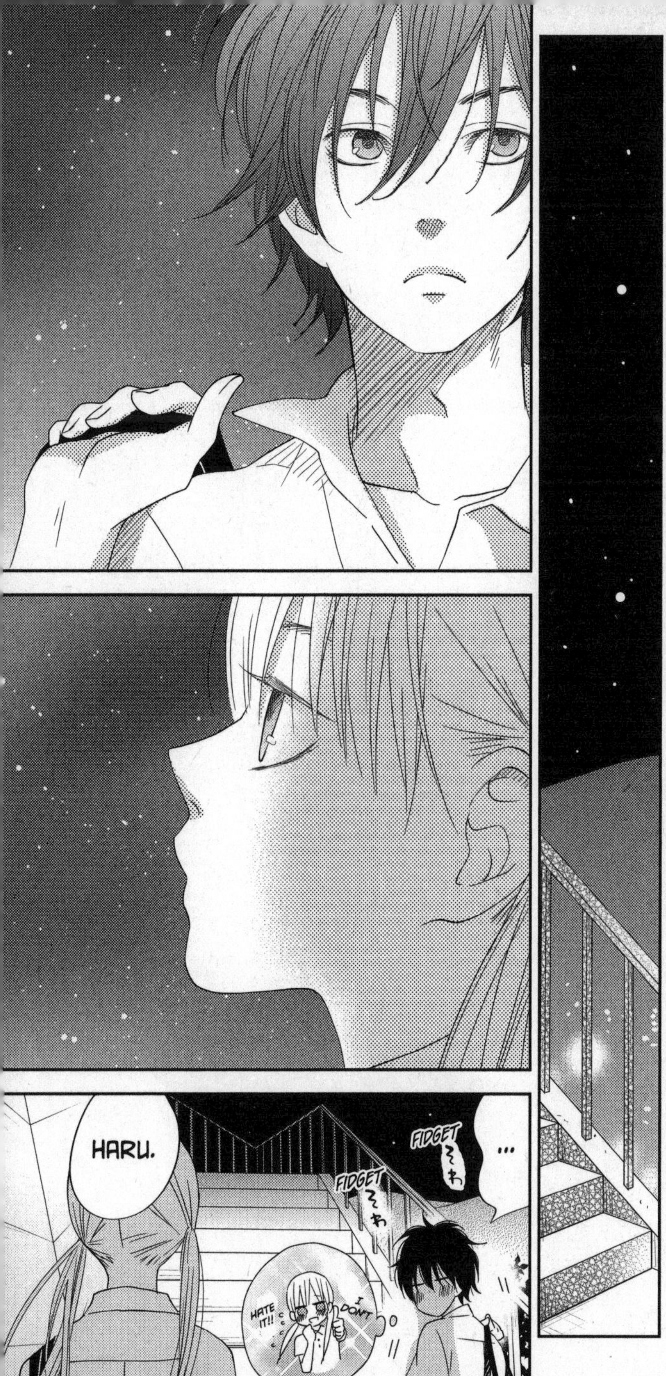
...
FIDGET
そわ
FIDGET
そわ
HARU.
I DON'T HATE IT!!

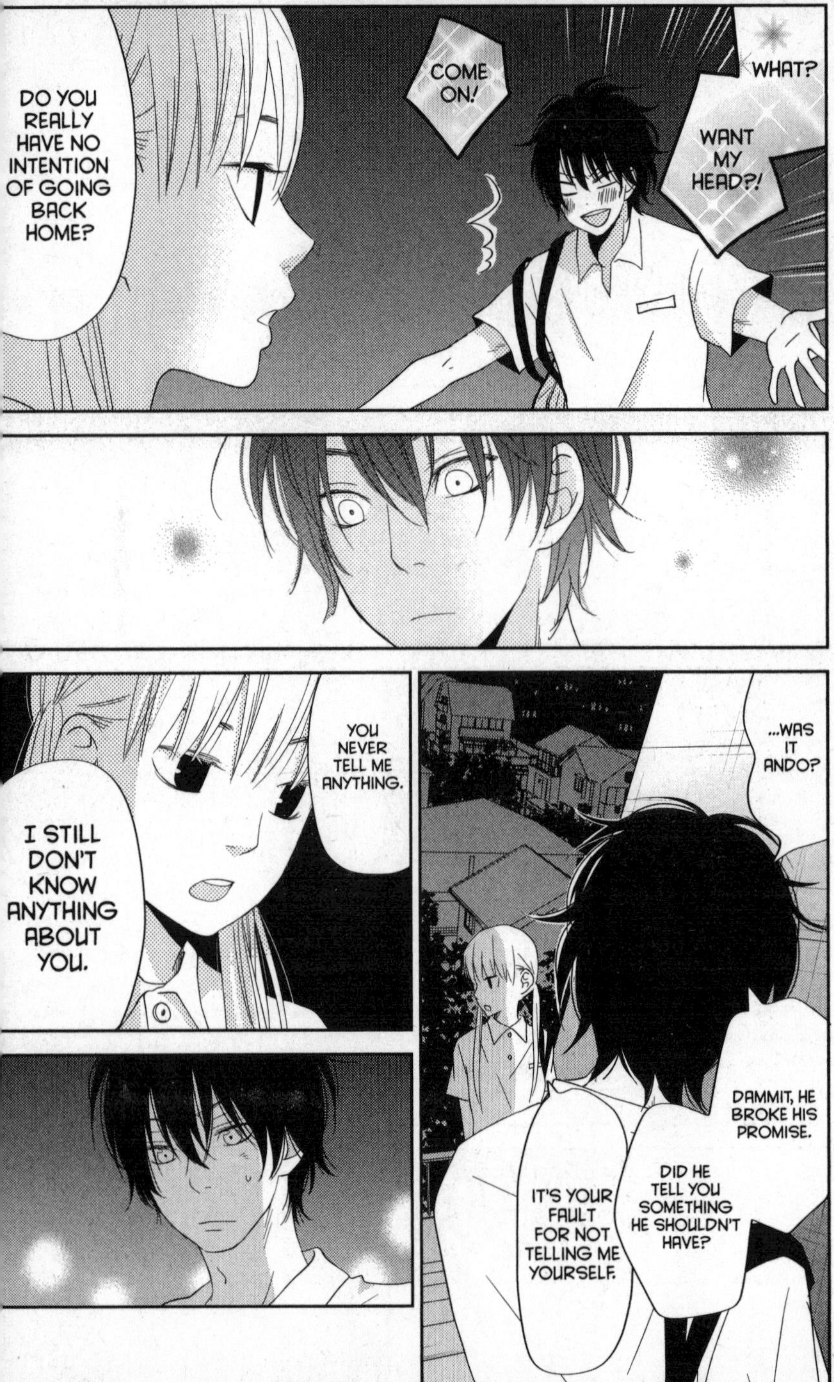
WHAT?
WANT MY HEAD?!
COME ON!
DO YOU REALLY HAVE NO INTENTION OF GOING BACK HOME?
...WAS IT ANDO?
DAMMIT, HE BROKE HIS PROMISE.
DID HE TELL YOU SOMETHING HE SHOULDN'T HAVE?
IT'S YOUR FAULT FOR NOT TELLING ME YOURSELF.
YOU NEVER TELL ME ANYTHING.
I STILL DON'T KNOW ANYTHING ABOUT YOU.

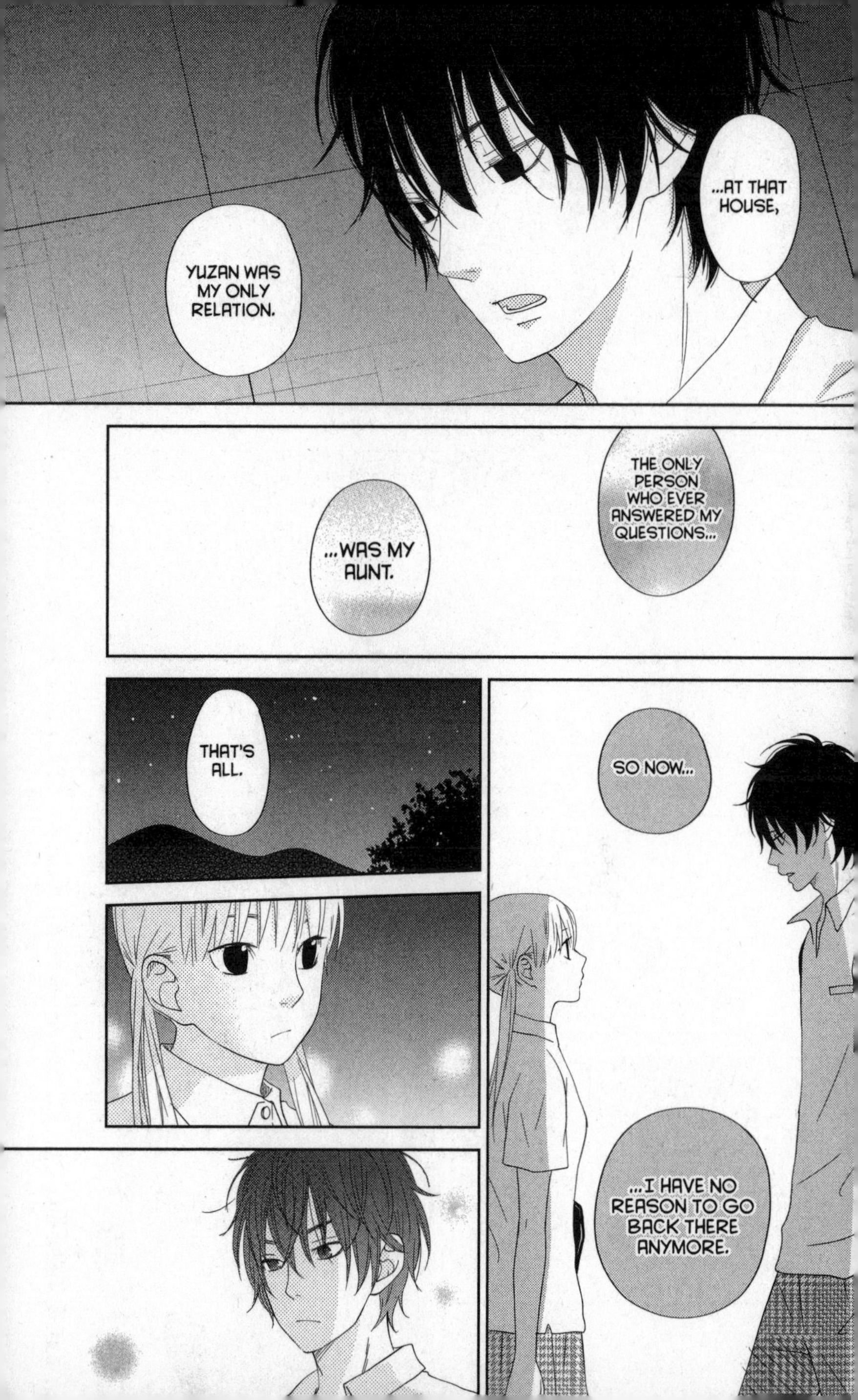
...AT THAT HOUSE,
YUZAN WAS MY ONLY RELATION.
THE ONLY PERSON WHO EVER ANSWERED MY QUESTIONS...
...WAS MY AUNT.
SO NOW...
...I HAVE NO REASON TO GO BACK THERE ANYMORE.
THAT'S ALL.

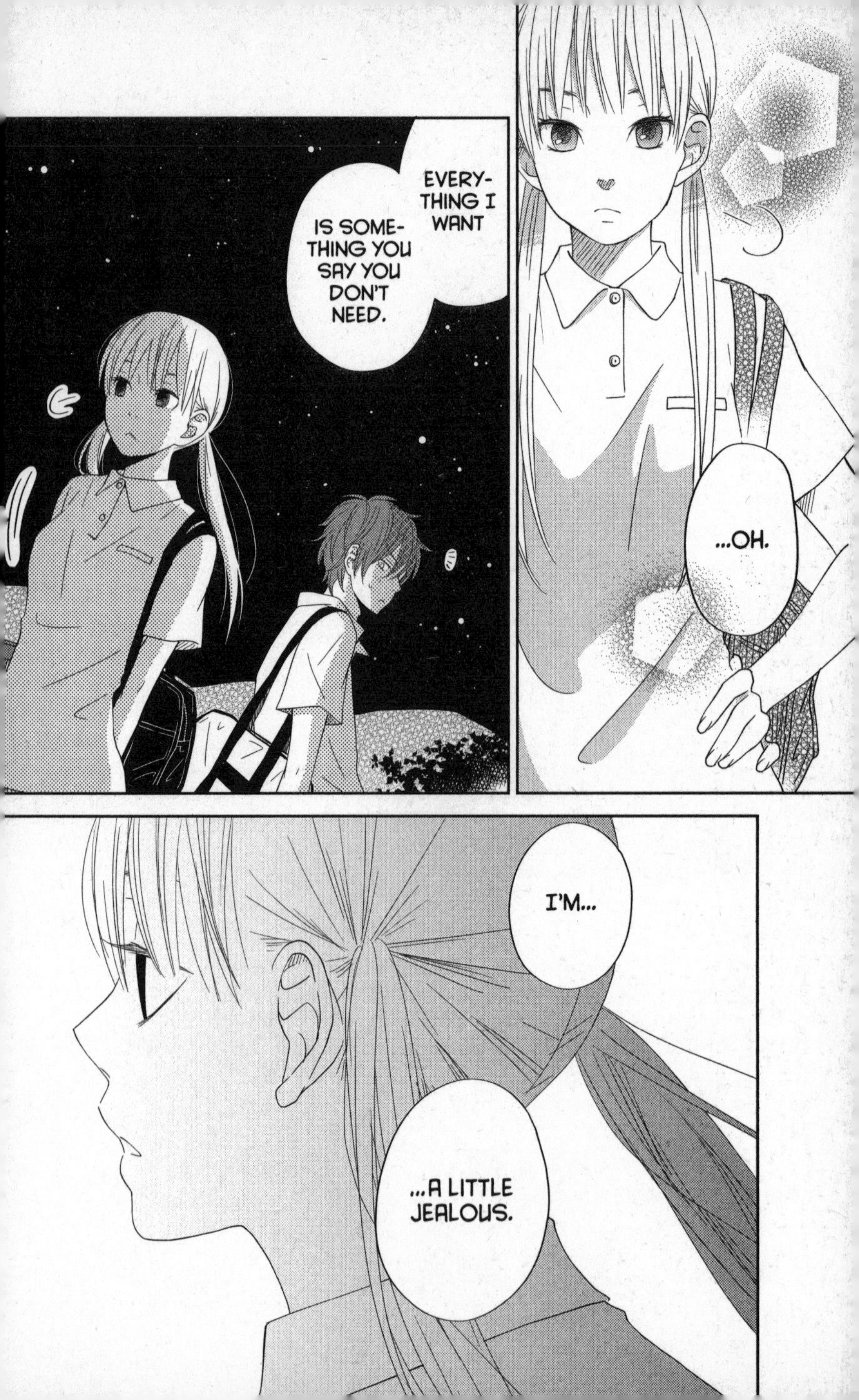
...OH.
EVERYTHING I WANT IS SOMETHING YOU SAY YOU DON'T NEED.
I'M...
...A LITTLE JEALOUS.

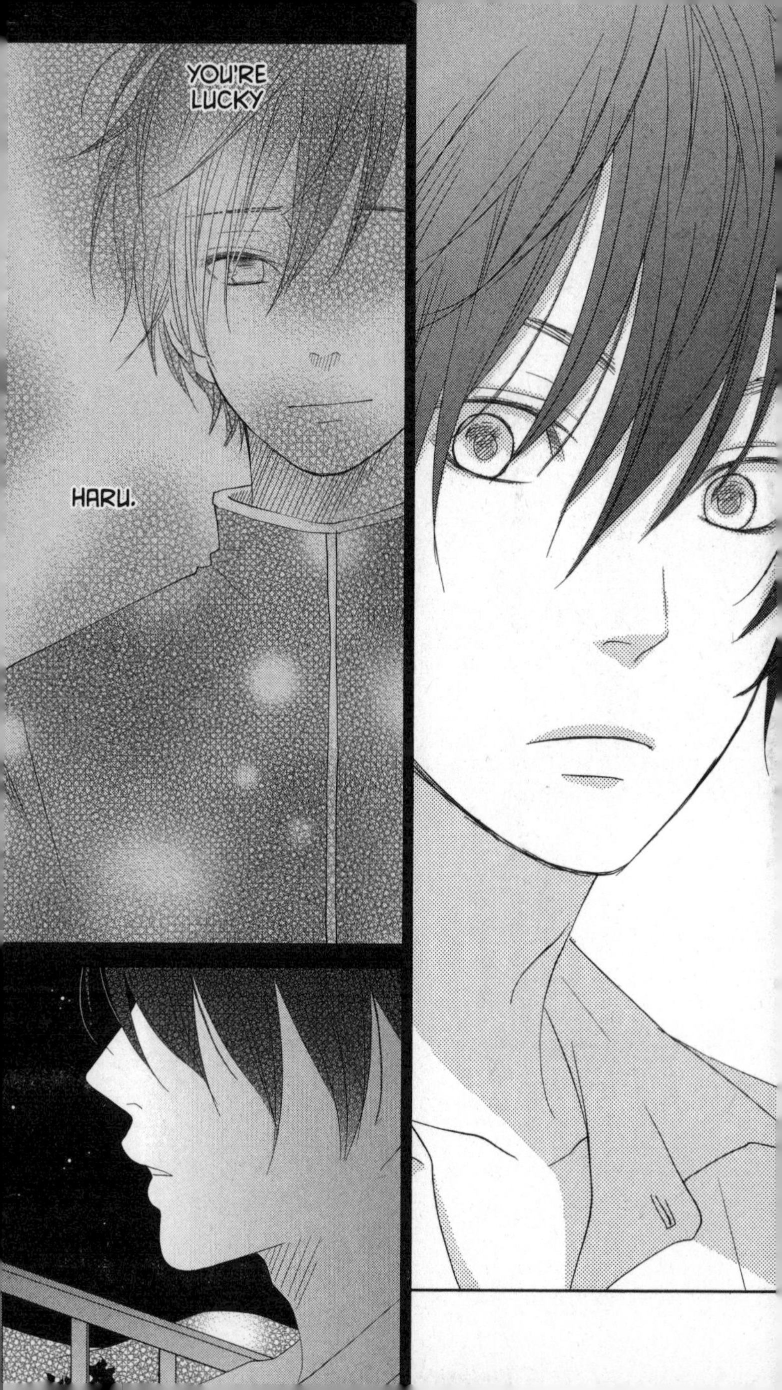
YOU'RE LUCKY
HARU.

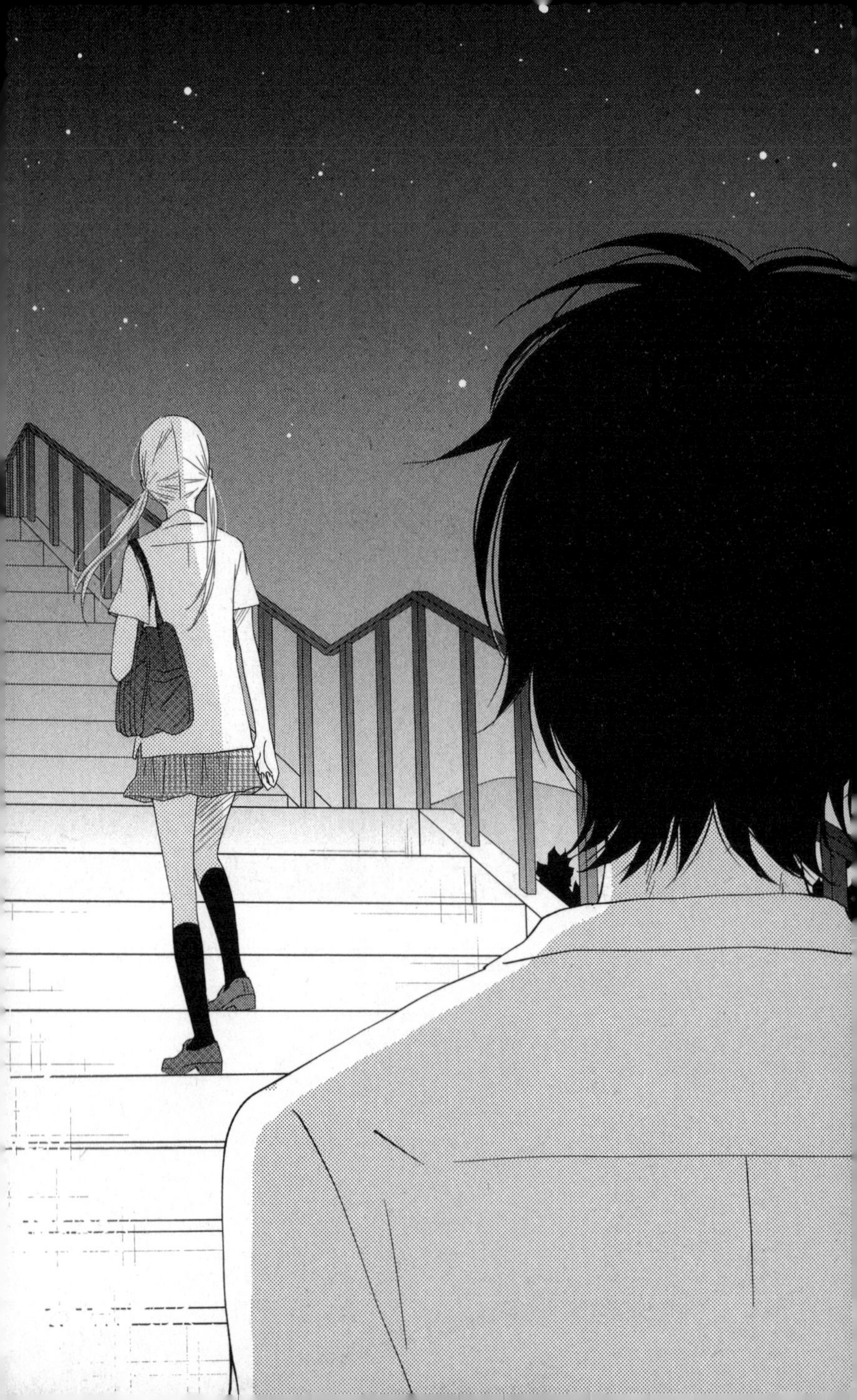

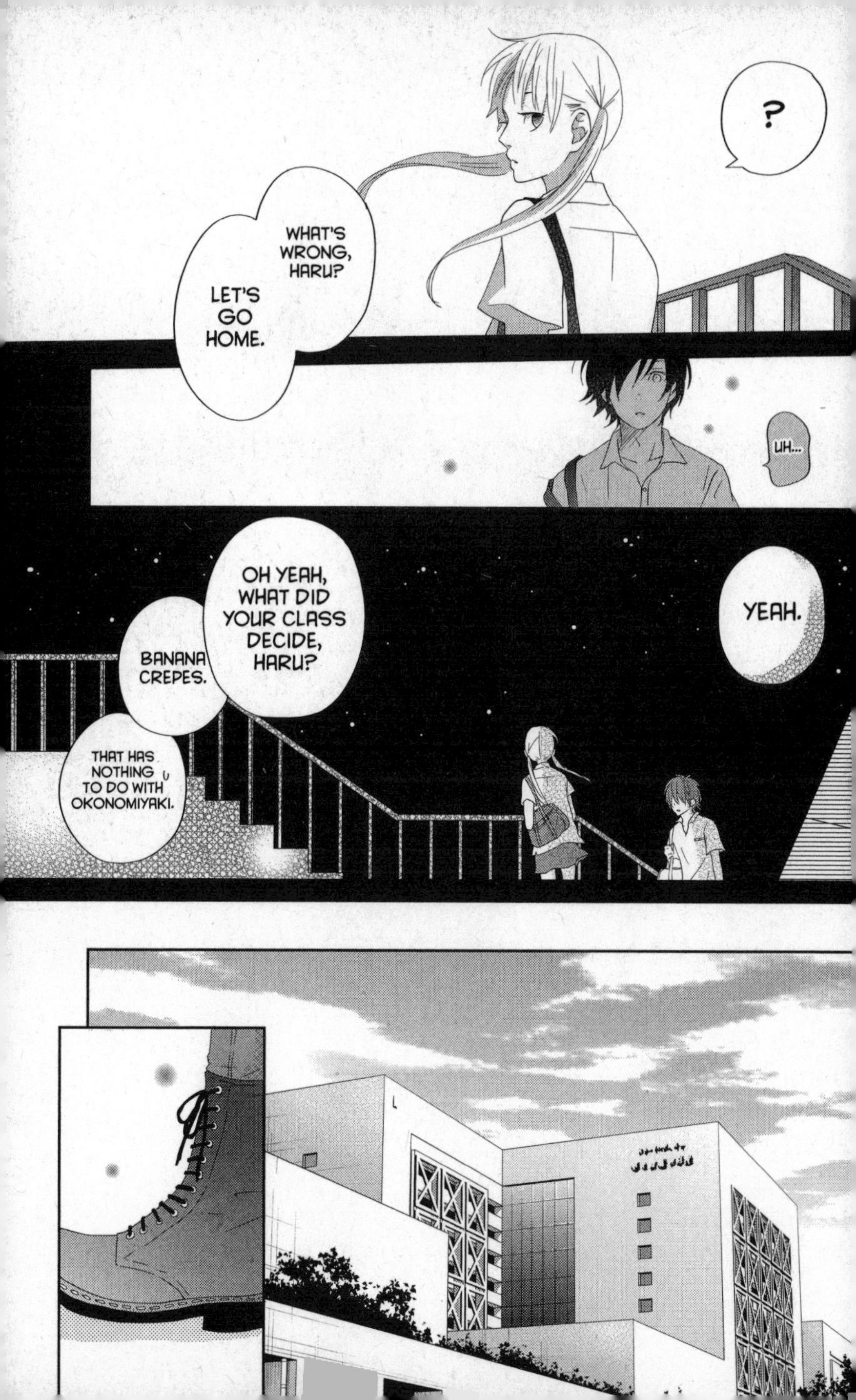
?
WHAT'S WRONG, HARU?
LET'S GO HOME.
UH...
YEAH.
OH YEAH, WHAT DID YOUR CLASS DECIDE, HARU?
BANANA CREPES.
THAT HAS NOTHING TO DO WITH OKONOMIYAKI.

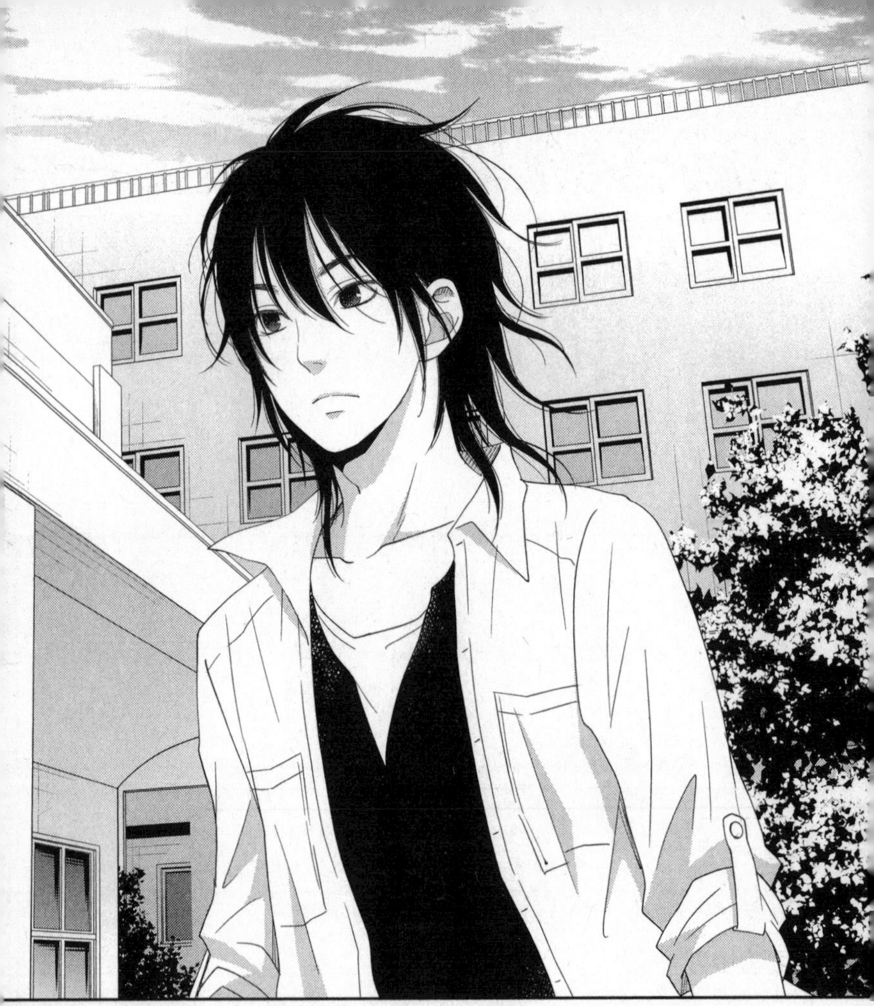
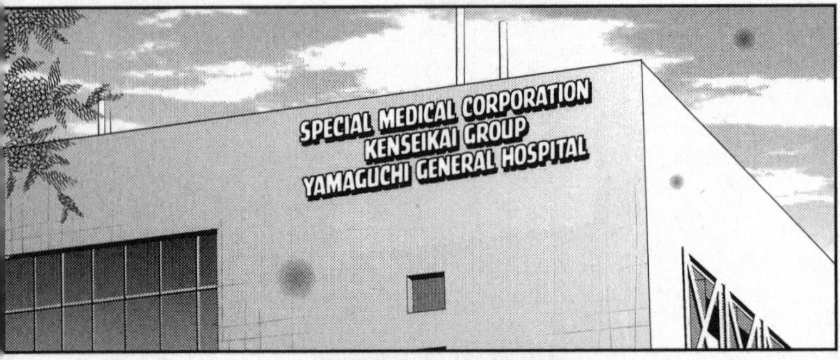
SPECIAL MEDICAL CORPORATION
KENSEIKAI GROUP
YAMAGUCHI GENERAL HOSPITAL
CONTINUED IN VOLUME 10!!

MONSTER GIRLS COLLECTION

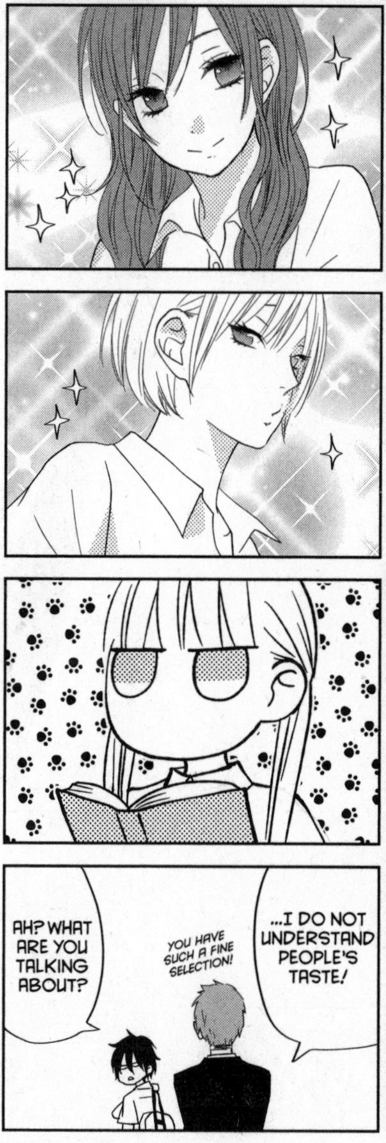
...I DO NOT UNDERSTAND PEOPLE'S TASTE!
YOU HAVE SUCH A FINE SELECTION!
AH? WHAT ARE YOU TALKING ABOUT?

AFTER THAT

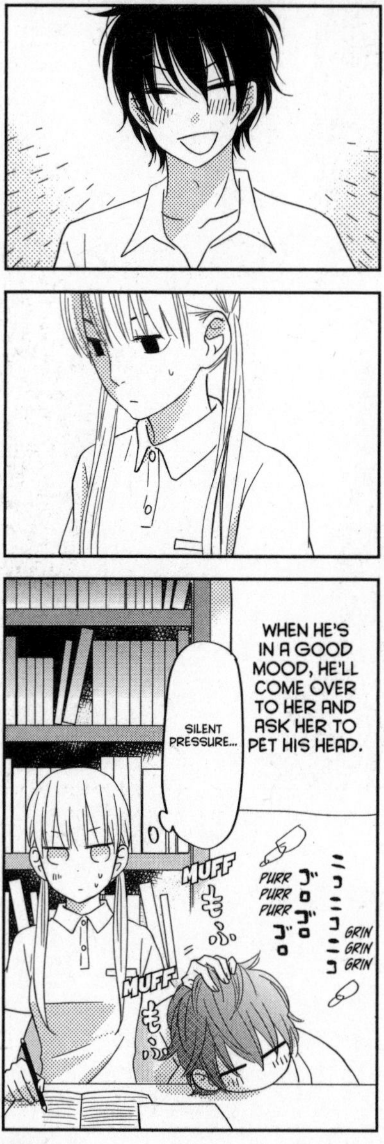
WHEN HE'S IN A GOOD MOOD, HE'LL COME OVER TO HER AND ASK HER TO PET HIS HEAD.
SILENT PRESSURE...
ニコニコニコ
GRIN GRIN GRIN
ゴロゴロゴロ
PURR PURR PURR
もふ
MUFF
もふ
MUFF

TO BE CONTINUED IN VOLUME 10.

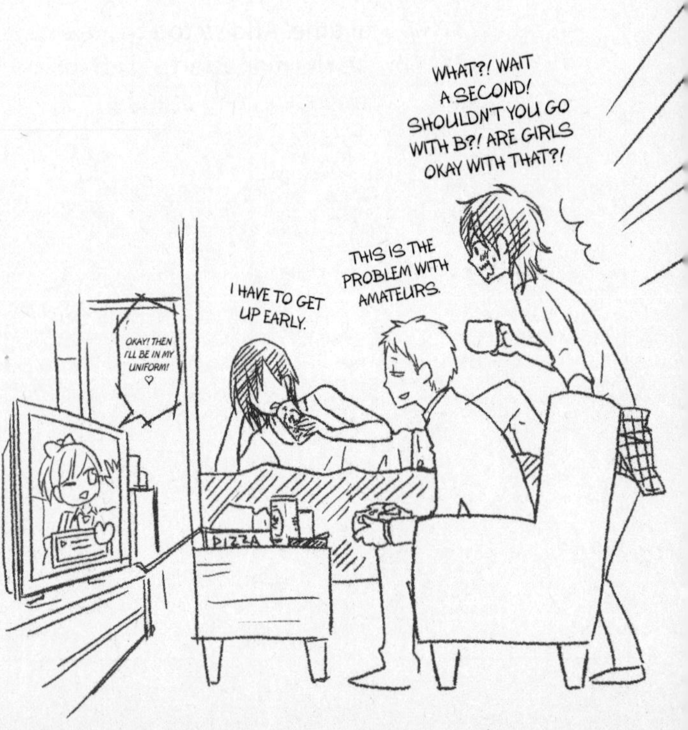
WHAT?! WAIT A SECOND! SHOULDN'T YOU GO WITH B?! ARE GIRLS OKAY WITH THAT?!
THIS IS THE PROBLEM WITH AMATEURS.
I HAVE TO GET UP EARLY.
OKAY! THEN I'LL BE IN MY UNIFORM! ♡
PIZZA

COMMENT

Robico

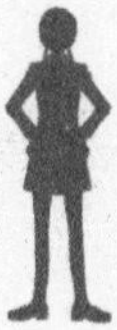

This is volume nine. Time definitely flies. Sometimes I don't know anymore if the time in the manga or the time in reality is the real time. And so today, I realize that I'm like the manga artist I imagined when I was a child.

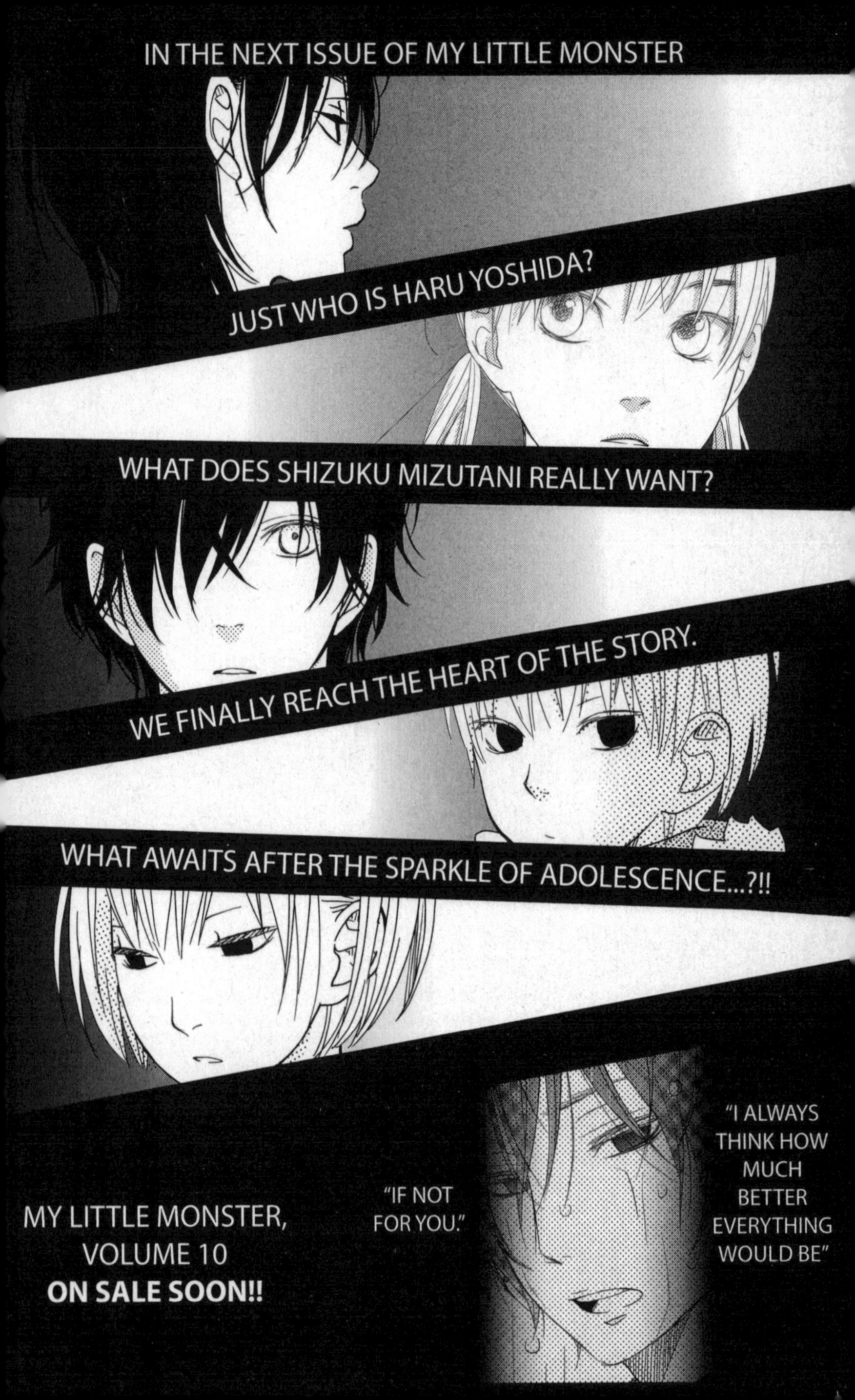
IN THE NEXT ISSUE OF MY LITTLE MONSTER
JUST WHO IS HARU YOSHIDA?
WHAT DOES SHIZUKU MIZUTANI REALLY WANT?
WE FINALLY REACH THE HEART OF THE STORY.
WHAT AWAITS AFTER THE SPARKLE OF ADOLESCENCE...?!!
"I ALWAYS THINK HOW MUCH BETTER EVERYTHING WOULD BE"
"IF NOT FOR YOU."
MY LITTLE MONSTER, VOLUME 10 **ON SALE SOON!!**

UNDER-THE-SLIPCOVER BONUS MANGA:
MOEBIUS ★ STORY

WE RECOMMEND READING
THE BOOK FIRST!!

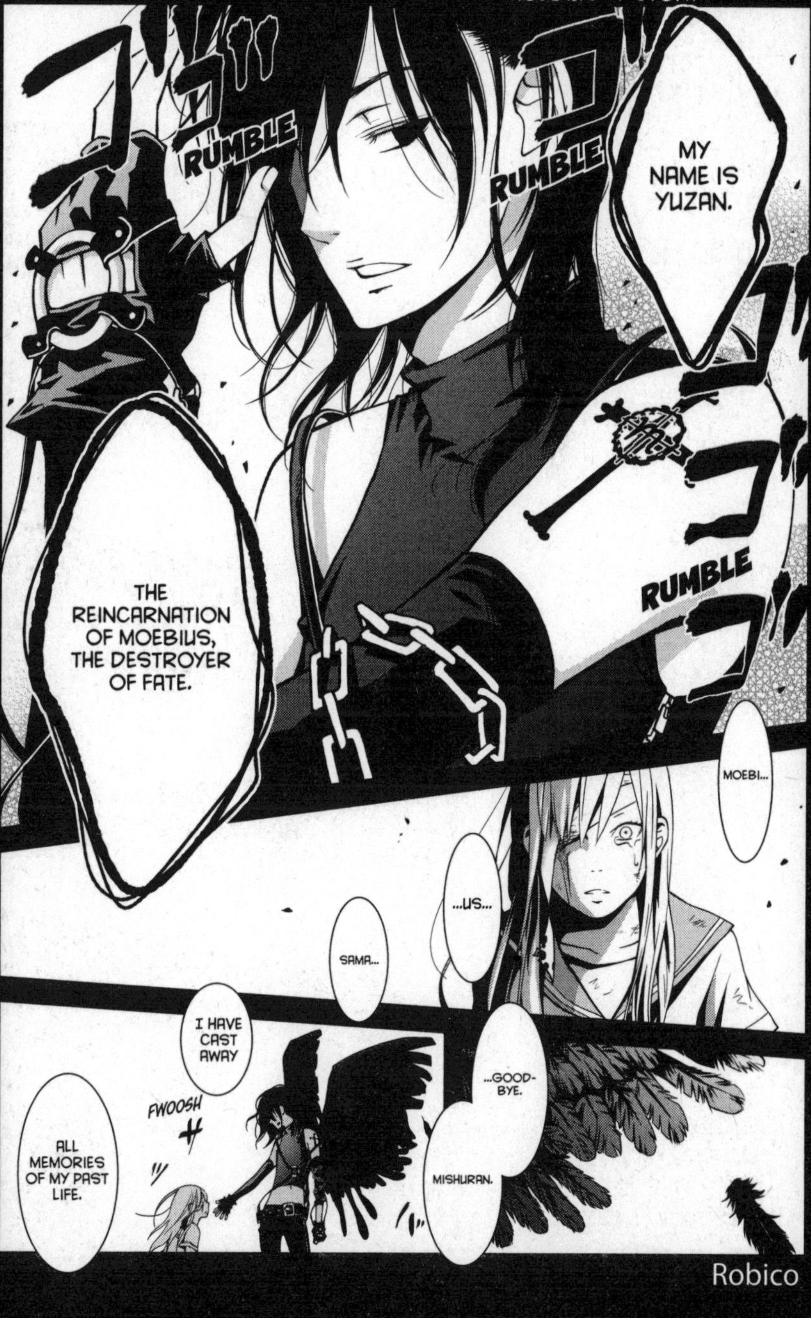
RUMBLE
RUMBLE
MY NAME IS YUZAN.
RUMBLE
THE REINCARNATION OF MOEBIUS, THE DESTROYER OF FATE.
MOEBI...
...US...
SAMA...
...GOOD-BYE.
MISHURAN.
I HAVE CAST AWAY
FWOOSH
ALL MEMORIES OF MY PAST LIFE.

Robico

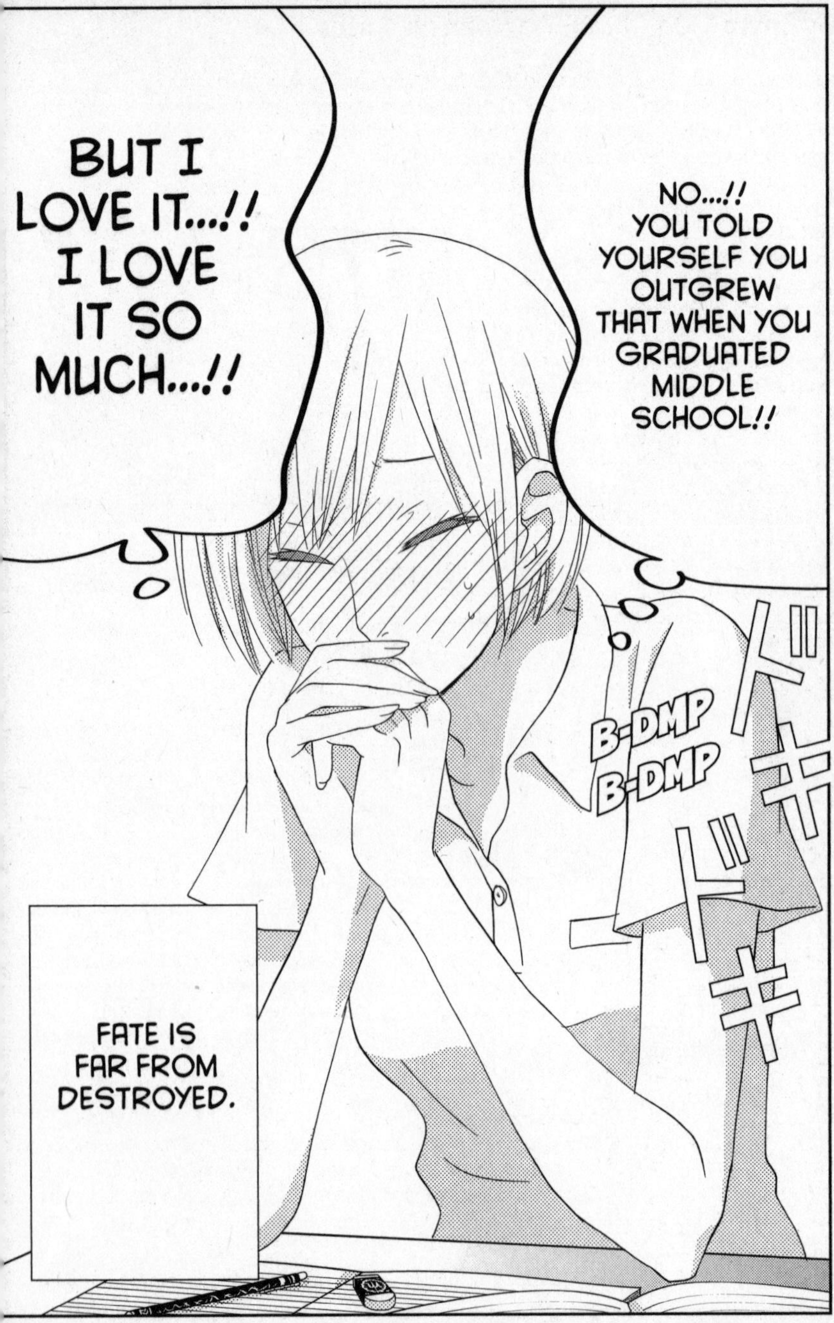
NO...!! YOU TOLD YOURSELF YOU OUTGREW THAT WHEN YOU GRADUATED MIDDLE SCHOOL!!
BUT I LOVE IT...!! I LOVE IT SO MUCH...!!
ドキ ドキ
B-DMP B-DMP
FATE IS FAR FROM DESTROYED.

My Little Monster 09 Translation Notes

Japanese is a tricky language for most Westerners, and translation is often more art than science. For your edification and reading pleasure, here are notes on some of the places where we could have gone in a different direction in our translation of the work, or where a Japanese cultural reference is used.

Test of courage, page 6

Although the test of courage was not portrayed in the story, it is a standard summer activity for manga characters. It usually involves pairing up and walking along a specified path in the dark to get to a goal before chickening out and going back to the safety of the campground. Meanwhile, non-paired members of the group are stationed along the path, waiting to jump out and scare the "unsuspecting" participants. Of course, the characters in My Little Monster can't let anything be as straightforward as that, and while we don't know exactly what happened, we can be pretty sure it was hilarious.

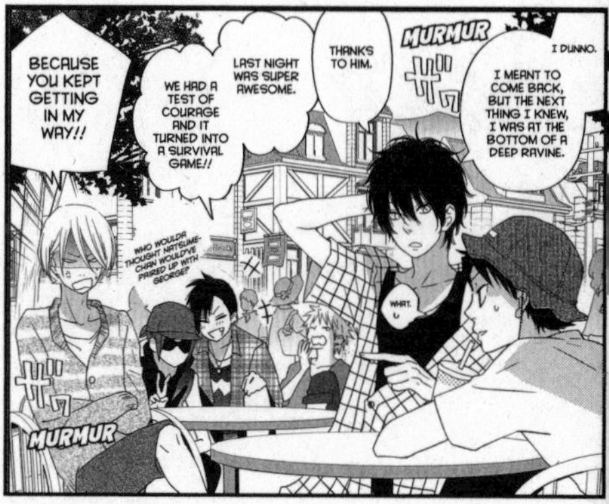
I DUNNO.
I MEANT TO COME BACK, BUT THE NEXT THING I KNEW, I WAS AT THE BOTTOM OF A DEEP RAVINE.
MURMUR
THANKS TO HIM.
LAST NIGHT WAS SUPER AWESOME.
WE HAD A TEST OF COURAGE AND IT TURNED INTO A SURVIVAL GAME!!
BECAUSE YOU KEPT GETTING IN MY WAY!!
WHAT.
WHO WOULDA THOUGHT NATSUME-CHAN WOULD'VE PAIRED UP WITH GEORGE?
MURMUR

Go eat buckwheat, page 7

This may be a reference to a famous quote by Japanese Prime Minister Hayato Ikeda. Apparently there was a scandal when something he said was interpreted as, "poor people, eat buckwheat!" In actuality, he was commenting on the financial state of things, and how those with lower incomes tend to eat wheat, while those with more money will eat more rice. Iyo might be suggesting that Yamaken's friends are lower class and should eat a food worthy of their station.

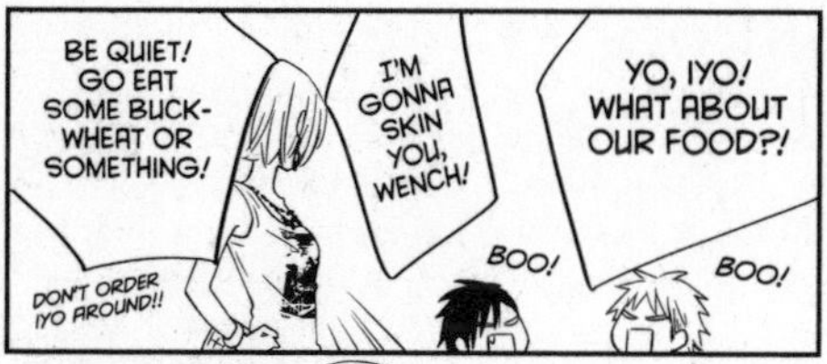
YO, IYO! WHAT ABOUT OUR FOOD?!
BOO!
I'M GONNA SKIN YOU, WENCH!
BOO!
BE QUIET! GO EAT SOME BUCK-WHEAT OR SOMETHING!
DON'T ORDER IYO AROUND!!

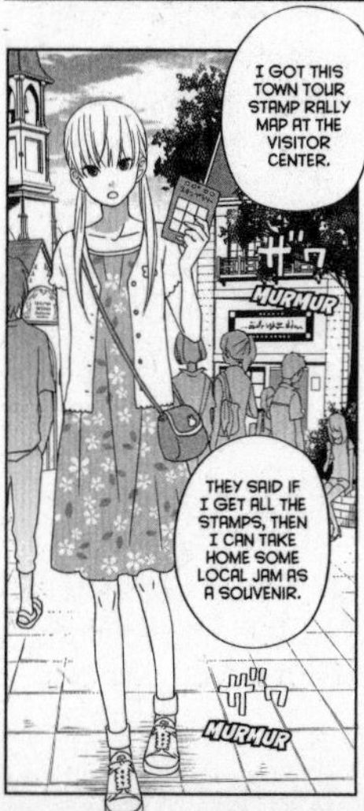
I GOT THIS TOWN TOUR STAMP RALLY MAP AT THE VISITOR CENTER.
MURMUR
THEY SAID IF I GET ALL THE STAMPS, THEN I CAN TAKE HOME SOME LOCAL JAM AS A SOUVENIR.
MURMUR

Stamp rally, page 8

A stamp rally is sort of like a scavenger hunt, and it's a way for tourists to see everything a town or a tourist spot has to offer. In this case, Shizuku has a map, marking all the places she can find rubber stamps. if she stamps all of them on her paper, she can collect a prize.

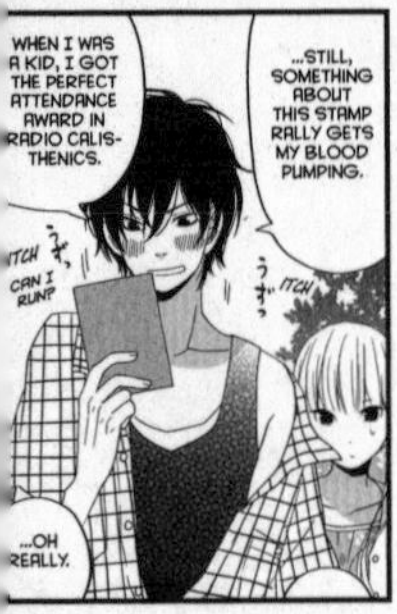
...STILL, SOMETHING ABOUT THIS STAMP RALLY GETS MY BLOOD PUMPING.
WHEN I WAS A KID, I GOT THE PERFECT ATTENDANCE AWARD IN RADIO CALIS-THENICS.
ITCH
ITCH
CAN I RUN?
...OH REALLY.

Radio calisthenics, page 17

Radio calisthenics is an exercise program in Japan. In Haru's case, he probably went to a radio calisthenics program for kids over the summer. The program would have provided an attendance card, which would have a calendar on it. The calendar would get a stamp on every day he attended, filling up like a stamp rally card.

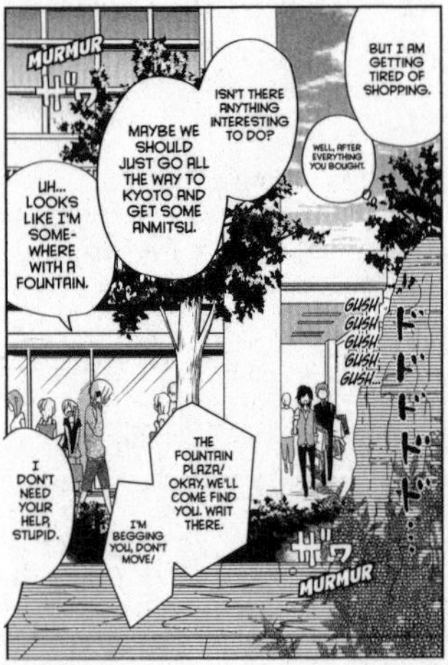
BUT I AM GETTING TIRED OF SHOPPING.
WELL, AFTER EVERYTHING YOU BOUGHT.
ISN'T THERE ANYTHING INTERESTING TO DO?
MAYBE WE SHOULD JUST GO ALL THE WAY TO KYOTO AND GET SOME ANMITSU.
MURMUR
UH... LOOKS LIKE I'M SOME-WHERE WITH A FOUNTAIN.
GUSH GUSH GUSH GUSH GUSH...
THE FOUNTAIN PLAZA/ OKAY, WE'LL COME FIND YOU. WAIT THERE.
I'M BEGGING YOU, DON'T MOVE!
I DON'T NEED YOUR HELP, STUPID.
MURMUR

Anmitsu, page 19

As you may have guessed from the fact that Yuzan is making the suggestion, anmitsu is a type of dessert. It's made of agar jelly and served with sweet bean paste and fruit.

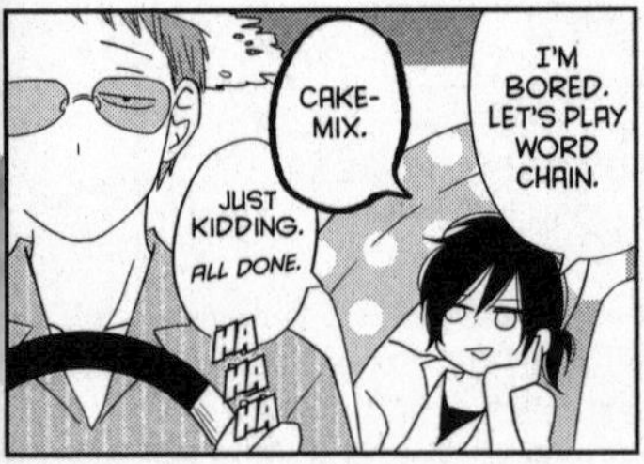
I'M BORED. LET'S PLAY WORD CHAIN.
CAKE-MIX.
JUST KIDDING.
ALL DONE.
HA HA HA

Word chain, page 43

A common game to pass the time in Japan is called shiritori, or "take the end." A similar English-speaking game is called word chain. In both games, the idea is to take the last letter of the previous players word and start a new word. In Japan, the writing system is a syllabary, so the next word will start with the next syllable. But if a word ends in the syllabic n, then the game usually ends because no words in the Japanese language start with the syllabic n. (They may start with n, but because each written character represents a vowel sound or a consonant followed by a vowel (except for syllabic n), it would be written with the character for na, ni, nu, ne, or no.) Yuzan cruelly crushes his own idea by starting with the word purin (pudding or flan). The translators attempted to replicate the effect his choice would cause by choosing a word that ends in x.

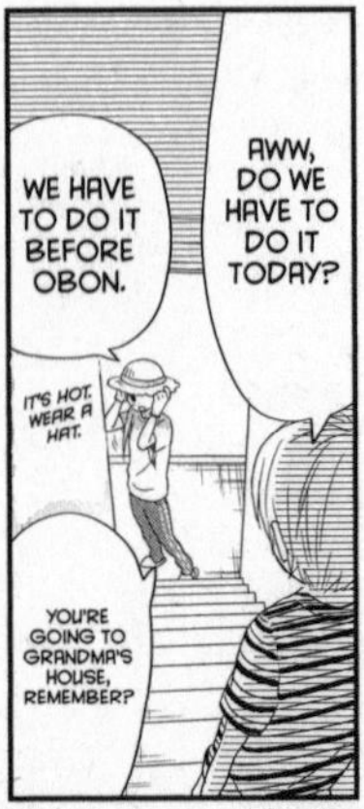
AWW, DO WE HAVE TO DO IT TODAY?
WE HAVE TO DO IT BEFORE OBON.
IT'S HOT. WEAR A HAT.
YOU'RE GOING TO GRANDMA'S HOUSE, REMEMBER?

Obon, page 50

Obon is a Japanese holiday that honors the spirits of the dead. It's celebrated in the summer and is a time for family reunions.

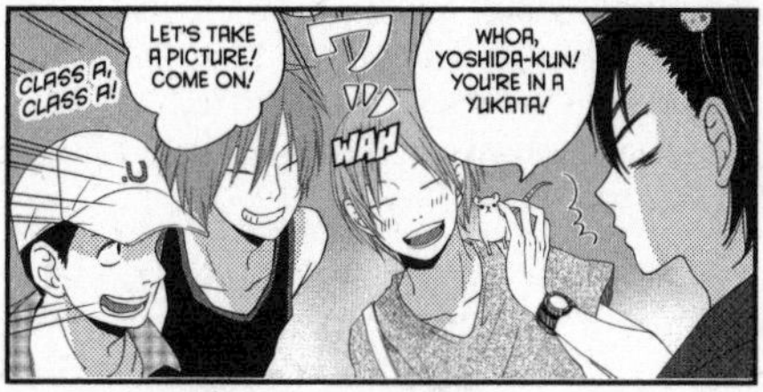
WHOA, YOSHIDA-KUN! YOU'RE IN A YUKATA!
WAH
LET'S TAKE A PICTURE! COME ON!
CLASS A, CLASS A!

Yukata, page 59
A yukata is a light summer kimono. Traditional Japanese clothing isn't as commonly worn in Japan these days, but they still bring it out for special occasions like summer festivals.

Two aaay, page 60
When taking pictures in English-speaking countries, we often ask people to say "cheese," because the "ee" sound causes people to natural move their lips into a smile. In Japan, the sound of a smile is ni, for the same reason. So when taking pictures, sometimes the photographer will ask the subjects what one plus one is, because the answer, in Japanese, is ni (two). Since these are pictures of the members of class 2-A, they can't resist adding the rest of their class name.

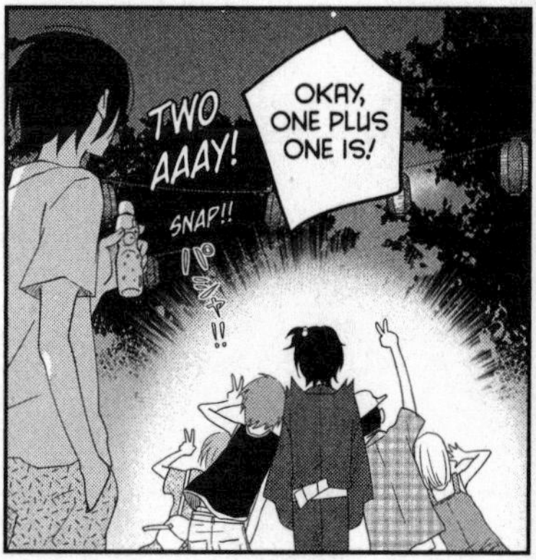
OKAY, ONE PLUS ONE IS!
TWO AAAY!
SNAP!!
パシャ!!

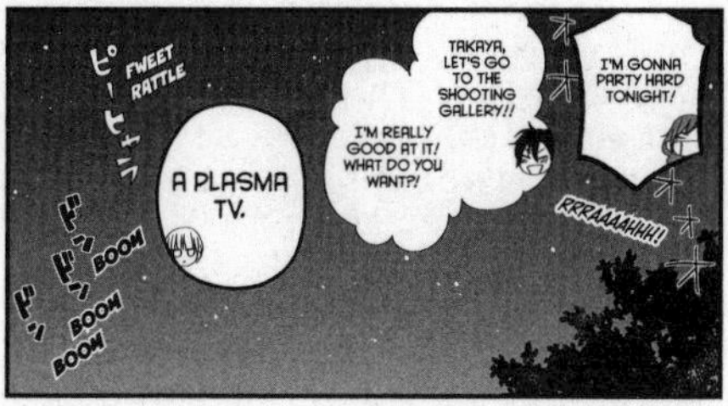
I'M GONNA PARTY HARD TONIGHT!
TAKAYA, LET'S GO TO THE SHOOTING GALLERY!!
I'M REALLY GOOD AT IT! WHAT DO YOU WANT?!
RRRAAAAHHH!!
A PLASMA TV.
FWEET RATTLE
BOOM
BOOM
BOOM

Shooting gallery, page 61
A shooting gallery at a Japanese festival is just a little bit different than what the reade may be used to in North America. In Americ shooting galleries usually involve shooting targets that are worth prizes. At a Japanese festival, the prizes are the targets; if you can knock it over, you can take it home. Prizes such as plasma tvs may be on display, but because the guns are toys and the bullets ar lightweight, the odds of knocking one over are very slim.

Household altar, page 63
As the name suggests, a household altar, or butsudan, is a Buddhist altar in the home. It is a wooden cabinet with religious objects and a place to put offerings of flowers and food. They often hold memorial tablets of deceased relatives, so Mitchan's probably has one of his late mother, and the lady from the takoyaki stand probably has a picture of her late husband in her butsudan. Taking flowers from a household altar can be roughly equivalent to taking them from someone's grave.

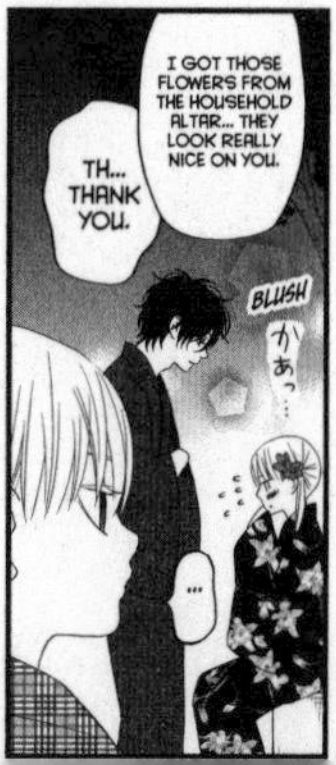
I GOT THOSE FLOWERS FROM THE HOUSEHOLD ALTAR... THEY LOOK REALLY NICE ON YOU.
TH... THANK YOU.
BLUSH
かぁっ…
...

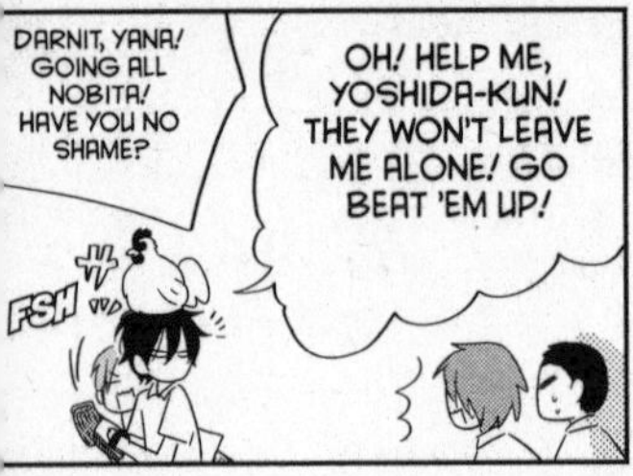
OH! HELP ME, YOSHIDA-KUN! THEY WON'T LEAVE ME ALONE! GO BEAT 'EM UP!
DARNIT, YANA! GOING ALL NOBITA! HAVE YOU NO SHAME?
FSH

Going nobita, page 125
Nobita is the main human character of the super popular Japanese manga and anime, Doraemon. One of his most notable traits is his cowardice.

The problem is this, page 128
The "this" Ando is referring to is explained by the gesture he is making with his hand. In Japan, the pinky finger signifies a woman. When someone holds up a pinky and says "this," that person is usually referring to a lover or mistress.

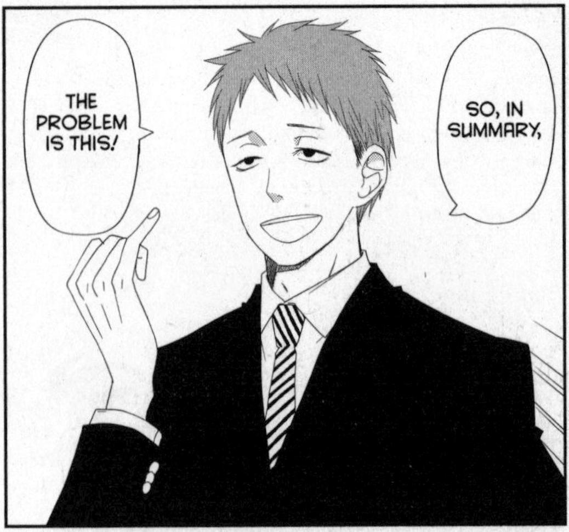
SO, IN SUMMARY,
THE PROBLEM IS THIS!

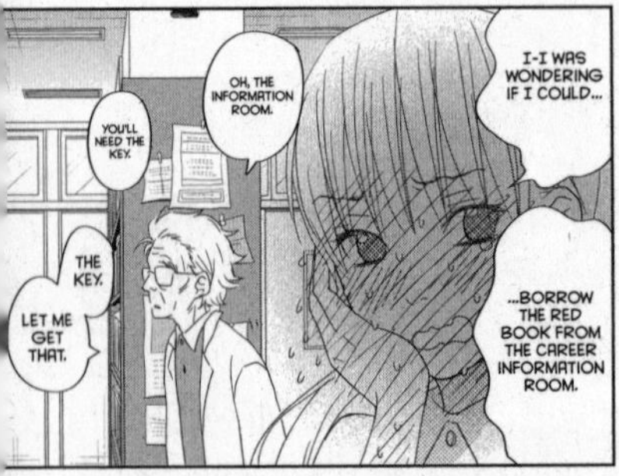
I-I WAS WONDERING IF I COULD...
...BORROW THE RED BOOK FROM THE CAREER INFORMATION ROOM.
OH, THE INFORMATION ROOM.
YOU'LL NEED THE KEY.
THE KEY.
LET ME GET THAT.

The red book, page 143
The red book that Shizuku is referring to is an akahon (red book) collection of college entrance exam questions.

Say I Love You.

Mei Tachibana has no friends — and says she doesn't need them!
But everything changes when she accidentally roundhouse kicks the most popular boy in school! However, Yamato Kurosawa isn't angry in the slightest—in fact, he thinks his ordinary life could use an unusual girl like Mei. But winning Mei's trust will be a tough task. How long will she refuse to say, "I love you"?

A Kodansha Comics Trade Paperback Original.

My Little Monster volume 9 copyright © 2012 Robico
English translation copyright © 2015 Robico

All rights reserved.

Published in the United States by Kodansha Comics, an imprint of Kodansha USA Publishing, LLC, New York.

Publication rights for this English edition arranged through Kodansha Ltd., Tokyo.

First published in Japan in 2012 by Kodansha Ltd., Tokyo, as *Tonari no Kaibutsu-kun*, volume 9.

ISBN 978-1-61262-993-3

Printed in the United States of America.

www.kodanshacomics.com

9 8 7 6 5 4 3 2 1

Translator: Alethea Nibley & Athena Nibley
Lettering: Paige Pumphrey